CHRISTIANITY
Outside the Box

Samuel
with best wishes

Nigel Scotland

21/02/2015

CHRISTIANITY
Outside the Box

Learning from Those Who Rocked the Boat

NIGEL SCOTLAND

Foreword by George Kovoor

CASCADE *Books* · Eugene, Oregon

CHRISTIANITY OUTSIDE THE BOX
Learning from Those Who Rocked the Boat

Cascade Books
An Imprint of Wipf and Stock Publishers
199 W. 8th Ave., Suite 3
Eugene, OR 97401

www.wipfandstock.com

ISBN 13: 978-1-61097-360-1

Cataloguing-in-Publication data:

Scotland, Nigel.

Christianity outside the box : learning from those who rocked the boat /
Nigel Scotland, with a foreword by George Kovoor.

xiv + 330 pp. ; 23 cm. Includes bibliographical references and index.

ISBN 13: 978-1-61097-360-1

1. Montanism. 2. Donatists. 3. Celtic Church. 4. Waldenses. 5. Lollards.
6. Moravians. 7. Puritans. 8. Quakers. 9. Methodism—History. 10. Salvation
Army—History. 11. Church work with the poor—England—London—19th century. 12. Pentecostalism—History. 13. Vineyard Christian Fellowship. 14. Church
history. I. Kovoor, George. II. Title.

BR150 S36 2012

Manufactured in the U.S.A.

For my wife, Anne,
for her loving support and encouragement

Contents

Foreword

IT IS A GREAT pleasure for me to write a foreword to *Christianity Outside the Box*, written by my colleague and friend the Reverend Doctor Nigel Scotland, who is a wonderful teacher of Church History and a faithful disciple of Jesus Christ. We at Trinity College Bristol, UK, are committed to the vision for a re-evangelization of Britain and Europe. This requires imagination, courage, audacity, biblical faithfulness, and a genuine openness to the Holy Spirit. The presence and activity of the Holy Spirit have led men and women down through the ages to break through traditions and think and act outside the box!

In the context of the twenty-first century we are confronted with the huge challenges of poverty, injustice, a global financial crisis, the confusion of sexual identity, ecological disasters, the fragmentation of the family and the polarization of society between the haves and the have-nots! The church as an institution seems to be paralyzed and almost impotent to respond to the new opportunities and challenges confronting it. Its life and witness are predictable, unimaginative, and seem to be out of touch. Young people are voting with their feet! This to me is scandalous because Jesus Christ, who is the Lord of the church, arrested me when I was a teenager and I have witnessed the power of his gospel to transform lives, homes, and communities all over the world. As the leader of Trinity College Bristol I am committed to Christian discipleship and the formation of transformational leaders who make a difference on the ground. I have been very conscious that within the history of the global Christian tradition there are very significant resources and lessons to be learned from the past. How could we incorporate this learning into our missional curriculum? I therefore asked Nigel Scotland to consider distilling from the history of mission, case studies of men and women who were led by the holy Spirit to think and act outside the box. This book is a response to my invitation to bless the church with real life stories of faith in action from the history of the church, which include being misunderstood, being persecuted, and sometimes even martyrdom. I have enjoyed reading the book and am blessed, inspired, and encouraged.

In this book the author draws significant lessons for contemporary Christians from a number of vibrant orthodox Christian movements that operated and promulgated their vision outside the bounds of the established Christian churches, hence the title "Christianity Outside the Box." So here there are fourteen missional movements, rather than churches, which span the history of Christianity from the first century to the present day. Each chapter presents us with sections on the group's origins, development and key doctrines, and goes on to indicate the core reasons for their considerable success in attracting ordinary working people to Christ and to the work of his kingdom.

Each group had particular emphases and concerns that are considered within the separate chapters but there were a number of key factors that were common to them all. Most apparent was the fact that the leaders in every case were men and women of vision who dreamed dreams and pursued them with seriousness. They were also people of passion who were wholly committed to Christ and intentional when it came to sharing their faith and encouraging others to do the same. They were also men and women of integrity who were loved and respected by their followings. None of them got trapped by the temptation of money, sex, or power. They did not work from existing ecclesiastical structures; rather they developed strategies that facilitated the vision they felt God had given them. They were men and women of the Spirit and prayer who practiced a deep spirituality and who cared seriously about the poor and needy. Many of these movements took up human rights issues with great seriousness showing major concern over issues such as the role of women, slave trading and ownership, conditions in the work place and the state of the dwellings in which people lived, often in very poor cottages or, in more recent times, sub-standard tenement blocks in slum areas. Here also were movements that took education seriously and regarded and used it as a necessary and vital adjunct for their goals to be realized. As the author points out, the fact that not all these movements survived to the present day should not be taken to imply that they should be regarded as failures. They were movements that invested in people rather than structures or institutions and some, like the Waldensians and the Lollards, merged with other larger groups that emerged at a later date with a similar vision.

This is a serious and scholarly book that is informative and highly readable. It is written by a Christian scholar who knows his material well and uses it to make Christian history relevant to the present age. Many of the core issues confronting the declining churches in Western Europe and North America can be faced with a true confidence in the gospel of Jesus Christ by learning from those who have been faithful and imaginative in their context. I commend it wholeheartedly and without reservation as an important resource for our own growth in discipleship, but also as a textbook for those who want to grow in missional leadership.

Canon George Kovoor
Principal of Trinity College, Bristol
Chaplain to Queen Elizabeth II

Preface

THIS BOOK CAME INTO being when my college principal, Canon George Kovoor, knowing my interest in New Religious Movements, said to me, "Nigel, why don't you write something on Christianity outside the box" to see if there are any common success factors from which the historic and denominational churches can learn? So what follows attempts to do just exactly that.

This is an examination of fourteen groups spanning the entire history of Christianity. Each of them were theologically orthodox in that they based their beliefs and practices on New Testament principles and endorsed the doctrines of the early catholic rules of faith and the historic creeds. Some of these movements prospered only for a time and then declined, and in some cases came to an end. That in itself should not necessarily mean that contemporary Christianity has nothing to learn from them. Indeed there are often vital lessons to be drawn from groups who, like the early Wesleyan Methodists, had a powerful impact on church and society only to lose their cutting edge in the centuries that followed. The origins and historical development of these movements are examined using primary and classic secondary sources. Key features that accounted for their effectiveness are identified and highlighted at the end of each chapter.

Significantly, a number of success factors common to all of these "outside of the box" movements emerges, perhaps the most significant being "enthusiasm." The word enthusiasm derives from the Greek *en theos*, meaning literally "in God" and it well describes the ethos and experience of the groups studied in this volume. Their expressions of the Christian faith were essentially personal and experiential and touched what the American philosopher and theologian, Jonathan Edwards, termed the "religious affections." It led to their being passionate and serious for the God they served.

Other common threads emerged, the most obvious being leadership. All were led by men and women who had what the sociologist of religion, Max Weber, termed "charisma"; that is, they had the ability to magnetize their following, bring them on board, and then persuade them to run with their message and agenda. A seemingly integral part of this leadership was what might be termed a protest of spirit that resulted in a reaction against nominal, establishment religion, which was often perceived to be soulless, lifeless, and without a positive impact in the world of suffering and injustice. They all, without exception, saw Jesus as a reformer and challenger of ineffectual status quo religion. Each one had a Spirit inspired and biblically faithful vision that harnessed a dynamic social energy and resulted in a transformational change, which in almost all cases impacted the lives of the poor and marginalized.

Other shared features included plain, straight-forward teaching in the language of the people, a deeply disciplined and resolute spirituality, identification with the cultural context, and a strong focus on the poor and marginalized. These features are developed in detail in the concluding chapter. It is my hope that what emerges will not merely be of academic interest to historians and sociologists of religious movements, but will be a practical and personal challenge and inspiration to church planters and leaders within the denominational Christian churches who have a vision to extend the kingdom of God.

Nigel Scotland
Tutor at Trinity College, Bristol
Honorary Research Fellow, University of Gloucestershire

1 | The Montanists

MONTANISM WAS A MOVEMENT within Christianity that originated in Phrygia in the middle years of the second century. It became known by some of its opponents as "the Phrygian Heresy" despite the fact that its beliefs were orthodox and creedal. Others referred to it as "the New Prophecy." One of the problems when it comes to studying Christian groups who were "outside of the box" is that very often most of what we know about them comes from the pens of their opponents.[1] It is therefore necessary to do some reading between the lines of their writings in order to get closer to the truth of what they believed and practiced. This fact is immediately apparent when we come to study the Montanists, who Eusebius, the church historian, denounced as "heretics influenced by the devil" and "poisonous reptiles"—descriptions that do little to recommend him as an unbiased observer.

When the aged apostle John had a vision from the risen Jesus of the seven churches of Asia Minor, only one of them received any real encouragement and that was Philadelphia.[2] This church—situated on the boarders of rural, pagan Phrygia—was commended by the Lord for its faithfulness in tribulation as a result of which "an open door was set before them." They were also given the hope of Jesus "coming soon"[3] and the expectation of "New Jerusalem coming down out of heaven from my God."[4] Two Philadelphian Christians who took an active part in this early missionary outreach were the prophetess, Ammia, and the prophet, Quadratus.[5] They were doubtless inspired by Jesus' promise "to make all

1. Trevett, "Montanus, Priscilla, Maximilla and Their Teachings." In Esler, *The Early Christian World*, 938: "what we know of these prophets stems almost entirely from hostile sources . . ."

2. Rev 3:7–13.

3. Rev 3:11.

4. Rev 3:12.

5. Eusebius, *History of the Church* 5.17. Here Eusebius cites a work by Miltiades

things new."[6] Reading between lines of an account by Miltiades it seems that Montanus and his female followers took up their mantle[7] about the year A.D. 156, though the style of their ministry was evidently somewhat more fervent. Despite his hostility to the movement, Eusebius, the early church historian, noted that "the sect" flourished in Phrygia."[8] This success was also attested to by Apollonius, Bishop of Ephesus, writing thirty-nine years after the beginning of Montanus' ministry. Apollonius indicated that in his day the Montanists were still making a considerable impact on the people of the province.[9]

The second century apologist, Miltiades, wrote a pamphlet against the Montanists entitled, *How a Prophet Ought Not to Speak in Ecstacy,*[10] but their enthusiasm and commitment to Christ was not going to be quickly extinguished by the writings of a hostile philosopher who denounced them for their ignorance. The early Montanists were active and urgent in proclaiming the gospel message. Calder's work on Phrygian gravestones in the Tembris valley illustrates their boldness, showing that their gravestones have Montanist Christian inscriptions in a period when, out of fear of the authorities, most Christians made their burial place look like pagan ones.[11] Hippolytus, a bishop in Rome, recorded that they produced books that spelled out their message. These may well have been an effective aspect of their rapid growth though it has to be said that Hippolytus wasn't greatly impressed by them. Indeed, he wrote that "the supernatural is discerned in the normal ministry of the sacrament, not in the irrational ecstasies which lead people to pride and censoriousness."[12]

The New Prophets were forthright in their stand against the persecuting Roman authorities. Tertullian later noted that "those who receive the Paraclete, know neither to flee persecution nor to bribe."[13] The movement therefore expanded and their popularity increased. Montanism is

---

who recorded Ammia and Quadratus as orthodox Christians who "prophesied under the New Covenant."

6. Rev 21:5.

7. Miltiades wrote, "For if, as they claim, after Quadratus and Ammia at Philadelphia Montanus and his female disciples succeeded to the Prophetic gift . . ." Cited by Eusebius, *History* 5.17.

8. Eusebius, *History* 5.18.

9. Ibid., 5.16–18. Apollonius (c.211) had no office in the church.

10. Cited by Eusebius, *History* 5.17.1.

11. See Calder, "Philadelphia and Montanism."

12. Chadwick, *The Early Church*, 53.

13. Tertullian, *De Fuga*, 14.

known to have been strong in Thyatira until about A.D. 260. It also took root and flourished in North Africa at least until end of the third century. Montanus' most notable follower was Tertullian,[14] the first great Latin theologian of the church. He was born about the year A.D. 160 and trained in law. He became a Christian about the year A.D. 195 and, like Montanus before him, he was serious in his commitment to Christ as well as being a rigorist by nature. Jerome suggested that he returned to his native Carthage shortly around his conversion where he was ordained a priest. He was doubtless disenchanted at the way some of his fellow Christians were compromising their faith and witness in the sporadic outbreaks of persecution. He also warmed to the Montanist call for stricter holiness of life. His first work as a Montanist was a defense of the new prophecy in six books entitled *De Ecstasi*. The book was lost but fragments of its contents were preserved in the writings (entitled *Praedestinatus)* of an unknown author and found among Augustine's works.

It is very likely that Perpetua (d. 203) and other catechumens who were imprisoned for their faith and condemned for execution in the arena at Carthage, were members of the New Prophecy. *The Passion of St. Perpetua*, which records her story also makes mention of the fact that she faced the crowd and the beasts in the spirit of ecstasy.[15] Interestingly, in North Africa the New Prophets appear to have been accepted as part of the mainstream church congregations much in the way that Charismatic Christianity gradually found acceptance in the historic denominations in America, Britain, and parts of Europe in the 1970s and 1980s. There are no indications either during Tertullian's lifetime or in the years immediately following his death that Montanism was condemned or rejected. The "Tertullianists" so called are generally regarded as being another name for the later Montanists of North Africa.[16] It seems they continued to play an active role in the life of the Carthage Christian community well into Augustine's day, and there was even a report of their handing over one of their buildings in the city to Catholics during his time.[17]

Montanism found its way to Rome at an early point in time. Eusebius reported that they were led by two unfrocked presbyters of that city, Florinus and Blastus, and that many from the local diocese joined their

---

14. Trevett, *Montanism*, 941.

15. See The Acts of Perpetua and Felicitas. In Foakes Jackson, *The History*, 73.

16. Barnes, "The Chronology of Montanism," 43.

17. Augustine, De Hearesibus 1.86. In Trevett, *Montanism*, 43.

fellowship.[18] About the same time Tertullian stated that "the Bishop of Rome had in fact acknowledged the prophetic gifts of Montanus, Priscilla, and Maximilla and, in consequence of that recognition, had bestowed his peace on the churches of Asia and Phrygia."[19] Later however, Tertullian recorded that Apollinarius, Bishop of Hierapolis, whom he nicknamed "Praxeas" (meaning "busybody"), persuaded the Bishop of Rome to recall his irenic letter and "to refrain from affirming their prophetic gifts." Tertullian went on to state that in so doing Praxeas[20] had done two pieces of significant work for the devil, since by driving away prophecy he had "put to flight the Paraclete" and "he had crucified the Father." The latter statement referred to the bishop's teaching that God the Father, as opposed to Jesus the Son, had been put to death on the cross at Calvary. The result of the bishop's pronouncement was that Montanus was excommunicated and his movement became known as "The Phrygian Heresy."

Hippolytus (c.170–c.236), another Roman bishop, wrote somewhat scathingly of the Phrygians suggesting that they do not judge what their prophets are saying and that "the majority of their books are silly, and their attempts [at reasoning] weak."[21] Notwithstanding these criticisms, Montanism was still an active force in Rome at the close of the fourth century.[22]

A firmly orthodox expression of Montanism took root in Asia Minor and other missionaries carried the new teachings into Spain where it was active until the end of the fourth century. It was also known in the third century at Iconium and in Syrian Antioch. There were still reports of Phrygian activities in Armenia as late as the ninth century.

MAN OF THE HOLY SPIRIT

Montanus had been a priest of the cult of Cybele,[23] the Phrygian Earth Mother, whose priests ritually castrated themselves as an act of total commitment to her. This fact may well explain some of Montanus' later strong views on celibacy. The Cybelian priesthood were assistants to the priestesses and served in particular by teaching the rituals. About the year A.D.

18. Eusebius, *History* 5.14.

19. Tertullian, *Against Praxeas*, 1.

20. The identity of this bishop is not clear but it may well have been Eleutherus (174–189) who was known to have received letters from Gaul.

21. Hippolytus, *Refutation of All Heresies* 8.12.

22. Praedestinatus, Haer. 1.86.

23. Montanus' connection with the Cult of Cybele is reported by Jerome.

157 Montanus became a Christian in what was in all probability a dramatic and powerful conversion experience in which he was overwhelmed by the Holy Spirit. Montanus was almost certainly baptized at the time of his conversion and sensed his call to preach very early on. He began his prophetic ministry in the village of Ardabau in Phrygia.

Montanus appears to have been particularly captivated by the passage in the Gospel of John where the evangelist speaks the Holy Spirit as the "Paraclete," a person who would stand beside the people of God to strengthen and help them in their daily life and work. On occasion, Montanus spoke as if he himself was the Paraclete and this has led to some misunderstandings. For instance, Didymus recorded that "Montanus says, 'I am the Father and I am the Son and I am the Paraclete,'"[24] but this need not be taken to imply anything other than that he was claiming to speak in God's name, in much the same way that preachers sometimes preface their sermon with the words "in the name of the Father and the Son and the Holy Spirit." Montanus was quite possibly seeking to allow the Spirit of God to speak through him in the same way that many other men and women of the Spirit have done. It needs to be kept in mind that Tertullian, who was the first Christian to use the word "Trinity" and to articulate a doctrine of the Trinity, wrote nothing to indicate that Montanus held an erroneous doctrine of the Holy Spirit. Indeed, if anything, it is entirely possible that he had come to grasp that the Holy Spirit was as much "person" and as equally deserving of worship as the God the Father and Jesus the Son.

Montanus early claimed to be the mouthpiece of the Paraclete with a gospel that was charismatic, revivalist, and anticipated the coming of God's kingdom on earth; indeed—to be precise—beginning at Pepuza in Phrygia! Here he and his followers taught and believed that the New Jerusalem would descend as they believed the Lord had indicated in his vision to the Apostle John on the island of Patmos.

MONTANUS' MESSAGE

This central aspect of Montanus' message was that the millennium would be inaugurated with the coming of Christ and the descent of New Jerusalem at Pepuza in A.D. 177, and so he and his fellow leaders set up their headquarters in that town. In order to prepare for the anticipated advent many believers migrated there, including some bishops and other church

24. Didymus, *Concerning the Trinity* 3.41.1.

leaders. However, the time of predicted advent came and went without an intervention of any kind, but remarkably, instead of marking the collapse of the movement, the prophecy was interpreted in a spiritual light and was held to be the beginning of a new age of the Spirit. This aspect of Montanist teaching, which was developed at a later stage by Tertullian, was an early form of "dispensationalism," which in this case asserted that following the dispensation of Christ the church had entered on the day of Pentecost into a new and final dispensation or era of the Spirit. This was a simpler version of dispensationalism than that which was later taught by John Nelson Darby and adopted by Charles Schofield in the nineteenth century, according to which biblical history was analyzed into seven dispensations.

Montanus was endorsed and revered by his later followers of Tertullian's day as one of the heralds of this new era of the Holy Spirit. The Montanist emphasis on spiritual gifts, the imminent parousia at Pepuza, and the dispensation of the Spirit has been regarded as an early form of fundamentalism. Some of those who had migrated to Pepuza in anticipation of New Jerusalem settled there while others moved out into the surrounding areas and began to live out the new life-style they had been taught.

This was a serious and radical message and it required total commitment and rigorous discipline on the part of Montanus' following. He therefore urged demanding forms of holiness that included celibacy and periods of strict fasting. On occasion "dry fasts" were observed in addition to the regular fasts enjoined by the Catholic Church. Montanists were enthusiastic in their missionary zeal and were quite prepared to face persecution and martyrdom if need be. Later Montanists were known for their high standards of behavior. In the area of sexual relations, marriages could, if necessary, be dissolved and second marriages were forbidden. Tertullian wrote: "Among us, however, whom the recognition of spiritual gifts entitles to be deservedly called 'Spiritual,' continence is as religious as license is modest; since both the one and the other are in harmony with the Creator. Continence honors the law of marriage . . ."[25]

In all of this the Montanists were motivated and inspired by their charismatic experience of the Holy Spirit who they believed would lead them into all truth and strengthen and equip them to witness to their faith in Christ. Montanus was not only a prophet but he spoke in tongues as had been common in the early churches since the day of Pentecost. It was for these reasons that he in particular was met with hostility from the early Catholic hierarchy. On occasion his enthusiasm was such that he appeared

25. Tertullian, *On Monogamy*, 1.

frenzied and seemed to speak in ecstasy. Epiphanius (c.315–403), a monk who later became Bishop of Salamis and was a rigid opponent of anything that seemed the least bit fringe or unchurchy, gives the content of one of his prophecies as follows:

> Behold, man is like a lyre,
> And I [the Spirit] rush like a plectrum.
> Man sleeps and I awake.
> Behold, the Lord is he who arouses the hearts of men,
> And gives a heart to men.[26]

As we have already noted, Didymus (c.313–98), who supervised the Catechetical School in Alexandria, recorded that Montanus proclaimed, "I am the Father, the Word, and the Paraclete."[27] This and other reported prophecies in which Montanus began with the word "I" and "I the Lord have come," doubtless rattled the ecclesiastical status quo of the day.[28] In reality, however, Montanus was simply expressing his conviction that it was the Lord who had prompted his utterance and it was the Lord who was speaking through him—playing him like a plectrum strumming a lyre.

Despite these rather different views on the Holy Spirit and prophecy, Montanus was doctrinally in harmony with the orthodox "rule of faith" and the baptismal creeds. His beliefs were those of the Catholic Church, a fact endorsed by Hippolytus, who recorded that "in respect of what appertains to the origin and creation of the universe, the Phygians are supposed to express themselves correctly and in regard to Christ they have not irreverently formed their opinions."[29] In another place, Hippolytus stressed that they conformed to the rule of faith and "acknowledge God to be the Father of the universe and creator of all things; . . . they receive what the Gospel testifies concerning Christ."[30]

---

26. Epiphanius, *Panarion* 48.4. The Panarion is commonly known as *Refutation of all the Heresies*. See also Aune, *Prophecy*, 314.

27. Didymus, *De Trinitate* 3.41.

28. See also Epiphanius, *Haer.* 48.11.1 where he reports Montanus as saying "I the Lord, the Almighty God, remain among men" and 48.11.9, "Neither angel, nor ambassador, but I, the Lord God the Father, am come."

29. Hippolytus, *Refutation of All Heresies* 8.21. In *Ante-Nicene Fathers*, vol. 5, 147.

30. Hippolytus, *Phil* 8.19.

WOMEN LEADERS

Alongside Montanus, two significant leaders were the prophetesses, Priscilla and Maximilla, whose authority was soon widely acknowledged. Indeed Montanus not only valued them but treated them as equals. He wrote of Priscilla as being "the mouthpiece of the Paraclete."[31] Both Priscilla and Maximilla were noble women whose prophetic gifts Montanus encouraged and nurtured. Epiphanius stated that by the fourth century the "ordination" of women in Montanism was common practice and the unknown author of Praedestinatus stated that "the Pepuzians are giving leadership to women, so that among them these are honored like a priest."[32]

Montanus' call for chastity and abstinence from sexual relationships should come as no surprise in view of his emasculated condition, which dated from his years as a priest in the cult of the goddess, Cybele. Jerome suggested his castration was out of devotion to her.[33] It was on account of this injunction to celibacy that Priscilla had left her husband when she joined the movement. Eusebius cited Apollonius who wrote, "It is evident that these prophetesses, from the time they were filled with the Spirit, were the very first to leave their husbands. How then could they lie so blatantly as to call Priscilla a virgin?"[34] It was possibly for this reason that on one occasion at Pepuza, Maximilla was forced to submit to an unsuccessful exorcism of the spirit within her by Bishop Zoticus who "planted himself in front of her and tried to silence the spirit at work in her." He was prevented from doing so by Themison and some of her "partisans."[35] She was, however, revered and respected by those to whom she ministered and with whom she enjoyed a reputation for holy living. She was assured in her calling, declaring on one occasion, "The Lord has sent me as adherent, preacher, and interpreter of this covenant and promise; he has compelled me, willingly or unwillingly, to learn the knowledge of God."[36] It seems that she may well have been hounded by the local bishops and accused of sheep stealing, for she said on at least one occasion, "I am chased like a wolf from the sheep; I am not a wolf; I am word and spirit and power."[37]

---

31. Tertullian, *Concerning the Resurrection of the Flesh* 11.2.
32. Anon, *Praedestinatus*, 27.
33. Jerome, *Letter* 41.4. In Trevett, *Montanus*, 939.
34. Eusebius, *History* 5.18.
35. Ibid.
36. Epiphanius, *Panarion* 48.13.1.
37. Asterius Urbanus, *Ante-Nicene Fathers*, vol. 7, 336.

Indeed her central message—recorded for us in the writings of Bishop Epiphanius, an opponent of Montanism—would arguably have been acceptable to anyone in the early Catholic Church as she declared, "Listen not to me, but listen to Christ."[38] Again she said on another day, "Do not hear me but hear Christ."[39]

Montanism was criticized by early Catholic officialdom on account of the place it accorded to women in its leadership. In this regard, the teachings of Montanism were clearly out of harmony with some of Apostle Paul's instructions (1 Tim 2:12), although it is evident that the apostle exhorted *all* the Corinthian Christians, both men *and women*, to prophesy (1 Cor 11:3–11). Chadwick noted that it was the role the Montanists accorded to women that led to their exclusion by Catholic bishops.[40]

OPPOSITION TO MONTANISM

The majority of groups that, like the Montanists, believe in and proclaim an imminent advent frequently develop a fervent concern with spiritual gifts, simply for the reason that biblical text declares that "in the last days God will pour out his Spirit on all flesh." As has been noted, the Montanists were particularly focused on the prophetic and other works of the Spirit such as speaking in tongues, dreams, and visions.

This emphasis on "freedom in the Spirit" sometimes produces moral and social libertainism. Such was the case for a few of the sixteenth-century Anabaptists in Europe, some of whom shared all things in common, practiced polygamy, and pooled their money in a common purse. A less frequent response to a perceived imminent coming of the Lord is the demand for a high level of holiness so that the waiting group will "be prepared like a pure and spotless bride ready for the arrival of the bridegroom." It was this thinking that led Montanus to operate his strict and austere regime. Indeed, his rejection of marriage and advocacy of celibacy needs to be seen in the light of his strong conviction that the return of Jesus was close at hand. It was in line with the apostle Paul's injunction to the Corinthians "that since the time was short . . . those who had wives should live as if they had none."[41] Doubtless, Priscilla was impacted by this when she made it clear that her spiritual life had been considerably sharpened after she was

38. Ibid., 336.
39. Epiphanius, *Panarion*, 48.12.4.
40. Chadwick, *History of the Early Church*, 53.
41. 1 Cor 7:29.

freed from a lifeless marriage. According to Tertullian, she said that sexual purity enabled Christian believers "to see visions and . . . hear distinct voices which are as saving as they are mysterious."[42] Tertullian later wrote that the Montanists were rejected, not for their unorthodox views, but rather because "they plainly teach more frequent fasting than marrying."[43]

Tertullian's comment here leads us to consider another aspect of Montanism that resulted in strong criticism—the way in which they practiced fasting. The church normally fasted on Wednesdays and Fridays, but Montanism increased this from half a day to the whole day and additionally for two week-long periods during the year. Montanus' advocacy of dry fasts with radishes probably meant abstinence from alcohol and a vegetarian diet, since wine was a basic drink. Tertullian defended the Montanist practice in his treatise *On Fasting*. In this he wrote: "On this account the New Prophecies are rejected: not that Montanus, Priscilla, and Maximilla preach another God, nor that they disjoin Jesus Christ (from God), not that they overrun any particular rule of faith or hope, but that they plainly teach more frequent fasting than marrying."[44]

Related to these austerity measures was the accusation made by Apollonius against Montanus that he "appointed agents to collect money, who contrived to make the gifts roll in under the name of 'offerings,' and who has subsidized those who preach his message, in order that gluttony may provide an incentive for teaching."[45] This comes across as an ad hominem exaggeration, it being wholly unlikely that Montanus, who practiced austerity, would promote such excesses. It also seems perfectly reasonable that Montanus should have given financial support to those who were actively engaged in supporting his mission.

It could possibly be that this strict regime resulted in Montanus and his inner circle of leaders living Christ-like lives, which contrasted sharply with a rather more stultified mainstream Catholic Church and hierarchy. It is well known that many of the early Christians were attracted to the rigorous and serious Christian commitment that was exemplified by the cult of martyrdom, and individuals—possibly including Origen of Alexandria—voluntarily castrating themselves.

---

42. Tertullian, *On Exhortation to Chastity* 10.5.

43. Ibid., 8.1.

44. Tertullian, *On Fasting*, 8.1.

45. Eusebius, *History* 5.18.

THE KEY ISSUES

It was inevitable that Montanus and his followers would clash with the local bishops because they had little time for those who emphasized the importance of the office of ecclesiastical leaders and the institutional structured life of the Catholic Church. They were also dissatisfied with the worldliness and moral laxity of some of its congregations.

It is most likely, however, that the church turned against Montanus and his associates when the descent of New Jerusalem failed to materialize in A.D. 177. Some bishops had been captivated by Montanus' preaching and had gone to Pepuza to await the parousia. When it didn't happen they turned their backs on him and he was denounced as a false prophet. Doubtless, he was seen by some as an ecstatic enthusiast who had been led astray by the devil. Some of the local churches pronounced Montanism as a heresy and went as far as excommunicating him from their fellowship. Montanus, needless to say, did not accept their judgment and appealed to the Bishop of Rome who proved sympathetic to his cause, at least in the first instance. But his opponents went one step higher (at least, that is how it was seen at the time) and appealed to a group of Christian confessors who were awaiting martyrdom in the province of Gaul. Their leader, Irenaeus, sent various letters in response in which he made it clear that he himself stood in unbroken line from the apostles and therefore had the mind of Christ in such matters.[46]

Despite the fulminations of some local bishops and church leaders against Montanus and his followers it is a mistake to imagine that the movement was now a despised and rejected minority. Quite the reverse was the case and for a long time in a number of places the movement co-existed alongside the Catholic hierarchy. Part of the problem was that the official church was already grappling at this very time with external threats from groups such as the Gnostics and Marcionites. Having yet another problem in the shape of the Phrygians was perhaps felt to be one too many. In other words, the defensive attitude taken against the other heretical groups may have spilled over into the mainstream churches' attitude towards the Montanists.

46. Ibid., 5.20.

PROPHECY

The nub of the issue was that the level of Montanus' experience and understanding of the Holy Spirit was beyond that of most of the churches in his local area. Clearly, his critics had forgotten the day of Pentecost when the early disciples staggered like drunken men and women on the streets of Jerusalem after the Holy Spirit had come upon them. They rejected Montanus either because they found his fervent ways distasteful or for the reason that their own people might be drawn away by him.

It seems then that a number of bishops and church leaders turned against Montanus and his fellow leaders particularly on account of the failure of A.D. 177. But they also professed to be disturbed by the trance-like, whirling, and dervish manner of his prophecies. Once again, however, it needs to be said that these may have been no more outrageous than the shakings of the early Quakers or the early Pentecostals and therefore no necessary reason to condemn him.[47] Leaving aside the day of Pentecost, it needs to be remembered that there was a long-standing tradition of ecstasy in the Hebrew prophetic tradition.

Montanus clearly should not be denigrated as a false prophet on the basis of one failed prediction since he called people to follow the God who revealed himself in Jesus and was still well regarded by considerable numbers of people in after years. Hermas, a second-century church leader from Rome, wrote that "prophets receive divine revelation while the church is at worship and as a response to prayer. . . . False prophets avoid such cultic settings and give oracles in response to questions in private consultation and are paid for it."[48] In this statement Hermas was underlining a key apostolic principle that prophecies should be carefully scrutinized by the hearers. In encouraging his followers to prophesy, Montanus was merely obeying the injunction of the Apostle Paul who urged the Corinthian church not to be ignorant of spiritual gifts, but earnestly desire them—in particular the ability to prophesy.[49]

Montanus' anonymous opponent, cited by Eusebius, was critical of the fact that "he fell into a kind of trance and unnatural ecstasy" and that "he raved and began to chatter and talk nonsense [possibly glossolalia], prophesying in a way that conflicted with the practice of the Church

---

47. The anonymous opponent of the sect asserted that at times he appeared distraught with terror. Eusebius, *History* 5.17, 2–3.

48. *Shepherd of Hermas* 11.

49. 1 Cor 14:1–3.

handed down."[50] The majority of Phrygians, however, do not appear to have been turned away from following Montanus on account of what were reported as his displays of excessive emotion. Many of them must have been aware that the Apostle Paul claimed to speak in tongues more than all the Corinthians and experienced at least one moment of ecstasy when he was caught up in the third heaven.[51] Nor did the failure of his prophecies relating to New Jerusalem result in the demise of the movement. In fact, his following grew in numbers and developed and spread after the events of A.D. 177 It was the case that Cyprian, Bishop of Carthage, condemned the Montanists in a later period but it was not for prophesying but "for separating themselves from the Church of God . . . where the elders preside."[52]

Montanism was in most respects what sociologists of religion have regarded as a typical sectarian group. Its doctrines were in conformity with those of the proto-orthodox churches but it had become separate from the established church, not because it had made a conscious decision to do so but rather because the church had excluded it. Tertullian took the view that the church (rather than the Montanists) was schismatic in this particular matter. However, Augustine later defined heretics as "those who claim to confess the sound faith but have broken off and hold services in opposition to their canonical bishops," in consequence of which Montanism came to be seen by many as the "Phrygian heresy."[53]

The West has perhaps more to learn from the Montanists than might at first be apparent. We need to reflect that many of the so-called confessing churches of the sixteenth-century Reformation were themselves the product of schism. It is important that members of churches, such as the Anglican church and the Presbyterian church, don't self-righteously and disdainfully push away orthodox expressions of the Christian faith that they find not to their liking or style. Many of the leaders of these churches have become totally submerged in the surrounding secular culture and values and in consequence have lost almost all credibility, and the laying on of hands by bishops and presbyters has in many cases become a dead symbol of a powerless ritual.

50. Eusebius, *History of the Church* 16.3.

51. 2 Cor 12:2.

52. Cyprian, *Letter* 68.8. In *Ante Nicene Fathers*, vol. 5, 392.

53. Greenslade, *Schism in the Early Church*, 17.

FACTORS THAT MADE MONTANISM SUCCESSFUL

Dynamic Leadership

Montanus was clearly a powerful preacher and a leader with charisma. He had the ability to both set out a Christian vision that people were able to respond to and to persuade them to run with it. Montanus was undoubtedly a man with what Max Weber termed "charisma." That is, he had natural, inbuilt gifts of personality that attracted people both to him and to his cause. He was a man with high moral standards who was known for strong personal discipline and holiness of life. There is no suggestion that he ever fell into immorality of the kind we have seen in recent times in the lives of some televangelists and charismatic revivalist preachers. The fact that Montanus had charisma is obvious for the reason that he was able to sustain and re-envision the movement even after the failed promise of the coming of the Lord in A.D. 177.

Christine Trevett states that Montanus was said to have the "Pauline charisma of administration."[54] Certainly there seems no doubt that, like John Wesley after him, he was both a gifted organizer of men and women and had a real ability to handle money and finance his leadership teams and missionary endeavors.

Every Member Ministry

Although there were significant key leaders—Montanus, Priscilla, Maximilla, and later Tertullian, the movement was essentially one in which all the membership was actively engaged in ministry. The emphasis was on the gifts that the Holy Spirit had given to each person. Montanus moved away from the emerging tendency among the churches in Asia Minor, who were putting energy into developing ecclesiastical hierarchy, the office of priesthood, and the sacraments. As he perceived it, the official church was moving away from the first-century every-member ministry of the body model of church. His desire was to retain to the charismatic Christianity of the Apostolic age.

---

54. Trevett, "Montanism, Priscialla, Maximilla, and Their Teachings," 939.

Equality for Women

Montanus, as has been seen, not only appointed women to the leadership of his movement, he treated them as equals, allowing them to speak and regarding what they uttered as authoritative. Priscilla was clearly a woman of deep commitment to Christ and may well have been the one who spoke the anonymous sayings recorded by Tertullian and linking women with martyrdom: "Do not wish to die in your beds or in miscarriages and mild fevers, but rather in martyrdom that he may be glorified who has suffered for you."[55] This undoubtedly must have turned a few heads but Montanus could have reminded his congregations that in Christ there is neither male nor female but all are one in Christ Jesus. He could have impressed on them the fact that Jesus not only treated women as equals, but he also had women who travelled and worked with him as he preached the good news, healed the sick, and cast out demons. Montanus' followers took this aspect of Scripture seriously and at its face value and this must have been a particularly appealing aspect of his ministry.

Emphasis on Spiritual Gifts

Montanus was living and preaching at a time when the church was undergoing harsh persecution. This led in some areas to the development of bishops as leaders and the growth of ecclesiastical organization so that the congregations could stand united against the hostile and often persecuting authorities of the Roman Empire. Montanus' emphasis on spiritual gifts must have seemed to many as a welcome opportunity to those who were beginning to yearn for something more akin to the experience of the disciples on the day of Pentecost. In particular, the sharp focus on prophecy gave the opportunity to all to participate in worship, ministry, and service. Furthermore it was in conformity with the Apostle Paul's injunction to "eagerly desire spiritual gifts, especially the gift of prophecy,"[56] which meant speaking to others "for their strengthening, encouragement, and comfort."[57]

55. Tertullian, *De Fuga* 9.4.

56. 1 Cor 14:1.

57. 1 Cor 14:3.

A Christianity That Wasn't Merely Cerebral

Much of recent and contemporary Christianity, particularly in the West, has either been too grounded in the intellectual and in dry biblicism or, conversely, it has been a form of rootless experience. Montanism appears to have taken Scripture seriously, and fostered a disciplined spirituality, while at the same time giving freedom to the Spirit of God in worship, ministry, and service.

In the end it has to be said that the New Prophets were simply promoting a renewal movement that sought to safeguard important teachings and aspects of the New Testament gospel. They strove to establish a Christian faith that was apostolic in its organization, gave equal rights and place to women in its life and leadership, was alive in the Holy Spirit, practiced the gifts of the Spirit, and kept a strong Christian morality and values.

2 | The Donatists

BLOOD AND MARTYRS

IN THE YEAR A.D. 303 the Roman Emperor, Diocletian (284–305), began one of the most fierce and brutal persecutions of Christians that had been witnessed by that time; one in which Alban, the first British martyr, was put to death on the outskirts of Verulamium. Diocletian had recently attended a pagan sacrifice at which the augers were unable to discern any signs in the animal entrails. The oracle of Apollo had put the blame on some Christians who were present at the occasion and had crossed themselves. This, for him, was confirmation that action was needed to restore homage to the pagan gods of the Roman Empire. Diocletian therefore ordered that all church buildings were to be destroyed and the Scriptures were to be handed over and burnt. At the same time those who held official positions in the government or had other positions of public honor were stripped of their office if they continued to profess the Christian faith.[1] All citizens were required to appear before the local magistrate and offer incense while at the same time declaring "Caesar is Lord!" Those who refused or were unwilling to hand over sacred books were thrown into prison, tortured, and murdered. Eusebius, the church historian, who personally witnessed some of the persecutions, recorded that many believers had to face brutal floggings at the hand of the military, which were then followed by "the ordeal of facing man-eating beasts when they were attacked by panthers, bears of different kinds, wild boars, and bulls goaded with red-hot irons."[2] Some of the punishments meted out under the Diocletian tyranny were barbaric in the extreme. Eusebius reported the following episode, "Words cannot describe the outrageous agonies endured by the martyrs in the

1. Eusebius, *History,* 8:2.2.
2. Ibid., 8.7.

17

Thebais. They were torn to bits from head to foot with potsherds like claws till death released them. Women were tied by one foot and hoisted high in the air, head downwards, their bodies completely naked without a morsel of clothing, presenting thus the most shameful, brutal, and inhuman of all spectacles to everyone watching."[3]

Eusebius ended this same paragraph by remarking that "there were occasions when on a single day a hundred men as well as women and little children were killed, condemned to a succession of ever-changing punishments."[4] Christians reacted in different ways in response to these terrors. Many church leaders "bore up heroically under horrible torments, an object lesson in endurance of fearful ordeals," while countless others, "their souls already numbed with cowardice, promptly succumbed to the first onslaught."[5]

The issue that brought the Donatists to the fore was how to handle those Christians who had denied their faith in Jesus rather than die amid such terror and bloodshed. During the conflict some church leaders had not only handed over sacred books to be burned but had even made known the whereabouts of some of their fellow Christians. These people were known as "traditors," a name derived from the Latin word meaning "to hand over." Following Constantine's conversion in A.D. 312 many of these so called traditors returned to positions of authority in the church.

The touch paper of this dispute was ignited by the compromising behavior of Mensurius, the Bishop of Carthage. It was alleged that he had cooperated with the Roman authorities during the persecution. In particular, the local Roman officials had been lenient and allowed him to hand over heretical books to the authorities to be burned instead of copies of the Scriptures. He, in turn, had agreed to suspend public worship in the hopes that he could lie low until the persecution died away. At the same time, some of the more forthright Christians in the city who had boldly professed their faith found themselves in prison and denounced Mensurius as a cowardly, compromising traditor.

When Mensurius died towards the end of 311 there was an unseemly struggle to appoint his successor. By tradition new primates at Carthage were consecrated by twelve bishops, including the current primate of the province of Numidia. Two main factions emerged, each with their own candidates: one representing the more cultured city elements and the

3. Ibid., 8.9.

4. Ibid.

5. Ibid., 8.2.

other the more ordinary working people. Eventually Mensurius' archdeacon, Caecilian, was chosen as his successor. Contrary to the established
tradition, however, he was quickly consecrated by only three bishops, one
of whom was Felix of Aptunga in Byzacena who was also believed to be a
traditor.

Although Caecilian had the support of most of the Roman citizens
he was regarded with suspicion by many of the local church leaders. They
thought him cowardly, cruel, and intolerant, particularly of the confessors and martyrs. There were strong rumors that Caecilian was himself a
traditor, or if he wasn't, that he had indeed been consecrated by a traditor.
There seemed a distinct likelihood that bishop Felix was also guilty on this
score. As far as many in the city were concerned, this was a good enough
reason to reject Caecilian's appointment. Strife began in earnest when the
opposition party sent an invitation to Secundus of Tigisis, the primate of
Numidia, to intervene. He duly arrived together with seventy Numidian
bishops and a council was held that declared the consecration of Caecilian
to be invalid on the grounds that correct procedures had not been followed and that Felix was a traditor. The Council appointed Marjorinus
in his place. His candidature had been strongly supported by Lucilla, a
wealthy and devout lady whom he served as her private chaplain. Caecilian, it emerged, had offended her by publicly rebuking her for kissing a
relic during a communion service. Marjorinus (311–315) did not remain
in office for very long and on his death Donatus (died c.355), the Bishop
of Casae Nigrae, was immediately elected Bishop of Carthage in his place.
It is after him that the Donatists were named.

Caecilian and his followers widened the whole issue still further
when they appealed to the Emperor Constantine in Rome, claiming that
the schism was likely to cause a public disorder. Probably in the Spring
of A.D. 317 the Emperor Constantine put in place the most severe law in
North Africa decreeing that the Donatist churches should be confiscated
and their leaders sent into exile. But Donatus was made of sterner stuff
and refused to surrender the churches he held in Carthage, and the Christians of that city were at once a divided community. Away from the city, all
the old Donatist bishops were left untouched and continued to minister to
their clergy and people. Finally in May 321 Constantine saw the light and
realized it was going to be no easy matter to restore unity to the churches
in North Africa and he therefore granted the Donatists toleration. In a
subsequent letter to the Catholics he urged moderation and patience.

Meanwhile, Donatism spread rapidly with many new churches being constructed. Their basilica at Theveste was reckoned as one of the

finest monuments in Roman Africa; its massive stone blocks still stand unweathered.[6] Donatist worship was vigorous and lively and made use of the same Latin text of the Bible current in Cyprian's time. The reading of Scripture and Bible-based sermons played a central part in the proceedings. Agapē meals, particularly in conjunction with the anniversary of a martyr's death, were highly valued. It has been pointed out that many of the inhabitants of North Africa lived in fear of evil spirits and believed that there was a constant and dire need to propitiate the gods on this score. The strong Donatist emphasis on the Holy Spirit and the power of the third person of the Trinity over malevolent forces was therefore a particularly attracting feature of their message.[7] Their view of baptism was that the Holy Spirit was actually present in the water and had a powerful cleansing and protecting impact on those who received the sacrament.[8] Such was the appeal of Donatism that it even gained a foothold among the African community in Rome, and Donatus dispatched Victor of Garba to establish himself as the true bishop of Rome.

DONATIST CONCERNS

The big issue that the two sides hotly debated was whether or not the sacrament of penance could effect a reconciliation that was sufficient to allow a traditor back into full communion. The Catholic Church took the view that the sacrament of penance was exactly designed and effective for this purpose. The Donatists, on the other hand, maintained that such a crime of denying Jesus disqualified a person from any leadership role in the church.

The Donatists for their part were clear that such defectors could not celebrate valid sacraments because their denial of Jesus had lastingly tainted them. Put another way, their denial of Jesus meant that no grace or blessing could flow through them when they ministered the sacraments. In short, they were permanently corrupted individuals and no spiritual grace could be conveyed through their ministries. As far as the Donatists were concerned the conscience of the priest was crucially important. If a priest stood at God's altar spotted with vice or sin, how could God possibly hear his prayers? He could in fact only baptize people with evil. The Catholic Church argued that what made the sacrament valid was not

6. Frend, *The Donatist Church*, 162.

7. Ibid., 113.

8. Ibid., 119.

dependent on the spiritual state of the church leader but on God alone. This meant that even if a priest was in mortal sin the sacrament would still convey God's presence and blessing simply for the reason that the right form of words had been recited by a legitimately authorized priest. As far as the Catholic Church was concerned a person who received the bread and wine from the hands of even an unrepentant priest could still receive the presence of Christ.

The result of this major disagreement was that the church in many towns and cities of North Africa became divided. This matter also brought the very recently converted Roman Emperor, Constantine, into the controversy and in A.D. 314 he called together the Council of Arles. The decision of the assembled Christian leaders, which included representatives from Britain, went against the Donatists who, needless to say, did not accept the judgment. In fact, they despised those compromising bishops who collaborated with Rome, and they strongly opposed the notion of a state church over which the recently converted emperor was exerting a growing influence. In consequence, the Donatists rapidly became a second branch of the church, setting up their own hierarchy in A.D. 316. In fact, their threat was to grow so rapidly that a later emperor, Valerian I, passed further laws against them. By A.D. 350 they outnumbered the orthodox Christians in Africa, and each city had its own opposing Donatist bishop. It wasn't until the time of Bishop Augustine of Hippo's campaigns against them that the official church began to gain the upper hand. Augustine's view was that it was the office of the priest that was important, rather than his character. He argued on the basis of legal documents that the emperor Constantine had chosen the Catholic Church of the empire rather than the Donatists as the official church of the empire. The result of all this was that the Donatists faced considerable persecution.

The two sides had completely opposite views regarding the nature of the church. The Catholics held the church to be an inclusive and mixed body consisting of both saints and sinners. They saw this pictured in Jesus' parable of the wheat the tares[9] and the dragnet[10] and possibly symbolized in Noah's taking both clean and unclean animals into the ark. The Donatists, on the other hand, saw those very same passages as referring to the world and therefore held that the sorting and separation happens here and now to produce a pure body of Christ. At heart, therefore, the Donatists

9. Matt 13:24–30, 36–43.
10. Matt 13:47–50.

were a holiness movement and declared themselves to be the true church on the ground of holiness.

THE SPREAD OF DONATISM

Unlikely though it seemed, it was the Donatist church rather than the official Catholic Church under the Emperor that grew rapidly across the North African provinces of the Roman Empire. As W. H. C. Frend observed, "Within a generation, Donatism was the religion of nearly all Africa and neither force nor argument could root it out";[11] and again, "Southern Numidia remained for three centuries the heart of Donatism."[12] This rapid spread was borne out by a 1930s excavation that studied seventy-two Romano-Berber villages and brought to light over 200 Donatist churches and chapels with a uniform local culture and distinctive art forms[13] based on veneration of the martyrs.[14] There were a number of reasons for this burgeoning movement. Perhaps most obvious was the fact that many of the North African peoples were readily convinced by the Donatist view that traditors who had renounced Christ could not have the Spirit of God in them. Conversely, they quickly saw the Donatists as the true church who were wholly committed to following Jesus and standing without fear in times of persecution.

The Donatist gospel also found a ready hearing on the part of the tribal peoples who lived southwest of Carthage, between the sea and the Aures mountains. In pre-Christian times they had been fanatical and rigorous worshippers of the pagan god Saturn. The uncompromising stance of the Donatists and their willingness to face martyrdom had an immediate appeal to their serious-minded natures. Symbols such as the palm, dove, lion, and crown were common in both Saturn and the Donatist worship that they subsequently embraced. The acceptance of Christian teaching from Donatist evangelists did not appear to them as a radical rejection of the African tribal religion but rather as a transformation of it.[15]

11. Frend, *The Donatist Church*, 23.

12. Ibid., 24.

13. Ibid., 66.

14. Ibid., 53.

15. Ibid., 104.

DONATUS OF CARTHAGE

Donatus' literary works have not survived and little is known about his personal life and friendships. What is clear from the writings of Augustine, however, is that he was a great orator and leader of men. Wherever he went he stirred enthusiasm and his charisma was remembered even fifty years after his death.[16] As Frend aptly put it, "He seems to have personified popular loathing for the worldly ecclesiastics who thought that they would do well in this life and the next." Optatus stated that Donatus "claimed for himself sovereign authority at Carthage, he exalted his heart and seemed to himself to be superior to other mortals, and wished that all, even his allies, should be beneath him." He was rarely called "bishop" but was known as "Donatus of Carthage." Frend described him as "a prophet and religious leader who could converse directly with the Lord and maintain stringent control over his following."[17] According to Augustine, he was known as the man "who purged the church of Carthage from error."[18] He was clearly sold out for Christ and the work of his kingdom and found it difficult to comprehend why anyone would deny the Lord he served. He had a vision for a church that would stand strong in times of persecution and whose members would not capitulate from their faith. Donatus wrote several forthright pamphlets against the followers of Caecillian and sent a whole series of pastoral letters to his clergy, even those in the remotest parts. Augustine noted that towards the end of Constantine's reign Donatus' authority was acknowledged by nearly 300 bishops.[19] Indeed, when the emperor died in May 337 Donatus was at the height of his power with strong and solid support in Carthage and Numidia and his authority extending to every corner of Roman Africa. Donatism remained the predominant religion in North Africa for another fifty years. Frend noted that many literate Africans regarded the Donatist church "as the true Catholic Church in Africa and the successor of the Church of Cyprian's time."[20]

Many of the Donatists found it difficult to come to terms with the fact that the Emperor and the Roman authorities were now on the side of the church. Thus when Constantine pronounced against them in 314 they

---

16. Ibid., 153.

17. Ibid., 165.

18. Augustine, *Contra Cresconium*, 3:56, 62. In Frend, *The Donatist Church*, 154.

19. Augustine, *Letter* 93.43. In Frend, *The Donatist Church*, 167.

20. Frend, *The Donatist Church*, 170.

began to repeat Tertullian's question, "What has the emperor to do with the church"?

THE CIRCUMCELLIONS

Among those who were bemused by this new situation were groups of people known as Circumcellions who began to attach themselves to the Donatists about the year A.D. 340. They shared the Donatist concern for the poor and were fanatical in their concern for social justice.[21] Their name derived from the fact that they lived "around the shrines" (*circum cellas*). It is not altogether clear whether they grew out of the Donatist movement or attached themselves to it. However, one thing is clear—they proved to be a double-edged weapon as far as the Donatists were concerned. They were bands of social revolutionaries who hailed from Upper Numidia and Mauretania. Combining religious enthusiasm with violence they protested against the poverty they believed resulted from the harsh taxes of the Roman establishment, who they perceived as working hand-in-glove with the newly emerging state church.

Optatus, the Catholic Bishop of Milevis, warned of the threat they sometimes posed in the countryside when he wrote: "Even journeys could not be made with perfect safety, for masters were thrown out of their own chariots and forced to run in servile fashion, in front of their own slaves, seated in their lord's place. By judgment and command of these outlaws, the condition of masters and slaves was completely reversed."[22] It was perhaps not surprising therefore that Augustine later denounced them as "crazy herds of abandoned men" and accused them of a whole range of violent acts. Frend was of the view that in the present era they would be regarded as "terrorists." The fact was, however, that many Numidians had an intense dislike of the armies of Roman tax collectors who, as the historian Lactantius noted, frequently descended on them for money. Circumcellions found they had a natural affinity with the Donatist rejection of imperial authority. Significantly, inscriptions that have been uncovered in Donatist village churches hail Jesus as the champion of justice and the refuge from toil and hardship in the world.[23] Donatists found that whenever

---

21. Frend notes that Monceaux suggested that the Circumcellion movement may have begun as early as A.D. 316–17 but that he could find no evidence to support this. See Frend, *The Donatist Church*, 171 note 1.

22. Stevenson, *Creeds*, 202.

23. Frend, *The Donatist Church*, 111.

there was tough work to be done, such as sacking a Catholic Church or Roman villa, the Circumcellions could be relied on but at other times the Donatists found it necessary to reject their extreme behavior.

The religious life of the Circumcellions focused on living round the tombs of saints and martyrs, from whom they drew spiritual strength and protection for their souls. Pilgrimages to these shrines and burial by a martyr's tomb were key aspects of Circumcellion spirituality. Many Circumcellions, who prized martyrdom highly, represented Donatist doctrine in its extreme form.

The Catholic Church on a number of occasions found itself unable to deal with the threat posed by the Circumcellions and appealed to the secular power in the person of the Emperor to come to their aid. On one occasion in A.D. 405 the Cirucmcellions made the whole diocese of Hippo unsafe, destroying villas, attacking churches, and ambushing and beating church officials. Not only were the Roman authorities unable to deal with their threat in a decisive manner, their interference was resented by the Donatists as the state interfering with religion. In many ways interference of this kind convinced the indigenous population that the Donatists were a pure church whereas the Catholics were in league with "Babylon," the persecuting Roman authorities, and tainted by the relationship. The attempts to use force against the Donatists, in fact, simply hardened their wills and made them more determined to stand firm against the Catholics. Petilian, the Donatist bishop, was scathing about the Catholic participation in this persecution, writing that:

> The Lord Jesus Christ commands us, saying, "When they persecute you in this city, flee ye to another; and if they persecute you in that, flee to a third; for verily I say unto you, you shall not have gone over the cities of Israel, till the Son of man be come." If He gives us this warning in the case of Jews and pagans, you who call yourself Christian ought to not imitate the dreadful deeds of the Gentiles. Or do you serve God in such wise that we should be murdered at your hands? You do err, you do err, if you are wretched enough to entertain such a belief as this. For God does not have butchers for his priests.[24]

The Catholic desire for unity was understandable and praiseworthy, but the use of state power and the eventual designation of Donatists as "heretics" were highly questionable. Augustine, as we have seen, did see Donatists as heretics and later cited Jesus' words from the parable of Great

---

24. Ibid., 223.

Supper, "Compel them to come in." He defended his stance in 408 in a letter written to his friend Vincentius who had recently become a Donatist bishop.

> Your also read how he who was at first Saul and afterwards Paul, was compelled, by great violence with which Christ coerced him, to know and to embrace the truth. . . . You are also of the opinion that no coercion is to be used with any man in order to deliver him from the fatal consequences of error; and yet you see that in examples which cannot be disputed, this is done by God, who loves us with more real regard for our profit than any other can, and you hear Christ saying, No man comes unto me, except the Father draw him, which is done in the hearts of all those who, through fear of the wrath of God, betake themselves to him.[25]

In A.D. 361 the Donatist church came under the leadership of bishop Parmenius who wrote a long treatise against the Catholic Church. The Donatist position was that the sacraments operated on account of the moral fitness of the minister. This view was rebutted by bishop Optatus, who penned *Optatus of Milevis against the Donatists*. Optatus' main point was that the sacraments derived their validity from God and not from the minister. True baptism was therefore conferred by the name of the Trinity and not in the name of the minister. The Donatists strongly disagreed and took the view that those who had been baptized in the Catholic Church should be re-baptized after penance, a practice that bishop Cyprian of Carthage had used in previous times when restoring the lapsed into the church. The Donatist also advocated the re-ordination of leaders who joined their ranks from the Catholic churches. Augustine was later to express his disagreement and to contend that baptism could be conferred outside the Catholic Church as well as in it. His point was that the sacraments are God's sacraments even when administered in schism.[26] Donatus was strongly of the view that there was no true baptism outside his communion and yet he was still able to be flexible. Thus when he discovered that a number of congregations in Mauretania were willing to join him if they could do so without undergoing what they considered to be a second baptism, Donatus allowed himself to be persuaded by them.[27]

---

25. Stevenson, *Creeds*, 220.

26. Augustine, *Writings*, 3.

27. Frend, *The Donatist Church*, 168.

The end of Donatus' influence and the decline of his movement began about the year A.D. 346 when he decided to appeal to the Emperor
Constans for recognition as the sole Bishop of Carthage. Unlike his father,
Constans did not reject his request outright but sent a commission to
investigate the matter. Unfortunately for Donatus, the African Catholic
bishops had primed the members of the Commission even before they
set off to meet him and it was clear on their arrival that they were not
going to support Donatus or his followers. Several violent clashes ensued
in Carthage and various parts of Numidia with imperial troops locked in
combat with Circumcellions in some places. Donatus himself was exiled
and never again set foot in Africa. His death (which probably took place in
A.D. 355, away from his homeland) did, however, enable his followers to
claim him as a martyr as well as a reforming religious leader.

Donatus was clearly a dynamic and strong leader. Indeed, Augustine
went so far as to call him a "precious jewel in the Church."[28] He was gifted
with spiritual and administrative talents and shared a high view of the
office of a bishop.

DONATISM IN THE YEARS AFTER DONATUS

After Donatus' departure, Gratus, the Catholic Bishop of Carthage, summoned a council in the city (probably in A.D. 348 or 349), which enacted
canons forbidding the practice of rebaptism and venerating "unworthy
persons" as martyrs. Gratus also condemned traditors, those who had
handed over sacred Scriptures to the authorities. That said, it soon became clear that he lacked the skills to exploit the Catholic victory to the
full. There was little significant doctrinal difference between themselves
and the Donatists, and some Donatist bishops found little or no Catholic
Church members in their dioceses. Following Donatus' death the leadership passed to Bishop Pontius and Macrobius, the Donatist bishop in
Rome who had previously been a presbyter in the Catholic Church. Macrobius sent encouraging letters to the North African churches.

Then in A.D. 361 Julian, who was a pagan, became the Roman Emperor and he immediately allowed all those who had been banished to
return home. The return of the Donatist leaders was greeted with wild
enthusiasm as Donatism was rekindled in a frenzy with Catholic mitres,
vestments, and vessels being smashed or destroyed. Justices were kept

---

28. Augustine, *Sermon* 37.3 In Frend, *The Donatist Church*, 181.

busy restoring Donatist churches that had been seized by the Catholics during the previous fourteen years.

As long as Julian remained Emperor the Donatists were secure in North Africa, but when he died on 26th June, 363, the situation changed once more. However, this time and for nearly thirty years the Donatists were led by Parmenian, the Donatist Bishop of Carthage. He was a man of integrity who strongly opposed violence and brutality. He was also a powerful speaker and preacher who stood firm against the Catholics while at the same time taking care that the essential teachings of Donatism were imbibed by the mass of his followers. Parmenian also wrote "new psalms," probably in rhyming couplets, that proved very popular and were still sung in Augustine's day and in much later times.[29]

Parmenian also possessed considerable teaching gifts, and under his instruction Donatist theology was developed and strengthened. Parmenian set out his ideas in a five-volume set entitled *Adversus Ecclesiam Traditorum*. The work has not survived but snippets of it were quoted by Optatus of Milevis. From these it seems likely that the main themes were baptism, church unity, and the crimes of the persecutors and the traditors. Among other points he was clear that the Donatist claim to be the true church rested on the fact that they did not have among their leaders those who had denied their faith in Christ during the persecutions. Parmenian was adamant that African Catholics had proved themselves to be false Christians because they had betrayed their Lord. Return to the true church could only be gained by penance followed by a new initiation by baptism at the hand of a pure minister. Parmenian therefore reinforced the views of Donatus that the Christian church must be separated from the state. Such opinions would inevitably result in persecution, for which true Christians must always be ready. Optatus replied at some length, but, as Frend has pointed out, it is doubtful that the Numidians were convinced by him since they still had strong memories of Donatus' death in exile and the brutality of the imperial troops.

There were a few harsh times for the Donatists as the Roman authorities tried to exact heavy taxes from the people. On a number of these occasions the Circumcellions were drawn into the fray, sometimes bringing shame to the Donatist cause on account of their unruly behavior. On the whole, however, the Donatists enjoyed peace from outside interference during Parmenian's time in office while the Catholics continued to decline in number and influence.

29. Augustine, *Letter* 55.18, 34. In Frend, *The Donatist Church*, 194.

RADICAL DONATISM UNDER OPTATUS
AND GILDO AD 386-98

In the year A.D. 386 the Emperor Theodosius appointed Gildo as his commissioner to Africa and just two years later a priest named Optatus was elected Bishop of Thamagadi, which was the most important see in southern Numidia. These two men were to be partners in thrusting the Donatist cause forward. Optatus was fanatically attached to the Donatist agenda and was bent on establishing a social and religious revolution by violent means. He built one of the largest Cathedrals ever erected in Christian Africa, measuring some 200 feet long by fifty feet wide with a richly adorned baptistery standing alongside. He was a powerful orator who could sway the emotions of a crowd, and under his influence the Circumcellions became a military force to be reckoned with. Their clubs and staves were supplemented with swords, spears, and other more effective weaponry. In what was essentially a period of social deprivation, Optatus set about creating a more just social order aided by Circumcellion forces. Augustine later related that he redistributed land, settled marriage disputes, evicted unpopular heirs, and punished oppressive landowners by forcing them out of their estates. In this period there were reports of villas being destroyed and Circumcellions ruling the countryside. That said, it is clear from Augustine's letters that, generally speaking, the Catholics were left in peace during this time and that the Donatists did not oppress their Catholic neighbors. Indeed, they were left free to hold councils even in towns such as Hippo where there was a Donatist majority. Frend commented that "in these ten years between 388 and 398 Donatism came nearest to achieving complete mastery in Africa."[30] In this period there is evidence that many literate Africans continued to prefer Donatism to Catholicism and even Augustine himself was unable to dissuade some of his own clergy from leaving the Catholic fold. To this day, the ruins of many village churches speak of the enthusiasm the Donatists leaders must have inspired. Thus it was that in the last decade of the fourth century that Donatism reached its pinnacle of influence.

The end of their supremacy came when Gildo gambled on trying to force the imperial authorities to recognize their right to be the official church of Northern Africa. The method he chose was to hold the corn-fleet back in North African ports until his request was granted, in consequence of which he fully expected conflict with the Emperor Honorius' troops.

---

30. Ibid., 210.

As things turned out, he was trapped by a small expeditionary force as he sought to escape. His friend and ally, Optatus, suffered the same fate. Their deaths marked the end of the Donatist bid for supremacy in Africa just when it seemed they were almost on the brink of becoming a national church like the Copts in the Nile Valley. They had, nevertheless, been hugely successful. They had won the battle for popular support, they had set up their own diocesan structures and raised up many able leaders and strategists of considerable ability and spirituality. Their problem was that though they were highly successful in many ways, they never finally succeeded in finding an alternative to the state church. Although Donatism was to live on for many years to come, the future for Africa was to be quite largely in the hands of pro-Catholic administrators and church leaders. In their Primate, Aurelius, and Augustine of Hippo, the Catholics had finally found men who could debate the issues with them in a convincing way.

AUGUSTINE AND THE DECLINE OF DONATISM

It was their teaching and the writings, the public debates of Augustine, Bishop of Hippo, and the conferences he organized between the orthodox and Donatist bishops at Carthage in 411 that finally turned the tide for the Catholics. For ten years Augustine poured his energies into combating them both by tracts and books and by organizing major conferences to debate the issues. He entered into correspondence with leading Donatist laymen as well as highly placed Donatist clergy. Augustine reached out to the Donatists, referring to them as "brothers" who shared the same gospel and enjoyed the same worship. On this basis, he appealed to a text in Luke's Gospel, "Compel them to come in" as justification to come over to his side. Together with Aurelius, Bishop of Carthage, Augustine gathered 286 Catholic bishops. They were joined by 284 Donatist bishops led by Primian (the Donatist Bishop of Carthage) and Petilian (Bishop of Constantine). Their discussions lasted for three days. The Catholics had agreed beforehand to give up their sees to the Donatists if the decision went against them. They had also covenanted to recognize any Donatist bishops who were prepared to declare their allegiance to the Catholic Church. The debate inevitably focused on whether Bishop Felix had been a traditor and whether or not the church could welcome back into membership those who had denied Jesus during the persecution. At the end of many heated deliberations, Marcellinus, the imperial commissioner, decided in favor of the Catholic party. The Emperor Honorius then pronounced an edict that made Donatism a criminal offense punishable by fine and a requirement that all Donatist property was to be handed over to the Catholics. This strong state suppression contributed to what was to be a gradual but by no means total decline.

DONATISM AFTER THE CARTHAGE CONFERENCE, A.D. 412–429

The aftermath of the council did not bring immediate and total supremacy to the Catholics. As things turned out, Augustine's activities were confined to the Romanized cities along the coast and some of the river valleys where the Catholics had previously predominated. Augustine's major point— that the visible church contains both true believers and reprobates—was probably lost on the majority of the Berber population. They could readily understand the idea of the church as the Ark—the saved inside and the ungodly drowning outside in the waters of worldly compromise—but anything more complicated was beyond them.

While Donatism declined in influence after the conference it was by no means dead and buried. In the seventeen remaining years of Roman rule in Africa the Donatists did not return to the Catholic fold in large numbers as Augustine had hoped. Petilian remained in Numidia and was able to keep in contact with his fellow bishops by holding occasional councils. Donatist bishops remained in control in centers such as Caesarea and Thamugadi. There were also new Donatist ordinations and a fresh spate of pamphlets against Catholic practices. It is clear from Augustine's correspondence that Donatist leaders stood firm and that they continued to influence the mass of the Berber peoples. Frend noted that in the countryside archaeologists had yet to find clear evidence for the transformation of a single Donatist church into a Catholic one.[31] Excavations have revealed that a new Donatist church was built at Benin between A.D. 434 and 439. In Numidia there is evidence of continuing Donatist communities throughout the Vandal and Byzantine periods. Significantly, as late as A.D. 594 we find Pope Gregory writing to the new Bishop of Carthage urging him to hold a council against the Donatists. Little decisive action could have taken place, however, since Donatism continued in many areas until the Arab conquests of the seventh and eighth centuries.

Donatism and Catholicism were clearly two fundamentally opposite ways of doing church. While it is plain that the Catholic approach was

31. Ibid., 299.

both practical and inclusive, it failed—like most state religion—to deliver on a number of key issues and most obviously the social evils and injustices that were being meted out to the slaves and poverty-stricken workers on the big estates run by the Roman authorities. For all its inclusiveness, a Catholic church that sided with the oppressors could never appeal to the Berber poor of northern Africa. In short, the issue was whether these injustices were to be tolerated for the sake of Christian unity or challenged in the name of Jesus. For the Donatists there could only be one answer!

The issues raised by the Donatists resonate with some of the issues the contemporary church has faced in more recent times. The consecration of Gene Robinson as Bishop of New Hampshire has raised questions that may well end in schism. The issues arising out of the scandal of Roman Catholic pedophile priests has been seen by some as a mandate for a Donatist-style separation.

FACTORS THAT MADE DONATISM SUCCESSFUL

Leaders

There is no doubt that both Donatus and Parminian were remarkable primates and leaders. They, along with other bishops, were for several generations believed to be able to perform miracles. In addition, it is clear that many hundreds of other Donatist bishops were men of the Spirit who were wholly committed to scriptural teaching, and who were pastorally sensitive and caring. It is also the case, as Ronald Knox pointed out, that Donatist bishops were non-hierarchical in their practice and addressed letters to their clergy as "fellow presbyters who have been appointed with us to minister in the gospel."[32] Many Donatist leaders were cultivated men (such as Emeritus of Caesarea) and moral preachers (such as Macrobius of Rome), but they were also adaptable such that they were able to give powerful, scriptural sermons in the language of the local people.

Clear Teaching

One of Donatism's great strengths was its straightforward teaching. This is manifestly obvious in Petilian's *Letters to Presbyters*. Writing about baptism he is adamant that "he who knowingly receives faith from the

---

32. Knox, *Enthusiasm*, 67–68.

faithless receives not faith but guilt." The true church is that which main-tained the purity of the sacraments. Catholic clergy who received their ordination from traditors were not clergy at all since their ordination was invalid. They were, in fact, following in the steps of Judas. Petilian was also quick to point out that Augustine himself had been a Manichee priest and, he said, remained one at heart.

The Poor

A theoretical debate over Scripture was one thing, but the rigorist ethic of the Donatists challenged the actions and day-to-day attitudes of many in the Catholic Church as well as the wider pagan Roman society. Outside the main towns and cities there were many large estates worked by slaves who, needless to say, were not readily drawn to the Catholic Church and its alliance with the state. The Donatists were those who had a real heart for the poor. Frend suggested that Donatism was a vehicle for Berber pa-triotism and for socio-economic protest. It was "the protest of the urban poor and the rural peasants in the name of Jesus and on the basis of his teaching against a Church increasingly identified with the landowning classes and imperial authority."[33]

Identity with Local Culture

There is no doubt that Donatism drew strength on account of its close identity with local culture. They made full use of the local languages rather than Latin. This meant they were able to communicate with ordinary tribal groups who lacked education and other benefits of citizenship. In contrast, it is said that Augustine required an interpreter as he travelled round the countryside surrounding Hippo, since the indigenous population only spoke Berber or Punic.[34] Frend commented that he was out of touch with the agricultural workers from whom the Donatist drew so much of their strength.[35]

33. Frend, *Saints and Sinners*, 20.

34. Sundkler and Steed, *History of the Church*, 27.

35. Frend, *The Donatist Church*, 233.

Spiritual Vigor

For generations the Donatists had been taught to expect persecution and when it came to stand firm. There is evidence a plenty that in the towns and villages across North Africa the Berber peasants remained resolute in their faith. Their worship was fervent and touched people's emotions at a deep level, a fact born out by an inscription from the church at Thamallula that reads, "Praise the Lord you righteous, and let us glory in the Lord with a true heart." The same note is also sounded in the Donatist pamphlet entitled *Acta Satunini*, "In our church, the virtues of the people are multiplied by the presence of the Spirit."[36] Martyrdom and love for God's word were at the heart of Donatists.

36. Ibid., 318.

3 | The Celts

BEFORE THE ROMANS SET foot on British soil, at some point in the early part of the first century the major inhabitants of the land were the Celts who had come originally from the area around the Black Sea. It seems likely that some of the military and administrative personnel, who were sent to establish the Roman province of Britannia, possibly as early as A.D. 50, were practicing Christians who shared their faith with their new neighbors. They evangelized and began to establish church life based on the administrative organization of the Roman Empire, with its dioceses and parishes. This fact is clear because in A.D. 314, when Christianity became officially recognized throughout the Roman Empire, three British bishops represented the English church at the Council of Arles with the newly converted Emperor Constantine paying their travelling expenses.

It wasn't until later in 381 when the Emperor Theodosius made Christianity the official religion of the Roman Empire and the bishops of Rome began to increase their influence. This, however, was only for a brief period since in A.D. 409 Rome was invaded by the Goths, and the soldiers who were garrisoned in Britain were called back to defend the heart of the empire and the Eternal City. Yet even at this point in time the English churches were still only loosely attached to the practice of the Roman church and not fully under the authority of its bishops.[1] Roman influence over the British churches did not begin to forcibly assert itself again until A.D. 597 when Pope Gregory sent one of his monks, Augustine, to re-evangelize the British nation, which by that time had large Saxon settlements in the south and east of the country. Even then, however, the bishops of Rome had no universal authority. Indeed there were five bishops who were recognized as patriarchs of the church but no agreed head. The extent to which supervision could be exercised from Rome varied according to distance and the number of personnel and their loyalty.

---

1. Hood, *St Patrick,* 5 and 9.

All this meant there was a loss of Roman influence in the English church for the best part of two hundred years, from the Roman withdrawal at the beginning of the fifth century until Augustine's arrival at the close of the sixth century. It was during this period in particular that Irish Celtic missionaries began to bring their particular brand of Christianity to Scotland, England, and Wales. Much of its character derived from Patrick.[2]

PATRICK

Patrick (c 389–461)[3] was the son of a British local official who was also a deacon in the church. While still a teenager he was captured by pirates from his father's farm, which was probably in what is present day Glamorgan, and taken to Ireland where he was held captive for six years. He eventually escaped to Gaul where he came into contact with the monastic movement under Martin of Tours. Patrick is generally believed to have studied in the monastery of Lérins, possibly between 412 and 415, shortly after which he was made a deacon. He eventually returned to Britain in 432, Germanus having consecrated him in that year as a bishop to work in Ireland, following the death of bishop Palladius. He went to the court of the High King Laoghaire (d. 458) at Tara, Meath, where he gained toleration for Christianity despite strong opposition from the Druids. He preached widely in Connaught, Leinster, and Meath where he established numerous churches and a number of monastic communities. Following a visit to Rome in 440 he was consecrated Archbishop and returned to Ireland in 444 to establish a church hierarchy and a Cathedral church at Armagh, which shortly afterwards became an educational, training, and administrative center for the Irish church.

Ireland at the time of Patrick was a largely rural society with very few large towns. It had never been part of the Roman Empire, so the country wasn't organized to fit with the secular Roman administrative system of diocese and parish. Patrick therefore developed a more informal strategy that was based on establishing small monastic communities close to the existing scattered village settlements. Here they lived alongside and served

2. It should be noted that Professor Donald Meek rightly drew attention to the recent enthusiasm of searching for roots and justification for new spiritualities in the life and worship of the early Celtic Christians. This has created a romanticized version of Celtic Christianity, some of which cannot be found in the early classic Celtic sources. See Meek, *Quest for Celtic Christianity*.

3. The main sources for Patrick's life are his *Confessions* and his *Letter to Coroticus*.

the local people in a system in which the Abbot or ruler of the monastic community became the leader rather than a bishop. Priests in the Celtic system could be married men. The distinctive Celtic spirituality, which emerged from Patrick's Irish missions, was rooted in the rural, the domestic, and every-day living.

In A.D. 432 Patrick wrote *The Book of the Law of Moses (Liber Ex Lege Moisi)*, which came to be used by the local chieftains. Around A.D. 565, Columba, a disciple of Patrick's teaching, evangelized Scotland and translated the *Liber* into the Scottish language. The writings and teachings of these pioneer missionaries attest to the early introduction of biblical concepts of local Christian self-government and the rule of law. The *Liber* still survives in four tenth- and eleventh-century manuscripts and is a distilled compilation of the law of Moses. It covers matters of diet, and following the ceremonial Levitical law many Celtic Christians did not eat pork. It also included guidelines about when a woman is unclean and when a married couple might have sexual relations. Money lending had to be in accordance with Jewish practice and tithes had to be paid to the church in the same way that offerings were made to the Jewish temple. The *Liber* also detailed a penitential system involving restitution that had to be carried out for breaches of law.

Thus from the time of Patrick through to the Synod of Whitby in 664 a large number of Celtic congregations emerged in the British Isles that were largely independent of the Roman church. They were remarkable for their distinctive spirituality, evangelism, church planting, and monastic communities on account of which they grew and expanded rapidly. Significantly, many of the Saxons who invaded Britain following the departure of the Roman armies were themselves converted to this ancient British form of Christianity. The fifth to the end of the seventh century was probably the "golden age" of Celtic Christianity, although some of their congregations continued a separate existence up to the time of the Norman Conquest. In short, theirs was an outside-the-box Christianity, from which there is much that the contemporary churches can learn. Indeed, twentieth-century Charismatic Christians in particular soon began to recognize that there was good reason to revisit and learn from Celtic Christianity.

The major sign of the increasing influence of the Roman tradition over the Celtic practice first became visible at Synod of Whitby. There, with strong help from King Oswy, the Celtic and the Roman churches of Northumbria finally reached agreement over the date of Easter. The decision, it should be said, was by no means unanimous, with Bishop Colman, the Celtic spokesman, leaving British soil in protest. This did not mean that Celtic influence was suddenly lost at a stroke from British Christianity. In other parts of Britain, Celtic churches continued to exist apart from Rome for varying lengths of time. Aspects of Celtic spirituality—pioneer missionary work, learning, and calligraphy—continued for many years in those churches that did not conform to Whitby, but overall the Celtic and Roman churches gradually and eventually fused together. The Celtic churches in North Wales did not come into line with the Anglo-Saxon church until A.D. 768 and the supremacy of the See of Canterbury was not established until the twelfth century. The British church in Somerset and Devon surrendered its independence at the beginning of the eighth century. This happened largely on account of the influence of Aldhelm, who Bede tells us became Abbot of Malmesbury in A.D. 671 and Bishop of Sherborne in A.D. 705. The Cornish churches finally submitted to Archbishop Wulfhelm at the beginning of the tenth century when the area was conquered by the West-Saxons.

THE SPREAD OF CELTIC CHRISTIANITY

The Celts spread their brand of Christianity so effectively on account of their many forthright pioneer evangelists. They were men and women of prayer and compassion and a heart for the poor. In addition to Patrick, there were many other able and saintly evangelists and leaders. Among them was Ninian (c. 360—c. 432),[4] an English monk who studied under Martin at Marmoutier in France. He was consecrated as a bishop in 394 and came to Britain as a missionary about the year 397. He eventually settled at Whithorn in Galloway, where he founded a monastery that became a training base and from which he and his monks sought to convert their neighboring Britons and the Picts.

David (died c. 601), the patron saint of Wales, is one of the most celebrated British saints, although there is no reliable biography of him. His earliest life by bishop Rhygyfarch or Ricimas was written in the eleventh century to support the view that Welsh bishops were independent of the See of Canterbury. David is believed to have come from Cardigan and to have founded a monastery at Menevia (now St. David's). Another tradition relates that he acquired the nickname "aquaticus" or "waterman,"

---

4. There are two main sources for Ninian's life: Bede's *Ecclesiastical History* and a more elaborate but less reliable twelfth-century life by Ailred.

possibly because of his teetotalism but more likely because he was said to stand in the sea chanting the psalms oblivious of the incoming tides.

Columba[5] (c. 521–597) came from a noble Irish family and was trained in Irish monasteries by Finian and others. After founding a number of churches he left his homeland in 563, setting out with twelve companions and landing on the island of Iona. There they built a monastery and spent time tilling the soil, fishing in the waters, copying manuscripts, and keeping a daily round of prayer. He lived and worked from his community base for thirty-four years, evangelizing the mainland and setting up monastic communities on some of the neighboring islands. Although he remained in priest's orders he was regarded as the chief ecclesiastic in the whole area. His fame spread far and wide and he succeeded in converting Brude, the King of the Picts. Later, in 574, the new monarch of Dal Riada, the western Scottish kingdom, came to him to receive his "sacrying."

Among those who were trained in Iona was Aidan (d. 651).[6] He was sent at the request of King Oswald of Northumbria to revive the missionary work of Paulinus. Consecrated a bishop in 635, Aidan established his headquarters on the island of Lindisfarne from where he made long journeys on the mainland, strengthening existing monastic communities and founding new ones. Coming from Iona his spirituality and praxis were inevitably those of the Celts. He carefully mentored a group of twelve English boys to be future leaders of the church among whom were Chad (d. 672)[7] and his brother, Cedd (c. 620–664),[8] both of whom served for a brief period as Abbot of Lastingham in Yorkshire. Chad became Bishop of the Mercians in 669 with his See at Lichfield, while Cedd was consecrated Bishop of the East Saxons in 654. He founded many churches and established monasteries at West Tilbury and Ythancester (Bradwell-on-Sea). Columbanus (c. 550–615) was a native of Ireland who went via England to Gaul about the year 590 where he set up monasteries with very strict rules at Anegray and Luxeil in the Vosges. He experienced harsh persecution but eventually fled to Milan and settled at Bobbio, where he built a monastery between 613 and 615 with a famous library.

Alongside these well-known and influential missionary figures there were literally hosts of other, less familiar mission-orientated men and women whose names cover Devon, Cornwall, Wales, and parts of

---

5. The principal source of Columba's life was written by St Adamnan (c. 627–704).

6. The main source for Aidan is in Bede, *History*, 3.3–5, 14–17, and 25.

7. The main source for Chad is ibid., 3.23, 28.

8. The main source for Cedd is ibid., 3.21–23, 25, and 4.3.

the northeastern area of England. Among them were Brigid (c. 450–523), Abbess of the convent at Kildare and Hilda (614–680), who founded a monastery at Streanaeshalch. Bede states, "So great was her prudence that not only ordinary folk, but Kings and Princes used to come and ask her advice in their difficulties, and take it."[9] Colman (d. 676), the leader of the Celtic party in Northumbria and Bishop of Lindisfarne, Cuthbert (d. 687), a monk from Melrose who later became Prior and Bishop of Lindisfarne, and Hilda (614–680), who was later Abbess of Whitby.

DOCTRINE AND WORSHIP

The Celts were thoroughly immersed in the Scriptures of the Old and New Testament and were avid copyists of the Bible and of biblical commentaries. The famous Lindisfarne Gospels, which were written sometime before 698 in honor of Cuthbert, owed its text to the monastery of Wearmouth and Jarrow. Patrick's *Confessions* typify the Celtic devotion to the Scriptures being full of biblical references. Patrick was emphatic that he sought only to follow only what was written in the Scriptures. He wrote: "the words are not mine, but of God and the apostles and prophets who have never lied."[10] In all matters of theology and morality the Celts were thoroughly grounded in the Scriptures. The rules that were followed in Celtic monastic houses were also based in Scripture. Aidan taught his monks to meditate on the Scriptures and learn the psalms as they walked through the countryside of northern Britain. The Celts used many of their songs as a vehicle to teach doctrine and this was particularly helpful as a means of instruction for those who were not able to read. Bede related that Caedmon, a brother from the monastery of Streanaeshalch, had a gift of being able to set creedal teachings to music. He "sang of the Lord's incarnation, Passion, Resurrection and Ascension into heaven, the coming of the Holy Spirit, and the teaching of the Apostles."[11]

Although the Celts had a vivid sense of the presence of Jesus they also thought of God the Father in strong and majestic terms. Indeed, in Patrick's breastplate he is described as "the High King of Heaven," and Celtic Christians approached him with a sense of awe and wonder. The Celts had a strong doctrine of the Trinity with a deep sense of the Holy Spirit's presence in their lives. Their pagan background, in which triads

9. Bede, *History* 4.23.

10. Patrick, *Letter to Coroticus*, 20.

11. Bede, *History* 4.24.

featured, may well have helped them to grasp the Trinity more easily than those who encountered Christianity in the Roman Empire. When Patrick was once asked by some Irish princesses to explain the doctrine of the Trinity he didn't enter into a theological discussion, but simply bent down and picked up a shamrock and pointed to its three leaves growing on one stem.[12] The Celtic understanding of the Trinity is clearly articulated in his Breastplate hymn.

> I bind unto myself today
> The strong name of the Trinity
> By invocation of the same
> The three in One and One in Three.

Patrick urged that with "faith in the Trinity . . . we ought to spread God's name everywhere confidently and fearlessly."[13]

The Celts seem to have had a high view of baptism. Celtic bishops were wont to speak of baptism as "the waters of salvation for the forgiveness of sins"[14] and of being "cleansed in the life-giving waters of baptism."[15] Families were baptized on conversion and babies soon after birth. Baptism was done in the name of the Trinity and, when possible, in the flowing water of a river. There is also an interesting reference in Bede's *History* in which Bishop John re-baptized a man on the grounds that the priest who had baptized him "was so slow-witted that he could not have learned how to catechize and baptise." The bishop was categorical that "if you were baptised by that priest, you were not validly baptised."

The Celts were a sacramental people who knew the immanent presence of the Lord in all aspects of their living. They were able to drink in the presence of God while they worked, walked through the countryside, or joined in common meals. The Eucharist was an important part of their sacramental living, which they sometimes celebrated in the open air. They valued the Eucharist at special moments in their life. Thus when Caedmon was about to die he requested that the Eucharist be brought to him and asked the brothers "whether they were all charitably disposed towards him and whether they had any complaint or ill-feeling against him." When it

---

12. Bradley, *The Celtic Way*, 44.
13. Patrick, *Confession*, 14.
14. Bede, *History* 5.6.
15. Ibid. 5.6.

was apparent that they were at peace, he took the sacrament and passed away very shortly afterwards.[16]

Something of the character of the Celtic Eucharist has become apparent through recent archaeological discoveries, the most important being the *Derrynaflan Hoard*,[17] which was discovered in 1980 and includes a chalice and paten (a small plate used to hold consecrated Eucharistic bread) dated as either late eighth or early ninth century. The Derrynaflan paten is significantly different from modern patens, which usually measure no more than 18–20 centimeters since they are designed only for a token breaking of bread, the actual communion wafers already being pre-cut. The pre-cutting arguably diminishes the original symbolic force of the Eucharist as taught by St. Paul in 1 Corinthians 10:16–17 and the Didachē 9. In contrast, the Derrynaflan paten approximates to a good-size dinner plate and measure about 36 centimeters in diameter. This measurement (alongside other additional evidence) makes it clear that they were still using a single loaf at the Eucharist and then breaking it symbolically for each communicant. The Irish homily in the *Stowe Missal* states that the bread was broken symbolically into five, seven, eight, or however many breakings were necessary for each person present to remind themselves that they were partakers. The number of breakings allowed could be as many as sixty-five at Christmas, Easter, and Pentecost. This suggests that Celtic communicant fellowships were about this figure; in other words, they were not large congregations. The size of the Derrynaflan paten shows that the Celtic Eucharist still had an appreciation of the symbolism of "the one loaf" broken into pieces to establish unity among all those who shared that one loaf (1 Cor 10:17). The Derrynaflan chalice is also significant, its dimensions being 21 centimeters in diameter and 11 centimeters in depth. This is the capacity of a medium-sized mixing bowl so that when it was full it could hold one and a half liters of wine. The emphasis of the Stowe Missal is clearly in union with Jesus through eating and drinking— in other words, a Eucharist which resonates with the Eucharist at Tiberius in John's Gospel chapter 6.[18] All of this indicates that the Celts built their church fellowships on the Pauline model of the "household" (Eph 2:19).

Singing played an important part in Celtic life and worship. The Celtic Christians loved to sing while they were out walking in the open

---

16. Ibid., 4.24.

17. Derrynaflan is near Cashel in County Tipperary.

18. Information derived from O'Loughlin, *Celtic Theology: Humanity, World and God in Early Irish Writings*, 135–36.

countryside or while they engaged in manual labor in the monastic community. Singing, particularly antiphonal singing, was central to the monastic worship. Bede tells of Caedmon who lived in the monastery at Streanaeshalch and described him as "a brother singularly gifted by God's grace." He continued: "so skilful was he in composing religious and devotional songs that, when any passage of Scripture was explained to him by interpreters, he could quickly turn it into delightful and moving poetry in his own English tongue."[19] His verses, according to Bede, "have stirred the hearts of many folk to despise the world and aspire to heavenly things." Others, he noted, "at that time tried to compose religious poems in English but none could compare with Caedmon for he did not acquire the art of poetry from men or through any human teacher but received it as a free gift from God. For this reason he could never compose any frivolous or profane verse; but only such as had a religious theme fell fittingly from his devout lips."[20]

SPIRITUALITY

The Celts were people of the Spirit. Patrick for example, related at the beginning of his *Confession* that Jesus "poured out on us abundantly His Holy Spirit, the gift and pledge of immortality, who makes those who believe and obey to be sons of God and heirs along with Christ."[21] Patrick related how, when he first reached Ireland as a captive, he was able to pray before dawn in all weathers—snow, frost, and rain—"because the Spirit was fervent within me."[22] On occasion Patrick was profoundly conscious of the Holy Spirit praying from deep within his own spirit. His description of this experience is not dissimilar from that recounted by people who pray in tongues or who enter a state of constant intercession by praying the Jesus Prayer. Patrick related:

> I saw Him praying within me and I was, as it were, inside my own body and I heard His above me, that is to say, above my inner self, and He was praying there powerfully and groaning; and meanwhile I was dumbfounded and astonished and wondered who it could be that was praying with me, but at the end of the prayer He spoke and said, that He was the Spirit. . . . The Spirit

19. Bede, *Ecclesiastical History*, 4.24.
20. Ibid., 4.24.
21. Patrick, *Confessions*, 4
22. Ibid., 16.

helps the weakness of our prayer, for we do not know what to pray for as we ought; but the Spirit Himself intercedes for us with unspeakable groans which cannot be expressed in words (Rom 8:28) and again: "The Lord our advocate intercedes for us."[23]

When Patrick later reflected on his time in Ireland as a captive exile he wrote that God protected him from all evils "because of His Spirit dwelling in me."[24] Bede, in his life of Cuthbert, stressed the work of the Spirit in the bishop's life. He related that the bishop was in the habit of "going round the diocese giving saving counsel in all the houses and hamlets of the countryside, and laying his hand on the newly baptised so that the Grace of the Holy Spirit might come down upon them."[25] On another occasion, Bede reported that Cuthbert arrived in a certain village where "he preached twice to the milling crowds and brought down the grace of the Holy Spirit by the imposition of hands on those newly regenerated in Christ."[26] It is clear therefore that in the years up until the time of Bede, Christian people sought for and cultivated a conscious awareness of the Spirit's presence in their lives. Additionally, they expected the charismata or gifts of the Holy Spirit to feature in the church's life, ministry, and worship.

Ancient Britons were people of prayer. They prayed constantly throughout the day, often in short one-sentence prayers. As far as the Celts were concerned nothing was too small to pray about and no situation too insignificant to bring to God. They knew what George Herbert was later to discover and articulate in his hymn "Teach me my God and King in all things Thee to see and what I do in anything to do it as for Thee." In his *Confessions* Patrick related:

after I had come to Ireland I used to feed cattle, and I prayed frequently during the day; the love of God and the fear of Him increased more and more, and faith became stronger, and the Spirit was stirred; so that in one day I said about a hundred prayers, and in the night nearly the same; so that I used to remain in the woods and in the mountains; before daylight I used to rise to prayer, through snow, through frost, through rain and

23. Ibid., 25.
24. Ibid., 28.
25. Bede, *Life of Cuthbert*, 28.
26. Ibid., 32.

felt no harm; nor was there any slothfulness in me, as I perceive, because the Spirit was then fervent within me.[27]

The result of this was that Celtic Christians had a very vivid sense of the presence of Jesus with them. This sense of God's omnipresence is very marked in Patrick's celebrated *Breastplate*.

> Christ be with me, Christ within me,
> Christ behind me, Christ before me,
> Christ beside me, Christ to win me,
> Christ to comfort and restore me,
> Christ beneath me, Christ above me,
> Christ in quiet, Christ in danger,
> Christ in hearts of all that love me,
> Christ in mouth of friend and stranger.

An important aspect of Celtic prayers were blessings. These included blessings for special occasions such as baptisms, journeys, and death, but also prayers said over everyday domestic situations. Ian Bradley noted that among other Celtic prayers were blessings for the house, for taking a bath, for hatching eggs, clipping sheep, and tending the loom.[28] Celtic spirituality was a spirituality of the everyday, which caused Bradley to remark that "one of the most important lessons we can learn from the Celts is to reinvest the ordinary with a measure of sanctity, to value again the importance of little things, and to find God once more in the trivial round the common task."[29]

The Celts' spirituality was rooted in the creation for which they had both a great love and a healthy respect. They enjoyed the elements to the full. If God had seen fit to bless the earth with wind and rain they were happy to walk in it and pray as they did so. They understood that human beings need to have a delicate and close relationship with the natural world around them. They sought to glorify God by valuing and appreciating his creation. They did not, however, confuse God and his creation nor see them submerged into one another as certain elements of the New Age movement have done. The Celts did not regard the created world as a living, self-regulating being, which many New Agers call "Gaia," the Earth Goddess. The Celts did however strongly emphasize God's immanence or very presence in his creation.

---

27. Patrick, *Confessions*, 16.
28. Bradley, *The Celtic Way*, 49.
29. Ibid., 39.

It seems that the Celts also took seriously the command to rest as an important part of their spirituality. The Celtic church kept their Lord's Day or Sabbath as the Jews did from Friday night to Saturday night and then worshipped on Sunday with no restrictions about working or making journeys. Patrick records in his *Letter* that on one occasion, when he was resting on the Lord's Day on the sea-shore by the salt marsh a short distance from the place known as the Ox' neck, he was disturbed "by a noisy din coming from pagans who were working on the Lord's Day making a rampart." Patrick remonstrated with them but they paid no heed. He rebuked their leader, Mudebrod, saying, "However much you work, may it get you nowhere." So it proved during the following night when rough seas destroyed their work.[30]

The Celts took seriously the biblical injunction about praying for the healing of the land. Bede related how Cuthbert went to live on Farne Island, a few miles to the southeast of Lindisfarne. He was, says Bede, "the first brave man to live there alone," for the island "had no water, corn, or trees and being the haunt of evil spirits was very ill-suited to human habitation." However, when Cuthbert arrived he ordered all the evil spirits to withdraw, and the island became quite habitable and "a rich crop quickly sprung up."[31] Aidan demonstrated his delight in the land by encouraging his monks to learn the Psalms as they walked through the countryside. Such was their delight in God's creation that the Celts often celebrated the Eucharist outside in the open air and both Martin and David were known to have transportable tables ready to perform the task![32]

Art, particularly the copying of manuscripts and decorative design, was an important aspect of Celtic spirituality. They delighted in intricate patterns and knots and were famous for their beautifully carved stone crosses. Pagan art forms and culture were transformed for the glory of God.

EVANGELISTIC STRATEGIES

Following the example of Jesus, whose works incarnated his words, the Celts evangelized with signs and wonders. Patrick wrote, "It is our duty to fish well and diligently, as the Lord urges and teaches us, saying: 'Follow me, and I shall make you fishers of men' (Matt 4:19). . . . And so it was

30. Muirchu, *Life of Patrick*, 24.

31. Bede, *History* 4.28, and Bede, *Life of Cuthbert*, 18.

32. Leatham, *Celtic Sunrise*, 20.

our bounden duty to spread our nets, so that a vast multitude and throng might be caught for God and there might be clergy everywhere to baptise and exhort a people that was poor and needy."[33] This was often most visible in their emphasis on healing and wholeness. We see this exemplified in the ministry of Brigid (c. 450–523) of Ireland who cured a blind child who was mute.[34] We see it also played out on a number of occasions in the life of Cuthbert who, for instance, brought healing to a woman who had been desperately ill. He told the woman's husband, "God will grant her a speedy recovery, or if she must die, put an end to agony and take her without delay." Cuthbert asked for the water to be brought, blessed it, and gave it to the priest to sprinkle over the sick woman. The priest entered her bedroom and found her lying there and looking like a corpse. He sprinkled the bed, sprinkled her, opened her mouth, and poured a little of the life-giving water down her throat. She revived and thanked the Lord, rose from her bed and thanked those who had ministered to her.[35]

On another occasion, Cuthbert ministered to a bed-ridden man named Hildmer who had been confined to bed with a dangerous illness. His friends had crowded round the bed fearing the worst when one of them remembered that he had in his pocket a piece of bread, which Cuthbert had shortly beforehand blessed and given to him. The men, none of them ordained, filled a cup with water and dropped the tiny piece of bread in and gave it to the man to drink. The moment "the water the bread had made holy entered his stomach, all internal pain left him and his body was no longer in pain."[36] Bede wrote of Cuthbert, "He became famous for miracles, for his prayers restored sufferers from all kinds of disease and affliction. He cured some who were vexed by unclean spirits not only by laying on of hands, exhorting, and exorcising—that is by actual contact—but even from afar, merely by praying or predicting their cure."[37]

Bede gives many similar instances in his *Ecclesiastical History*. Among them he related the case of a youth whose arm was healed by the power of the cross that King Oswald (605–642) had erected before going into battle in 634. Some years after the king's death, a brother named Bothelm from the church at Hebron—who Bede stated "is still living"—slipped on the ice and fractured his arm, which caused him agonizing pain. At length,

---

33. Patrick, *Confession*, 40.

34. De Paor, *St Patrick's World*, 212.

35. Bede, *Life of Cuthbert*, 29.

36. Ibid., 31.

37. Ibid., 16.

another brother went up to the site of the cross and brought back a piece of its revered wood. At supper he passed a few strands of the old moss that grew on the surface of the cross to the injured man. He had nowhere to put it and so thrust it next to his breast. When he awoke next morning he was perfectly healed. Bede went on to relate several other miraculous cures that took place at the site of Oswald's death, among them a young paralyzed girl was healed on being laid down at the place of Oswald's death. "Many people," he wrote, "took away the very dust from the place where his body fell, and put it in water, from which sick folk who drank it received great benefit."[38]

Bede noted a number of healings that took place at the hands of Bishop John of Hexham, then of York. On one of these occasions a dumb youth who had many scabs and scales on his head and was particularly bald, began to speak freely after "the bishop took him by the chin and made the sign of the cross on his tongue." Later, with the assistance of the bishop's blessing and prayers, "his skin was healed and a vigorous growth of hair appeared." At York he prayed for a young nun and her badly swollen arm, which was then restored.[39] On another occasion he brought healing to one of his clergy who had fallen from his horse and cracked his skull and broken his thumb. He was carried home and lay speechless all night vomiting blood as a result of internal injury. Bishop John spent the night in prayer for his restoration. In the morning he went to the man and called him by name and he was awakened from what seemed a heavy sleep. He then laid his hand on the man and blessed him and then found on his return a short while later that the man was sitting up and well enough to talk.[40]

It is, of course, possible that some of these stories may have been embellished or added to, but taken as a whole they are too numerous to discount in total. De Paor criticized Bede on the ground that he took some of his information from Gildas, a Welsh monk who wrote about A.D. 540 and whose knowledge of events a century and a half before his time was very far from perfect.[41] Ian Bradley expressed the view that Bede "almost certainly over-exaggerated both the peculiar missionary zeal and the monastic character of the Irish church." To support his contention Bradley, not altogether convincingly, instanced the way in which Bede took a modest source about Fursey, an Irish monk who journeyed from Ireland to the

38. Bede, *History*, 3.9.

39. Ibid., 5.3.

40. Ibid., 5.6.

41. De Paor, *St Patrick's World*, 11.

province of the East Angles. There he preached the gospel as he always did, following which "many unbelievers were converted to Christ, and many who had already believed were drawn to greater love and faith in him."[42] Against this skepticism, it should be noted that Bede did have access to the library at Jarrow, which was almost unequalled by any in England, and he did crosscheck his evidence with other sources and with individuals whom he knew personally. To this can be added the fact that Bede (673–735) has been shown to be accurate in many of the historical facts that he records and is careful to mention the sources he is using.

Another aspect of their mission strategy was to make an early visit to the local king or chieftain. This not only demonstrated respect but it often provided protection and a welcome. Sometimes the conversion of a local leader led to the people under his rule following his example. Bede's accounts document King Oswald translating God's word to his people [43] and King Peada's baptism by Bishop Finan with all his earls and soldiers and their servants who came along with him.[44]

THE PROPHETIC

The Celtic congregations displayed a marked concern to listen to what they took to be the voice and instruction of the Lord and to follow it through in their actions. In his *Confessions* Patrick recounted eight visions that he saw in dreams, all of which were direct messages from God. The most vivid and most important in so far as the direction of his life was concerned was his call to return to Ireland and proclaim the gospel. Patrick described it in terms that resemble the apostle Paul's Macedonian call in Acts 16:9.

> And then I saw, indeed, in the boom of the night, a man coming as it were from Ireland, Victorinus by name, with innumerable letters, and he gave one of them to me. . . . And while I was reading aloud the beginning of the letter, I myself thought indeed in my mind that I heard the voice of those who were near the wood of Foclut, which is close by the sea. And they cried out thus as if with one voice, "We entreat you, holy youth, that you come, and henceforth walk among us."[45]

---

42. Bradley, *Celtic Christianity*, 27.

43. Bede, *History*, 3.3.

44. Ibid., 3.21.

45. Patrick, *Confessions*, 23.

At another point in *Confessions* Patrick tells us that he was frequently warned and guided by prophecy. [46]

Columba, like Patrick, was a man of prophetic disposition, his biographer, Adamnan, reporting that he "often saw, by revelation of the Holy Spirit, the souls of some just men carried by angels to the highest heaven."[47] Adamnan went on to relate that Columba "very often foretold the future deserts, sometimes joyful, and sometimes sad, of many persons while they were still living in mortal flesh."[48]

Bede furnishes us with a number of similar instances of other Celtic church leaders who were guided in similar ways. He tells us that Cuthbert "grew strong in prophecy foretelling the future and revealing to those near him events that were happening elsewhere."[49] Bede also related that Bishop Aidan sought God's guidance for a priest named Utta who had been instructed by king Oswy to go to Kent and bring back Eanfled the daughter of the King of Kent who was to be his wife. His plan was to travel by land to Kent and then return by sea. Having prayed for them, Aidan gave them some holy oil, saying: "When you set sail, you will encounter a storm and contrary winds. Remember then to pour the oil that I am giving you on the sea, and the wind will immediately drop, giving a pleasant, calm voyage and safe return." Bede commented: "Everything happened as the bishop foretold." After giving details of the stormy voyage Bede ended the chapter by stating: "The story of this miracle is no groundless fable; for it was related to me by Cynimund, a most faithful priest of our own church [Jarrow], who had it from the mouth of the priest Utta, on and through whom the miracle was performed."[50] Bede also related how, on one occasion, Aidan burst into tears and prophesied the imminent death of King Oswin. "I know," he said, "the king will not live very long; for I have never before seen a humble king. I feel that he will soon be taken from us, because this nation is not worthy of a king." Bede commented: "Not very long afterwards, the bishop's foreboding was borne out by the king's death."[51]

---

46. Ibid., 35.
47. Adamnan, *Life of Columba*, I.1.
48. Ibid., I.1.
49. Bede, *Life of Cuthbert*, 11.
50. Bede, *History*, 3.16.
51. Ibid., 3.14.

SPIRITUAL CONFLICT

The Celtic missionaries were acutely aware that extending God's kingdom was a battle against unseen and sometimes dark forces. While it is true that they have often been praised because they did not destroy the culture of those to whom they preached the Christian message, they certainly did not go along with beliefs and practices they found to be incompatible with orthodox teaching. Indeed, they were always at the ready to stand against pagan powers and strongholds. This is perhaps nowhere better seen than in Patrick's confrontations with the Druids who were based at their stronghold in Tara. He and his companions incurred the wrath of their king by their presence in the area. As one of the king's henchmen came out to meet Patrick reviling the name of Jesus and the Trinity as he walked, Patrick called out to the Lord in a loud voice to destroy the man, who was indeed smitten and died.[52] Patrick recorded another occasion during his labors in Ireland when he was attacked by the devil, writing in his *Confession*, "I was asleep, and Satan attacked me violently, something which I shall remember as long as I am in this body; and there fell on top of me a huge rock, as it were, and I was completely paralysed." However, after shouting out, aided by Christ and his Spirit, he was set at liberty.[53]

Cuthbert, like Patrick, was acutely aware of the presence of the devil and evil spiritual forces. On one occasion, when he was preaching the words of life to a great crowd in a small village, he realized that "the ancient enemy, the devil, was present, come to hinder his work of salvation." He at once broke off from his discourse and said: "My dear brethren you must be on your guard to listen with complete attention and not let the devil distract you with foolish worries from hearing what concerns your eternal salvation."[54] Bede related how the wife of Hildmer, King Egfid's sheriff, was possessed by a devil. She was, according to Bede, "so sorely vexed that she would gnash her teeth, let out frightful howls, and fling her arms and legs about. But as Cuthbert, a man full of the Holy Spirit, came up to her, the evil spirit departed."[55] Bede wrote of Cuthbert, "He became famous for miracles, for his prayers restored sufferers from all kinds of disease and affliction. He cured some who were vexed by unclean spirits not only by laying on hands, exhorting, and exorcising—that is by actual

---

52. Muirchu, *Life of Patrick*, 17.
53. Patrick, *Confessions*, 20.
54. Bede, *Life of Cuthbert*, 13.
55. Ibid., 16.

contact—but even from afar, merely by praying or predicting their cure, as in the case of the sheriff's wife."[56]

Celtic Christians developed a range of strategies and rituals to invoke God's protective powers against evil and danger. At such moments some Celts would draw a circle round themselves and their loved ones or using their index fingers they would point and turn round sun-wise reciting a prayer of protection.[57] The breastplate prayers, of which the one attributed to Patrick is the most well-known, seek in a similar way to surround those who pray with the protective clothing of God. This, of course, has clear scriptural precedent in Ephesians 6:10–18. The verses from Patrick's breastplate illustrate the wide range of powers that the Celts invoked for protection: the strong name of the Trinity, the life, death, and resurrection of Jesus, the angelic hosts, the faith of the confessors, and the word of the apostles. It has even been suggested that the pattern known as the Celtic knot was designed and used to ward off the devil's powers. Wherever they went Celtic Christians erected crosses, locating them in market places and around churches and monastic communities. The crosses functioned in two ways, reminding people of the protection that came through the death and resurrection of Christ and acting as a symbol of the faith to those outside the Christian community.

MONASTIC HOUSES

A key feature of Celtic Christianity was the importance of monastic houses. A frequent Celtic mission strategy was to ask permission from the local leader if they could live near the local Druid community. They would then build a small monastic settlement, often on the Egyptian model, from which they would serve the neighborhood who in time would come to embrace the Christian faith. In this way, sometimes, whole communities believed and were baptized together with their children. On some occasions it happened that the former Druid leader became a Christian Abbot. The Celts believed in belonging before believing and it was often the case that pagans came to faith simply as a result of being served and cared for in very practical ways. Celtic Christians were particularly strong on hospitality and Abbots were known to break their own fasts if visitors came to the doors of their monastery. This concern probably originated from the rule of Benedict which stated that "All guests who present themselves are to

56. Ibid.

57. Bradley, *Celtic Way*, 47.

be welcomed as Christ, for He himself will say: 'I was a stranger and you welcomed me.'"[58]

The Celts developed the monastery to work as a hub that could function as a worshipping and caring community, a place for instruction and training, and a base from which to reach out into the surrounding community. Much of this vision came from Patrick, the principal apostle of Ireland who encouraged monasticism for both men and women. Within a century of his death the monasteries became the most important aspect of the Christian church in Ireland. Indeed monks who were trained in Ireland began to find their way to both England and Scotland. The central place given to the monastery was ideal in Ireland, which, as already mentioned, was a country without towns and which had never been part of the Roman Empire. It therefore never had the Roman civil government structure of dioceses into which the post-Constantinian church so easily fitted.

Because of this absence of towns the Irish episcopate did not flourish. Irish society was essentially tribal, with the extended family as its essential unit. When a family became Christian, it was natural for it to stay together, and it was from this that the early Irish monastic communities developed. These were of several different types. There were often large numbers of married people, still part of their family unit but attached to the monastery and engaging in agricultural or craftsmanship of one kind or another. They would live by a set of written rules such as that of Columbanus and under the authority of an abbot. Bede and Cuthbert both valued the Rule of St. Benedict. The importance of the Abbot in Irish Christianity often resulted in bishops having much less influence by comparison. This system, which was established by Columba in Iona on the west coast of Scotland, was certainly different from the Roman system where the town at the center of the local diocese served as the hub from which training and evangelism emanated. This was the place where the bishop had his cathedra or chair and from which the surrounding area was pastored and evangelized.

CONCERN FOR THE POOR

A major function of the monasteries was to care for the needs of the poor. Bede reported that during his lifetime King Oswald "never failed to provide for the sick and needy and to give them alms and aid."[59] Although Cuthbert kept himself under an austere monastic regime he was conspicu-

---

58. Hunter, *Celtic Way*, 42.

59. Bede, *History*, 3.9.

ous in his compassion for the poor, for feeding the hungry and consoling the afflicted. Bede recorded of him that on his pastoral visits "he made a point of searching out those steep rugged places in the hills that other preachers dreaded to visit because of their poverty and squalor. He was so keen to preach that sometimes he would be away for a whole week or a fortnight, or even a month, living with rough hill folk, preaching and calling them heavenwards by his example."[60]

FACTORS THAT MADE CELTIC CHRISTIANITY SUCCESSFUL

Their Positive Attitude to the Indigenous Culture

There is no doubt that the way in which the Celtic Christians lived close to the soil and their happy delight in the beauties of creation enabled them to convey the Christian message effectively among their pagan neighbors, most of whom were Druids who both worshipped the sun and held the earth in great reverence. The Christian Celts shared their Druid neighbors' love for the poetic and the creative arts, as well as healing and wholeness, and this meant that they had something of a common basis on which to share the message of Christ. As G. G. Hunter observed, "When the people know that Christians understand them, they infer that maybe the High God understands them too."[61] All too often in later times, not least the Victorian era, it was part of mission strategies to put down the indigenous local culture as being demonic and needing to be immediately obliterated as a perquisite to receiving Christianity. The consequence of such action was to demonstrate disrespect for those they had come to and to create a barrier between them. By contrast, Celtic Christians did not distance themselves from the culture of those they sought to evangelize. As Ian Bradley explained:

> The Celtic missionaries had a wholly different attitude towards those with whom they were seeking to share the light of Christ. For them evangelism was more a matter of liberating and re-leasing the divine spark which was already there in every person than imposing a new external creed. They did not see the primal pagan religion of the people as a threat to Christianity or a dangerous heresy to be eliminated. Rather it represented,

60. Bede, *Life of Cuthbert*, 10.
61. Hunter, *The Celtic Way*, 20.

however imperfectly, a stirring of the spiritual and a reaching
to the eternal.[62]

Community

Perhaps the greatest reason why Celtic Christianity flourished was their
understanding and practice of community. Pre-Christian Celtic society,
as has been observed, was a tribal society in which people lived in clusters of what were, to all intents and purposes, extended families in which
individual married couples and their children lived as separate units, but
worked and shared in a common life. They labored together, cultivating
the land, pasturing their flocks and herds, and banding together for protection against the elements and hostile invaders. The Celtic missionaries
who had themselves been nurtured in this environment recognized that
though many of these communities worshipped the various Druid deities
that was no reason for trying to oppose or attempt to dismantle the communities. In fact, they recognized that there was much in these communities that resonated with St. Paul's teaching that the church is the whole
household of God. The Christianity of the Celtic missionaries served to re-
enforce the existing communities with their corporate prayers and singing together with their regular Communion services. As has been noted,
it seems likely that their communal worship was in smallish groups of
less than seventy people. The Christianity of the Celts therefore acted as a
bonding agent that drew communities together more deeply. People living
in these Celtic communities quickly came to recognize the fact Christianity was in effect enhancing the quality of their existing social life.

Leadership

One of the obvious causes of the success of the Celtic congregations in
England, Wales, Scotland, and Ireland was their servant leadership, which
was not only able to establish Christian communities but also to nurture
them. Indeed Celtic Abbots were quickly observed to have achieved greater
respect than the Druid tribal leaders who held sway in earlier times. Such
a leadership role demands skills that are altogether different from the up-
front pioneer leader with a team that is breaking new ground in virgin territory. To successfully lead a community requires gentle leadership from

62. Bradley, *The Celtic Way*, 94.

behind that is humble in attitude, non-hierarchical in structure, and pastoral and nurturing in spirit. Men like Patrick, Aidan, and Cuthbert possessed these qualities in marked degree. Patrick, for example, was always open about his poor Latin and lack of formal theological expertise while at the same time always ready to be compassionate and caring. Similarly, Cuthbert spent weeks at a time tramping through the isolated hamlets and villages of Northumbria to visit and heal the sick, cast out the demons, and befriend the needy. Much of what they and their contemporaries were about resonates with secular contemporary "brand management" in which the leaders resist the temptation to impose their personal style and instead concentrate on embodying the corporate ideals of the business they lead. These pioneering Celtic Christian men and women leaders were acutely focused on nurturing a brand that was devoted to establishing small, caring, extended family tribal units built around Christian faith and worship.

4 | The Waldensians

As far as is known, the Waldensians—who are also sometimes known as the Vaudois—first emerged into public prominence in the twelfth century as a reaction against the dominating clergy of the Roman Church. They are orthodox, creedal Christians who were well known for their strong biblical morality and purity of life.

Various claims have been made that their roots can be traced back to antiquity and it has even been asserted by some that they were founded by St. Paul and that they alone had preserved the primitive Christian faith and discipline through the dark Middle Ages. Among scholars who take this view was J. A. Wylie who wrote that the Waldensian traditions "invariably point to an unbroken descent from earliest times, as regard to their religious beliefs." Wylie's point, which is a reasonable one, is that the Bishops of Milan, whose diocese included the Waldensian territory, did not come under Papal authority until 1059.[1] This submission was brought about when Petrus Damianus of Ostia and Anslem, Bishop of Lucca, were dispatched by Pope Nicholas II to bring about the submission of the Lombard churches. Although the plains were conquered, many of the Waldensians retreated into the seven valleys of the Piedmont Alps, while others escaped into the Rhineland where they were able to practise their faith with less chance of persecution. We may also note that two of the Waldensians' greatest opponents—Claude Seyssel of Turin and Reynerius Saccho, the Inquisitor—both considered them to be among the most dangerous of heretics on account of their ancient Christian roots. Another tradition suggests that they separated from the Catholic Church at the time when Constantine granted land and status to Pope Sylvester. Some even go so far as to suggest that the Waldenses are directly descended from persecuted Novatians who separated from the church of Rome in A.D. 251 and left

---

1. Wylie, *The History of Protestantism*, Vol. 1, 23. See also Muston, *The Israel of the Alps*, 3.

Italy for the valleys of Piedmont sometime after A.D. 325.[2] (Waldensians still exist today in what is known as the *Waldensian Evangelical Church* and active congregations can be found in Europe, South America, and the United States. They are strong advocates of religious toleration and social justice.)

So there were traditions suggesting that the roots of the Waldensians were ancient. However, the first really authentic evidence of the Waldenses dates from the middle of the twelfth century, and most historians trace their origins to Peter Waldo (or Valdo) (c. 1140–1218), a wealthy merchant from the city of Lyons. It is, of course, possible that there were orthodox sectarian groups in the Piedmont valleys before Waldo's time. The name Waldenses or Vaudois seems most likely to have come either from Waldo himself or from the woodland character of the local area—"pagus Waldensis," meaning forest or woodland. It has been thought that Peter's surname, Valdo, may have been derived from the fact that he was born in Valdum in the marquisate of Lyons or from the district of Walden.

Waldo became a believer about the year 1160, but the precise details of his conversion are not known. It seems that the unexpected death of a close friend and a devotional meeting in which he heard the story of St. Alexius, an early Christian father who gave up everything to serve the poor, had a dramatic effect on him and led to his becoming a wholehearted follower of Christ. It also prompted him to give up his large property and to devote himself to the service of the poor. He declared: "I am avenging myself upon those enemies of my life who have enslaved me, so that I cared more for gold pieces than for God and served the creature more than the Creator."[3] Waldo employed a poor scholar to translate some of the books of Scripture into the vernacular together with some passages from the early church fathers. He set out to live a life of full-surrender to Christ based on poverty and care for the needy. In biblical fashion he organized some of his followers to go out into the neighborhoods and preach, which provoked considerable anger and hostility on the part of the archbishop and clergy of Lyons. Little details of Waldo's life are known, but it is generally believed that he died in Bohemia.

Waldensian pastors were named "barba," the Vaudois term for *uncle*. They were trained in their college, which was situated in the solitude of the Pra-del-Tor, an isolated gorge in Piedmont. There they learned by heart the Gospels of Matthew and John, the catholic epistles, and some of Paul's

---

2. Ray, *The Baptist Succession*, 179.

3. Saxby, *Pilgrims*, 92.

writings. They were given instruction in Latin, Romane (old French), and Italian.[4] The barbas were also known locally as the "Poor Men of Lyons" and sometimes called the "Sabatati" on account of the large wooden shoes or sabots which they customarily wore. An annual synod was held and a president or moderator was appointed for the year. The barbas visited all the homes every year in their respective district to hear and receive the confession of each individual inhabitant.[5]

Lay preaching had not featured in the Roman church of the time and the practice of the Waldensians roused a good deal of opposition. Two of their number were bold enough to appear in Rome in 1179 and requested permission from Pope Alexander III to do so. He approved of their poverty but denounced their taking on what he regarded as the role of the clergy. When they persisted in asking for permission Alexander referred them to their own local clergy who met them with the same degree of hostility. The Archbishop of Lyons went so far as to issue a formal injunction against Waldensian preaching, but Waldo responded with apostolic firmness that they ought to obey God rather than men. At this point, their doctrine was in accord with the Catholic creeds to which the Roman church also adhered, but Alexander's successor, Pope Lucius III, nevertheless declared them to be heretics at the Synod of Verona in 1184. This decision was reiterated at the Fourth Lateran Council in 1215. More than eighty Waldensians were burned as heretics in Strasburg in 1211. They were nevertheless recognized by their opponents as men and women of piety who lived upright, honest, and sober lives. Not surprisingly therefore their numbers grew rapidly, which caused considerable concern to Reinerius, the Dominican Inquisitor who had been sent to restrain their activities.

MISSIONARY STRATEGY

The Waldensian missionary strategy was based on Jesus' example of sending out the seventy and consisted of commissioning missionary bands that preached a message of repentance. Both women and men played an active role in these missionary bands and displayed great zeal in sharing the faith. *The Passau Anonymous* recorded the zeal of one missionary who swam up the river Ibbs in winter to visit a potential convert and of others

---

4. Muston, *The Israel of the Alps*, 3.

5. Ibid., 7.

who spent time speaking to lepers.[6] There were also Waldensian celibate female communities in Montcuq and Beaucaire. As was later to be the case in English Lollardy, some who were clerics of the Roman church endorsed and supported the Waldensian movement and a small number even sought to build links with them. Their usual method of preaching was to travel in pairs under the guise of a secular profession. Many of them were in fact merchants or peddlers who carried silks and items of jewelry for sale and some of their number were surgeons and physicians.[7] In this way they often found an open door, and when the opportunity arose they were able to recite or read passages of the New Testament to those who had either purchased or shown interest in their goods and services.[8]

Like the Lollards in England, the Waldensians engaged in bookselling and distributed tracts and portions of Scripture in these secret or largely private gatherings. Typical of their number was Barthelemy Hector of Poitiers who travelled the valleys, where he recited biblical passages and sold Reformation pamphlets. He was eventually caught by papal agents in the year 1556 and taken to Turin where he was burned at the stake.[9]

DISTINCTIVE BELIEFS

The Waldensians had no desire to separate from the Catholic Church. They simply wanted to live as wholehearted followers of Jesus who confessed their belief in the Scriptures of the Old and New Testaments. They acknowledged the sacraments instituted by Jesus and accepted the creeds that had been agreed by the first four general councils and also the creed of Athanasius. Many of the Waldensian beliefs and customs can be readily ascertained from their celebrated work entitled *The Noble Lesson*, a poem in rhyming verse written in the Provencal dialect. It is thought to have been composed in 1100 but some scholars have suggested a later date of between 1190 and 1240. It contains Old and New Testament biblical history and ends with an attack on the papacy.

Waldensians were strongly trinitarian in their teaching and experience. One passage in the *Noble Lesson* states that in the doing of good works and Christian service, "The honour of God the Father ought to be his first moving principle. He ought likewise to implore the aid of His

6. Murray, "The Waldensians," 14–15.

7. Muston, *The Israel of the Alps*, 4.

8. Wylie, *History*, Vol. 1, 30.

9. Ibid., Vol. 3, 452.

glorious Son, the dear Son of the Virgin Mary, And the Holy Ghost which lightens the true way. These three [the Holy Trinity] as being but one God, ought to be called upon." The Waldensians accepted the Ten Commandments as their rule of life and professed submission to those placed over them. The problem was that they frequently showed up the laziness and lack of commitment of the local clergy.

The Waldensian belief that the church must be separate from the state and their devoted study of the Scriptures soon led them to oppose many of the practices of the Roman church. It is generally accepted that the Waldensians possessed the New Testament in the Romaunt tongue, which was the common language of the south of Europe from the eighth to the fourteenth century.[10] The translation that they used was most probably made under the supervision of Peter Waldo, not later than 1180.[11] Significantly, this was before any complete version of the New Testament had appeared in Germany, France, Italy, Spain, or England. As the Waldensians continued to study the Bible they recognized that the Roman church had moved a long way from the days of the apostles and they sought in consequence to root out practices for which they believed there was no Scriptural precedent. In effect, they were a kind of restoration movement seeking to restore the church back to its pre-Constantinian days.

They adhered strongly to the doctrines of the Apostles' Creed and therefore cannot be dismissed as theologically heterodox. A Confession dating from 1120 declares: "We believe and firmly hold all that which is contained in the twelve articles of the symbol, which is called the Apostles' Creed." The same document states in Article 2: "We do believe that there is one God, Father, Son and Holy Spirit." A third Article is explicit as to Jesus' divinity declaring: "that Jesus Christ is the Son and image of the Father. That in Him dwells all the fullness of the Godhead, by whom we have knowledge of the Father." Article 3 is clear that "the Holy Spirit is our Comforter, proceeding from the Father and the Son."[12] Their main objections centered on the papacy and the ecclesiastical hierarchy, the sacraments, the saints, and various ritual practices. In summary, they threw off the authority of the Pope and bishops generally and strongly objected to the compulsory celibacy of the clergy. As far as the saints were concerned,

10. Ibid., Vol. 1, 28. In note 5 he references *The Romaunt Version of the Gospel according to John* preserved in Trinity College, Dublin. Six copies of the Romaunt New Testament are known to be in existence.

11. Ibid., Vol. 1, 28.

12. Moreland, *The History*, 37.

the apostles were the only ones who could be held in honor. They asserted the right of the laity to preach, including women on the grounds of Anna (Luke 2:36–38) and Paul's injunction in Titus 2:3 ("Teach the older women . . . to teach what is good"). In keeping with the convictions of the Donatists, the Waldensians maintained that the unworthiness of the minister rendered the sacraments of no effect. In fact, they held that absolution by a good layman was effective and that confession could be made to any godly person. Waldensians refused to pay tithes and protested against religious endowments and the temporal power of the clergy.

The organization of the Waldensian church was a simplified expression of the Roman church in that they organized themselves into districts but there was no hierarchical structure. Each parish or local area was placed in the care of a pastor who was assisted by a consistory of lay people. A synod composed of pastors and an equal number of laity was held annually, the most usual meeting place being at the head of the Angrogna valley. On some of these, occasions more than a hundred and fifty pastors and the same number of lay members were present.

THE SACRAMENTS

When it came to the Eucharist some of the early Waldensians held to a subjective presence of Christ in the bread and wine, but maintained that transubstantiation took place, not in the hand of the priest, but in the mouth of the believer. However, with the passing of time they came to reject the concept of the Mass with its central focus of offering up consecrated bread and wine as a sacrifice for the sins of the living and the dead. Increasingly, Waldensians came to share Communion in their homes without any barbas being present. They held that any godly and respected person was qualified to lead such occasions.[13] Practice varied from one region to another, but the emphasis was on "simplicity rather than solemnity."[14] The Waldensians came to regard the Lord's Supper as a memorial and not a sacrifice. The thirteenth-century inquisitor, Reinherius Saccho, stated that "they do not believe the body and blood of Christ to be the true sacrament, but only blessed bread, which by a figure only is called the body of Christ, even as it is said, 'and that rock was Christ.'"[15] In the post-Reformation era the Waldensian view of the sacrament became more explicit, the *Piedmont*

13. Murray, "The Waldensians" In *Radical Christian Groups*, 14.4.

14. Ibid.

15. Moreland, *The History*, 22–23.

Confession of 1655 asserting "that Jesus Christ having fully expiated our sins by his most perfect sacrifice once offered on the Cross, it neither can, nor ought to be reiterated upon any account whatsoever, as they pretend to do in the Mass."[16]

It seems clear enough that the Waldensians practiced believers' baptism. One passage in the *Noble Lesson* emphasizes that the apostles "spoke without fear, of the doctrine of Christ . . . and baptised those who believed in the Name of Jesus Christ."[17] The contemporary writers Eberhard and Ermengard in their book entitled *Contra Waldenses*, written near the end of the twelfth century, repeatedly refer to immersion as the form of baptism among the Waldensians.[18] Reinerius Saccho, who had himself in earlier times been a Waldensian for seventeen years, condemned their rejection of infant baptism in his book *Of the Sects of Modern Heretics*, published in 1254. "Secondly," he wrote: "they condemn all sacraments of the Church; in the first place as to baptism, they say that the Catechism is nothing—also that the ablution which is given to infants profits nothing."[19] The creed of the Bohemian Waldensians published in 1532 is categorical that "infant baptism does no good, and is not ordered by Christ, but invented by man. Christ wants His baptism based upon his word for the forgiveness of sins, and He promises, 'he that believeth and is baptised shall be saved.'"[20] As late as the sixteenth century, Cardinal Hosius, who presided at the Council of Trent, noted that the Waldenses rejected infant baptism and re-baptized all who embraced their sentiments.[21] However, that said, it is clear that in the years following the Reformation the Savoy section of the Waldensians adopted the practice of infant baptism. Vedder has suggested that this took place at the Synod of Angrogne under the guidance of the Basle Reformation leaders, William Farel (1489–1565) and Johannes Oecolampadius (1482–1531).

In the matter of the church's rituals and ceremonies the Waldensians were against all alms, masses, fasts, and prayers for the faithful departed. They denied purgatory and maintained that departed spirits go either

---

16. Ibid., 65.

17. *The Noble Lesson*, extracted from Moreland, *The History*. Sir Samuel Moreland, a Cambridge academic, was sent by Oliver Cromwell on a mission to Italy in 1655 to protest at the actions taken against the Waldensians.

18. Christian, *A History*, Vol. 1, 81–82.

19. Tierney, *The Middle Ages*, 223.

20. Everts, *The Church*, 37.

21. Orchard, *A Concise History*, 304.

straight to heaven or hell. They rejected the canonical hours of prayer and opposed the use of crosses, images, and ornaments in churches. They also rejected the ceremonies of Candlemas, Palm Sunday, all benedictions, and indeed all ecclesiastical customs and ceremonies that did not have an explicit scriptural precedent. They denied the mystical sense of Scripture and called pilgrimages "useless." Some of their number refused to worship in official church buildings, preferring instead to worship in smaller groups in barns, homes, or other small locations. Lambert noted that many groups "rejected wholesale the sacraments and apparatus of the Church, vestments, chants, bells, organs, hierarchy and relics."[22]

Waldensians vehemently rejected the doctrine of purgatory, asserting that the Bible taught that there are only two destinies, heaven and hell. They were clear that there was no such thing as purgatory and were thus adamant that certificates of pardon were simply a form of financial racketeering. The *Noble Lesson* underlined the fact that it is God alone who can pardon.

> For, I dare say, and it is very true,
> That all the Popes which have been from Silvester to this present,
> And all Cardinals, Bishops, Abbots, and the Like,
> Have no power to absolve or pardon,
> Any creature so much as one mortal sin;
> Tis God alone who pardons, and no other.[23]

In other matters Waldensians denied the lawfulness of capital punishment, of oaths and bearing arms in self-defense, a position which was rejected by their later successors the Vaudois.

WALDENSIAN ECCLESIOLOGY

The Waldensian church kept themselves away from politics and wished only to be able to practice their faith in quiet and undisturbed. Waldesnsians held to a believers' model of the church that had traces of the earlier Donatists in that some of their congregations argued that converts from the Roman Catholic Churches should be re-baptized.[24] They shared the Donatist conviction that the unworthiness of the minister prevents the grace of God from coming to the believer through the sacraments.

22. Lambert, *Medieval Heresy*, 159.

23. Moreland, *The Noble Lesson*.

24. Murray, *Radical Christian Groups*, 12.

The later medieval Roman Catholic Church denounced the Waldensians as a recent schismatic group. In response, however, the Waldensians contended, possibly with some truth in their claim, that they could trace their history back to the time of Jesus and his apostles. The Waldensians went further and turned the offensive on the papal establishment, claiming that they had been fatally compromised by the so-called Donation of Constantine, a document that asserted Sylvester, the Bishop of Rome, had accepted lands, money, and recognition as the true church from the Emperor. In 1440, however, the document was finally shown to be an eighth-century forgery. The Waldensians therefore felt justified in claiming they were the true successors of those who rejected the "donation." They were adamant that their predecessors in the remote northern parts of Italy had never been tainted by the growing worldliness and corruption that had developed during the post-Constantinian centuries.

Waldensians held strongly to the doctrine of the priesthood of all believers and there was no clergy/laity divide in their communities. Both men and women played an active role in preaching, teaching, and leading worship. There was no leadership hierarchy that resembled anything approaching the Catholic system of bishops, priests, and deacons. The laity were divided into two categories: "the Perfect" and the "Imperfect." The first group gave up all their property and practiced a strict rule of fasting. The latter lived in society but without any of the trappings of luxury. Their rules concerning property were fairly soon relaxed. The poor or "perfect" brothers who were chosen by the community committed themselves to celibacy and were trained for a period ranging from one year to, in some circumstances, as many as six. On the completion of their studies they were sent out in pairs to visit, instruct, and care for the people in their allotted area. Early Waldensians were strong in their advocacy of non-violence but some later adherents in the post-medieval period were more ready to resist those who attacked them or raided their property. According to Wylie, there was no kingdom in Southern or Central Europe that these missionaries did not visit in their quest to share their faith. In the West they penetrated Spain, while in Southern France they labored among the Albigenses at Dauphiné, and Languedoc. On the East they descended into the regions alongside the Rhine and the Danube. Some of their number penetrated as far as Poland.[25]

The preachers exercised a strategic role, providing teaching and encouragement. Their regular visits, which might only be on one or two

---

25. Wylie, *The History,* Vol. 1, 32.

occasions during the year, provided vital encouragement to the many Waldensians who lived in isolated rural contexts. Open evangelism was often dangerous and so preachers frequently had to resort to gathering their followers and potential converts together, where they read or recited biblical passages and explained their meaning.

After Valdes died there was no overall leader of the Waldensians (in a way that was paralleled by the English Lollards after the death of Wycliffe). The strength of the Waldensians lay in the large numbers of their lay preachers who had thoroughly grasped the vision that Waldo had proclaimed. They were not only well-trained, but they were regularly encouraged in their work by gatherings intended specifically for that purpose, which were held once or twice a year.

In terms of their eschatology there is some evidence that they held to an imminent second return of Christ. At the beginning of the *Noble Lesson* we find these words.

> O Brethren, give ear to a noble lesson.
> We ought always to pray,
> For we see the world nigh to a conclusion.
> We ought to strive to do good works,
> Seeing the end of the world approacheth.
> There are already a thousand and one hundred years fully
> accomplished,
> Since it was written thus, for we are in the last time.
> We ought to covet little, for we are at what remains, viz. at the
> later end.[26]

Significantly, this passage in the *Nobel Lesson* goes on to mention that "In the Gospels and St Paul's Writings . . . no man living can know the end."

THE SPREAD OF THE MOVEMENT

The early followers of Waldo made strenuous efforts to spread their understanding of the Christian message. At some point in the twelfth century the Waldensians were granted refuge in Piedmont by the Roman Catholic Count of Savoy, a move which provoked the anger of the papacy. Beginning from this refuge in Southern France they spread out through Arragon, on one side, and into Milan, on the other, and further afield in France, Italy, Germany, and Bohemia. They were most successful in Piedmont and Dauphiné, and established permanent communities in the Cottian

26. *The Noble Lesson* extracted from Samuel Moreland, *The History.*

Alps. They attracted not only the poor and the newly emerging middle classes, but found acceptance among certain members of the aristocracy. For example, in 1207 the wife of Count de Foix joined them. There were also a number of other high-ranking individuals in Metz, Milan, and Arragon who threw in their lot with the movement. With the passing of the years their numbers gradually declined in France, but they extended their influence into Lower Germany, Brandenburg, Pomerania, and Mecklenburg, where in later times they helped to pave the way for the Protestant Reformation. Indeed, J. A. Wylie was of the view that the Reformation church was in the loins of the Waldensian church well before the birth of Luther. However, it was in Italy, where they were sometimes referred to as the Vaudois, that they developed most strongly and became renowned for their courage and refusal to take up arms even when they were persecuted. It is possible that some of those who followed Waldo may have existed in a community before he encountered them. Even if such is the case he was undoubtedly responsible for extending and developing them. Soon after this early point in time Waldo disappeared from the scene, possibly settling in the Cottian Alps. Other sources relate that he died in Bohemia, but the date of his death is uncertain.

PERSECUTION AND SURVIVAL

It was inevitable that a movement such as the Waldensians, which spread rapidly and put out a strong challenge to the dominant Roman church, would experience persecution. Such indeed proved to be the case. Pope Innocent III was one of the strongest earlier persecutors. Becoming Pontiff in 1198 he attempted to distinguish between those who were clearly heretics and those who were merely discontented with the institutional church. The latter he did his best to draw back into the fold. After a decade had passed Innocent took the view that all the necessary persuading had been done and he subsequently devoted his attention to rooting out the remainder. The Roman persecutions continued throughout the following century and between 1307 and 1323, out of a total of 607 sentences handed out by the Roman church's Inquisition in France upon heretics, ninety-two were Waldensians.

Those Waldensians who lived on the western slopes of the Alps were subjects of the King of France while those to the East, who occupied the district between Mount Viso and Mount Geneva, were under the Dukes of Savoy. The fact that the Waldensians were under two governments was to their benefit because the French kings were often engaged in much weightier concerns. In contrast, the Dukes of Savoy were often ready to take action against those who resided in their territory. It often happened that when those on one side of the mountains were attacked they could take refuge with their brethren on the other side. The French Waldensians were in the territories of the Archbishop of Embrun and the diocesan records contain details of the persecutions and the costs that they incurred. The accounts for 1335 have the following entry: "Item for persecuting the Vaudois, eight sols and thirty deniers of gold." An extensive Inquisition in Bohemia conducted by Gallus of Neuhaus discovered and punished at least 2,500 Waldensians between 1335 and 1355.[27]

The history of the Italian Waldensians is complex. They suffered a whole series of invasions and persecutions during which they held on to their faith with great courage and determination. Indeed, their staunch Christian commitment illustrates well how persecution often has the effect of strengthening people's existing beliefs. The establishment of a branch of the Inquisition at Turin brought danger much closer to home for the Italian Waldensians. They were accused by Pope John XXII in 1332 of having murdered the rector of the parish church of Engravia. In 1403 St. Vincent of Ferrers entered their lands and made an unsuccessful attempt to convert them. In 1487 Innocent III launched a crusade against the Waldensians and plenary indulgences were granted to all those who joined with it. Eighteen thousand regular troops and six thousand volunteers poured into the country plundering and laying it to waste. Soldiers made their way into the valley of Loyse where more than 3,000 Waldenses who had adopted a non-resistance stance were butchered. Those in the neighboring valleys of Argentière and Fraissinière quickly learned the lesson and took on a more aggressive role, barricading the mountain passes and fiercely opposing the papal troops. Seven hundred soldiers of the papal legate were killed in battle at the hamlet of Pommiers.[28] Several thousand more were trapped in a thick mist in the valley of Angrogna and killed by the Waldensians, Wylie observing "that of 18,000 regular troops . . . few ever returned to their homes."[29] Unexpectedly their ruler, the young Charles

27. Murray, "The Waldensians." In *Radical Christian Groups*, 13.

28. Wylie, *History of Protestantism*, Vol. 3, 440.

29. Ibid., Vol. 3, 443.

II,[30] Duke of Savoy,[31] then took up their cause and defended them, and even went as far as to express his admiration of their faith and good living.

Stuart Murray has pointed out that in certain areas Waldensians survived by keeping a low profile on account of official indifference. Some Waldensians attended Catholic services, paid tithes, swore oaths, and took part in various Catholic ceremonies. Wylie cites examples of this in Savoy during the closing years of the fifteenth century.[32] The survival of the movement into the sixteenth century in some parts was simply due to the resilience of small local groups that were little more than extended families and the bravery of the travelling preachers who visited and encouraged them.[33] It is clear, as Wylie and others have pointed out, that the dispersion of Waldensians over France, the Low Countries, Germany, Poland, Bohemia, Moravia, Calabria, and Naples sowed the seeds of what was eventually to become the European Reformation. It was, therefore, no surprise that in 1530 the churches of Provence and Dauphiné commissioned George Morel of Merindol and Pierre Masson of Burgundy to visit the Reformers of Switzerland and Germany in order to try to understand their doctrine and manner of life.

Among those they met were Berchtold Haller (1492–1536) and William Farel. They then went on to Basle where they presented the city's Reformation leader, Johannes Oecolampadius, with a complete statement of their doctrine and church order asking him to specify whether or not he held it to be defective in any way. He replied in a letter addressed to the churches of Provence and dated 13 October, 1530: "We render thanks to our most gracious Father that he has called you into such marvellous light, during ages in which such thick darkness has covered almost the whole world under the empire of Antichrist. We love you as brethren."[34] The Waldensian leaders also went on to Strasburg where they had similar meetings with Martin Bucer (1491–1551). Following these conferences the Waldensians convened a Synod in the town of Chamforans[35] in the Angrogna Valley to consider whether or not to throw in their lot with

30. Wylie points out that Leger and Gilles are of the opinion that this Duke was Philip II but that Monastier maintains that they "are mistaken, for this prince was then in France, and did not begin to reign till 1496." This peace was granted in 1489. See ibid., Vol. 3, 444, note 3.

31. Ibid., Vol. 3, 444.

32. Ibid., Vol. 3, 446.

33. Murray, *Radical Christian Groups*, 13.8.

34. Wylie, *The Waldensians*, Vol. 3, 446.

35. This town later ceased to exist.

the Reformers. Prominent among the Protestant leaders who attended the assembly, which began on 12th October, 1532, was William Farel.

William Farel, who knew the Waldensians and spoke their languages, urged them to join the Reformation and to leave secrecy. The synod sat for six days, and a Confession of Faith with Reformed doctrines was formulated with seventeen articles. Following these exhortations to courage from the Reformers, the Waldensians decided to worship openly and it was also resolved to print the Old and New Testaments in French. The new version first appeared three years later in 1535 and the entire expense was met by the Waldensians. However, this new openness resulted in their being harshly persecuted by King Francis I, with hundreds dying in the Massacre of Mérindol. A treaty of 5th June, 1561, finally granted amnesty to the Protestants of the valleys and allowed freedom of worship. During the 1560s the German Protestants contributed to the relief of the Waldensians and made representations to the Court of Turin on their behalf. This checked persecution against them for a considerable period. In consequence the Waldensians became more strongly aligned with the Protestant groups and in 1655 accepted the *Confession of Augsburg*. Most historians take the view that the Waldensian movement came to an end at the time of the Reformation when it merged with Protestantism. Significantly, as early as 1631 Protestant scholars had begun to consider the Waldensians as forerunners of the Reformation.

WALDENSIANISM SINCE THE REFORMATION

Waldensianism has continued in various Protestant forms and exists today in countries as diverse as France, Uruguay, and the United States. During the first two hundred years following the Reformation, the Waldensians, even in their more Protestant form, continued to battle with hardship and persecution. Another attempt against them was made by the Marquis de Pianesses who marched up the Angrogana Valley at the head of some fifteen thousand men. After an inconclusive struggle, he proposed a peace treaty with the proviso that a regiment of infantry and two companies of cavalry should remain with them for a short period of time. The Waldensians agreed to what turned out to be treachery as the billeted soldiers massacred the greater part of their community. At this point Oliver Cromwell intervened on their behalf and put pressure on Cardinal Mazarin to threaten the Duke, who was compelled to withdraw, and a period of peace ensued. In England a sum of £40,000 was collected, half of which was immediately sent to them with the remainder kept in an interest-bearing fund that was intended for future needs. The fund was subsequently lost as a result of the changing political situation in England.

The Edict of Nantes, which was issued by King Henry IV of France in 1598, afforded the Waldensians a lengthy period of toleration with substantial civil rights during which they erected church buildings and worshipped openly, but its subsequent revocation was followed by bitter persecution and the destruction of their churches and the suppression of much of their worship. It wasn't until comparatively recent times that renewed religious freedoms allowed them to surface in a public manner once more.

Other persecutions followed in the succeeding decades. The peace lasted only until 1685 when Louis XIV revoked the Edict of Nantes and his cousin, Duke of Savoy, Victor Amadeus II, made a concerted attack to crush them. In what followed both the French and the Italian Waldensians suffered harsh treatment as they were forced to surrender with many of them incarcerated in dungeons where they either died of disease or were executed. Following this conflict the Waldensian believers found refuge in Switzerland, Holland, Brandenburg, and the Palatinate. However, in 1689 about 800 of them went back to their mountain homeland under the command of their pastor, Henri Arnaud, in what was styled "the Glorious Return." They were, however, especially ruthless in removing those who had settled on their land and had taken over many of their homes.

After the French Revolution of 1789 the Waldensians of Piedmont-Sardinia were given liberty of conscience. In the early years of the nineteenth century they were much helped by the labors of Felix Neff (1798–1829), a Swiss Protestant pastor and philanthropist. Born in Geneva, he decided in 1819 to devote himself entirely to evangelistic work. He was ordained to the ministry in 1822, and soon afterwards settled in the valley of Freissinières where he was at one and the same time pastor, schoolmaster, engineer, and agriculturist. He was so successful that he changed the character of the district and its inhabitants.

In 1848 the situation further improved when the ruler of Savoy, King Charles Albert of Sardinia, restored their civil rights and what became known as the Waldensian Evangelical Church spread across Italy. On the French side they also enjoyed a brief period of peace under Napoleon I, who removed all restrictions and granted aid towards the maintenance of their pastors. They were, however, confined within a small mountainous area near the sources of the river Po, between the Clusone and the Pelice.

As their population increased many of them began to suffer poverty and restrictions were placed on their activities. They were not allowed to practice law outside their own territories and all civil and military occupations were forbidden to them. During World War II Waldensians played a significant role in hiding and protecting Jews from Nazi extermination. In 1975 the Waldensian church joined the Italian Methodist church to form the Union of Waldensian and Methodist Churches, which is a member of the World Council of Churches. Waldensian immigrants settled in Uruguay and Argentina in the middle years of the nineteenth century. Many also emigrated to the United States, settling in New York City, Chicago, and Rochester.

The legacy of the Waldensians is twofold. They undoubtedly helped to swell the movement that resulted in the Protestant Reformation in Europe, but perhaps of greater significance was the fact that they inspired the Catholic orders of the Franciscans and the Dominicans who emerged a generation or so later. Of the former (Reformation) influence, it has been pointed out that the spread of the Hussite movement after Huss's death in 1415 brought them into contact with the Waldensians, some of whose practices they adopted. These included baptizing converts and sharing the bread and wine of Communion in barns and other unauthorized places. There is little doubt that the Waldensian ideas provided fertile ground for the growth of Anabaptist ideas and practices in the sixteenth century. On the latter (Catholic) impact, it has been pointed out by a number of historians that both Dominic and Francis adopted Waldensian lifestyle and practice with only minimal changes. Francis, for example, founded an association committed to poverty and preaching and based on the sending out of the seventy.

FACTORS THAT MADE WALDENSIANS SUCCESSFUL

Their Biblical Faith

The Waldensians were from the earliest times straightforward people of the book, which they took at face value as is witnessed by the strong opposition to war and the strict codes of honesty in all things. They were a close-knit community who gathered round the Scripture in small study groups. Waldensians had a deeply personal knowledge of the Scriptures and spent much time learning passages by heart, which they applied to their daily living. It was reported that poor men and women members who were unable to read could nevertheless recite much of Luke's Gospel and repeat the Apostles' Creed.

A Minimalist Church

Waldensians, along with others, were deeply concerned at the worldliness of the Catholic Church's ecclesiastical hierarchy. The sought to retain what they saw as the simplicity of New Testament Christianity. Along with the English Lollards they were strong advocates of lay preachers. The Waldensians had two types of membership. The "society" members were those who renounced all worldly property and a lengthy period of probation was required before the commitment was made. "Friends" were allowed property but were expected to be generous givers. Their lifestyle was both plain and appealing. Waldensians were humble people who worked hard with their hands, dressed modestly, and were known for their truthfulness, integrity, and caring attitudes. They avoided taverns, dances, and company, which were likely to lead to un-Christ-like behavior.

A Deep Concern for the Poor

One Waldensian explained that the reason why goods were shared in common was not "to buy souls," as the Inquisition claimed, but out of love for Christ to assist the poor, regardless of whether or not they were Waldensians. Even the Inquisitors were compelled to acknowledge that "they are recognisable by their customs and speech, for they are modest and disciplined. They take no pride in their garments, which are neither costly nor vile. . . . They live by their labour as artisans. Their teachers are cobblers. They are chaste, temperate, and restrain themselves from anger, avoiding baseness and light speech, lies and oaths."[36] In this regard they were, of course, close to the heart of the Lord, whose kingdom they sought to proclaim. It was to be a kingdom with good news for the poor.

Total Commitment to Jesus

There can be no doubt that the sheer unswerving dedication and total abandonment of many Waldensians drew many to their ranks. "The blood of the martyrs," as Tertullian had observed, "was indeed the seed of the

---

36. Saxby, *Pilgrims*, 94.

church." Alexis Muston gives the following examples of some of those who died amid terrible and inhuman suffering for their faith in Jesus in the valleys of Peidmont in the middle years of the sixteenth century. Hugo Chiamps of Finestrelle had his entrails torn from his living body at Turin. Peter Geymarali of Bobbio suffered the same fate at Luzerna and a fierce cat was thrust on him to torture him further. Maria Romano was buried alive at Rocco-patia and Magdalen Foulano suffered the same fate at San Giovanni. Daniel Michelini had his tongue torn out for having praised God. James Baridari perished covered with sulfurous matches that had been forced into his flesh and under the nails, between the fingers, in the nostrils, in the lips, and all over his body, and then set alight. Daniel Revelli had his mouth filled with gunpowder which, when lighted, blew his head off. Maria Monnen had the flesh cut from her cheek and chin bones so that her jaw was left bare and she was left to perish. Sarah Rostagnol was slit open from the legs to her breasts and left to perish on the road between Eyral and Luzerna. Anne Charbonnier was impaled and carried on a pike, as a standard from San Giovanni to La Torre. Daniel Rambaud at Paesano had his nails torn off, then his fingers chopped off, then his feet and his hands, then his arms and his legs, with each successive refusal to deny his biblical faith.[37]

Waldo's Gift of Leadership

Peter Waldo was a man with a unique gift of leadership. He was a visionary with a clear vision from God, but his strength lay in the fact that he was able to make it plain enough for the most humble and illiterate rural mountain folk to understand, embrace, and share. It is one thing to have a vision, but quite another to be able to persuade others to run with it. Not only did Waldo succeed in this, but he had the necessary abilities and resources to produce the right literature and Scripture, and the management skills to set up an organization and training scheme that could function when he had gone. Although other leaders came and went, such was Peter's legacy that the movement was in many senses self-perpetuating.

37. Muston, *Israel*, 45–46.

5 | The Lollards

ABOUT THE YEAR 1328 a man who was later to be called the "Morning Star of the Reformation" was born in the Yorkshire village of Hipswell, not far from the town of Richmond. His name was John Wycliffe (1324–84). He proved to be an able scholar and went to study at Balliol College, Oxford, later becoming its Master in 1358. Four years later he became Warden of the recently founded Canterbury Hall. During these early years he was in favor with the Roman church and held a number of ecclesiastical positions, including Fillingham (1361), Ludgershall (1368), and Lutterworth, which he received as a gift from the crown. In 1372 Wycliffe proceeded to the degree Doctor of Divinity, which appears to have been a turning point in his theology, teaching, and lecturing in the university.

About 1375 Wycliffe spoke in support of King John, who had declined to pay tribute money to the papacy. His argument was that the monarch held his kingdom directly from Christ and that the popes had, in any event, forfeited any claim to tribute money on account of their worldliness and moral corruption. This action marked the beginning of Wycliffe's public career. Up until that time his writing had been confined to theology and philosophy. He was strongly committed to realism and denied the possibility of anything being annihilated. This impacted his thinking on the Eucharist and led him to reject transubstantiation, which implied a change in the substance of the elements. He did not, however, deny the presence of Christ in the sacrament, nor did he reject the seven traditional Catholic sacraments, though he held confirmation to be only of limited value. He made strong accusations against the behavior and teaching of the friars and became a staunch opponent of corruption in the church, writing stinging words against the promotion of clergy to positions of state. He was strongly opposed to the wealth and power of the Roman church and worked for a return to the apostolic gospel and compassionate concern for the poor.

In September 1376 John of Gaunt, who resented the interference of churchmen like William Wykeham[1] in politics and administration, invited Wycliffe to preach in London. His sermons resulted in a summons to appear before Convocation,[2] but the presence of John, along with Lord Percy, saved him. Nevertheless, by the end of the following year the University of Oxford examined his doctrines and decided that his views were both unorthodox and dangerous. In consequence, he was ordered to remain silent on what were considered to be his erroneous doctrines. However, the growing freedom of thought in many European universities intensified his questioning of holy orders and the sacraments. Some of his writings are strongly anti-clerical, particularly concerning monks and immorality among the priesthood. In 1378 he published his *De Veritate Sacrae Scripturae* in which he appealed to the Bible against the abuses of his time. The book was significant because it demonstrated that there was no bar on translating the Scriptures into the vernacular. Indeed there were already translations of parts of the Bible, including Richard Rolle of Hampole's Psalms.

Wycliffe was adamant that the Bible should be in English and the translation that he and his close friends and colleagues made from the Latin was racy and vigorous. In consequence, it soon became widely read and sought after. While it is the case that statements were made by Archbishop Thomas Arundel[3] and John Huss of Bohemia that affirm Wycliffe translated the whole Bible, some questions have been raised about the matter. It seems quite likely that Wycliffe may have been largely or wholly responsible for an initial and almost unreadable translation that was followed some time later by a more polished version. This second version, which has a strongly Lollard prologue, is thought by most historians to have been the work of John Purvey (c. 1353–c. 1428),[4] a close friend and colleague from Wycliffe's Lutterworth days, and Nicholas Hereford (died

---

1. William Wykeham (1323–1404) was made Chancellor on 17 September, 1367, and consecrated Bishop of Winchester on 10th October in the same year.

2. Convocation was the name given to the church's parliament. The two archdioceses of Canterbury and York had their own Convocation.

3. Thomas Arundel (1353–1414) was a prominent politician in the reign of Richard II. He was Bishop of Ely in 1374 and translated to York in 1388 and Canterbury in 1396.

4. John Purvey was curate to Wycliffe in the latter part of his time at Lutterworth. Hudson, *Lollards and their Books*, 109, questioned the evidence for Purvey's role as translator.

c. 1420), a West Country Lollard who was a resident at Queen's College, Oxford.

At some point during his time at Oxford, probably about 1377, Wycliffe appears to have begun to train certain priests and laymen to spread the message of his teaching. Known as his "poor" preachers they were in some ways reminiscent of the friars. They went about in blue or russet gowns and depended on the hospitality of their hearers. In addition to their knowledge of the Bible they were known for their sincere and vibrant spirituality. Wycliffe had major doubts about the validity of priestly ordination such that by the time he died his preachers were almost entirely laymen.

When the Peasants Revolt took place in 1381 Wycliffe's sympathies were strongly in favor of the poor, and some of the leaders of the uprising may have been impacted by his views. Although Wycliffe did not offer any overt support to the rebels, their protest and its defeat may have cost him the support of some of those in authority. This, coupled with the fact that his great supporter, John of Gaunt, fell from power, meant that he and his Oxford colleagues were silenced. In the same year, Wycliffe expressed his doubts concerning the doctrine of transubstantiation, which in part led to his dismissal from the university. Wycliffe, however, boldly appealed to the king and nation and refused to go to Rome to answer for his condemnation of the doctrine. He was also cited to appear before an assembly of eight bishops and fourteen doctors at Grey-Friars in London but declined to attend. The investigation proceeded in his absence and out of his twenty-four writings ten were condemned as heretical and fourteen as erroneous. Wycliffe, for his part, simply remained at Lutterworth preaching and teaching until his death on 31st December, 1384.

Wycliffe was primarily an academic and should probably be regarded as a radical rather than a revolutionary. His criticisms of corruption rather than error should be seen as a plea for reform rather than as an excuse to set up an alternative church. Although his sympathies were often on the side of the poor Wycliffe had no thoughts of stirring social unrest.

THE LOLLARDS

Wycliffe's struggle in Oxford had been primarily academic and its influence had a powerful impact on the university. However, his ideas and teachings were far from being at an end. His followers, known as Lollards, developed into a popular movement and continued to preach, teach, and circulate tracts and portions of the Scriptures throughout the course of the next hundred and fifty years.

Wycliffe's vision was not to start a new movement or plant new congregations, but rather to supplement the work of the parishes by raising up teachers and evangelists to work alongside the local priest. Some of the movement's early leaders were scholarly individuals such as Thomas Brightwell in Leicester and William James in Oxford. Philip Repingdon preached in the areas between Oxford and Northampton and also formed groups in Leicester and Brackley. He later returned to the established church, eventually becoming Bishop of Lincoln in 1405, in which position he was a prominent opponent of Lollardy. Most Lollard preachers and leaders, however, knew little of Wycliffe's scholarly pursuits and presented a simplified but biblical version of his teachings, which found a ready hearing among artisans, peasants, and some of the country clergy, such as William Sawtree from Norfolk and William Northwold, an archdeacon from Sudbury. The Lollards were a diverse group of people comprising of knights, merchants, and peasants. Among the noble supporters was a group on ten "Lollard Knights," which included Sir John Montague, who removed images from his private chapel in Shenley, and Sir Thomas Latimer, who protected Lollards around Northampton. Their most effective leaders, which soon becomes clear from John Foxe's detailed accounts, were the ordinary laymen and women who made their living as tanners, textile workers, and weavers. Many of them memorized New Testament books, such as the letter of James, and gathered small groups of friends and neighbors together in homes and out of the way places.

There have been several suggestions as to the origin and meaning of the word "Lollard," the most likely one being that it is derived from the German word "lollen," meaning "to talk in a low voice," "to mumble," or "mutter under one's breath." The core of Lollardy stemmed from Wycliffe himself, but there were other independent spirits, such as William Swinderby, who attached themselves to the movement. The Lollard ranks were also undoubtedly swelled as a result of the general ferment in thought and social life that accompanied the rise of individualism and a growing desire for personal salvation. The extent of Wycliffe's disciples at the time of his death was described by one of his contemporaries, Canon Knighton, who reported: "The number of those who believed in Wycliffe's doctrine very much increased, and were multiplied like suckers growing from the root of a tree. They everywhere filled the kingdom; so that a man could scarcely meet two people on the road but one of them was a disciple of Wycliffe."[5] Knighton went on to write, "they so prevailed by their laborious urging of their doctrines, that they gained over half the people, or a still greater proportion to their sect. Some embraced their doctrines heartily, others they compelled to join them from fear or shame."[6]

While Knighton's statement that every other person in the kingdom was a disciple of Wycliffe was probably an exaggeration, the fact was that the king and Parliament had been in a longstanding conflict with the papacy. This meant that British people were not afraid to throw in their lot with a radical Christian group who were protesting against the Roman church. By 1384 the threatened church authorities had issued injunctions against Lollardy over a wide area of England. In 1392 King Richard II reported in a letter that "Lollardy had spread in divers places within the diocese of Hereford and parts near adjoining, both privily and openly."[7] The following year a number of Lollards were reported in the town of Leicester for holding opinions contrary to the church of Rome.[8] John Foxe noted that in 1428: "a great number both of men and women from Norfolk and Suffolk and especially from the towns of Beccles, Ersham and Ludney were cast into prison for Lollard beliefs." He gave a list of one hundred and twenty of their number.[9] Punishments were often humiliating and severe. Roger Dexter and his wife, Alice, were made to walk through the streets to the collegiate church of St. Mary-in-the Newarks, Leicester, carrying a crucifix in their left hand and a taper weighing half pound weight in their right, he in his shirt and breaches and she "in her chemise alone."[10] In 1428 John Beverly was required "to fast upon the Friday and Saturday and on the Saturday to be whipped from the palace of Norwich, going round about by Tomblands, and by St Michael's Church . . . and about the market, having in his hand a wax-candle of two-pence, to offer to the image of the Trinity after he had done his penance."[11]

Early sixteenth-century punishments meted out to Lollards were equally as brutal. At Amersham, about the year 1506, thirty individuals "who spoke against the superstition and idolatry of the church and were

5. Anon., *Lives*, 51.

6. Ibid.

7. Foxe, *The Acts and Monuments of John Foxe*, Vol. 3, 196.

8. Ibid., Vol. 3, 197.

9. Ibid., Vol. 3, 587.

10. Ibid., Vol. 3, 200.

11. Ibid., Vol. 3, 593.

desirous to hear and read the Scriptures, were burned on their cheek, their necks being tied fast to a post and their hands holden fast that they might not stir; and so the iron, being hot, was put to their cheeks."[12] In 1508 Laurence Ghest was burned in Salisbury in front of his wife and seven children, the authorities hoping by this means to persuade him to recant his biblical convictions.[13]

LOLLARD DOCTRINE

Lollards believed that Christianity should be closely based on the Bible and that everyone should have access to a Bible in the vernacular and be free to interpret its meaning for themselves. For this reason Wycliffe's prime objective was to produce an English Bible for his preachers and those who listened to their teaching. Much of the translation work was probably done by Nicholas of Hereford, with revision possibly being carried out by his secretary, John Purvey. Lollard leaders and followers became increasingly critical of church practices that could not be supported from the Scriptures, which they held to be the supreme source of authority. Out of this fundamental building block, Anne Hudson has argued, sprang the other aspects of their theology.[14]

Prominent among Lollard doctrines was their belief in an invisible church that was a community of the faithful, which overlapped with the visible Catholic Church but which was not identical with it. Wycliffe was a predestinarian and believed that only those who were pre-selected in the sovereign will of God would enjoy salvation in heaven, beyond the grave. All of this ran strongly counter to the teaching of the Catholic Church, which taught a doctrine of works that insisted that salvation could only be achieved through behavior and charitable works. By the same token Wycliffe found himself in conflict with the Catholic priesthood, who saw their function as helping the laity on their journey by dispensing grace through the sacraments, such as confession and the Eucharist.

In their theology of the Eucharist the Lollards denied that God's body could leave heaven by virtue of the priest's words and become enclosed in the bread that is given to the people at the altar. Francis Funge was punished about the year 1520 for saying: "If the sacrament of the altar be very God and man, flesh and blood, in the form of bread, as priests say

12. Ibid., Vol. 4, 124.

13. Ibid., Vol. 4, 127.

14. Hudson, *The Premature Reformation*, 389.

that it is, then have we many gods; and in heaven there is but one God."[15] At the same time Thomas Clerke was charged with speaking against the real presence of Christ in the sacrament.[16] Later Lollard teaching, which was encapsulated in a tract entitled *The Wicket,* held that the Eucharist was a simple commemoration meal. This was certainly a development on Wycliffe's ideas.

A clear idea of Lollard doctrines can readily be gained by examining the accusations brought against Lollard preachers and teachers before diocesan bishops from Wycliffe's time to the second and third decades of the sixteenth century. It is clear that although most of them were believers in the doctrine of the Apostles' Creed, they held major doubts about many of the practices of the Roman church. This was particularly evidenced at Archbishop Thomas Arundel's examination of William Thorpe in 1407.[17] It is plain that the Lollards denied that the "very body of Christ was present in the sacrament of the altar." Some of their number, such as Walter Brute, held the elements as "a sign and a memorial only."[18] They regarded the Pope as the anti-Christ and asserted that he cannot grant pardons. They shared the views of William Swinderby who was adamant that "contrition only putteth away sin if any man shall be duly contrite; and that confession and exercise is superfluous, and not requisite of necessity for salvation."[19] They also asserted that no man is bound to give tithes. A number of Lollards were of the view that the New Testament did not require tithes.

Although Wycliffe was ambivalent about images, Lollards were strongly opposed to the abuse of them in the Roman church, maintaining that they were objects of superstition and idolatry. Richard Belward of Ditchingham in Norfolk for example, held that "such as go on pilgrimage, offering to images made of wood and stone" should be excommunicated "because they ought to offer to the quick and not to the dead."[20] John Blomstone of Coventry taught that there was as much virtue in a herb as in the image of the Virgin Mary and that prayer and alms avail not the dead. He also maintained that it "was foolishness to go on pilgrimage to the image of our lady of Doncaster, Walsingham, or even the Tower of Coventry: for a man might as well worship the blessed virgin in the kitchen,

---

15. Foxe, *The Acts*, Vol. 4, 233.

16. Ibid., Vol. 4, 233.

17. Ibid., Vol. 3, 252–53.

18. Ibid., Vol. 3, 132.

19. Ibid., Vol. 3, 112.

20. Ibid., Vol. 3, 585.

as the aforesaid places."[21] Both the practice of going on pilgrimages and the use of paintings in churches were also opposed by Lollard groups and individuals. Lollards had little time for excessive singing, bell-ringing, and auricular confession. They were also strongly opposed to the sale of indulgences, the cult of the Saints, and trading in relics.

Women were equally forthright in Lollard convictions. Margaret Backster, the wife of William Backster of Martham in Norfolk, said during her interrogation "that she would never confess herself to any priest, neither obey him; because they have no power to absolve any man from his sins, for that they offend daily more grievously than other men; and that therefore men ought to confess themselves only unto God, and to no priest." She also asserted that "holy bread and holy water were but trifles of no effect or force."[22]

LITERATURE AND PAMPHLETEERING

Initially, Lollardy spread because a number of the nobility, such as Sir Thomas Latimer and Sir John Montague, gave the movement their active support. These two knights, together with eight others, were known as the "Lollard Knights." Even some who were members of the king's court took Wycliffe's ideas out into the everyday world of politics. Among their number was the London Mayor, John of Northampton. In the early days following Wycliffe's death Lollard influence was noted in the dioceses of Canterbury, Rochester, London, and Hereford. It's not clear exactly how much support Lollards received in late fourteenth-century England, but one thing is clear and that is that it flourished in the middle years of the fifteenth century and was perceived as a significant threat in the early decades of the sixteenth century.

The scattering of pamphlets was one of the chief means of spreading the Lollard message. Between 1384 and 1396, a major Lollard collection known as *The Floretum* was produced and widely circulated. A Lollard man named Aston was brought to trial before Benedict Williams in 1405 for distributing literature in this way and William Pateshull was similarly condemned for handing out tracts during the London riots in 1405.

A major Lollard tract was *The Twelve Conclusions*, which they fixed on the gates of St. Paul's and Westminster Abbey and presented to Parliament in 1395. It complained of the wealth and power of the clergy,

21. Ibid., Vol. 4, 133.
22. Ibid., Vol. 3, 596.

attacked endowments, the hierarchy, clerical celibacy and immorality, transubstantiation, the Mass, prayers for the dead, chantries, pilgrimages, the worship of images and relics, auricular confession, indulgences, and capital punishment. Referring to the worship that comes from Rome they stated: "It consists in signs and ceremonies, and not that which Christ has ordained." They called on Parliament to bring the church into line with Scripture and even to deal with minor practices such "the blessing oil, salt, wax, incense, stones, mitres, and pilgrims staffs."[23] To this document should be added the *Thirty Seven Conclusions* and *The Remonstance* published by Forshall. Another way in which the Lollards used publicity to spread their message was by attaching Lollard prefaces to translations of the Psalms and Canticles.

PREACHING AND TEACHING

In the early days in particular, preachers received protection from local knights, which meant that manual craftsmen such as William Smith of Leicester were able to spread Lollard teachings to a wider audience. In his later writings Wycliffe had put forward a plan to train up "poor preachers," laymen who would be able to carry and teach the Scriptures across the nation. The Lollard groups who emerged soon after his death quickly expanded in numbers. As early as 1382 unlicensed preachers were noted as causing trouble, drawing in the crowds and refusing to respond to summons issued by the bishops. In the years immediately following the Peasants' Revolt there was anxiety over rumors of ordinations by certain Lollards in the Salisbury diocese.

Some of the Lollards were particularly able preachers. Such was Walter Brute, who was charged with heresy by John Trevenant, Bishop of Hereford, in 1391. Described in the official citation as "a lay person, learned of our diocese," it was asserted that he "hath laboured to inform men and companies" and "hath many years laboured to advance things erroneous and schismatical, and also heresies and implant them in the hearts of faithful people."[24] William Swinderby, who was also brought before Bishop Trevenant, was accused of having "preached at divers places and times before a great multitude of faithful Christians."[25] Reinerus, a thirteenth-century writer, who for a while had Lollard sympathies, related that "by

23. d'Aubigné, *The Reformation*, Vol. 1, 101–2.

24. Foxe, *The Acts*, Vol. 3, 132.

25. Ibid., Vol 3, 133.

offering jewellery and other artefacts for sale, the Lollards obtained opportunities to repeat and read passages from the gospels and to explain the doctrines which they held dear."[26] William Thorpe was brought before the Archbishop of Canterbury in 1407 for "travelling about in the north country and in other diverse counties of England, sowing about false doctrine . . . to poison all this land."[27]

In 1434 a certain Richard Belward was brought before the Bishop of Norwich on account of his keeping "schools of Lollardy in the English tongue in the town of Ditchingham" and for the reason that "a certain parchment-maker bringeth him all the books containing that doctrine from London."[28] There were other Lollard schools such as that run by Thomas Moon, a glove-maker from Loddon, Norfolk. In 1518 William Sweeting, a cowherd of St. Nicholas parish in Colchester, was accused of reading Lollard literature to local people while out in the field minding cattle. His friend, James Brewster, was accused of having "a certain little book of Scripture in English," which he was doubtless reading to friends and neighbors.[29]

It is clear that many Lollards memorized portions of the New Testament, which they then recited to others either outside in quiet or hidden locations or more often in their homes. These "reading circles" proved a successful means for attracting new followers to the movement. Thus Agnes Wellis, who was brought before John Longland (the Bishop of Lincoln) in 1521, was found to have learned the epistle of St. James in English by heart. Another woman, also Agnes, Agnes Ashford of Chesham, was questioned in detail for having on five occasions taught James Morden passages from the Sermon on the Mount and, on two occasions, the Beatitudes.[30] A certain Richard Bartlet had also learned from Thurstan Littlepage "some of the same epistle of St. James, thus beginning 'James the servant of God, to the twelve kinds,' & co."[31] Nicholas Durdant was found guilty about the year 1518 of reciting parts of the epistles of St. Paul in his home at Iver-Court.[32] John Barret, a goldsmith from London, was detected in his own

26. Anon, *Lives*, 52.

27. Foxe, *The Acts*, Vol. 3, 252.

28. Ibid., Vol. 3, 585.

29. Ibid., Vol. 4, 216.

30. Ibid., Vol. 4, 225.

31. Ibid., Vol. 4, 222.

32. Ibid., Vol. 4, 226.

house reciting the epistle of James, which epistle, with many other things, "he had perfectly without book."[33]

PERSECUTION

While there is evidence that Richard II (1367–1400) was sympathetic towards the Lollard agenda, this may have been exaggerated. Richard certainly had a strong orthodox Christian faith but nevertheless tolerated a wide spectrum of belief among his courtiers. John Foxe reported that he found no evidence of anyone being put to death in his reign for Lollard beliefs.[34] In 1382 Archbishop Courtenay had instigated a purge against Lollards in Oxford following the Peasants' Revolt, but it wasn't until the last years of the fourteenth century that a strong reaction set in against their activities. The authorities were alarmed at the growing influence of the Lollard preachers, particularly in the light of the unrest among the poor. The publication of the *Twelve Conclusions* shocked Archbishop Thomas Arundel and Robert Braybrooke, the Bishop of London. In October 1395 Pope Boniface IX issued a papal Bull against the Lollards. Addressed to "our well-beloved son in Christ, Richard, the noble King of England," it spoke of "a certain crafty and hair-brained sect of false Christians in the same your kingdom" who "do rise up and inveigh against the determination of the holy fathers and publicly preach very many erroneous, detestable, and heretical articles." The Bull went on to urge the archbishops of Canterbury and York "that they stand up in the power of God against this pestilent and contagious sect, and that they lively persecute the same in the form of law."

Richard's endeavors to take matters in hand were short-lived since he was deposed by his cousin, who became Henry IV and whose intervention resulted in Parliament passing an Act in 1401 entitled, *De Heretico Comburendo* (Concerning the Burning of Heretical Persons). This Act spoke of a new sect that usurped the office of preaching, held conventicles and schools, and circulated books and evaded episcopal jurisdiction. The Act gave diocesan bishops the right to suppress all of these activities. Offenders were to be held for three months and purged. If they proved unbending they were to be handed over to the secular courts and burnt. In March 1401, to show that they meant business, the church hurried through the burning of the first Lollard martyr, William Sawtree, a clergyman from

33. Ibid., Vol. 4, 228.
34. Ibid., Vol. 3, 202.

the Norwich diocese. He had recanted before his bishop but had then preached in London where he had also presumed to say; "Instead of adoring the cross on which Christ suffered, I adore Christ who suffered on it."[35] That said, the number of burnings were relatively few. The knights of the shires prayed that convicted clerks should not be placed in bishops' prisons and that the statute might be changed, but they were disappointed because a further Act of 1414 made heresy a common law offence and judges were made to swear to exterminate it. Persons who offended were now required to be handed over to the secular courts.

Archbishop Thomas Arundel (1397 and 1398–1410) emerged as one of the harshest persecutors of Lollardy. He publicly bewailed that "our province is being infected with divers and unfruitful doctrines, and defiled with a new and damnable name of Lollardy."[36] He tightened up the regulations on preachers requiring that "no person shall presume to preach, except he give faithful signification, in due form of his sending and authority."[37] He also ruled that "no book or treatise made by John Wycliffe, or others whomsoever, about that time, or since, or hereafter to be made, be read in schools, halls, hospitals, or other places whatsoever, within our province of Canterbury aforesaid, except the same be first examined by the University of Oxford or Cambridge."[38] Also included in this provision was a law that "no man hereafter, by his own authority translate any text of Scripture into English or any other tongue, by way of a book, libel or treatise."[39]

In 1417 Sir John Oldcastle, who had become Lord Cobham by marriage and had been in high favor with the King, was put to death on account of his having caused numerous copies of Wycliffe's writings to be made. He was one of the most prominent Lollard leaders who had gathered support for an armed rebellion that had been set up in 1414 with the intention of forcing the church to accept the movement's reforms. He was brought before Henry V who did not share his father's tolerant ways and ordered him to be taken to the Tower of London. He was subsequently brought before an ecclesiastical tribunal at St. Paul's at the conclusion of which Archbishop Arundel pronounced the sentence of death. He was returned to the Tower and given forty days to repent. He succeeded in escaping and

35. Ibid., Vol. 3, 103.
36. Ibid., Vol. 3, 246.
37. Ibid., Vol. 3, 243.
38. Ibid., Vol. 3, 243.
39. Ibid., Vol. 3, 243.

took refuge in Wales where he began to raise support for an armed rebellion. He was then recaptured and carried back to London where he was burnt on a slow fire in St. Giles fields. Others who had worked with him were hanged. The debacle made it clear to the authorities that Lollardy had spread over a wide area, but it also acted a set-back to the Lollard cause.

Through the course of the fifteenth century the church hierarchies worked to suppress Lollard activities and there were occasional Episcopal purges. Bishop William Alnwick of Norwich, for example, carried out a thorough investigation of his diocese in 1428–29, which brought to light "about sixty heretics" who lived and worked in the vicinity of Loddon and Beccles. They had been organized and led by William White who was burned at the stake with two other organizers. The rest were made to recant and do public penance.[40]

During the years that followed Oldcastle's death, and indeed throughout most of the fifteenth century, the crown and the church united against the Lollards and drove them underground. Oldcastle's death had lost them the support of almost all the gentry and intellectuals. They now found themselves compelled to hold their meetings in secret. In the 1450s, however, there was a brief lull in the clamp down on the Lollards, who began to re-surface and plant new groups and resurrected some of their reading meetings. Lollard beliefs remained strong in many family circles and were passed down through the generations and through trade contacts.

Despite the best efforts of the authorities to suppress them, there is clear evidence that Lollardy survived in England right up and into the early decades of the sixteenth century and the time when Lutheran ideas began to penetrate East Anglia and Cambridge. A. G. Dickens is among those scholars who have maintained that they provided a seedbed for the sixteenth-century Reformation. "That Lollardy survived," he wrote, "and contributed in some significant degree towards the Protestant Reformation is a fact based upon massive and incontrovertible evidence."[41] Philip Hughes, the Roman Catholic Reformation historian, concurred[42] and cited the fact that there were 365 "processes" for heresy in England in the thirteen years before Martin Luther made his appearance as a religious leader in Europe. Hughes wrote: "Our native heretics [the Lollards] of the early sixteenth century may indeed have been a feeble people, but the ideas to which they clung [were] handed down from generation to genera-

---

40. Thomson, *The Later Lollards*, 117–38.

41. Dickens, *English Reformation*, 37.

42. Hughes, *The Reformation*, Vol. 1, 126.

tion in obscure hamlets of the Chiltern hills and there is evidence that . . . the name of Wycliffe was still revered in the days of More and Fisher by these English craftsmen."[43]

In the end, the full extent of Lollard strength and influence on the eve of the Reformation will probably never be fully known. There is, however, some first-hand evidence of individual Lollard activities in the areas close to London. In 1506 Thomas Man of Amersham in Buckinghamshire had, with his wife, turned six or seven hundred people into sympathizers. Archbishop William Warham's 1511 purge of the Lollard communities in Kent resulted in five burnings and thirty abjurations and Bishop Smith's attacks in the same year considerably weakened the Lollard cause in Buckinghamshire. Smith succeeded in getting sixty recantations and four others were burned.[44]

In 1514 Richard Hunne, a London merchant tailor, was arrested and imprisoned after Lollard books were found in his home. We also have the testimony of Robert Hemsted of Steeple Bumpstead to the Bishop of London's court in 1518 that the curate, a man with Lollard sympathies, sought to persuade him during his Lent confession that he must not believe "that in the blessed Sacrament of thaulter [sic] is the very body of Christ."[45] Robert Bartlett was known to have organized a Bible study meeting in Amersham.[46] The Vicar of Windrush near Burford shared his Lollard convictions with Roger Dods after he had first sworn him to secrecy.[47]

The most rigorous sixteenth-century investigation into Lollardy was that of Bishop Longland in 1521–22. He began by questioning those who had been dealt with in his earlier purge of 1511. From their number Longland was able to round up nearly 400 hundred suspects from the towns of Amersham, Chesham, and Missenden, along with others who lived in and around Burford. Four were burned for heresy and about fifty made a public recantation and submitted to penance.[48] Significantly, Longland's interrogations revealed that one of the Lollards, Richard Saunders, was by far the wealthiest inhabitant of Amersham and that the bulk of the town's membership were from the middle ranks of society and represented about

43. Ibid., Vol. 1, 126.

44. Haigh, *English Reformations*, 53.

45. Parker, *The English Reformation*, 20.

46. Haigh, *English Reformations*, 52.

47. Elton, *Policy and Police*, 353.

48. Haigh, *English Reformations*, 53.

25 percent of tax payers.[49] Thomas Harding, another Amersham Lollard, was seen reading a book in a wood near Chesham. He was brought before Bishop Longland, tried, and burned at the stake.[50] In 1527 another Lollard, John Tyball, also of Steeple Bumpstead, was arraigned on a charge of heresy. It seems to have been the case that during Michaelmas in the previous year he and Thomas Hilles had visited the Cambridge Lutheran, Robert Barnes, in London, taking with them some of their Lollard books, doubtless expecting him to be impressed. Instead of which Barnes was able to sell them for three shillings and two pence, a copy of Tyndale's New Testament in flowing English.[51] Christopher Haigh has emphasized that Tyndale's Testament found a ready market among old Lollards.[52]

LEADERS

Nicholas Hereford is generally held to be the first Lollard leader. In 1382, before Wycliffe's death, he preached in Oxford calling for major reforms in the church and for his endeavors he was excommunicated by the Pope. Among other leading figures in the movement were William Swinderby and John Purvey, who is believed to have been the author or reviser of the second and later Wycliffe version of the Bible. Purvey was born at Lathbury and worked near Bristol. Nicholas Hereford was also involved in the translating of the Old Testament of the second version of the Bible. John Aston was one of Wycliffe's Oxford disciples who, along with Purvey, Hereford, and others, was inhibited by the Bishop of Worcester in 1387. It seems that they had set up an illegal and unlicensed college. Significantly, the Rolls of Parliament for 1401 and 1414 both speak of Lollard Schools. All three men travelled widely and established small communities across the countryside. Their message was readily received by sections of the artisan class who were becoming literate and were open to new ideas.

LITERATURE DISTRIBUTION

Literature distribution was one of the most effective methods used by the Lollards to spread the message. They had no access to printing presses

---

49. Brigden, *London*, 228.

50. Haigh, *English Reformations*, 51.

51. Parker, *The English Reformation*, 28–29.

52. Haigh, *English Reformations*, 60.

and the majority of their literature came from Flanders and France from men such as Richard Pynson and Wynkyn de Worde.[53] As literacy had increased in England in the later years of the fourteenth century, so the appetite for books and pamphlets had increased. Thomas Matthew, a fishmonger from Colchester in Essex, was typical of many. Not only was his house a refuge for meetings, it was also a book distribution center.[54] John Pykas, who was one of the teachers at the Colchester Lollard meeting, had been introduced to their teaching in his earlier years when his mother had given him an early translation of the letters of St. Paul and told to put his trust in their teaching and not the sacraments of the Roman church. A certain John Hacker attended the meetings for six years. Robert Necton of Colchester imported books from across the North Sea. During the course of an interview he also revealed that had received books from Robert Forman, the Rector of All Hallows in Honey Lane. Forman was found to have two sacks of Lutheran books but made out that he had collected them in order to refute their errors. John Foxe, the martyrologist, reported that a number of men were charged with heresies in 1531–32 after they had been found with banned books in their possession.[55] Richard Bayfield, a Lollard teacher who had also imported books, was burned in London in December 1531.[56] Lollards also played an active part in the dissemination of Protestant books, especially William Tyndale's New Testament, which was printed and distributed from Antwerp in 1526.

THE IMPACT OF LOLLARDY

The Lollards did not attract a huge following, although Thomas More may well have underestimated their strength. He was of the view that if anyone checked out the English dioceses "except London and Lincoln he shall scant in anyone of all the remnant find punished four persons in five year." The main areas of Lollard influence, as More knew well, were the small towns and villages in the Chiltern hills and some of the London parishes and parts northern Essex and East Anglia. Others groups were to be found in Bristol, Coventry, and parts of Kent. There were also activists in some of the villages of Gloucestershire, Wiltshire, and the Stour valley in Suffolk.

53. Loades, *Revolution in Religion: The English Reformation*, 56.
54. Haigh, *English Reformations*, 63.
55. Foxe, *Acts and Monuments*, Vol. 5, 38–39.
56. Haigh, *Reformations*, 67.

It is clear that the Lollards had anticipated much of what the Protestants stood for. Joel Hurstfield pointed out that "even in the [fourteen] forties and fifties many prosecutions for heresy recorded in our episcopal records show the survival of a proletarian radicalism stemming from Wycliffe rather than Luther."[57] Hurstfield suggested that the Lollards still flourished between 1490 and 1530 in the Chilterns, in London, Essex, East Anglia, West Kent, and the upper Thames valley.[58]

John Foxe, who is the chief primary source for Lollardy, regarded their impact as significant. Referring to them as "the secret multitude of true professors,"[59] he wrote: "I find that the light of the Gospel began to appear . . . especially about Buckinghamshire and Amersham, Uxbridge, Henley, Newbury, in the diocese of London, in Essex, Colchester, Suffolk and Norfolk and other parts more. And this was before the name of Luther was heard of in these countries among the people."[60]

Foxe lists more than 150 individuals by name who were brought before Bishop Longland of Lincoln between 1518 and 1521. Their places of residence included Amersham, Ankerwick, Ashley Green, Asthall, Beaconsfield, Burford, Betterton, Burton, Charney, Chesham, Denham, Dorney, Ginge, Harrow-on-the-Hill, Henley, Hungerford, Iver Court, Little Missenden, London, Great Missenden, Newbury, Staines, Stanlake, Upton, Uxbridge, Walton, Ware, Windrush, Windsor, Witney, Woburn, Woodrow, and Wycombe. The occupations of some of those who were brought to the Bishop's court were listed by Foxe as brick-maker, carpenter, husbandman, serving man, shearman, smith, tailor, weaver, wire-drawer, and wheeler.[61] "Few of these good men and women," wrote Foxe, "were learned, being simple labourers and artificers . . . but it pleased the Lord to work in them knowledge and understanding, by reading a few English books, such as they could get in corners."[62] Their crimes included reading Wycliffe's *Wicket*, holding meetings in their homes, learning, reading, and reciting the Scriptures in English, either in their homes or to gatherings in the open-air or in barns. Others were punished for speaking against worshipping images, pilgrimage, penance, and purgatory, or for knowing the Ten Commandments in English. Such was the cruelty of the Bishop's

57. Hurstfield, *The Reformation Crisis*, 47.

58. Ibid., 46.

59. Foxe, *The Acts*, Vol. 4, 218.

60. Ibid., Vol. 4, 220.

61. Ibid., Vol. 4, 225.

62. Ibid., Vol. 4, 240.

court that many were terrified into giving testimony against their own family members in the hope that they themselves might escape burning or other punishments. Some of these men and women were seen to have been remarkably effective leaders and evangelists. Such for example, was Thomas Man who was brought to trial in 1518 for Lollard activity in the Home Counties, East Anglia, and London. He and his wife claimed to have made over 500 converts.[63]

Lollardy had largely disappeared by the 1530s, but the reason for this was simply that their program had merged with the much greater and more powerful Reformation agenda, which had finally begun to break the strangle-hold of the papacy and the Roman Catholic hierarchy. Many of their secondary concerns over issues such as the sacraments, images, and pilgrimages were taken up by the Puritans in the Elizabethan and Stuart period. Lollard beliefs had indeed come to be deeply embedded in English culture.

FACTORS THAT MADE LOLLARDY SUCCESSFUL

Its Domestic Setting

One important aspect that aided the success of Lollardy was its domestic setting. Church leaders such as Bilney and Barnes who preached Lutheran teaching could be rounded up and burned as heretics, but Lollard conventicles, which were tucked away in rural cottages, were very much harder to find and pin down. A typical instance was the home of William Russell in Bird's Alley, near Colman Street in Colchester. William Swinderby was another who used his house as a Lollard meeting place. One of the articles brought against him in 1391 by the Bishop of Hereford was that "the same William [Swinderby], unmindful of his own salvation, hath many and often times . . . in a certain chapel not hallowed, or rather a profane cottage, hath, in contempt of the keys [ecclesiastical discipline] presumed of his own rashness to celebrate, nay rather to profanate."[64] Humphrey Monmouth, a London draper, used his home as a Lollard base and was investigated on the grounds that he held a combination of Lollard and Lutheran doctrines "that faith without works is sufficient to save a man's soul" and "that we should pray to God and not to saints."[65] Lollards also

63. Knox, *The Lord's Supper*, 29–30.

64. Anon., *Lives of British*, 58.

65. Davis, *Heresy and Reformation*, 63.

paid particular attention to house to house visiting and made those intentional occasions for reading the Scriptures and speaking of Christ to those who welcomed them in.

The Use of the Laity

The Lollards wanted a simpler and purer church with a larger role for the laity and to that end they translated the whole of the Bible into English. The Lollards attracted many adherents because theirs was a lay person's religion in what was essentially an anti-clerical era dominated in some significant measure by a corrupt, brutal, callous, priesthood ruled over by a financially-driven papacy. Many ordinary country folk in the fifteenth century found the wealth of the monasteries distasteful and they rejected pilgrimages as being of little or no spiritual value. They were also dismissive of many of the saints' days as well as the official fast days and requisite visits to the confessional. Most Lollards disliked priestly ordination and some opposed clerical celibacy. They were strongly committed to the New Testament doctrine of the priesthood of all believers, the doctrine that Luther was later to emphasize so forcefully. Lay people were involved at every level in the Lollard communities, including preaching, teaching, organizing, and hearing confessions on an informal basis.

It is not clear whether Lollards regarded their communities as alternative or separate congregations, although they certainly operated separately from the parish churches. They do not appear to have established any form of ecclesiastical hierarchy or organization, preferring rather to operate on an informal basis. Lollard mission was not restricted to their commissioned preachers; it was held to be the responsibility of every member to engage in evangelism. They clearly made many converts through house-to-house visitation where they were intentional about wanting to read the Scriptures and instruct those who had invited them in.

Christ-Centered Bible-Based Living

The Lollards were seeking to be first and foremost biblical people. They hand copied the Scriptures and later printed them. They learned whole books of the New Testament by heart, a particular favorite being the epistle of James. They encouraged and promoted personal study of the Bible and organized readings from the Scriptures that enabled those who were unable to read to understand Jesus' teaching and the messages of the gospel.

93

They also taught the ordinary and poor people to memorize Scripture and to live it out in their work and homes.

Lollards were men and women with an active trust in Christ who took great risks to share their faith. C. S. L. Davies wrote: "By the end of the fifteenth century Lollardy was largely a movement of certain artisans and tradesmen: rigorous, independent-minded, prepared to take great risks for their beliefs (at least seventy-four were put to death between 1414 and 1520)."[66] As was the case in the early church, "the blood of the martyrs proved to be the seed of the church."

There is no doubt that many Lollards were men and women who were serious for God and died bravely for the faith. Some were clearly inspiring examples of godly living. Among their number was William White, described by Foxe, as being of "so devout and holy life, that all the people had him in great reverence, and desired him to pray for them: insomuch that one Margaret Wright confessed, that if any saints were to be prayed to, she would rather pray to him than any other."[67] John Foxe was deeply impressed by the ways in which Lollard people resorted and conferred with their neighbors and "did win and turn their minds to that wherein they desired to persuade them, touching the truth of God's word and his sacraments. To see their travails, their earnest seekings, their burning zeal, their readings, their watchings, their sweet assemblies, their love and concord, their godly living, their faithful demeaning with the faithful, may make us now, in these our days of free profession, to blush with shame."[68]

Among those who came before Bishop Longland was Thomas Pope, who was described by the wife of Bennet Ward as "the devoutest man that ever came in their house; for he would sit reading in his book to midnight many times."[69]

The Use of the Printed Word

There is clear evidence that the invention of printing considerably helped the spread of Lollard ideas. John Foxe recorded how Nicholas Belward purchased a New Testament about the year 1450 for four marks and forty pence, whereas after the invention of printing the same money would buy

---

66. Davies, *Peace, Print, Protestantism*, 147.

67. Foxe, *The Acts*, Vol. 3, 591.

68. Ibid., Vol. 4, 218.

69. Ibid., Vol. 4, 226.

for forty persons.[70] Foxe went on to state that "whereas Almighty God, of his merciful providence, seeing what lacked in the church, and how also to remedy the same, for the advancement of his glory, gave understanding of this excellent art or science of printing, whereby three singular commodities at one time came into the world." These were cheaper books, more people who were able to read, and an increased number of good authors.[71]

70. Ibid., Vol. 3, 721.
71. Ibid., Vol. 3, 721.

WHO WERE THE PURITANS?

PURITANISM IS A BROAD category that is not easy to define in a precise way. In very general terms it described all those who were of the view that the Reformation in England had not gone far enough and still contained elements that were unreformed and needed to be brought into line with biblical teaching. They regarded the Anglican Church of Elizabeth I as a compromising Laodicean church. All ceremonies, as far as they were concerned, must have a biblical warrant. For this reason they believed the church's practice, ministry, and worship needed to be "purified" from what they perceived as Romish traditions, customs, and ceremonial. Many of their number in England regarded the *Book of Common Prayer* as "an imperfect book culled from the popish dunghill." A large section of Puritans disliked the use of the ring in the marriage service, which they regarded as pagan. They also felt that confirmation and exorcism at the baptism service were evidence of unbiblical superstition. Radical Puritans wanted to abolish church courts and all other vestiges of priestly control.[1]

It is not easy to identify the Puritans in a precise way because some of their number broke away from the Anglican, Lutheran, and other national reformation churches to form separate communities. Among their number was Robert Browne (c. 1550–1633), who established independent congregations in Norwich and elsewhere. There were others, however, who remained loyal to their institutions with the hope of purifying them from within. An early glimmer of Anglican Puritanism was seen in the ministry of Bishop John Hooper of Gloucester during the reign of Edward VI. For some time Hooper had even postponed his acceptance of the See of Gloucester because he could not in conscience wear what he regarded as "Romish" episcopal robes at his consecration service. Hooper

1. Hill, *The World*, 161.

was committed to the Puritan pastoral ideal of having a group of godly laity and clergy to oversee the discipline and behavior of the congregations of a local area. He was a strong advocate of an educated clergy and went to great lengths to instruct the ordained ministers of his diocese. A little later in time Edmund Grindal, who was Elizabeth I's second Archbishop of Canterbury, declared his strong support for the Puritan agenda. In particular, he refused the Queen's request to close down "prophesyings," which were informal meetings organized by many Puritans at which Bible passages and other literature were discussed and then followed by prayer. There were other Anglican bishops with strong Puritan sympathies. Among their number were John Jewell (1522–71) and Richard Cox (1499–1581). Most Puritans were followers of John Calvin, but there were Arminian Puritans such as John Goodwin (1594–1665), who was for a time incumbent of St. Stephen's Coleman Street in the city of London. In 1651 he published *Redemption Redeemed*, which was a powerful critique of the doctrine of limited atonement.

In the Elizabethan period there were several determined attempts to try and model the church on Puritan lines. Thomas Cartwright who authored *Admonition to Parliament* made strident efforts to introduce a voluntary form of Presbyterian government, but his endeavors were suppressed by the powerful influence of Archbishop Whitgift. His successor Richard Bancroft, when Bishop of London, had added further weight by his attacks on the Puritans at the Hampton Court Conference held in January, 1604. He made it clear that conformity was to be the order of the day and that the Prayer Book rubrics were to be adhered to.

By the later years of the sixteenth century it was clear that the efforts to "Puritanize" the Church of England's liturgy and practices were not succeeding, though many clergy and laity with Puritan convictions remained within the establishment with the hope that reform might eventually come. Inevitably, the inertia resulted in the emergence of a growing number of separatist churches, particularly in the early years of the reign of James I. In the early Stuart period some escaped the persecuting authorities and settled in parts of Europe and in the New England colonies in North America. Among them were the Pilgrim Fathers, who set sail from Holland and England in the *Mayflower* in September 1620 and established a settlement at Plymouth in Massachusetts.

Although the Puritans had made their presence felt from the very first months of Elizabeth's reign there was undoubtedly a flowering of the movement in the 1580s and 1590s, which eventually came to make a powerful impact during the Cromwellian period in the middle years of the following century. It was in these last Elizabethan decades that Richard Rogers (c. 1550–1618), Richard Greenham (c. 1535–94), and John Dod (1565–1645) began to come to the fore. These men have been seen as the cream of Puritanism. They were not so much writers as good pastors and preachers. They held their secret presbytery meetings, they preached the word, and they studied and prayed together. In the following century their mantle was taken up by Richard Sibbes (1577–1635), Richard Baxter (1615–91), and John Owen (1616–1706). In America, prominent Puritans included Jonathan Winthrop (1588–1649), Increase Mather (1639–1723), Solomon Stoddard (1643–1729), and Jonathan Edwards (1703–58).

Notwithstanding the diversity of opinions regarding liturgy and practice, Puritans shared a number of common ideals that had a powerful influence in private and public worship, in morality, and perhaps above all in the work place. Coming out of this there also emerged a new piety, a new approach to preaching and to doctrine as they sought to apply the classical teachings of Calvin to their own spiritual life. Many of these men were Cambridge trained and left the university with a passion to spread the gospel among the common people.

Puritan Ideals

The Reformation had produced doctrines that were simpler than Catholic doctrine and arguably closer to the text of the New Testament. The teachings of the Reformers had certainly inspired and strengthened the martyrs, but it had not revitalized everybody's Christian life on an individual and personal basis. In Elizabethan times many Christians lacked the sense of a personal daily walk with Christ that impacted the way they lived, worked, and related to others.

By the end of the sixteenth century Counter-Reformation literature was flooding into England, much of it devotional in character. To some extent it challenged the Puritans to produce something of comparable quality that was experiential and practical in emphasis, rather than the theoretical. The Puritans well knew that the greatest piety in church history had come from the pens of the early church fathers, most notably Origen, Clement, and above all St. Augustine. In their writings the English Puritans quote these men above all other sources.

The heart of the Puritan Christian life was their understanding of the doctrine of regeneration. Alan Simpson, in his volume *Puritanism in Old and New England*, maintained that regeneration is the key factor.[2] In the medieval period, regeneration had been taught by the Roman church as a life-long endeavor in which individuals could lose the saving presence of Christ in their lives on account of their sin but be re-infused with grace through the sacraments, particularly those of the Mass and confession. In consequence medieval Christians lacked any sense of certainty as to their standing with God. However, Luther and the Reformers were able to demonstrate from Scripture that believers could be *certain* of salvation. Calvin in particular stressed that regeneration was a sovereign work of God in which the individual was totally secure.

In contrast to the medieval church, the Puritan concern was therefore that all believers should experience and know themselves to be regenerate. One of the reasons why the "separatist" strand emerged in Puritanism was that the presence of goats among the sheep tended to obscure who the regenerate actually were. The separatists wanted to have a church that was for believers only.

Gordon Wakefield points out that for the Puritan regeneration was a conscious and continuous experience that often began with "a tremendous first act." Many of their number wrestled for weeks grieving over their sins before they finally felt the beginnings of this assurance and salvation. Puritan conversion experiences were often overwhelming and deep affairs that issued in immediate holy living of a high order. What they were often like was well captured in the following lines penned by Nicholas Byefield.

> The Holy Ghost at some time falls upon him, & sets him all on a fire . . . both of sudden and violent indignation at sinne . . . as also the fire of holy affections. . . . He doth feele his heart oftentimes on a sudden surprised with strange impressions, sometimes of sorrow, sometimes of feare and awefull dread of God; sometimes of fervent desires after God; sometimes of strong resolutions of holy duties to be done by him. . . . He feeles at some times the unspeakable and glorious joyes of the Holy Ghost . . . such as by effect make him more humble, and vile in his owne eies, and do inflame him to a high degree of the love of God and goodnesse, which illusions can never doe.[3]

For the Puritans that were committed to the theology of Calvin the emphasis in regenerations was always on God taking hold of the individual, rather than the believer reaching out to the Lord of his or her own

---

2. See Simpson, *Puritanism*.
3. Byefield, *The Marrow of the Oracles*, 172.

volition. In order to achieve this experience of "new birth" some Puritans developed a *Busskampf* or "scheme of conversion," which involved several preparatory steps. There needed, for example, to be a deep work of the law that involved detailed preaching of the Ten Commandments, with a view to enabling the hearers to grieve over their sin. As part of this process Puritan preachers sometimes held the threat of hell and punishment over their congregations. Often when men and women were grieving over their sins in this way, Puritan preachers, because of their strong belief in the sovereignty of God, reminded them that they couldn't repent in their own strength. The Puritan stress was not that the individual reaches out and takes hold of God but rather that they must simply wait until they know that they had been seized by the grace of God.

Once having experienced this "first act of regeneration" Puritans were urged to maintain their initial assurance of it by inspecting their works. Were they displaying the virtues or fruits of the Spirit in their living? Were they overcoming bad habits? More importantly for many, were they prospering in their business and family lives? If they could answer in the affirmative then it was indeed probable that they had been "born anew"! On a negative side, this practice of inspecting your works tended to lead to over-introspection and sometimes self-righteousness. Puritans often kept overly detailed accounts of their spiritual experiences and diaries of their daily events and work.

PURITAN LIFESTYLE

Hard Work

In order to help themselves live effectively as Christians they developed a distinctive lifestyle that was based on hard work and limited to strictly controlled leisure activities. Part of the background to this was the growing amount of idleness on the part of village communities in Elizabethan England, particularly on saints' days. The fact was made clear by the *Statute of Artificers* of 1563, which laid down regulations about the hours of employment required by various callings on such days. A later Act of 1597 stated in its pre-amble that "agricultural production was being hindered by idleness, drunkenness and unlawful games." Puritan preachers emphasized that labor was a duty to one's neighbor, to society, and to mankind as a whole. About the year 1588 the separatist Robert Browne went so far as to suggest that an idle person ceased to be a member of the church of God.

William Perkins (1588–1602), a leading Puritan theologian, was perhaps more in line with the movement as a whole when he declared that "such as live in no calling, but spend their time in eating, drinking, sleeping, and sporting were guilty of disobedience and rebellion against God."[4]

For the Puritans there was no separation between the sacred and the secular and they applied their faith in Christ to every aspect of their business and working lives. Because of their insistence on a strict work ethic some writers—notably Max Weber (*Protestant Ethic and the Spirit of Capitalism*) and R. L. Tawney (*Religion and the Rise of Capitalism*)—have tended to give the impression that the Puritans were ruthless men of business who justified the profit motive on the ground that economic opportunities had been entrusted to them because they were God's elect. Other writers, however, including A. G. Dickens[5] and M. M. Knappen, have taken an opposite view and regard the Puritans as basically "other-worldly" people who had a genuine distrust of any capitalist system. The issue is whether capitalism was an intended or in sociological terms a "manifest function" of Puritanism or whether it was a "latent function" or unintended by-product.

In many ways it could be argued that the Puritans seemed to be attempting to live a monastic life, but in the *outside* world; because alongside their hard work they stressed the need for a series of daily meetings with God. It was almost as if they were trying to modify and adapt the monastic canonical rule of prayer for everyday use in the world of work, business, and education. The Puritan man would start the day with meditations on the mercy of God. Then he would pray by himself and with his family. At work he would be exhorted to meditate on God and to be careful to witness by an upright life and standard of behavior. On his return home supper would be preceded by grace and prayers. After eating was over there would be a period of reading and catechizing the family. Before bed there would often be prayers and even in bed meditation as exhorted by the psalmist was enjoined.

Structured Leisure Activities

Puritans were instructed to be very careful about how they spent their time. They were recommended to keep diaries so that they could organize

4. C. Hill, *Society and Puritanism in Pre-Revolutionary England*, 140.

5. Dickens, *The English Reformation*, 431.

themselves more efficiently and profitably. Reading was very important and John Foxe even suggested they should read when travelling on horseback.

Elizabethan entertainments, such as the theatre, received strong condemnation. The Puritan Henry Barrow objected to English bishops keeping fools to entertain them.[6] To the Puritan mind the theatre meant an atmosphere of immorality, drunkenness, and time wasting. Deuteronomy 22:5, to the Calvinistic mind, prohibited men wearing women's clothes, a characteristic of sixteenth-century theatre when only men acted and women's parts were often taken by boys. Dr. John Reynolds (1549–1607) of Queens College, Oxford, was greatly offended by the performance of a play at Christchurch and published in consequence *The Overthrow of Stage Plays* (1593), in which he held that the theatre led morally downwards. Among other things, he was particularly incensed by "the sin of small boys wearing the dress and affecting the airs of women." Although he was no enemy of poetry and reasonable recreation, he doubted whether some of the hours spent at the theatre ought not to be spent at sermons.[7] A far more vigorous denunciation of the stage came from the pen of William Prynne (1600–1669), who published his *Histriomastrix; or the Player's Scourge* in 1633. It was a ruthless assault on the stage and all who patronized it but it was also libelous and offended the Queen, whose Court masques he denounced. He was forced to stand trial in the Star Chamber and sentenced to stand pillory, to lose both ears, to pay a heavy fine, and suffer imprisonment for life. The severity of his sentence later caused the Puritans to deal harshly with the acting fraternity.

Card playing or any activity that wasted time could not be approved of, along with shuffleboard, the alehouse, and betting and gambling. William Perkins of Cambridge drew up a list of permissible activities based on the Scriptures. To this end hath the Word of God permitted shooting (2 Sam 1:18); musical consort (Neh 1:10); putting forth riddles (Judg 14:12); hunting of wild beasts (Can 2:15); searching out or contemplation of the works of God (1 Kgs 4:33).[8]

6. Carson, *Writings of Henry Barrow*, 192–93.

7. Chadwick, *The Reformation*, 118–19.

8. Cragg, Puritanism, 133.

The Sabbath

Another aspect of Puritan lifestyle that related to the issue of leisure was their Sabbatarianism. The Puritan Sunday was often a strictly kept Sabbath—a day of rest—not merely a celebration of the Lord's Day. While it is the case that in general the Puritans kept a strict Sabbath many were perhaps not quite so picky when it came to dos and don'ts, as has sometimes been supposed. For example, it is known that even John Calvin played bowls on the Sabbath. One major motivation that caused the Puritan to keep the Sabbath was simply as a form of self-protection. The Puritan who worked hard for six days needed a strict Sabbath day that forbade Sunday work and travel to and from markets. For example, in 1583 the Dedham Classis in Suffolk was concerned about clothiers "setting their woad vats on the Sabbath" and decided to talk to "the godliest of that trade" about it.[9] Two books that were influential as far as Sabbath keeping was concerned were Richard Greenham's *Treatise on the Sabbath*, published in 1592, and Dr. Nicholas Bownde's *The Doctrine of the Sabbath*, published in 1595. Bownde argued that the Sabbath as Sunday was a "natural, morale and perpetual" law binding on all humanity. It was not merely a ceremonial law binding only on ancient Israel. Therefore, the adoption of Sunday as a Sabbath was a divine mandate that came ultimately from Christ himself and was transmitted through the apostles. Again he asserted, "The Sabbath was appointed for no other purpose than to render men conformable to their Creator." Bownde demanded that the fourth commandment be incorporated into the laws of land. "It behoveth," he wrote, "all Princes and Magistrates, that be in higher authority, to provide that lawes be enacted for the preservation of the rest, with civil punishments to be inflicted upon them that shall break it." Furthermore, Bownde asserted: "It is . . . certain that we are . . . commanded to rest . . . from . . . all . . . things which might hinder us from the sanctifying of the Sabbath. . . . We must not think it sufficient that we do not work on the Sabbath, and . . . be occupied about all manner of delights, but we must cease from the one as from the other."[10]

Calvin had asserted in his *Institutes* that the Sabbath was a day on which "believers were to cease from their own works and allow God to work in them; . . . a stated day on which they should assemble to hear the law and perform religious rites. . . . The Sabbath was appointed for no

---

9. Hill, *World Turned Upside-Down*, 169.

10. Bownde, *The Doctrine of the Sabbath*, 95. In Eskenazi, *The Sabbath*, 108–9.

other purpose than to render men comfortable to their creator."[11] William Perkins opined that: "It is a notable abuse of many to make the Lord's Day a set day of sport and pastime, which should be a day set apart for the worship of God and the increase in duties of religion."[12] On a more positive note, John Dod asserted: "The Sabbath is the market-day of the soul, on which we lay in spiritual food for the following week; a day that doth enrich the saints."[13] It is a day, he continued, "that doth the saints enrich."

Sunday, for the Puritan, was a family day as well as a day of worship. It was particularly a time for review, for prayers and for reading. It seems fairly clear that the practice of daily private prayer and Bible reading has its origin in the Puritan Sabbath.

Puritan Casuistry

Closely related to these aspects of Puritan lifestyle we have been considering, yet meriting separate consideration as a distinctive entity, is their casuistry. A casuist is someone who quibbles over points of behavior. The Jesuits of the Counter-Reformation were casuists and the Puritans who emerged during the same historical period of history shared their concern for precision.

Part of the reason for Puritan casuistry was their desire for a disciplined church. Great importance had been attached to this by Martin Bucer, the Continental Reformer, during his stay at Cambridge during the reign of Edward VI. A little later, in 1566, Lawrence Humphrey and Thomas Sampson, who objected to the use of vestments, complained that discipline, "the sinews of religion," was utterly lacking in the Elizabethan church. Still later a petition to Parliament in 1584 called for "the suppression of blasphemy, looseness of life, bribery . . . and for a sharper law against fornicators." One of the key documents that expressed this concern for discipline was Walter Travers' (1548–1635) *Book of Discipline*, which was published in 1587. The *Book of Discipline* was separate from his earlier work, *Ecclesiastical Discipline*, which was first published in Geneva in 1574. Travers contended that each church should appoint a group of elders who should assist the pastor and "watch over the life and behaviour of every man."

---

11. Calvin, *Institutes*, Vol. 1, 239–41. In Hill, *World Turned Upside-Down*, 170.

12. Hill, *World Turned Upside-Down*, 174.

13. Ibid., 175.

Part of the reason for this Puritan insistence on discipline and casuistry was their desire to serve God as precisely as they could. John Dod, whose parish was in north Oxfordshire, was nicknamed "Decalogue Dod" because of his commentary on the Ten Commandments, which gave such precise applications on their meaning. On one occasion the local Lord of the Manor was riding out with Richard Rogers, the Puritan pastor of Wethersfield in Essex, and asked him what made him so precise? "O Sir," Rogers replied, "I serve a very precise God."[14] The Puritans were very precise about a range of activities and behavior. Rogers, for example, listed as forerunners to adultery "painting, the unchaste foot (legs were covered in those days), certain perfumes and a rolling eye." Drugs, tobacco, and sac (alcohol of a strong kind) were all prominent in Puritan denunciations, as were cards and dice, which were condemned because of their association with chance and lotteries.

To subsequent generations of Christians, Puritan casuistry sometimes appeared to be bondage and deadness. To the Puritans themselves this sort of precise behavior was the backbone on which they could develop spiritual muscle, moral strength, and tenacity of purpose. (This is not to say, however, that, on occasion, Puritans do not appear extremely morbid and over-introspective.)

The Puritan practice of caring for the soul is expressed in some of their "manuals." These are of interest because they recognize that attacks on Christian behavior come from the "flesh" (that is, fallen human nature) as well as from the devil. One point of particular interest is that some of these documents attempt to distinguish between problems deriving directly from the devil and problems arising from psychosomatic disorders. They recognized, for example, that eating and glandular functions could be a root cause of depressions.

It is important, having examined the Puritan concern for the inner-life, not to allow ourselves to imagine they were insular or unconcerned for the needs of those around them. In fact, Thomas Cartwright (1535–1603) believed firmly that if there was a better disciplinary system fewer men and women would have fallen into poverty and idleness. By the same token there would have been more money available to be used for the needs of the poor.

---

14. Packer, *Among God's Giants*, 149.

PURITAN ECCLESIOLOGY

The heart of Puritanism was the life, worship, and practice of their church and here it will be observed that the Puritans had a distinctive ecclesiology. Their ideal was expressed in the *Admonition to Parliament*, which was published in 1572. The work of two Puritan clergymen, John Field and Thomas Wilcox, it demanded a non-episcopal constitution for the English church and made a number of other lesser demands, such as an end to the use of wafer bread and the practice of kneeling to receive the bread and wine at communion. It included the following lines: "May it therefore please you however to understand, we in England are so far off from having a church rightly reformed according to the prescripts of God's word that as yet we are not come to the outward face of the same. . . . The outward marks whereby a true Christian Church is known are preaching of the word, ministering of the sacraments sincerely and ecclesiastical discipline which consists in admonition and correction of faults in a severe manner."[15] Strictly speaking, the 1559 Ornaments Rubric of the Elizabethan Prayer Book allowed the wearing of the alb and chasuble at the Eucharist and the surplice at the services. Nevertheless, most Puritans strongly objected to these ecclesiastical garments, which they denounced as "popish rags," and many of their number refused to appear in a church wearing a surplice. Puritans and those who sympathized with them raised strong objections in Convocation in 1563 in what became known as the "Vestiarian Controversy." Following this, in 1566, Archbishop Matthew Parker issued his *Advertisements*, which required the use of a "four-cornered cap, a scholar's gown priestly, and in church a linen surplice, and a cope in cathedrals and collegiate churches." Thirty-seven London clergy refused to comply and were deprived of their ministry. In some dioceses, however, the bishops did not enforce Parker's mandate and the situation was somewhat confused.

In terms of church buildings, the Puritans wanted premises with plain walls. Medieval wall paintings were whitewashed over and moveable objects, such as crucifixes and chalices, were removed. Stained glass windows—especially those with imagery, which it was felt could lead to idolatry—were destroyed. This was because "shrines in all ages suggested prayers to the saints, pilgrimages and purgatory."[16] When it came to church-based worship, the Puritan ideal was a corresponding simplicity.

---

15. *Amonition to Parliament 1572*. In Murray, *The Reformation Church*, 85–86.

16. Knappen, *Tudor Puritanism*, 434.

This was made perfectly clear in 1571 when a Puritan member of the House of Commons, William Strickland (d. 1598), and others, applied for "All things to be brought back to the purity of the primitive church." Strickland produced a bill to reform the *Book of Common Prayer* and to abolish the use of surplices, the practice of confirmation, baptism in private houses, kneeling at communion, the ring in marriage, and other practices regarded as superstitious. The bill was rejected.

Puritans also took strong objection to ecclesiastical titles, which, in their view, militated against the doctrine of the priesthood of all believers. As the Puritans saw it: "Instead of an Archbishop or Lord Bishop, you must make equality of ministers. Instead of Chancellor, Archdeacons and the rest, you have to plant in every congregation a lawful and godly seignior . . . and these three jointly, that is the minister, seignior and deacon is the whole regiment of the church committed."[17]

Puritans liked Sunday worship that was organized, disciplined, moral, and rational. Psalm singing held a particular appeal and was greatly encouraged, although it was felt that pleasure should not be the primary aspect. In 1562 a whole book of psalms was published. John Northbrook, a Bristol Puritan clergyman, wrote in 1577 that "we must take heed that in music be not but the whole sum and effect of godliness and of worshipping God."[18] He continued to attack the papists saying that they think "that they have fully worshipped God when they have long and much sung and piped. Singing and music must not take up invaluable time which could be used for preaching the word of God belief doctrine."

Preaching and Prophesyings

A. G. Dickens stated that throughout Elizabethan England Puritan preachers dominated the pulpits, even though many of them were intermittently engaged in disputes with their bishops.[19] Dr. Irvonwy Morgan wrote, "the essential thing in understanding the Puritans was that they were preachers before they were anything else."[20] For the Puritans the sermon was the centerpiece or apex of the Sunday service. Nothing brought more honor to the Lord than the clear preaching and obedient listening to the word of God.

17. McGrath, *Papists and Puritan*, 134.

18. Northbrooke, *A Treatise on Dicing, Dancing, Plays and Interludes*. In Knappen, *Tudor Puritanism*, 432.

19. Dickens, *The English Reformation*, 428.

20. Morgan, *The Godly Preachers*, 11.

Puritan sermons were often lengthy affairs, sometimes lasting for as much as two hours. Puritans believed it not to be a church service without a sermon. Puritan preachers were to be well educated and were instructed to be plain and "deliver the message without rhetorical or literary flourishes." Richard Baxter wrote in the preface to his *Treatise on Conversion* that "the plainest words are the profitablest oratory in the weightiest matters."[21]

Sermon reading also became a pastime. One Puritan wrote: "every sermon was orthodox and useful and therefore after supper I busied myself in enlarging and correcting such notes as I had taken at the afternoon sermon."[22] Puritanism, particularly in its extreme Calvinistic forms, had an inbuilt tendency to neglect evangelism and proclamation. In the earlier Elizabethan phase, however, there does seem to have been a concern both for the lost and for clear preaching of Christian truths. Robert Bolton in his *Directions for Comfortable Walking with God* wrote that "Our hearts must bleed within us for those around cast into the miseries of hell."

Puritans organized meetings known as "prophesyings" where sermons were analyzed and where the Scriptures were expounded and discussed. Although they were usually intended for local ministers, lay people were frequently admitted. On some occasions these meetings were "subversive" of church order; at their best they raised the standard of clerical education and increased personal discipline and the quality of spiritual life. Elizabeth I was strongly opposed to them, partly because in some areas of the country they appeared to be becoming a substitute for the Prayer Book service of Evening Prayer. Elizabeth asked Archbishop Edmund Grindal to put a stop to prophesyings and in consequence of his refusal to do so he was suspended from his ministry for five years until his death.

Pastoral Work

Puritans were as much good pastors as they were good preachers. Anglican Puritans modeled their practice on the ordinal in the Book of Common Prayer that called on clergy "to teach, and to premonish, to feed and to provide for the Lord's family." Richard Greenham, the incumbent of Dry Drayton near Cambridge from 1570–90, was one who endeavored to carry out this ideal in his ministry. He toiled long hours rising at four

21. Baxter, *Treatise on Conversion* in Works, Vol. 2, 399. In Packer, *Among God's Giants*, 96.

22. Seaver, *The Puritan Lectureships*, 40.

o'clock in the morning and preaching a sermon at day break each Monday, Tuesday, Wednesday, and Friday in order to teach his parishioners before they went out to labor in the fields. On Sundays he gave two sermons and catechized the children. In the morning he studied and in the afternoons he visited the sick or walked out to visit the laborers in the field.[23] The most notable Puritan pastor was probably Richard Baxter (1615–91) who ministered in the parish of Kidderminster from 1641–60, with an interval of five years during the civil war. Kidderminster was a town of some 2,000 souls, most of whom were converted under Baxter's ministry. Baxter related that on his arrival at Kidderminster he found his parishioners to be "an ignorant, rude and revelling people who had hardly ever listened to any serious preaching." He was so impressed as to the importance of personal face-to-face communication that he and his curate set aside two whole days each week and visited fourteen families in their homes with the sole purpose of explaining the Christian faith to them. By that means he made contact with eight hundred families a year. In 1656 Baxter published *The Reformed Pastor* in which he set out all the details of his pastoral care. Such were the results of Baxter's care that, to use his own words, "the congregation was usually full, so that we were fain to build five galleries after my coming thither. . . . On the Lord's Days there was no disorder to be seen on the streets, but you might hear a hundred Families singing Psalms and repeating sermons, as you passed on the streets."[24]

A significant aspect of the Puritan pastoral care was their introduction of the *Classis* system on a voluntary basis. In this setup groups of local Puritan ministers and clergy formed themselves into a body and acted in certain matters of discipline, advice, and behavior. Among other things, Puritans who wanted to train for the ministry went before the local classis for approval. Once, having received a call from the classis they then proceeded to the bishop for preparation for their ordination.

PURITAN SOCIAL CONCERN

The tradition that those with money and property should dispense hospitality and relieve the poor goes back a very long way. The 1547 *Articles of Visitation* inquired whether ministers kept hospitality and relieved their parishioners. Care for the poor and needy was certainly a Puritan concern, though some of them seem to have been a little harsh on the unemployed

23. Packer, *Among God's Giants*, 51.
24. *Reliquiae Baxterianae*, 84. In Packer, *Among God's Giants*, 62.

and poor, believing them to be idle, lazy, and in some cases wicked and therefore poor for their own fault. Both Dod and Perkins expressed this view on occasion. Dod, it should be noted, also stated that it was the business of the Judge to see that the poor were cared for. He also stated on another occasion that social injustice is as bad as sodomy. Downham asserted that "Affluence is good for only one thing, it enables you to better relieve the poor." William Perkins addressed himself to the question of slavery. He didn't quite reach the point of rejecting slavery altogether, but he did say that slave owners must take slaves into their own homes and treat them as equals.

EDUCATION

Education at all levels was a high priority among Puritans. In the 1580s the Dedham Classis recommended a scheme of universal education for their town, which included the provision of fees for poor parents from church collections.[25]

Lectureships were endowed by wealthy, Puritan, lay people in parish churches, which meant that able Puritans were given the opportunity to teach the reformed faith, usually in the form of an evening lecture. These became increasingly popular and many continued well into the nineteenth century because they were independent of the local rector or vicar and outside of their control.

In the seventeenth century the Puritan dissenters set up a number of academies where ministers who were unable to go to Oxford or Cambridge universities could have theological training. Oliver Cromwell's Durham College, which did not survive for long, was an early attempt to break the Oxbridge monopoly. Other noteworthy academies included those at Tewkesbury, Daventry, and that at Market Harborough, which began under the leadership of Philip Dodderidge in 1723. The education given was often of a high standard and many Anglicans sent their sons to be educated by them.

RELIGION IN THE HOME

Aside from their concern for the welfare of the poor and the lost, the Puritans were concerned to make Christianity the religion of their home.

25. Tawney, *Religion and the Rise of Capitalism*, 217.

J. I. Packer wrote, "It is hardly too much to suggest that the Puritans created the Christian family in the English-speaking world."[26] When a new home was occupied for the first time Puritans dedicated it to God and pledged all the members of the household to his service. Ties of mutual obligation bound the members of the household to one another. P. McGrath emphasized that "it was Puritanism which stressed an individual pietism, with the household as its essential unit rather than the parish."[27] Religious books were read to the family to promote piety. Puritan philanthropists were always eager to increase their number and donate them to poorer Puritan homes. It was a frequent custom in Puritan homes to read sermons as a method of religious education. Members were exhorted to listen carefully to the preacher so that they could write down parts of the sermon when they got home or repeat parts of it and other members would contribute filling in the forgotten parts. Among the many Puritans devotional writers Richard Baxter was one of the most significant. In 1650 he published *Saints Everlasting Rest*, which has endured as one of the classic devotional texts on the subject of heaven.

The singing of Psalms in the home was another feature of many Puritan families. Family prayers, however, occupied the largest place in the discipline of the Puritan household and it was generally accepted that in a well-ordered household family prayers should be held twice a day. The discipline of the individual soul was also felt to be the key to character, and private devotions were therefore a very important part of Puritan home-life.

PURITAN THEOLOGY

G. R. Elton says that "Puritanism was not in the main a theological movement: it produced no original ideas in theology and almost no treatises on divinity. It borrowed these things from abroad, at first from the Zwinglians and later from Calvin and Beza." Three doctrines that the English Puritans strongly emphasized were the authority of Scripture, the sanctity of human conscience, and the doctrine of predestination. This latter belief stemmed from their conviction that God was in sovereign control of every aspect of their lives and that everything was in his hands. The Puritans also laid stress on the covenant between God and his people. In this aspect they have sometimes been criticized (unfairly) for reducing God to the level of

26. Packer, *Among God's Giants*, 28.
27. McGrath, *Papists and Puritans*, 336.

a bargainer who only blesses on the condition that his people fulfill their obligations to him.

Puritan theology also displayed a particular interest in the ministry of the Holy Spirit. J. I. Packer wrote that "the work of the Holy Spirit is the field in which the Puritans' most valuable contributions to the church's theological heritage were made."[28] In their teaching they underlined the importance of the Holy Spirit's role of giving believers assurance of their faith. For the Puritans being a Christian was not simply a matter of believing or giving intellectual assent to the objective facts of the Christian faith; individual believers could know their reality in their experience. Puritans believed that this assurance was most often a gradual process that emerged in the lives of those who both sought for it and lived faithful Christian lives. Thomas Goodwin expressed the point in the following lines.

> Assurance comes in as a reward of faith. . . . A man's faith must fight first, and have a conquest, and then assurance is the crown, the triumph of faith . . . and what tries faith more than temptation, and fears, and doubts, and reasonings against man's own estate? That triumphing assurance, Rom. 8:37, 38 . . . , comes after a trial, as none are crowned till they have striven.[29]

The Puritans maintained that the Holy Spirit awakened the mind to receive spiritual things and impressed their reality on it. Goodwin put it as follows, "The Holy Ghost, when he doth work faith in us . . . doth two things: *first*, he doth . . . give us a new understanding . . . 1 Jn. 5.20 . . . a new eye to see Christ with. . . . *Secondly*, himself cometh with a light upon new understanding, thus bestowing a spiritual 'sight' of spiritual realities."[30] The Puritans emphasized the Holy Spirit's role in bringing alive the words of Scripture in a way that made believers aware that God had spoken specifically to them.

The great strength of Puritan theology was that it was always practical. It was the theology of experience and the everyday. Doctrine was not preached or taught unless it could be lived out in everyday experience. Thus, in the words of Peter Lewis, the Puritans "were masters of no divinity more than practical divinity, there was no doctrine that could not be practised, just as all good practice had to be founded on sound doctrine."[31]

28. Packer, *Among God's Giants*, 235.
29. Goodwin, *Works*, Vol. 8, 346. In Packer, *Among God's Giants*, 238.
30. Ibid., Vol. 8, 260. In Packer, *Among God's Giants*, 237.
31. Lewis, *The Genius of Puritanism*, 78.

Two of the great early Puritan theologians were William Perkins and William Ames. William Perkins stated on one occasion that "theology is the science of living blessedly forever."[32] William Ames asserted that "theology is the doctrine of living before God."[33]

In the wake of these men a whole generation of practical theological preachers grew up particularly at Christ's and Emmanuel College in Cambridge. They were sometimes called "searching painful preachers" because their doctrine struck deeply into the hearts of their hearers.

PURITANISM: AN ASSESSMENT

Some of the things the Puritans stood did not find favor with both their contemporary and succeeding generations. They were criticized among other things for their austerity, their introspection, their exclusive contempt for the medieval past, their inordinate concern with predestination and church discipline, as well as their over-scrupulousness about modest ritual externals such as the marriage ring, the sign of the cross, and the surplice. That said, the Puritans fostered a version of Christianity that was real and related to everyday life. They delighted in the small pocket-sized Bibles and helped to foster many Bible-reading laymen and laywomen. They also created an educated clergy who studied, wrote, and thought deeply. Their stress on the home and family life created generations of men and women who were secure in themselves and provided a significant stimulus to the industrial revolution of the eighteenth and nineteenth centuries. Their ideals of hard work and thrift, coupled with practical care of the poor, was thoroughly in keeping with New Testament Christianity.

FACTORS THAT MADE THE PURITANISM SUCCESSFUL

Their Focus on the Family

Puritans had a high view of the family, which they held to be the basic unit of society. They made their homes their church, regarding the husband as the pastor and the wife as his associate with an equally important role to fulfill. They worked in tandem so that all those who were born into their

---

32. Perkins, *A Golden Chain*, 1616 edition, 11, in Stoeffler, *The Rise of Evangelical Pietism*, 53.

33. Ames, *The Marrow of Theology*, 77.

home might also be born again. It was the husband's role to see that the whole family went to church on Sunday and to lead them in the home in family prayers. His other responsibilities included seeing how much of the Sunday sermon had been understood and to catechize the children. There can be no doubt that the contemporary church has seriously neglected the biblical emphasis on the home and has much to learn from the Puritans. Just to take note of the Puritan practice of praying together as families or sitting down to discuss important questions would go a long way towards strengthening family life and, in consequence, the spread of the Christian faith.

Seriousness

Puritanism was above all a spiritual movement that was passionately focused on Christ and godly living that impacted every area of their lives. Puritanism made men and women aware that they were accountable to God for every aspect of their lives. Theirs was a Christianity that was applied to every aspect of living. They were always doers of God's word and not mere hearers. While it is true that many were perhaps overly rigid, and at times introspective, Puritans were compassionate, caring, and socially concerned people with a heart for God and for the poor.

A High View of Work

The Puritans had a thoroughly biblical doctrine of work, which they believed and taught as a calling from God. Against a background of what many perceived as idleness, they laid stress on the biblical injunction that six days were to be set aside for labor followed by one day for rest. They taught that labor was "a duty to one's neighbour, to the commonwealth and to mankind."[34] Christopher Hill pointed out that "Puritanism held a particular attraction to small employers and self-employed men, whether in the town or the country, for whom frugality and hard work might make all the difference between prosperity and failure to survive in a world of growing competition."[35] There can be little doubt that this Puritan work ethic provided both a moral backbone and a stimulus to the developments in commerce and industry in the eighteenth and nineteenth centuries. It

34. Hill, *The World Turned Upside-Down*, 129.
35. Ibid., 134.

was their capital that helped to provide money for banking and investment, which in turn generated work and a living for the hugely growing population.

Plain Practical Religion

The Christianity of the Puritans was plain and practical. It was a religion of the everyday. Their worship was plain and unadorned, with clear biblical truths preached and taught in a way that was readily understandable. It was in many ways a layperson's church in which there were opportunities for laymen and women to participate in prayers and discussion in the home. They could also attend the prophesying meetings and discuss the content of the Sunday sermons and passages of Scripture. Puritans impressed on their congregations that living as a Christian was not just something that happened but required self-discipline and a determination of the will. At the present time too many Christians expect things to just happen or come easily in some quick-fix ministry session. Puritans also pointed out that to remain steadfast in times of doubt and difficulty can be the fuel of faith and indeed the subsequent experience of assurance.

$$7 \quad | \quad \text{The Moravians}$$

EARLY HISTORY

THE ORIGINS OF THE Moravian church date back to the later part of the fourteenth century and in particular to the followers of John Huss (1373–1415) of Bohemia. Huss was strongly opposed to some of the teachings and practices of the Roman Catholicism of his day. He wanted to bring the church in the territories of Bohemia and Moravia back into conformity with the Eastern Orthodox practice it had enjoyed in the earlier times. Among other things, this would mean having the liturgy in the Czech language, communion with both the bread and the wine, and married priests. Additionally, indulgences and the idea of purgatory on which they were based would be eliminated. In these desires Huss was influenced by the English reformer John Wycliffe (c.1325–84).

This English influence came about in 1382 when Richard II married Princess Anne of Bohemia and a number of Bohemians came to the English Court. In 1390 a group of students from Prague University visited Oxford and spent time studying Wycliffe's writings, some of which they took home with them. In 1406 and 1407 other students came to Kemmerton in Worcestershire and Braybrook in Northamptonshire for the same purpose. As a result of these visits there was widespread and growing interest in Wycliffe's teaching in Bohemia. Among other things, Huss came to share Wycliffe's doctrine of justification by faith alone. By these strange exchanges it happened that at the very time Wycliffe's English followers were being persecuted, and even in some cases burned as heretics, John Huss was preaching their doctrines from the pulpit of Bethlehem chapel in Prague. English Lollards did what they could to support and encourage the new movement in Bohemia. Richard Wyche sent a letter of support, which Huss read to his congregation. Peter Payne, the Principal of St. Edmund Hall, Oxford, settled in Prague, where he published and made Wycliffe's doctrines popular.

Huss was a gifted teacher and was made rector of the faculty of Arts at the Charles University in Prague in 1402. His new movement gained widespread support in the University and even received royal endorsement for a time but was eventually forced to submit to Rome. However, his fortunes began to change when Pope John XXIII began a campaign to raise money by selling indulgences. Huss felt bound to oppose this campaign on biblical grounds. The papacy responded harshly and Huss was given twenty-three days to recant. The University authorities changed their tune and bowed to the papal authorities. Huss was then forced to withdraw from the city and he and his supporters publicly insisted that the church consists of all who worship Christ and that the Popes are not infallible as they have lived ungodly lives and erred on many occasions. Huss publicly endorsed Wycliffe's views and called upon the state to reform the churches. Huss was imprisoned, during which time he was brutally treated for six months prior to his trial at the Council of Constance in 1415. He was sentenced to be burned at the stake. A paper crown with pictures of demons tearing his soul to threads was placed on his head and his books were piled up and burned. Huss was escorted to a meadow not far from the Cathedral where he was burned and his ashes thrown into the Rhine.[1]

Huss's movement did not die and as soon as the news of his martyrdom came to Bohemia 452 noblemen immediately denounced the harsh brutality of the faithless Council. Huss became a symbol of Bohemian nationalism and fifteen years of bloody civil war ensued. The main problem, however, was that no group accepted all of Huss's teachings. The moderates, who were know as Calixtines, wanted to preserve Catholic unity but insisted on four articles. They wanted (a) free preaching of the Word of God, (b) communion for the laity as well as for the priesthood and in both the bread and the wine, (c) reform of morals, and (d) deprivation of power and wealth from the clergy. The Taborites were a more extreme group who wanted to break away altogether from what they believed was an apostate church. As far as they were concerned, the Bible alone is the sole guide in all matters of faith and practice and the doctrines of transubstantiation, penance, purgatory, prayers for the saints and the dead, and the veneration of images and relics are all superstitious. Notwithstanding their differences, both parties acted together, socially and militarily, during the struggle

---

1. Cannon, *History of Christianity,* 307.

for independence. A compromise peace was effected in 1434, following the battle of Lipan.

In the years that followed a tailor by the name of Gregory, who came from the village of Kunwald in southeast Bohemia, established an independent brotherhood with the name "Unitas Fratrum," the Unity of the Brethren. Because this name conveyed little or no meaning, they came with the passing of time to call themselves Moravians. Gregory, who later became known as Gregory the Patriarch, taught that the Holy Scripture alone was the sole standard for Christian belief and practice and that neither the state nor the church should engage in war. The community at Kunwald aimed to bring every aspect of their lives into conformity with Christ's teaching. They also vowed not to be under any unscriptural authority. Their first spiritual leaders were ex-priests, but in 1467, following a meeting at Lhota, they took the decision to obtain their own Episcopal Orders. They did this by making application to the Waldensians who consecrated the first Moravian bishop.

In 1481 the Brotherhood suffered a further period of persecution during which they fled through Hungary and Transylvania settling in Moldavia. After a six year period the majority of their number returned to Moravia. The doctrines that they held at this time were set out in three documents, copies of which they sent to King Ladislaus (1272–90). Among other things, they rejected worship of the saints, Purgatory, and transubstantiation. They did, however, retain a Catholic understanding of the Eucharist, believing the consecrated bread and wine to be the body and blood of Christ. The strength of their convictions was made clear when, at the beginning of the sixteenth century, Luther and other leaders in Germany and Switzerland found the Moravians firmly established in biblical Christianity and ready to join with them in promoting the Reformation in Europe.

By the beginning of the sixteenth century the Hussite Brethren numbered around three hundred congregations in Moravia. About that time they were joined by many Calixtines and some of the Calixtine nobles built places of worship in the towns and villages where they were settled. The Brotherhood had worked hard and established a Protestant school in almost every town and village in the Czech lands. During this time even the University of Prague was also firmly in Protestant hands. However, this peace was not destined to last for long since, in 1566, the Jesuits arrived in the country and established the Catholic Academy at Olomouc in the capital. This marked the beginning of what eventually became another round of suffering. The Holy Roman Emperor, Matthias (1557–1619), installed the fiercely Catholic Ferdinand II of Styria (1578–1637) on the throne of Bohemia. This provoked Protestant Bohemian noblemen to start a revolt which ended in their defeat at the battle of White Mountain in 1621.

BISHOP COMENIUS AND THE HIDDEN SEED, 1621–1722

Many of their number were executed or expelled from the country and replaced by German speaking nobility. By 1622 the entire education system of the country was in the hands of the Jesuits. The estates, churches, and schools belonging to the Brethren were confiscated while they themselves left the country, many taking refuge in Poland. The sufferings of the Moravian Brethren in this period aroused strong sympathy among the British public and during the Cromwellian period £6,000 was collected for their relief. Later on, in 1683, a further subsidy was raised and endorsed by Archbishop William Sancroft (1617–93).[2]

The war and plagues had caused a considerable decline in the population, from more than three million to about 800,000 people. The last bishop to exercise a ministry in Moravia was the learned John Amos Comenius (1592–1671), who was consecrated at Lissa in Poland in 1632. Despite all that had happened he still believed that in God's time the Moravian church would be revived. In this faith he had his son-in-law, Peter Jablonsky, consecrated a bishop and he, in his turn, consecrated his son, Daniel Ernest Jablonsky. Bishop Daniel later consecrated David Nitschmann, the first bishop of the renewed Moravian church. After the death of Comenius the Brethren adopted an ordinary Presbyterian organization but held what were essentially Lutheran beliefs. The only vestige of episcopacy was the occasional use of the word "bishop" when referring to their presiding elder.

During this hundred year period, from 1621–1722, the few Brethren who remained in Moravia were inevitably forced to keep a very low profile much in the way that the Lollards had done in medieval England in the years following Wycliffe's death. They existed as a "Hidden Seed," holding their meetings in secret and passing on their traditions from father to son.

2. Hassé, *The Moravians*, 14.

REVIVAL UNDER NICHOLAS LEWIS, COUNT ZINZENDORF

A revival in the Moravian church began when Nicholas Ludwig (1700–1760), Count of Zinzendorf and Pottendorf and a legal adviser at the Court of Saxony, allowed a certain number of refugees from Moravia to settle on his estate in Saxony. Most of those who came were from the "Hidden Seed," who soon established a settlement at Herrnhut. Regarded as the greatest German evangelical since Luther,[3] it didn't take long for him to recognize that these exiles from Moravia were the direct descendants of the old Hussite Brethren. Zinzendorf, who had been ordained as a Lutheran minister at Tübingen in 1734, tried at first to establish the Moravians as a separate group within the Lutheran establishment under his leadership. Events did not, however, turn out in the way that he had hoped and he set up a headquarters in western Germany and then later in London (1751–55) and finally on his own estate in the village of Herrnhut.

Zinzendorf was nurtured in a deeply Christian environment. He said, while giving one of his *Discourses to Children*, that "he had had the happiness of knowing the saviour from my youngest years." His relationship to Jesus was both personal and very natural. His father, George Ludwig, was a close friend of Philip Jacob Spener, the leader of the Pietist movement and a man with a deep Christian faith. Pietists were noted for their earnest devotion to Christ. Theirs was a religion of the heart that began at conversion. Many of their number sought to strengthen their walk with Christ by denying themselves worldly pleasures. Zinzendorf, it should be said, was rather more world-affirming in his spirituality. He was nonetheless passionate in his devotion to Christ and had a burning desire to reach and revive the whole of the Christian church and to evangelize the heathen.

Zinzendorf entered University in 1716 where he studied law in order to prepare for a diplomatic career that he began in 1721 when he became a King's Councilor at the court of the King of Saxony. He carried out his government commitments with great care, but on weekends he opened his Dresden house from 3 in the afternoon until 7 in the morning! He spent a great deal of his life in travel as he earnestly sought to fulfill his missionary vision.

1727 proved to be a remarkable year in the story of the renewed Brethren. On the afternoon of the 11th May a significant number of Brethren came together and an extended singing meeting took place. On the following afternoon Zinzendorf's called all the inhabitants of Herrnhut

---

3. Drummond, *German Protestantism since Luther*, 72.

together and addressed them for about three hours. He then presented them with a series of regulations that were to govern their community life, after which he introduced *The Brotherly Agreement*. This was a voluntary commitment to live in Christian fellowship. There was no general community of goods but every member sought to detach themselves from the things of the world. There was, however, a strict business ethic. All new entrepreneurial activity required consultation and no competition in trade was allowed. On that same day twelve trustworthy elders were elected from the common class to oversee the running of the community and Zinzendorf was elected Warden of the community. On the 19th July Zinzendorf introduced "Bands," which consisted of two or three or more persons who met together for prayer and encouragement. A Communion service on 13th of August proved to be a powerful spiritual occasion with loud weeping and prayers of great power and fervor, which were described as "a baptism into one spirit." Zinzendorf soon realized the power of singing hymns, praying, and sharing food together and this led to his reviving of the Agapē meal or Love Feast, a vital feature of the early church.

About the year 1728 Zinzendorf sent three of his Brethren to London to see what could be learned from the work of the *Society for the Promotion of Christian Knowledge* and *The Society for Promoting the Gospel in Foreign Parts*. This eventually resulted in the arrival of other Moravian missionaries and the establishment of many Moravian congregations on English soil. The church planting began following Zinzendorf's visit to the English capital in 1737.

Zinzendorf's first significant missionary venture was to the West Indies in 1739 and this was followed by two years (1741–43) in America. There he devoted time and energy to the Moravian settlements in Pennsylvania and gave the name Bethlehem to the new town. General Oglethorpe, the governor of the recently formed colony of Georgia, welcomed Moravian missionaries into his territory. It was this that brought them into contact with John Wesley who later met Christ in a renewed and powerful way in their chapel at Aldersgate Street in the city of London. Zinzendorf also spent time in Switzerland, Holland, England, and Livonia. He developed a strong relationship with the Mennonite leader, Joannes Deknatel (1695–1759), whom he met on a visit to Amsterdam in 1739. He died at Herrnhut on the 6th May, 1760.

Zinzendorf was a man of deep devotion who was totally and fully surrendered to Jesus' will. On more than one occasion he declared, "I have but one passion and it is He [Jesus] alone."[4]

A PIONEER MISSION CHURCH

From their inception the Moravians have been a pioneer church in a number of significant and important ways. They were clearly the forerunners of the Reformation in Europe, with Martin Luther later declaring that he was another Johan Huss. Huss, as we have seen, was burned at the stake because he refused to surrender his belief that the Bible is the supreme authority and that its teachings should be followed by all Christians.

The Moravians were also pioneers in the matter of Christian missions. From the start of Zinzendorf's leadership the entire church recognized the call to witness as much as to worship. Men and women of rank, such Frederick von Watteville and Henry Cossart, and academics, such as August Gottlieb Spangenberg (1704-92), Peter Böhler (1712-75), John Gambold (1711-1771), and Jacob Rogers, who had been to Oxford University, took this calling with supreme seriousness. Zinzendorf had been inspired and motivated to evangelize by the pentecostal experience he had shared with the Brethren on the 13th August, 1727. It was his strategy and driving energy that thrust the movement forward.

The beginnings of this missionary outreach took place in 1732— which was some sixty years before William Carey founded the Baptist Missionary Society—and what then became known as the modern missionary movement was born. Before that time there had only been one or two very brave individuals who had ventured to take the Christian message to "the heathen," but the Moravians were the first Protestants to undertake missions *as a church body*. Following a New Testament pattern, they began their outreach in their immediate neighborhood and then extended their concern to Silesia, Moravia, Hungary, and Bohemia. Their first overseas endeavor came about when Zinzendorf learned that Hans Egede and his wife, a Danish couple from Copenhagen, had decided to abandon their Greenland mission. Zinzendorf immediately called on his brethren from Herrnhutt to step into the breach. In 1733 three young Moravian men set sail and landed on Greenland's Arctic coast and began a work among the Eskimos. They proved to be faithful missionaries and eventually built up an enduring Christian church. Stephen Neill in his *History of Christian*

4. Hassé, *The Moravians*, 22.

Missions wrote: "Under the leadership of Zinzendorf this small Church was seized with a missionary spirit which has never left it."[5]

While it is the case that the Moravian church was not the first Protestant church to come to America, it established a presence in the state of Georgia from 1735 to 1740 and maintained permanent settlements in Pennsylvania in 1740 and North Carolina in 1753. A number of men born in Moravia were detained in London on their way to the British colony of Georgia and the numerous documents that they presented led to Parliament giving official legal recognition to the *Unitas Fratrum* (Moravian Brethren) as an "ancient, protestant, Episcopal church."

The Moravians were men and women with a clear assurance of their conversion and faith. It was this calm sense of Christ's presence on the part of some Moravian missionaries that so impressed John Wesley during a storm on the Atlantic Ocean. While Wesley and many of the English passengers feared for their lives, the Moravians prayed and sang praises to God "knowing whom they believed, and being persuaded that he was able to keep that which they had committed unto Him." It was later, on the 24th May, 1738, that John attended the Moravian Chapel in Aldersgate Street and felt "his heart strangely warmed" and received assurance that his sins were forgiven and that "he did trust in Christ alone for salvation." After Greenland and America the Moravians focused their attention on Labrador, the North American Indians, South Africa, and Australia. Commenting on Moravian Missionary endeavor in 1808 Beilby Porteus (1731–1809), Bishop of London, expressed his opinion that "among other religious communities, they who have most distinguished themselves in the business of conversion are the Moravians, or United Brethren. These, indeed, have shown a degree of vigor, of perseverance, of unconquerable spirit, and firmness of mind, which no danger, no difficulties, could subdue, combined at the same time with the greatest gentleness, prudence and moderation, of which no example can be found since the first primitive age of Christianity."[6] At the present time there are still several Moravian provinces on the African continent.

---

5. Neill, *A History of Christian Missions*, 237.

6. Thompson, *The Moravians*, 486.

MISSION STRATEGIES

First and foremost, Moravian Brethren *lived* the faith before they preached it in words. Zinzendorf said: "Let the people see what sort of men you are and then they will be forced to ask, 'Who makes such men as these?'"[7] Missionaries were to exist as a pattern for life. They were also to be at all times humble. Zinzendorf was also adamant that they must never attempt to lord it over the heathen. Rather, they were to gain respect through the power of the Spirit, working in and through their lives and ministries. Moravian missionaries laid particular stress on healing the sick and engaging in medical work.

One piece of unusual and unique mission thinking was Zinzendorf's setting up of The Pilgrim Congregation, which he designed to function as an itinerant headquarters that would organize training, evangelism campaigns, and ecumenical witness. No one was appointed to it unless they were willing to go anywhere at any time. Its personnel, made up of people from all ranks of society, included members from other denominations. The *Pilgrims* changed fairly frequently as some of their number stayed put in some of the mission stations. The Countess of Zinzendorf supervised all the housekeeping that the Congregation required. Although The Pilgrim Congregation did not become a permanent institution in the Moravian church, it represented a truly forward-thinking vision, versions of which were adopted by other missional groups and societies in later times.

In their mission strategy the Moravians were always careful to avoid building on other missionaries' labors. "Ever guard against proselyting [*sic*]"[8] was enjoined on all Moravian missionaries. The Brethren were urged not to enter into disputes with other denominations and to ensure that any they converted who were already attached to a particular church were encouraged to return to it. If, however, it did happen that people from other churches were brought into contact with them by marriage or by virtue of moving house, then they were happy to receive them so long as they had a letter of commendation from their minister or pastor. Bishop Spangenberg wrote in 1768, "We never enter into controversy with any other denomination, nor do we endeavour to draw members over to us. Much less do we attempt to win over to our church any of the heathen who are already in connection with those of any other church."[9] Had this

---

7. Lewis, *Zinzendorf*, 91.

8. Thompson, *Moravian Missions*, 467.

9. Spangenberg, *A Declaration Relative to Labor*. In Thompson, *Moravian Missions*, 468.

clear-sighted Moravian injunction been adopted by other missionary societies a great deal of internecine struggling between churches, confusion on foreign soil, and damage to the cause of Christ could have been avoided.

The Moravian churches have focused much of their mission endeavor by founding societies for that purpose. Among the earliest was a *Society for the Furtherance of the Gospel*, which was organized in 1735 and was succeeded in 1787 by *The Society for the Propagation of the Gospel among the Heathen*, which became the leading missionary society in the Moravian church. This was later re-named of *The Foreign Missionary Society of the Moravian Church*, which now supervises all Moravian Missionary work. From a very early point in time women were taking an active part in Moravian missionary societies.

ECUMENISM

Zinzendorf's constant thought was that in Christ all men are one. The challenge that he had felt, even from his childhood days, was how to make that fact a reality. With five other schoolboys Zinzendorf had founded a little society called *The Order of the Grain of Mustard Seed*. Its first article was "the members of this society will love the whole human family."[10] An integral part of Zinzendorf's mission strategy was this same ecumenical spirit. Indeed Zinzendorf must rank as one of the greatest and most forward-thinking missionary strategists. He was deeply aware of the scandal of the divided church, but his solution was very far from trying to merge all the denominations into one. In fact, quite the reverse was the case. He regarded each separate denomination as a *Tropus* or "a school of wisdom," having a unique contribution to make to the worldwide body of Christ. In the days when Zinzendorf was planning his visit to the State of Pennsylvania, he said: "I cannot with my testimony confine myself to one denomination for the whole earth is the Lord's, and all souls are his."[11]

Zinzendorf was totally dedicated to Jesus, believing that there can only be true unity in him. The second statute of *The Brotherly Agreement* reflected this same all-embracing spirit, stating that "Herrnhut shall stand in unceasing love with all the children of God in all churches, criticize none, take part in no quarrel against those differing in opinion, except to preserve for itself the evangelical purity, simplicity and grace."[12]

10. Lewis, *Zinzendorf*, 26.

11. Ibid., 143.

12. Ibid., 53.

A major aspect of Zinzendorf's mission strategy was his formation of The Diaspora. The word was taken from 1 Peter 1:1, where Peter refers to the "diaspora of Pontus." It was through this group the Zinzendorf sought to make the Moravian Brethren the servant of all other churches. *The Diaspora*, which was born out of the pentecostal experience of 13th August, 1727, was a network of informal meetings and societies set up in the various denominations that had been brought into new life through the Moravians. Each missionary in The Diaspora had their own special district in which they went from house to house and organized gatherings for prayer and mutual encouragement. Those who became part of these small groups only sang, prayed, and talked together. They were to confine their discussion to sharing their Christian experience and strictly forbidden to engage in any kind of theological argument or dispute. Those who became part of one of *The Diaspora* groups were required to take the Lord's Supper in the church to which they belonged. No Diaspora meeting was allowed to continue if they were opposed by the clergyman of the parish in which it was situated.

SOCIAL CONCERN

There was a strong social content to their missionary concern, as was illustrated by the lives of Leonard Dober and David Nitschmann, who responded to the call to take the gospel to the black slaves of the West Indies.[13] For the next forty-four years the Moravians were the only missionaries in the islands. While Protestants in England and elsewhere continued to debate the slavery issue the Moravians were bringing the slaves to faith in Christ. When in 1739 Zinzendorf visited St. Thomas he was amazed to discover that more than thirteen thousand of the black slaves had been baptized on profession of their faith.

The same spirit of Moravian compassion was in evidence in the work of George Schmidt (1718–85), who left Herrnhut and went out single-handed to work among the Hottentots of South Africa. On arrival he found that the Dutch Huguenots, who had left the persecuting authorities on their homeland to obtain religious liberty, had done nothing to educate or care for the indigenous population. Indeed, they had shot them by the hundred and sold others by the shipload for work in India. A. C. Thompson observed that over the doors of one church was posted a notice

13. Hassé, *The Moravians*, 120.

which read, "Hottentots and dogs forbidden to enter."[14] However, Schmidt was not a man to allow himself to be overcome by these distressing events and began at once to share the Christian message. At first the Dutch were amused by his efforts, but later they became hostile and critical. Notwithstanding, Schmidt worked on quietly and mastered the native language and gained the respect of Hottentots. After five years his efforts were rewarded when he was able to baptize the first converts to the Christian faith. This event angered the local clergy who declared it an illegal act because Schmidt was not properly ordained and was not therefore permitted to perform baptisms. The result was that Schmidt was banished from the territory by the Dutch authorities, who were also clearly worried about what Schmidt's communications with Herrnhut might be revealing. Schmidt was never allowed to return to South Africa and it was a further fifty years before Moravian missionaries were allowed to return to work among the Hottentots.

The Moravians' strong ecumenical vision was exemplified in their attempt to establish a united fellowship of all German-speaking Christians in the colony of Pennsylvania in 1742. While Zinzendorf's endeavors in this project ended in failure there is no doubt that it represented an ideal that, had it been successful, could have resulted in a major expansion of the kingdom of God. The Moravian churches have been noted for their kindly and gracious spirit towards other denominations. This is well attested at an early point in time by the minutes of the synodical conference held in England in 1750. It urged a kindly feeling towards the Eastern Orthodox church because the gospel had come to them through the ministry of the Greek priests, Cyril and Methodius, in A.D. 863. It also declared that "we must not speak ill" of the Roman church because "we were once of their household," although "they have bidden us farewell." It went on to say: "We have particular connections with the Lutherans, many of whom have joined the Unity."[15]

MORAVIANS IN BRITAIN

As early as 1728 Zinzendorf had sent three Brethren to London and Oxford. Not long after that the Moravians established themselves in the capital and set up a chapel in Fetter Lane. Away from the capital their first attentions were focused on Yorkshire where John Töltschig began preaching

14. Thompson, *Moravian Missions*, 364.

15. Fries, *Customs and Practices of the Moravian Church*, 9.

in 1739. In a short space of time they had seventy regular preaching places, which included Bradford, Halifax, Wakefield, Leeds, Huddersfield, Sheffield, York, and Hull. It was a well-planned campaign that centered around open-air preaching. Elsewhere, Benjamin Ingham (1712–72),[16] one of Wesley's Oxford friends, did much to encourage the activities of the Moravians. In 1738 there was a serious outbreak of smallpox in the town of Bedford and many of the clergy fled the town. In response to an urgent call for help Ingham arrived with a number of members from London and Yorkshire congregations to help. A great awakening followed and very large crowds gathered to hear the word of God preached. Other Moravian societies were established in Nottingham, Leicester, Sheffield, Stratford-on-Avon, Wolverhampton, as well as Ockbrook, Matlock, and Belper in Derbyshire and a number of Northamptonshire villages. Moravian missionaries also reached Hampshire and Berkshire and penetrated parts of Cornwall. Wales also proved to be particularly fertile ground for the Moravian missionaries and by 1745 there were forty Societies under their pastoral oversight alone.[17]

One of the most prominent early Moravian missionaries in England was John Cennick (1718–55). He was born and brought up in Reading. He first met John Wesley in 1739 and became one of his first lay preachers in the Bristol area and was the cause of a considerable revival in Wiltshire. He recorded in his diary for 16th July, 1740, that "I preached for the first time in the street of Castle Comb to a vast concourse of people," and later at the invitation of some persons at Chippenham, "I preached to a prestigious multitude on Langley Common."[18] Cennick was hugely effective in Ireland in 1748, where he preached to crowds of between five and six thousand and was the instrument of a genuine revival.[19] Cennick focused his energies on Ulster, where he founded 220 Moravian communities.[20] An unusual feature of Cennick's work in Ireland was his work with children. He was, as Hassé pointed out, one of the earliest evangelists to organize special children's services.[21] After a visit to the Moravians in Germany he was ordained a Moravian deacon in London in 1749.

16. For Benjamin Ingham see Vickers, *A Dictionary of Methodism in Britain and Ireland*, 175.

17. Hassé, *The Moravians*, 69–70.

18. Ibid., 79.

19. Ibid., 96.

20. Ibid., 100.

21. Ibid., 99.

SPIRITUALITY

As far as Zinzendorf was concerned fellowship was essential to genuine Christianity. He said on one occasion, "I acknowledge no Christianity without fellowship."[22] In order to facilitate this concern the Moravians organized themselves into "bands." These were small groups of not less than five or more than ten persons who met to share their faith. It was these small groups that later gave Wesley the inspiration for the class meetings that he established among the Methodists.

Moravian spirituality was, from the first, built around a series of meetings. At Herrnhut there were at least three meetings for the whole congregation on each week day. On Sundays there was praise and worship from 5 in the morning until after 9 in the evening. Although Zinzendorf and the Moravians laid great stress on these occasions they were ever vigilant to retain their own private devotion consisting of prayer, Scripture reading, and meditation. Contemplation on Christ the Lamb was at the very heart of their thoughts and prayers. The slaughtered lamb spoke of sacrifice, love, commitment, and dedication to mission and service. These themes are echoed in the Moravian Lord's Supper, which was preceded by foot-washing to remind them of the need for service

The Moravian church has always, since the beginning, been a praying church. Zinzendorf rediscovered the Love feast or Agapé meal, which was common in the early church during the first and second Christian centuries. There was never any proscribed format for the Moravian Love Feast, but it was primarily a feast of singing and an address. In the early days the Brethren shared water and rye-bread. Later they shared wine and a special bread or bun to distinguish it from the Lord's Supper. Singing has played an important role in all aspects of Moravian spirituality. It has been observed that many of their hymns relate to the triumphs of Christ's kingdom.

Moravians value liturgy as a framework for their worship. In the prescribed Sunday morning liturgy there are petitions such as, "Prosper the endeavours of all to spread the gospel among heathen nations. Accompany the word of their testimony with power."[23]

---

22. *The Moravian Magazine* (1854) Vol. 1, 337. In Lewis, *Zinzendorf,* 67.

23. Thompson, *The Moravians,* 479.

AN EDUCATIONAL MOVEMENT

As has been noted, the Moravians had a long history of concern and interest in all aspects of education. It was a legacy that stemmed back to the time of Bishop John Amos Comenius. Indeed, he has been accorded the title, "the Father of the Elementary School." Of particular interest are his books, including *The School of Infancy*, which set out the basic objectives for teaching the young. Above all other considerations such schools had to be definitely religious. Children were also to be taught Latin and German and to be instructed in the grammar of their native tongue. High moral standards were a basic requirement and the Bible and the Catechism were basic texts. Comenius also authored *Orbis Pictis*, which made the case that pictures in a book increased its educational value. The *Informatorium*, the School of Infancy, was written to provide guidance for mothers of preschool children. Comenius was also interested in University education. As he saw it, a university should be international and comprehensive in more than simply name. It became a rule that all ministerial candidates would devote a period of time to teaching following the completion of their training. It was this combination of academic rigor and the personal knowledge of God that gave the school a definite religious purpose. On the continent of Europe Moravian schools flourished in Germany, Switzerland, Holland, and the Baltic provinces. In England there were flourishing schools in a number of places, including Fulneck in Yorkshire, Fairfield near Manchester, Ockbrook in Derbyshire, and Gracehill in County Antrim. On the mission fields Day Schools were a prominent feature of Moravian settlements and seen as a key means to winning the young for Christ and training them in ways of his kingdom.

In Germany and in England the Moravians built schools for girls as well as for boys. Pupils studied the geography of their land, learned practical trades, and read the Scriptures. They were also taught to care for the sick and aged. In their Greenland settlement they even introduced old age pensions. In America Gottlieb Augustus Spangenberg, a former professor at Halle and a Moravian bishop, devoted time and energy to the Moravian settlements in Pennsylvania ensuring there was adequate provision for girls as well as for boys. The very first Moravian school in this state was built at Germantown under the direction of Benigna von Zinzendorf (1725–86), Count Zinzendorf's daughter. It was a girls-only school and soon gained such a high reputation that President George Washington personally contacted the headmaster in an effort to get places for two of his great-nieces. The institution is still in existence as the Moravian

College and Theological Seminary, though it is now located in Bethlehem. A boys' school was also established in Bethlehem in 1742, which later became a men's college and finally combined with the girls' college in 1953, after two centuries of separate growth. Such was the Moravian priority for education that even in the frontier forests of North Carolina a school was established by three university graduates in the tiny village of Salem. With the passing of time the school was divided into a high school academy and a college, both of which are flourishing today.

Genuine revivals impact the whole person and in almost all cases they revive interest in education. It has been truly said that nothing quickens the mind more readily than the Spirit of God. Such renewed desire for learning and in particular knowledge of the truth impacted both adult and child learning. While it cannot be claimed that the Sunday School movement arose directly as a result of the revival, there is no doubt that revival prepared the way for the project that Robert Raikes (1736–1811) began in 1780 among the neglected boys of Gloucester and which is generally taken as the beginning of the Sunday School movement.[24]

One memorable children's tradition that the Moravians have given to the worldwide Christian Church is the Christingle service. It was first devised for the Moravian congregation at Mariernborn on 20th December, 1747, when John de Wattville gave each child a lighted wax-candle and with a red ribbon. The symbols were later developed to include an orange representing the world with the candle inserted at its center to represent Christ, the light of the world.

ECCLESIOLOGY

From the early Hussite era to the present time, the Moravian Brethren held to the doctrine of the "invisible church," composed of godly men and women across the globe, drawn by Christ from every race and denomination. The Brethren never separated from the church universal, merely from what they perceived as its unbiblical corruptions.

In 1457 when the first group of Huss's followers withdrew from Prague to the estate of Lititz there was no democratic government in church or state. Priests and laymen ruled their people with a firm and

---

24. That said, it needs to be acknowledged that as early as 1727, following an awakening among the children at Herrnhut, the Moravians were setting up schools to instruct the young in biblical principles. Zinzendorf loved children and did everything he could to bring light, color, and joy into their learning experiences.

often-brutal hand. Yet as they gathered in the little village of Kunvald they organized themselves on democratic lines. Members chose their leaders by a majority vote. Women as well as men were selected for office. As the movement spread and other congregations were established and developed, contact was maintained between them by means of conferences as well as by synods. They sought to demonstrate the reality of the democratic ideal, expressed by the model of the church as a body. Women as well as men were chosen to office as leaders. They sought to make Jesus' words in Matthew 23:8 a reality, "One is your Master, even Christ, and all of you are brethren." All major issues of doctrine and practice were discussed and debated by these synods. A synod made the decision that an independent ministry was necessary and went on to choose the first men to be ordained as bishops and priests. Throughout the early period known as the "Unitas Fratrum" the synod was the final decision-maker among their congregations.

After the end of the period in which the Brethren had been forced underground they reorganized the "Unitas Fratrum" in their new location in Herrnhut, Saxony. Once more they returned to the earlier practice of electing men and women to office by vote of members. At the present time the Moravians are divided into provinces, each of which holds their own conference, which consists of members who are elected by each local district. Today, the Moravian church is organized into seventeen provinces. Some of these are in developed, industrial nations while others are located on the poorer continents of the South.

The Moravian church still sets high store on the fact that its bishops are held to be in a direct line of succession from the apostles. This goes back, as has been noted, to the time when the Waldensian bishop Stephen consecrated three Moravian leaders. This continuity was acknowledged by Archbishop Randal Davidson in 1908 when he when he sent a greeting to the Moravian Synod at Dukinfield in Chester. "Your bishops," he wrote, "have come down in historical continuity through the first bishops, through Christ and the Holy Apostles down to the present time. That is what we call the historical succession or historic episcopacy, and something which you hold as precious and sacred. We recognise that, and that is a very strong point of kinship and alliance already between you and us."[25] Present-day bishops are elected from among the presbyters and are seen as "pastors of the pastors." Deacons are considered to be fully ordained and can baptize infants, preside at the Lord's Supper, administer confirmation and conduct marriage services.

25. Lewis, *Zinzendorf*, 185.

FACTORS THAT MADE MORAVIANISM SUCCESSFUL

Their Spirituality

From the earliest times, and certainly from the days of Zinzendorf, the Moravian Brethren have been a deeply spiritual people who have pursued the presence of Jesus with a seriousness and a heartfelt devotion not seen in many other Christian groups. At the very center of this has been constant meditation and contemplation of Jesus as the Lamb of God, the Lamb speaking of love, sacrifice, and compassion. Of equal importance is the Moravian emphasis on the Holy Spirit as the one who baptizes believers into the presence of Jesus. For the Moravians a head-knowledge of Jesus is insufficient. He must be known in the feelings and emotions: in short, in the heart. In order to sustain this deep presence of Christ in their lives Moravians are totally committed to fellowship, conversing, sharing, and praying in small groups known as "bands." These gatherings have been and are the very nerve center of Moravian spirituality from which social action and reform has issued.

Moravian spirituality was sustained by frequent, informal watchnight and day gatherings for prayer, as well as through Love Feasts, the Lord's Supper, and a rich and historical tradition of liturgies through the week and during the course of the Christian year. Like the Wesleyans, who they greatly influenced, Moravians, as has been noted, loved to sing. Zinzendorf, who wrote more than 2,000 hymns and knew the power of singing, once said; "There is more dogma in our canticles than in our prose."[26] In 1733 the Moravians stated that "Our little children we instruct chiefly by hymns; whereby we find the most important truths most successfully insinuated into their minds."[27]

Education

Integral to the Moravian church's success has been their strong insistence on the importance of education at all levels from pre-school to university. At the heart of education, as they see it, is the practical application of the Christian faith to the issues of living. For the Moravians, theology is applied theology. Their emphasis, which is always on applying the Christian faith to all aspects of education, has found an echo in the curriculum of

26. Ibid., 163.
27. Ibid.

some of the Christian colleges in United States, where an endeavor is made to articulate a Christian understanding and philosophy of each individual subject discipline. From Zinzendorf's time onwards the Moravians have operated what is, for all intents and purposes, an educational movement. Wherever they have established a mission they have set up a school in which those who are converted may not only grow in their new-found Christian faith, but be trained in caring for the sick and needy, and organized into teams to share in fellowship and engage in evangelism.

Mission

From the earliest times the Moravians were missionaries like no others. A. C. Thompson pointed out in 1883 that the Moravians were sending out "nearly one in every fifty of its communicants for foreign missionary work."[28] Though small in numbers, they ventured out across the globe, burning with a passion to share Christ with those who they contacted. Part of the reason for their willingness to obey the Lord's command "to go into all the world and preach the gospel" was the fact that they had long been a pilgrim people. The Moravian history was one of constantly being persecuted, uprooted, and forced to move on and then to re-establish themselves in a new location. Unlike the established state and denominational churches of Europe, they had not become settled and secure. They had little or no comfort zone in which to get stuck!

It is the case that it is the "pioneering mind-set" that stimulates missionary enterprise and concern, while the "settled mind-set," on the other hand, results in people becoming trapped in their comfort zones. In a short space of time the Moravians sent out missionaries from their base in Herrnhut to Greenland, Surinam, South America, the Guinea Coast, the Cape, as well as to the North American Indians. It is small wonder that Gustav Warneck and George Robson wrote in their *Outline of a History of Protestant Missions from the Reformation to the Present Time* that, "This small Church in twenty years called into being more Missions than the whole Evangelical Church had done in two centuries."[29] Moravian Christians, it seems, were always ready to give a prompt response when asked to engage in missionary service. On one occasion, at Marienborn, Zinzendorf sent for a Moravian brother and asked him, "Will you go to

28. Thompson, *Moravian Missions*, 487.

29. Warneck and Robson, *Outline of a History of Protestant Missions*. In Hassé, *The Moravians*, 123.

Greenland tomorrow as a missionary?" The man apparently had no previous intimation that he was about to be presented with such an opportunity, but after only a minute of hesitation replied, "If the shoemaker can finish the boots that I have ordered of him by tomorrow, I will go."[30] When William Chalmers Burns was appointed a missionary to China he was asked when he would be ready to start and he replied, "Tomorrow"![31]

Ecumenical Vision

Zinzendorf is without doubt one of the foremost Ecumenical pioneers and statesmen the Christian world has yet to see. His vision for the world-wide creedal faith churches to form themselves into a Commonwealth seems to be the only obvious and biblical way forward. As we have seen, Zinzendorf's vision of Christian unity was not one of uniformity, but of a unity-in-diversity with each denomination holding onto the precious jewel of its own particular insights. The contemporary church needs a trans-denominational Christianity and Zinzendorf's vision—whereby an individual Christian believer could remain a member of his or her denomination but be free without any restraints to fully participate in the life of any other creedal church in the Commonwealth—seems totally in keeping with Jesus' ideal that his followers might all be one.

LAST WORD

William Wilberforce wrote of the Moravians as "a body of Christians who have, perhaps, excelled all mankind in solid and unequivocal proofs of the love of Christ, and of the most ardent, active, and patient zeal in his service. It is a zeal tempered with prudence, softened with meekness, soberly aiming at great ends by the gradual operation of well-adapted means, supported by a courage which no danger can intimidate, and a quiet constancy which no hardship can exhaust."[32]

30. Thompson, *Moravian Missions*, 470.

31. Ibid., 470.

32. Ibid., 486.

8 | The Society of Friends

GEORGE FOX (1624–91) WAS not a man of letters or academic learning, but he had a powerful and compelling call to preach the Christian message. He was born at Fenny Drayton in Leicestershire where his father was a weaver and was apprenticed to a shoe-maker. In 1643, after a series of internal struggles, he felt the call to leave his family and close friends and spent the next few years travelling in search of enlightenment. At the time, Fox eventually became a public figure. The English nation was pulsating with life, but the established church was, for all intents and purposes, a dull reflection of the church of Rome, but with the king as the supreme ruler. In 1647 Fox gave up attending his local parish church, having developed a strange hatred for both the clergy and the establishment. Needless to say, his relatives and family were bemused. Fox's Christianity became a purely spiritual affair and he rejected the two sacraments of baptism and Holy Communion, believing them to be mere substitutes for the true and deep union with God. He recounted something of his early skepticism in the following lines: "As I was walking in a field on a First-day morning, the Lord opened to me that being bred at Oxford or Cambridge was not enough to fit or qualify men to be ministers of Christ; and I stranged [wondered] at it, because it was the common belief of people." Fox later put these feelings into words when addressing a gathering on the fell beside the Sedbergh chapel. He declared that Christ has "ended the temple, and the priests, and the tithes and said, 'Learn of me.'"[1] In short, Fox saw them as those who were suppressing freedom of religious thought.

Fox strove to come "to a knowledge of God" through diligently searching the Bible. However, while he was sure that the word of Scripture was a source of truth, he was clear that a mere knowledge of the Bible was not sufficient for him; he desperately desired an experience of God himself—"the Speaker of the Word."[2] Fox, like most sectarian leaders, was

---

1. Nickalls, *The Journal of George Fox*, 109.
2. Zarek, *The Quakers*, 37.

opposed to any attempt to intellectualize theology. Behind the word of Scripture, behind the gospel, he sought God, and he soon became convinced that God would make himself known to anyone who truly desired to know him. Fox's own deep, *inward* experience of God was preceded by a period of "waiting upon the Lord."[3] He did not want to believe anything simply because it was in the Bible, but only because it was true. To put it another way, he did not want to believe something simply because it was in Scripture, but only on the strength of a deep inward conviction. Fox therefore began to preach, teaching that the truth was found in the inner voice of God speaking to the soul. In the account of his experiences in his *Journal*, Fox often insisted that he was being guided by the inner light of Christ. For Fox, an intimate experience of the presence of Jesus was the very cornerstone of his movement. He believed that this inner light would shine for all who sought God and that this would give them an inner experience of his presence. This represented a strong belief in the priesthood of all believers, which was also reflected in the Friends' practice of refusing to take their hat off to any other person, whatever their social standing: all people were to be treated alike. It was this understanding of equality that enabled the Quakers to recognize that they all shared the responsibility of proclaiming the gospel message.

EARLY FRIENDS

Much of Fox's early success was due to the fact that, like all sectarians, he had what the sociologist, Max Weber, termed "charisma"—a gift of personality that drew people after him like a magnet. As William Penn (1644–1718) later put it, "His very presence expressed a religious majesty." People who encountered him said he came with "a weight of authority," and it was his certainty he possessed the truth that gave him the courage to proclaim his version of the Christian faith. Among other things, Fox appeared to have a gift of healing and cured a woman of lameness and restored a man "possessed" back to sanity. Late in 1683 he reported: "And as I laid my hands upon him, the Lord's power went through him."[4]

Quakerism was born when Fox launched his public mission at Dukinfield and Manchester in 1647. His message of the need to find peace and inner light overwhelmed the hearts of his hearers. Quakerism flourished for the next seven years, during a period of time that was characterized by

3. Ibid., 37.
4. Ibid., 42.

intense political ferment. This is not surprising, for sectarian movements often originate and flourish in times such as these. Fox led a life of apostolic simplicity, choosing to wear "leathern breeches and a doublet" and to be guided always by the prompting of the Spirit. The political circumstances of the age were ripe for the birthing of a new religious movement of the kind for which Fox had a vision. The British monarchy was in crisis and the countryside was the scene of bloody conflict between King Charles' forces and the New Model Army. Those who had rejected the Roman style of the Church of England came with growing boldness to "the man in the leathern breeches." As far as Fox was concerned, believers should come together for worship as equals but in such a way that each one should hear God individually and personally.

George Fox was convinced that God guided him in all aspects of his daily life, impressing on him when he needed to rest or sleep or set off in a new direction. Like most sectarian leaders, he sought direct guidance from God and then spoke on impulse. At times his utterances were very like those of Montanus, who believed himself to have been the mouthpiece of the Holy Spirit. On one occasion, Fox recalled, "The Lord's power was so mighty upon me and so strong in me, that I could not hold, but was made to cry out and say: 'Oh no, it is not the scriptures from which all teaching come, but the Holy Spirit.'"[5]

In his *Journal*, Fox explained a teaching that would become an essential principle of Quakerism: "The Lord taught me to act mercifully in two ways, viz., inwardly to God and outwardly to man."[6] Faith, as far as Fox was concerned, must be accompanied by works. His Christianity was concerned with putting the Sermon on the Mount into practical action. There is no doubt that he was a gifted teacher with an extraordinary presence. William Penn was struck by "his clear and wonderful depth, his extraordinary gift in opening the scriptures." Penn went on to describe him as "a discerner of other people's spirits, and very much a master of his own . . . above all he excelled in prayer. The inwardness and weight of his spirit, the reverence and solemnity of his address and behavior, and the fewness and fullness of his words, have often struck strangers with admiration."[7]

In his wandering, Fox did not set out to inspire a political protest, but because the church and state were so closely related, his protests against the ecclesiastical establishment were inevitably interpreted in this way.

5. Ibid., 50.

6. Ibid., 42.

7. Ibid., 50.

His first major brush with the authorities came on a visit to Nottingham, where having experienced "the mighty power of the Lord in the Meeting House" he left the Friends (the name the Quakers used for themselves) and entered the local parish church. He strode up the aisle and addressed the congregation. Fox described the moment in the following words: "When I came there, all the people looked like fallow-ground, and the priest, like a great lump of earth." In a powerful voice that filled the building, Fox declared: "It is not the Scriptures from which all teachings come, but the Holy Spirit."[8] Fox had, no doubt, intended his words as a spiritual challenge, but his outburst was seen as a direct attack on the church as an institution, with the rather inevitable result that he was thrown into gaol.[9]

This experience was a foretaste of many sufferings that were to follow. Following his preaching in Mansfield, he was dragged along the streets and brutally beaten with horsewhips, Bibles, and sticks. He was arrested in Derby in 1650 and imprisoned for six months, but his endearing personality impacted both his fellow prisoners and even the gaoler's sister who visited him. This young woman was so impressed with Fox's teaching that she subsequently declared that the Friends were innocent people who went about doing good. Fox became a strong advocate of justice and tolerance and was moved to write to some of the judges who were condemning people to death for stealing cattle money and other small matters. Fox's outburst in church was no isolated occurrence: other Quakers soon followed suit. When a Quaker interrupted a sermon in the Chapel Royal on the 15th February, 1655, Cromwell issued a *Proclamation against Quakers, Ranters and Others* "to avoid disturbing ministers." Later, during the reign of Charles II, many prisons were populated with Quakers: London alone had 500 Quaker prisoners in 1661. Quakers further agitated the system by refusing to take the oath in court, which resulted in the passing of an act the following year entitled, *an Act for preventing mischief and danger that may arise by certain persons called Quakers and others refusing to take lawful oaths*. In 1665, the year of the Great Plague, the number of Quaker prisoners in the capital numbered about 2,000.

TO ALL LANDS

Fox's remit was not limited to England. He had a clear vision to reach all the nations and he therefore began to send out messages to the rulers of

8. Ibid., 52.
9. Jail.

the world. He himself visited a number of countries: in 1671 Fox decided to visit the English settlements in America and the West Indies. Later, in 1677, and then again in 1684, Fox visited the Friends in the Netherlands. The first trip was the more extensive, taking him into what is now Germany. One of his early fellow workers was James Nayler (1618–60), who became a great favorite of people in the London area and the south. For a time Nayler and Fox appeared to be rivals, but that ended on a day in October 1656 when Nayler rode into Bristol in a re-enactment of Jesus' triumphal entry into Jerusalem, following which he was tried for blasphemy, imprisoned for two years, and severely punished. He died a broken man in 1660.

The Quaker message spread. In 1654 more than thirty Quaker ministers and elders set out to proclaim their message to the southern counties of England. Furthermore, some of Fox's persecuted followers, who had taken refuge in Holland, began to find their message was welcomed there. In 1661, William Caton and William Ames visited Germany, where they succeeded in winning many Mennonites over to the Quaker cause.[10]

Freedom of conscience and tolerance was one of the major pleas of the seventeenth century and many Friends began to seek refuge in the New World. The first Quaker missionaries to arrive there were Mary Fisher and Ann Austin who reached Boston in 1656. The early Quaker settlers experienced some persecution, but by the time George Fox and his twelve companions toured the colonies in 1672 it had more or less ceased and there were Quaker inhabitants in all the colonies from New Hampshire down to South Carolina. The number of Quakers emigrating increased in 1674 when Quaker proprietors gained control of West (New) Jersey.

Pennsylvania

One of the most important Quaker overseas ambassadors who facilitated this freedom on a large scale was William Penn.[11] Penn was from a distinguished family and can, without doubt, be considered among the most significant Quaker activists. Such was his standing that even though he

---

10. Hull, *William Penn and the Dutch Quaker Migration to Pennsylvania*, 267. In R. Smith, *The Friend*, Vol 13, (1840), 205.

11. There were others who preceded Penn, among them Ann Austin and Mary Fisher had some success in Barbados and in New England. Fox himself went to Barbados and then went to Maryland, where he made a deep impression on the people, including the Native Americans. See Zarek, *The Quakers*, 128.

was very open about his Quaker faith, Charles II readily welcomed him at court and granted his plea for the release of Fox in 1674. Since his early days as a student at Oxford, Penn had wanted to found a Quaker colony in America, which seemed to him to be a promised land. Prompted by the success of the small Quaker Colony of West Jersey and the respect accorded to them, Penn set his sights on the unsettled land to the west of the Delaware River and north of Maryland.

It happened that the crown owed his father a sum of money in the region of £16,000 and that William was the heir to this claim. Eventually, after some negotiation, Charles II agreed to grant him a vast area of land greater in extent than the whole of Ireland. It stretched between the 75th and 80th longitudes from the northern frontier of Maryland up to the northern lakes at the border with Canada. After a little further persuasion from his brother, James, the King added the whole of the Delaware Bay, which gave open access to the Atlantic Ocean. The new territory, which was established in 1681, was named Pennsylvania (meaning "Penn's Wood") and the land was given to the Quakers. The King tried to insist that Penn use the British military in any struggles that might occur with the Indian communities, but Penn was forthright in declining any use of force. Although Penn was the single owner of the land, he made every effort to ensure that no individual would be able to exercise sole authority over it and its peoples. To ensure this, Penn set up a Provincial Council of seventy-two members who would be elected by the freemen. The governor would simply be the chairman of the Council with no power to override any decisions. There was considerable tolerance in the new province and freedom of thought and action was guaranteed to the large numbers of non-Quakers who soon began to settle there. Perhaps inevitably, this resulted in the decline of Quaker influence, to the extent that by the end of the century it had become necessary to legislate against swearing and drunkenness.

Worse was to follow for Penn when the new King, William III, insisted that the Quaker state of Pennsylvania arm itself for the defense of English territories in America. Penn was willing to comply, even though it was against his beliefs and conscience. However, during his lengthy absence much had changed; now he was shocked to find that the inhabitants of his own land had little time for the English crown and they were certainly not willing to give money and arms to defend what they saw as a foreign cause. Penn returned to England in 1701, the year before the King died. He remained a broken and discouraged man, but significantly the seed he had sown in Pennsylvania bore fruit in the years after his death. His ideals of individual liberty, freedom of conscience, and respect for all, regardless of their race or religion, were gradually adopted as core values of the fledgling American society.

Quaker migration expanded rapidly and the census figures for 1843 made it clear that there were many more Friends in the new colonies than in their homeland. It has been pointed out that many emigrants did not venture to the colonies out of fear of persecution, but rather on account of the appeal of the new world.[12] The nineteenth century saw the birth of a number of Home Missionary societies in England and America and in 1868 British Quakers set up *The Friends Foreign Missionary Association*. An estimate of Quaker numbers at the middle point of the nineteenth century gave 8,000 in Pennsylvania, 11,000 in New York, 10,000 in New England, 18,000 in Ohio, and 30,000 in Indiana.[13] In Britain and Ireland Quaker numbers had declined in the eighteenth century, but by the middle years of Victoria's reign they numbered perhaps as many as 66,000 or 0.76 percent of the population.[14] The 1851 Religious Census for England and Wales showed the Society of Friends having 371 places of worship with a combined attendance of 18,172.[15] By the beginning of the twentieth century British Quakers numbered 20,000, with the Unites States having 120,000.[16]

The Society of Friends has suffered decline, and it is indeed still doing so. Clearly a variety of reasons have contributed to this, perhaps the most obvious being the general secularizing influences of the Enlightenment and postmodernism. But perhaps another key issue was that highlighted by Joseph Rowntree. In 1859, a prize had been offered for the best essay on the subject of the Quakers' declining numbers.[17] In his winning essay, Rowntree wrote: "The mistake of the early Friends" was "that of supposing that one form of worship . . . was the only one acceptable to God, or worthy of the adoption of his Church." He went on to assert that a much more effective course of action would have been to unite "the practice of silent worship with those other arrangements which, though not worship itself,

12. Dandelion, *An Introduction*, 50.

13. Zarek, *The Quakers*, 158.

14. Dandelion, *An Introduction*, 43.

15. Thomson, *Nonconformity in the Nineteenth Century*, 150–52.

16. Zarek, *The Quakers*, 198, and Dandelion, *An Introduction*, 81.

17. Paz, *Nineteenth-Century English Religious Traditions*, 91.

do at times prepare the way for it; as the audible reading of Holy Scripture, the teaching of Christian truth, etc."[18]

A DIVIDING OF THE WAYS

Like many sectarian movements, Quakerism had an inbuilt potential for division or fissuring. Although a gifted preacher of the Scriptures, Fox had a strongly mystical side to his faith and was guided by the "inner light" rather than by rational reflection on his experience. His followers, therefore, often found themselves without clear guidelines when it came to issues of belief. Certain changes in the internal life of the Society gave rise to what is now termed the "Quietist Period" of eighteenth-century Quakerism.[19] From the outset, Quakers had sought above all things to listen to the inner voice of God, but they usually relayed their experiences to others and, therefore, interacted dynamically with the people around them. During the Quietist period of Quakerism, however, many Friends became preoccupied with the life of their Society and they tended to be less involved with the affairs of the world "outside." Indeed, Quietist postures began to predominate in the period immediately following the restoration of the monarchy. The first generation of leaders, who saw themselves in the role of prophets, were followed by others who saw their roles in terms of nurturing and consolidating Quaker communities.

A new brand of leaders began to emerge who were of different stock and whose faith was more strongly intellectual in content. Among them were the previously-mention William Penn, the Son of Admiral Penn, a powerful influence under Charles II, and Robert Barclay who had studied in the Scottish Theological College in Paris. Barclay wrote what became a widely accepted volume on Quaker doctrine and practice, entitled: *An Apology for the True Christian Divinity: Being an Explanation and Vindication for the Principles and Doctrines of the People called Quakers.* In this volume Barclay taught a doctrine of Christian perfection,[20] and gave reasons for Quaker beliefs. Here, for example, was rule number four of six: "It is not lawful to use games, sports, plays, nor, among other things,

---

18. Ibid., 91.

19. Earlham School of Religion: http://esr.earlham.edu/support/comprehensive-case/the-vine/18th-century-quietism-19th-century-schisms.

20. Dandelion, *An Introduction*, 55. Barclay maintained, "There may be a state attainable in this life, in which to do righteousness may become so natural to the regenerate soul, that in the stability of this condition they can not sin."

comedies among Christians . . . which do not agree with Christian silence, gravity, and sobriety."[21] Penn, who was educated at Christ Church, Oxford, also engaged in serious writing in which he justified the plain and frugal lifestyle of the Quakers on economic grounds. He argued that if all the money spent on unnecessary entertainments, sinful fashions, taverns, horses, and coaches should instead be collected into a public stock, there would then be sufficient funds to provide labor for the unemployed and workhouses for the beggars.

Unlike the previous century, which had been one of struggles and persecution, the eighteenth century turned out to be one of prosperity and liberty, following King William's Toleration Act. The high value that the early Quakers placed on labor and modest living was maintained, and as a result many Quakers became prosperous. The Friends reinvested their surplus income in their businesses and entrepreneurial projects, but their sense of duty led a number of them to devote their attention to the needs of the poor. At the same time, entrepreneurial Quakers made the welfare of their workers a very high priority. The Quakers' altruistic focus resulted in many philanthropic ventures, which some have described as a form of religious socialism. Such ventures were epitomized in John Bellers' *Essay towards the Improvement of Physick*, in which he called for infirmaries to be built and care for the sick to be re-organized. For this reason, Bellers has been described as a pioneer of "Christian Humanism."[22] Indeed, he became a significant exemplar to those who came after him in the nineteenth century. Like the early Puritans, many Quakers came to the conviction that the measure of their Christian faith was the degree to which their philanthropic concerns impacted the lives of ordinary people. Notably, the context of this new emphasis was the Enlightenment, an era in which both basic Christian faith and humanitarian reason urged that men and women should live together in a spirit of unity and brotherhood. These were, of course, ideals that resonated strongly with Quaker convictions.

However, in the early eighteenth century, Quakers were often regarded with skepticism by their contemporaries; Friends were accused of being more interested in the business of making money than in anything else. This was a season of somewhat toned down enthusiasm, and emphasis was on building the movement's structure, defining doctrine, and promoting religious discipline. Throughout all the ages of Quakerism, Friends have shown an unusual sensitivity to those in need, but in the

21. Ibid., 55.
22. Zarek, *The Quakers*, 167.

early part of the century few Quakers spoke out *publically* against societal injustice. In the eighteenth century men were still hanged and transported for relatively small offences, and the vast majority of working people lived harsh, precarious lives. Generally speaking, Quakers did not confront the authorities about such things; rather they sought to make their own lives an expression of charity and they aimed for working practices that were above reproof. The London Yearly Meeting Epistle of 1689 advised Quakers as follows.

> Walk wisely and circumspectly towards all men, in the peaceable spirit of Christ Jesus, giving no offence nor occasions to those in outward government, nor way to any controversies, heats or distractions of this world, about the kingdom thereof. But pray for the good of all; and submit to that Divine power and wisdom that rules over the kingdom of men. That, as the Lord's hidden ones, that are always quiet in the land, as those prudent ones and wise in heart, who know when and where to keep silent, you may all approve your hearts to God . . .[23]

THE IMPACT OF EVANGELICALISM

Towards the later part of the eighteenth century, many Quakers in both England and America began to devote their energies to reformist activities. These Quakers were not deterred by warnings from their more introspective and reticent brethren, who feared that Quakerism would be tainted by too much involvement in worldly affairs. In fact, in many Quaker families there was a fresh surge of charitable enterprise and a "new fluttering of religious zeal."[24] It would appear that this new sense of energy was initially a response to the revival movements of George Whitefield in America, and John and Charles Wesley in England. Whitefield and Wesley's powerful brand of religious experience, which emphasized both the preaching of the Scriptures and social reform, had the effect of drawing many Quakers away from their world-denying spirituality. Indeed, in the Warrington area there was a group known as the "Quaker Methodists" who actively engaged with the needs of the working poor.[25]

23. Sykes, *The Quakers*, 177.
24. Ibid., 186.
25. See Lander, *Itinerant Temples*, 4.

The vigorous evangelical assertion of Scriptural authority challenged the Quietism of the earlier eighteenth-century Quakerism. Indeed, it was this Methodist influence that provoked Henry Tuke to write *The Principles of Religion,* in which he aimed to combine the mysticism of the early Friends with the evangelicalism of the Wesleys. Eventually, Evangelicalism provoked what became known as the "Great Separation" of 1827 in Quakerism. In America, two major groupings emerged: the Hicksites, who wanted to retain the emphasis on the "inward Light," and the "Orthodox Party," who held strongly to traditional evangelical tenets. In England their prominent leader was Joseph John Gurney.[26] The Hicksites were followers of Elias Hicks (1748–1828) of Jericho, New York. He held a number of views that were clearly at odds with orthodox Christianity. Among other things he rejected the fall, original sin, and the substitutionary atonement, which he considered to be "a vulgar error."[27] He held strongly to the inner light of "Christ within the hope of glory" as the sole source of authority. Eventually, there was split within the Philadelphia Yearly Meeting between the Hicksites and the Orthodox parties, and similar fractures took place at a number of other Yearly Meetings across America. In Britain there was a strong anti-Hicksite campaign with most of the Friends expressing their support, in varying degrees, with the Orthodox party. Among the more extreme opponents was Isaac Crewdson, who started a separatist faction in Manchester under the name of "Evangelical Friends." There, they erected a chapel in which there were elders and deacons, hymn singing, Bible reading, and prayers. There were other separations in the nineteenth century; among them was that led by John Wilbur (1774–1856) of Rhode Island. He held traditional evangelical convictions, but felt that too much emphasis was being put on outward form and religious practice and that the focus was moving too far away from "inward religion." Wilbur found sympathizers in both England and America.

Bryan Wilson analyzed this process in his classic text *Religious Sects,* observing that the Society of Friends changed from being an "introversionist sect" to become a "reformist sect."[28] As Wilson analyzed the situation he underlined the fact that George Fox "was disposed to be a prophet of doom" and that James Nayler took up these apocalyptic expectations

---

26. There were other further fissures within Quakerism. For example, in 1836 Isaac Crewdson led some 400 "ultra-evangelical friends out of British Quakerism altogether." See Dandelion, *An Introduction,* 7.

27. Dandelion, *An Introduction,* 86.

28. Wilson, *Religious Sects,* 178.

and even entered Bristol declaring himself to be a Messiah.[29] At the same time, Quakers learned to withdraw from the more worldly aspects of society and sought to receive inspiration from the "inward light" of the Spirit rather than the Scriptures. They tended in consequence to disengage with the world because they were expecting the arrival of an imminent millennium. This withdrawal or "introversionism" was, to some extent, reinforced by the persecutions of the Stuart period. Wilson goes on to point out that "as industry developed, Quaker manufacturers became noted as employers of exceptional integrity and high standards"[30] and they began to justify their newly created wealth by philanthropy. Quaker charity expanded hugely in the nineteenth century, the period when the Friends were starting to emerge from their world-denying stance. Their stress on the importance of conscience pushed many of them into reformist and political activities.

QUAKERS AND THE ANTI-SLAVERY MOVEMENT

Among the earliest Quaker reformist endeavors was the anti-slavery campaign on both sides of the Atlantic. In 1750 Anthony Benezet, a Philadelphia Friend, attacked the trade in a series of self-funded tracts, the most important of which was entitled, *A Caution and Warning to Great-Britain and her Colonies on the Calamitous State of the Enslaved Negros.* The Philadelphia Yearly Meeting sent copies to the London Friends and 600 copies were dispatched to members of Parliament. In 1775 an important and influential anti-slavery society was formed in the same city with the name of *The Pennsylvania Society for Promoting the Abolition of Slavery, for the Relief of Free Negros Unlawfully held in Bondage, and for improving the Conditions of the African Race.* The abolitionist task in America, as in England, was an uphill struggle against prejudice and vested interest.

Among those who gave themselves unstintingly to the fray was the New Jersey Quaker, John Woolman (1720–72), who proved himself a major figure. He did not eat sugar or make use of silver bowls or cutlery because of their connections with the slave trade. His sermons and pamphlets were also a powerful voice and he set out many of the arguments against the trade. Woolman recorded in his journal his deep distress on finding, during a visit to Newport, Rhode Island, that a large number slaves had been imported into the town and "were then on sale by a

29. Ibid.
30. Ibid., 179.

member of our society."[31] At a later point in his journal Woolman relates that he spent time engaging with Friends in Pennsylvania and elsewhere who kept slaves and that it led to his writing the second part of a work entitled, *Considerations on Keeping Negroes*.[32] In this document he wrote:

> To consider mankind otherwise than brethren, to think favours are peculiar to one nation, and exclude others, plainly supposes a darkness of understanding. For, as God's love is universal, so where the mind is sufficiently influenced by it . . . the heart is enlarged towards all men. . . . Whence it is that men, who believe in a righteous Omnipotent Being, to whom all nations stand equally related, and are equally accountable, remain so easy in the prerogative of the white colour; but for that they do not discuss this matter with that candour and freedom of thought, which the case calls for?[33]

The Quaker campaign against slavery continued unabated right up to the American Civil War. They founded schools for black people, one prominent example being the school founded by Anthony Benezet in Philadelphia for black people and their descendants.[34] In 1818 a petition for the abolition of slavery was sent by the North Carolina Yearly Meeting to Congress. Among those British Friends who campaigned against slavery, Joseph Sturge emerged as a forthright campaigner. He was a prominent member of the Birmingham Anti-Slavery Society, which organized numerous public meetings to inform the local people about the plight of the slave. The Birmingham Anti-Slavery Committee also campaigned against slavery in the local press. He later journeyed to America, where he supported anti-slavery societies in the North who challenged the apathetic, sometimes even complicit, stance of the American churches towards slavery in the South. Sturge himself wrote: "It is a distinguishing and beautiful feature of Christianity, that it leads us to recognise every country as our country, and every man as our brother, and as there is no moral degradation so awful, no physical misery so great, as that inflicted by slavery, I have felt it my duty to labour for its universal extinction."[35]

A number of prominent Quaker women were active in the anti-slavery campaigns on both sides of the Atlantic; among them was Mary Ann

31. Woolman, *The Journal*, 179–80.

32. Ibid., 194–95.

33. Zarek, *The Quakers*, 170–71.

34. Ibid., 194.

35. Richard, *Sturge*, 298.

McClintock (1799–1884). In 1835, she and her family moved to Waterloo, New York, and their home became a stop on the Underground Railroad, which was a network of secret routes and safe houses that enabled runaway slaves to get to free states or to Canada. McClintock participated in the founding of the Philadelphia Female Anti-Slavery Society and worked on the Society's first Anti-Slavery Fair in 1863.[36] One of the earliest, most enduring, and most important of Britain's numerous women's antislavery societies was established by the evangelical Anglican, Lucy Townsend, and the Quaker, Mary Lloyd. "The Female Society for Birmingham, West Bromwich, Wednesbury, Walsall, and their Respective Neighbourhoods, for the Relief of British Negro Slaves" was officially founded in 1825. This was a year before the all male "Birmingham Anti-Slavery Society" was established. Just like the men of the Birmingham Anti-Slavery Society, they were indebted to nonconformist religious views such as, Quakerism.[37] They were particularly influenced by Elizabeth Heyrick, a Leicester Quaker, who published "Immediate, Not Gradual Abolition" in 1824. Heyrick was one of the first people to propose the immediate emancipation of slaves in the British colonies, rather than the gradual abolition suggested by the Anti-Slavery Society. Sophia Sturge, the sister of the aforementioned Joseph Sturge, was the secretary of the female society, and this is just one example of the close connections between the men's and women's antislavery societies in Birmingham.[38] Eventually, the issue of slavery helped bring women to the fore in campaigns for the rights of slaves.

EVANGELICAL QUAKERISM

Prominent among those who wanted to emphasize the place of the Bible in Quakerism was Joseph John Gurney (1788–1847). He did not share the rigorous "sola Scriptura" views of Crewdson and emphasized the importance of the authority of both the word of God and the working of the Holy Spirit. He also recognized the value of the experience of silent worship. Gurney's teachings grew in influence in both England and America in the 1840s and moved many of the Friends on both continents to a more

---

36. National Women's History Museum, Alexandria, Virginia, http://www.nwhm .org/education- resources/activities/abolition-movement-tours/philadelphia.

37. Connecting Histories, Birmingham City Archives, http://www.connecting histories.org.uk/Learning%20Packages/Anti%20Slavery/antislavery_lp_03.asp. Midgley, *Women Against Slavery*, 198.

38. Midgley, *Women Against Slavery*, 85.

mainstream Protestant Evangelicalism. Indeed, by the later Victorian years Quakerism was predominantly evangelical in ethos. Gurney, it should be said, held that the Spirit was given at conversion and did not preach an imminent Second Coming. In England a number of Friends who shared his convictions became active in Parliament, social action, local government, and philanthropy. For instance, Joseph Pease (1799–1872), who managed the Stockton to Darlington railway, became MP for South Durham in 1832. He actively supported Thomas Fowell Buxton in the anti-slavery movement. John Bright (1811–89), one of the committee who founded the Anti-Corn Law League in 1839, was an MP for nearly forty years and is still regarded as one of the greatest orators of the nineteenth century. Among significant British Quaker social reformers was the previously mentioned Joseph Sturge (1793–1859). A Birmingham-based philanthropist, he was a major anti-slavery campaigner who pressed for the immediate and full emancipation of slaves in British territories. He organized the World's Anti-Slavery Convention in London in 1840 and in the following year travelled to America where he had a significant influence on the anti-slavery movement there. Although by this time slavery had been made illegal in the northern States, slavery was flourishing in the southern States and in the District of Columbia. By the end of the 1830s, it was clear that slavery would not gradually decline in the South, as many had previously predicted. Despite the end of the African slave trade in 1808, the slave population continued to grow, climbing from 1.5 million in 1820 to over 2 million a decade later.[39] A prevalent belief that blacks and whites could not coexist and that racial separation was necessary caused many people to call for the deportation of blacks to overseas colonies. In 1817 a group of prominent ministers and politicians formed the American Colonization Society to resettle free blacks in West Africa. Sturge supported those white and black abolitionists who condemned colonization and northern discrimination against African Americans; he also affirmed the abolitionists' argument that slavery in the South was a complete negation of the American principles of equality and freedom. Additionally, Sturge was by no means oblivious to the sufferings of the poor working people back in England. He also gave support to the peaceful elements of the Chartist electoral reform campaign of the 1830s and 1840s.

In both England and America Quaker businesses demonstrated genuine compassionate concern for their work force. One of the most prominent examples of this humane spirit was Cadbury's chocolate

---

39. http://www.digitalhistory.uh.edu/database/article_display.cfm?HHID=629.

factory founded by John Cadbury (1801–89) in 1831. He was joined in the business by his son, George Cadbury (1839–1922), in 1853. George had a strong Christian concern and almost from the start of his days he regularly took breakfast with the workers and before the day's work began led them in a short devotional service. It was called the "Daily Reading" and consisted of a passage of Scripture followed by a time of silence for prayer. George was keen on Moody and Sankey revivalist-style hymns and in later years the gathering often ended with a rousing song.[40] In 1900 it was decided to hold the service on just three days a week and it was estimated that a third of the 3,000 workers attended on each occasion.[41] The 3,200 workers in 1879 not only worked in a factory that was well-lit and well-ventilated, but they also benefitted from dining rooms, sporting facilities that included cricket and football, as well as drying and changing accommodation. Later there was a concert hall and an open-air swimming pool.[42] Then in 1895 George Cadbury purchased a 120-acre site beside the factory on which he built 370 houses, each of which had a substantial garden.[43] George set a very high priority on education and any worker was allowed to leave work an hour early if they were enrolled in a night school class. He himself was responsible for establishing five colleges in Selly Oak, where there was instruction on Christian social issues.[44]

It should be said that George Cadbury was, to use Ian Bradley's words, one of many Quaker "enlightened entrepreneurs." His fellow chocolatier, Joseph Fry (1777–1861) worked along similar lines, including starting the day with a short Christian service.[45] Joseph Rowntree (1836–1925) was another distinguished Quaker confectioner. At the time when he started work at his brother's cocoa, chocolate, and chicory works in 1869, the labor force numbered just twelve workers. When he retired in 1923 there were more than 7,000 men and women on the books.[46] Rowntree adopted some of Cadbury's successful ideas and relocated his chocolate manufacturing business away from the center of York, where he built a model village. He took a paternal interest in his employees and introduced medical and insurance schemes, a pension fund, and a minimum

---

40. Bradley, *Enlightened Entrepreneurs*, 125.

41. Ibid., 136.

42. Ibid., 126.

43. Ibid., 129–30.

44. Ibid., 132.

45. Ibid., 125.

46. Ibid., 140.

wage.[47] George Palmer (1818–97) took as his business partner his cousin, Thomas Huntley, and together in 1822 they founded the Reading-based biscuit company. Both were well-known men with a strong Quaker faith. By 1860 there were 500 employees. Jonathan Dodgson Carr was another Friend who founded Carr's biscuits in Carlisle. Other Quaker businesses included Clark's Shoes (founded by James and Cyrus Clark in Somerset), Bryant and May the match makers, Isaac and James Reckitt who built up a blue starch company in Norwich, Allen and Hanbury the chemists, and Colemans. Abraham Darby (1678–1717) was the most famous of three generations of Quaker pioneering industrialists based at Coalbrookdale.

Quakers were also prominent in the banking world. Barclays Bank derived its name from James Barclay who became a partner in 1736. The business then expanded considerably in 1896 when other smaller banks were incorporated into the business. The origins of the Lloyds bank also stretch back to 1765 when John Taylor and Sampson Lloyd set up a private banking business in Birmingham. In 1865 it became a joint stock company under the name Lloyds Banking Company Limited.

In America Quaker philanthropy developed in a similar way. The large Whitall Tatum Philadelphia Glass Company was founded in 1831 by John H. Whitall, a highly respected Friend. The same city's Bethlehem Steel Company was founded by the Quaker Entrepreneur, Joseph Wharton, but its roots went back to the earlier Saucona Iron Company of 1857. The famous New Jersey "Quaker Oats Company," which was founded in 1901, had its origins in the Quaker oat mills that had first been set up in the 1850s by Ferdinand Schumacher and Robert Stuart in Akron, Ohio. The Strawbridge and Clothier department stores in the northeastern Unites States had its origins in Philadelphia in 1862, where two Quakers, Justus Strawbridge (1838–1911) and Isaac Clothier (1837–1921), opened their first store. Macy's New York departmental store chain with 800 stores in the U.S. in 1910 was established by Russell Macy in Haverhill, Massachusetts, in 1851 to meet the need of the area's mill-workers.

THE LATER REJECTION OF DOGMATISM

Amid all the philanthropic endeavor and evangelical fervor of the middle years of the nineteenth century there was a resurgence of doubt following the publication of Darwin's *On the Origin of Species* in 1859 and *Essays and Reviews* in the following year. Darwin's findings caused many to doubt the

47. Ibid., 145 and 153.

historicity of the early chapters of Genesis, particularly the stories of the creation and fall. *Essays and Reviews* took on board the critical writings of the German critical scholars, who maintained that the historical Jesus was lost in what they took to be a cluster of mythical stories, of which the birth, resurrection, and ascension narratives were prime examples. The doubts led to the emergence of a liberal or modernist Quakerism, which emphasized conscience and the inner voice rather than submission to any form of scriptural authority or doctrinal teaching. The liberals, who were led by John William Rowntree (1878–1905) and Rufus Jones (1863–1948), began to take on board aspects of higher criticism and to reject doctrines, such as eternal punishment, that appeared to be morally offensive.

Dandelion suggests that many of the liberals were the sons and daughters of the earlier generation of Evangelicals.[48] If he is correct in this, it represents a similar pattern to that which took place in the Church of England. In general terms there was a shift towards pluralist thinking and an emphasis on the teaching of the Sermon on the Mount and Christian Socialist ideals. By the twenty-first century, it was even perfectly possible to hold Buddhist beliefs and be a Quaker. This led Dandelion to suggest that by the mid-1990s, this section of British Quakers were and are "Post-Christian."[49] Indeed, his 1989 survey found that only 39 percent claimed that Jesus was an important aspect of their Christian faith![50] Summing up the matter, Dandelion wrote, "Liberal Friends affirm their opposition to creeds. If pushed, they resist more firmly."[51] The heart of liberal Quakerism thus became silent and unstructured worship during which, it is believed, and the only genuine experience of God and his word is possible.

CONTEMPORARY QUAKERISM

Taking present-day Quakerism as a whole, it would be true to say that it reflects the elements of the past which we have been considering. The evangelical section of Friends is still actively engaged in promoting the biblical doctrines of justification by faith and personal commitment to Christ. Their worship is often in the style of other nonconformist churches with hymns, prayers, and a sermon. Liberal Quakers, on the other hand, have suffered a steeper decline than the theological conservatives, but have

48. Dandelion, *An Introduction*, 118.
49. Ibid., 135.
50. Ibid., 136.
51. Ibid., 137.

continued to pursue issues of social and economic justice. In particular, they have taken a prominent role against nuclear weaponry, exploitation of natural resources, environmental pollution, and have stood out strongly on human rights issues. Liberal friends are also liberal when it comes to sexual and family morality, while evangelical members adhere to traditional Christian values.[52]

QUAKER DOCTRINES

Belief in God

Quakers coming from a variety of backgrounds hold differing views about God. For those who are liberally minded there is often a debate as to whether God is a person and how closely the deity is to the presentations of God in the text of Scripture. On the other hand, the orthodox and evangelical Quakers see Jesus very much in New Testament terms and lay out creedal statements that encapsulate those views.

Kingdom

Dandelion has pointed out that although Quakers came from a variety of theological backgrounds, by the mid-1650s most believed that while the kingdom of God would only be fully realized in the future, or possibly near future, it was nevertheless already present in a limited sense in the Quaker movement.[53] Damiano and Tousley have made the point that Friends were still "realizing" the eschatology and "marginalizing" the future eschatological kingdom.[54] From the twentieth century onwards the majority of Quakers began to see the kingdom in social rather then apocalyptic terms. Their energies were spent in seeking to bring glimpses of the kingdom of heaven on earth as they worked with the Red Cross and campaigned for peace and Green issues. In this process creedal beliefs became less and less important.

52. Ibid., 242–49.
53. Ibid., 31.
54. Ibid., 57.

Ecclesiology

Like most sectarians Fox's understanding of the church was minimalist. The Lord who made the heavens and the earth did not dwell in temples made with hands. His people were his temple and his Spirit lived within them. Thus all that was required for worship were simple meetinghouses without steeples. Such premises were in the style and manner of ordinary houses. Within them there was no special dress code, no official leader, and no ritual or ceremonial. Worship, which was always held on Sundays and Wednesdays, was invariably plain and unadorned and could happen at any time and any place. Quakers were happy for music and singing without books, and their gatherings could last up to three hours and occasionally longer. In these worship rooms the believers sat in silence and waited for the "inner light" to make an impression on them. When the light was manifested the members were seized with jubilation and sometimes even began to tremble or quake. It was in Derby that Fox was first asked why his followers were called Quakers, to which he replied, "because we tremble at the word of the Lord." Another reason that has been given for the term was that the Society of Friends trembled under the power of the Holy Spirit at some of their gatherings for worship.[55] Quaker meeting places had no hierarchy or system of elected elders and there was no consensus or system of majority voting on matters of concern. To this day Quakers hold to what has been termed "a flat ecclesiology," in which any ministerial roles are decided on a consensual decision and held for a limited period of time. Following the practice of Jesus the Quakers called themselves "Friends." They always addressed each other with the words "Thou" and "Thee" and eschewed titles, rank, and status. Inevitably, when the monarchy was restored Fox found himself in conflict with the re-establishment of the social hierarchy.

Fox therefore rejected the notion of the visible church and held strongly to the notion of an invisible church. In an address he gave in Westmorland, Fox declared: "the church is only a place of limestone and wood. . . . You have given the title Church, which belongs to the people, to an old house, and you have taught the people to believe so."[56]

---

55. Dandelion, *An Introduction,* 29. In Punshon, *Portrait in Grey,* 71. "Quakerism was initially an insult coined by justice Bennett at Fox's blasphemy trial in Derby in 1650 but its usage spread, and it was soon adopted by the group."

56. Zarek, *The Quakers,* 80.

Pacifism

One belief about which all Fox's followers were adamant was that killing must always be wrong. Fox came early into conflict over the issue when he refused to enlist in Cromwell's army. His stand was a strong rejection of the view that killing can be justified, even if there is high motive behind it. Quakers were of the opinion that while armed conflict may compel the defeated enemy to bow to a new set of rules, it rarely succeeded in achieving loyalty and compliance of heart.

ORGANIZATION

In 1650 Fox and his followers commenced a systematic strategy to bring the inhabitants of Britain to an experience of light, Spirit, and grace. Fox pursued his earlier practice of preaching in churches and soon found that his behavior had brought him into conflict with the Quaker legislation of Charles II. Fox was particularly effective when preaching to large gatherings, but was also compelling in discussions with those who had been theologically trained. On occasion, Fox was seized with sudden overwhelming impulses to cry out in a loud voice. Such was the case when he paraded up and down the streets of Lichfield calling out, "Woe to the bloody city of Lichfield!" Fox by his very presence was nevertheless able to draw people into his cause. Such was the case when he met with the Seekers of Westmorland about the year 1652. They were a group not unlike the Quakers who had rejected church authority and sat in silent prayer at their meetings without either sacraments or priests. The Puritan preachers had been unable to reach them but Fox simply sat in silence among them and then finally stood up and spoke with irresistible and compelling power, such that the whole community was convinced that he was the one they had been waiting for.

George Fox took over from the Seekers the form of organization they had found effective, which was a system of monthly, quarterly, and finally a yearly meeting to which all were requested to attend. These meetings became an increasingly prominent feature among the Friends and Fox urged their importance on his followers.

About the time Fox had drawn the Seekers of Westmorland into his movement, a lady by the name of Margaret Fell, the wife of Judge Thomas Fell, Vice-Chancellor of the Duchy of Lancaster, heard him speak at Ulverstone. She was thirty-eight years old, but her husband was much older. She had borne him a son and six daughters and shared his Puritan outlook. She invited Fox to preach in her house and was converted along with many of her servants. Judge Fell was away on official business, but on his return to Swarthmore Hall he was immediately attracted by Fox's personality and offered him help and protection. Swarthmore Hall, a manor house in beautiful surroundings, thus became a refuge and a place of retreat for Fox whenever he needed one.

Margaret Fell (1614–1702) became very active in the movement and preached in public at a time when no church accorded women the right to preach. (Two other women, Elizabeth Heavens and Elizabeth Fletcher, also spoke in the streets, which prompted cartoons satirizing female preachers.) In 1664 Margaret Fell and George Fox were both sent to Lancaster prison for breaking the new restrictions imposed by the Restoration government. On their release they were married

LIFESTYLE

George Fox did not retreat from the world; in fact, he believed it was vital that God's people should express their Christian faith by active involvement in secular employment. Along with the Puritans, Fox was of the view that work was the sphere in which God's blessing and presence was manifested. Like the Puritans, he believed that it was important to live frugally, but at the same time to invest in business and to use profits for the welfare of employees and the local community. Quakers required endogamy, which amounted to "marrying under the care of the meeting." It was, however, not an easy matter to marry only a Quaker and over time there were a high percentage of "disownments" for breaking this particular rule. British Friends were also noted for prohibiting the marriage of first cousins even though the law of the land allowed it.

HELP FOR THE PRISONER

Fox was imprisoned on several occasions and knew from his own experience that people were often put in gaol unjustly. Early on he began to take an interest in his fellow prisoners finding out the reason for their sentences and demanding justice for the innocent. Fox was particularly incensed at people being condemned to death for stealing a cow or small financial dishonesty.

FACTORS THAT MADE THE SOCIETY OF FRIENDS SUCCESSFUL

Leadership

There can be no doubt that Fox was a man with remarkable "charisma." His preaching was always powerful and stirred the spirits of his hearers. He was particularly adept in his encounters with those who had formal theological training. William Penn noted that he "had an extraordinary gift of opening the Scriptures."[57] Along with many sectarian leaders, Fox was often guided in his actions by sudden impressions and on occasion he would make pronouncements in the street.

Early Quaker leaders included a number of able and talented women, among whom, most obviously, was Margaret Fell, who married George Fox in 1669. As we have noted, she was a woman of considerable means who put her resources at the disposal of Fox and the movement, but she was also a bold and forthright teacher. It has been argued that Gurneyite Quakers were not always positive in the public roles they gave to women.[58] Nevertheless, there were a number of effective female preachers and evangelists. Among their number was Rachel Metcalfe who left British shores for India in 1866 and Esther Butler from Ohio who engaged in work among the people of Nanjing in China. Prominent among Quaker reforming women was Elizabeth Fry (1780–1845), whose pioneering work in the prisons became known across the world. The third daughter of the London banker, John Gurney, devoted her life to the female prisoners of Newgate, and in her later years travelled widely in Europe promoting prison reform. She was also, in 1820, one of the founders of Nightly Shelter for the Homeless in London. An accomplished public speaker, she gave evidence on the state of prisons to the House of Commons select committee. Another prominent female, reforming Quaker was Catherine, the youngest daughter of Joseph Gurney. As a result of meeting a police officer and discussing the nature of his work, she founded the Christian Police Association. Her aim was to set before police officers the high ideal of life and service that is made possible through Christian faith and commitment. The work, which still continues to the present time, subsequently became international and an umbrella group known as the Federation of Christian Police Fellowships was later established.

---

57. Zarek, *The Quakers*, 78.

58. Dandelion, *An Introduction*, 158.

A Minimalist View of the Church

Fox was decidedly of the opinion that true worship must be, as Jesus declared, in Spirit and truth. His view of the church was minimalist. His meetinghouses were buildings without steeples and unecclesiastical in their appearance. There was no traditional or fixed service or ceremonial ritual of the kind that took place in the established church. Fox's congregations sat in quiet and waited until one or more of their number heard the Lord speak in the inner light of their heart. No one took the lead over the gathering or directed the others. Everyone who was present was capable of hearing God's voice. The organizational structure was also minimal and, as such, appealed to many in George Fox's day. For the most part, the Society of Friends has remained essentially a lay organization. Indeed, it is very possible that in the secularizing Western world of the twenty-first century, in which churchless Christianity is a growing phenomenon, this aspect of Quakerism will have an increasing appeal.

Emphasis on the Scriptures

As has been noted, Quakers set high store on the inner light of the Holy Spirit and regard this as the most authoritative source of God's word. Indeed, they maintain that truth was not closed off at the time when the New Testament was finally put together. That said, it is clear that Fox and the other leaders were devoted to the Scriptures of the Old and New Testaments and indeed affirmed that they were divinely inspired. Traditionally, Quakers were clear that standing behind the Scriptures is the living Jesus who speaks through them and in accordance with them.

Quaker Social and Political Action

Friends have a long tradition of doing what their consciences dictate is right and this has been strongly visible in their pleas for pacifism, an end to slave trading, and religious toleration. Perhaps above all, Quakers have demonstrated a fine tradition of caring compassion for the welfare of prisoners and employees on the factory floor. Nowhere was this more overt than in the great Quaker companies such as Rowntrees, Cadburys, and Frys. Not only were the laborers considered worthy of their hire, but the hire was made to be worthy of the laborers. This meant that employers were men of exceptional integrity. Individuals such as Henry Cadbury ensured that their workers were properly paid, housed in high quality cottages, and that they were given a good, cooked meal on site each day. During the First World War Quakers were active in relief and Red Cross work. They have also been at the forefront of a number of campaigns for reform, most obviously opposition to slavery, Corn Laws (in the nineteenth century), capital punishment, and harsh and unhealthy prison conditions. Quakers have reminded Christians that the kingdom of God needs to impact the working and social environment.

Courage and Conscience

The Friends were people of the Spirit who sought to hear God for themselves in the stillness of their own solitude and in the quiet of their worship. Their strongly experiential worship and spirituality led to their having compassionate hearts, particularly for the poor and needy. It was this fact, together with their determination to follow what their conscience dictated, that led to those who were employers exercising great care over their work forces.

9 | Early Wesleyan Methodism

THE SOCIAL SETTING

WESLEYAN METHODISM EMERGED IN the eighteenth century, an age that is well described by the opening words of Charles Dickens' novel, *A Tale of Two Cities*, "It was the worst of times and the best of times"—always depending, of course, on one's position on the social hierarchy. Dickens was actually describing the year 1775 and he wrote: "It was the best of times, it was the worst of times, it was the age of reason, it was the age of foolishness . . ." "We live," wrote the French philosopher, Voltaire, "in curious times and amid astonishing contrasts, reason on the one hand and the most absurd fanaticism on the other . . . a civil war in every soul."[1]

In the countryside the new progressive agriculture enabled the nobility to build gracious houses and, along with their tenant farmers, to live in ease and comfort and to eat from well-stocked tables. The rural laborers at their gates, on the other hand, lived in extreme squalor on a diet that consisted largely of bread, cheese, beer, and home-grown potatoes.

In the established church the Latitudinarians held sway with successive archbishops of Canterbury, John Tillotson (1630–94) and Thomas Tenison (1636–1715), calling the theological tune. The Latitudinarians believed that reason by itself could provide all that was needed in the way of truth. Reason could bring a person to faith in God. John Locke's volume, *The Reasonableness of Christianity*, published in 1695, marked this new emphasis on rationality, which meant that there was less emphasis on distinctive doctrines and greater emphasis on natural religion.

The wider Protestant church in Britain fell into two main groups: Anglicans and Dissenters. Neither was making any significant impact on the people. This was the age when Church of England clergy were preoccupied with hunting, shooting, and fishing. They were described by J. R.

1. Semmel, *The Methodist Revolution*, 6.

Green as "the idlest and most lifeless [clergy] in Europe."[2] Norman Sykes pointed out that half of all incumbents in the eighteenth century were absentees who lived away from their parishes.[3] The Dissenters were more conscientious, with a strong sense of duty, but their rationalism led many of them to deny the Trinity and preach Arian christologies.[4]

In London and the larger towns and cities the wealthy enjoyed an extravagant and often hedonistic lifestyle. The eighteenth century was the age of sinecures, bribery, and corruption. Prime Ministers Pitt and Walpole were sensuous and self-interested in their leadership. William Lecky wrote of Sir Robert Walpole's (1676–1745) brazen licentiousness as follows: "His personal habits were as gross and sensual as his mind was and his spirits were coarse. He was given to drunkenness and gluttony; he lived in open adultery; and having a taste for obscenity, the gross sensuality of his conversation was conspicuous in one of the coarsest periods of English history."[5]

This was an age in which the aristocracy protected themselves and maintained a semblance of order by means of a harsh and cruel penal system. Parliament ruled that there were more than 150 different offenses for which not only adults but children of both sexes could be hanged. A child could hang for stealing a gentleman's pocket handkerchief.[6] As late as 1820 Francis de Witt, the rector of Upper Slaughter in Gloucestershire and a local magistrate, recorded in his diary a visit he made to a young man he had committed to Gloucester gaol. His crime was sheep stealing. De Witt's entry read as follows, "visited the county hall and gaol. At the latter I had an interview with Joseph Palmer, a sheep stealer, whom I had committed and who had been tried, sentenced and left for execution. Though found guilty on the clearest and most direct evidence, this young man, persisted in denying his crime, at the same time he had every reason to believe he would be hanged the following Saturday."[7] Hangings were a frequent and popular spectacle with many of the rich willing to pay good money for a seat near the gallows. Criminals, so called, were dressed carnival style to add to the spectacle. In the year 1785 alone, nearly 500 people were

2. Green, *Short History of the English People*, chapter 10, sec 1.

3. Sykes, *Church and State*, 217.

4. Arianism took its name from Arius, a fourth-century Egyptian priest from Alexandria, who taught that Jesus was a godlike creation, but not himself God.

5. Lecky, *History of England in the Eighteenth Century*, Vol. 1, 365.

6. Trevelyan, *English Social History*, Vol. 3, 55.

7. Verey, *Diary of a Cotswold Parson*, 21.

sentenced to be hanged. In the absence of an efficient police force, violence, smuggling, and highway robbery were the order of the day.

In the eighteenth century slave trading reached its height. The practice had begun way back in 1562 when Sir John Hawkins took a cargo of slaves from Sierra Leone and sold them in St. Domingo. In the eighteenth century slave trading expanded hugely following the Treaty of Utrecht in 1713, which gave England a virtual monopoly of the trade with an agreed contract to supply 144,000 slaves in a thirty-year period. Horace Walpole, the fourth son of Sir Robert, noted in a letter that about 46,000 slaves were sold to the English plantations every year.[8]

These were years of drunkenness. In 1751 the English nation consumed 500 gallons of alcoholic drink per annum per head of the population. Signboards advertised, "Drunk for a penny, dead drunk for two pence. Free Straw." The huge consumption of liquor contributed to a downward spiral of poverty, starvation, and ill health. The high death rate was further increased on account of infants being breast-fed by mothers who had imbibed an excess of gin. Something of the extent of the problem can be gauged by the fact that when John Wesley was forty-seven years old, 506 of 2,000 houses in the parish of St. Giles, Holborn, in London were gin shops. In addition, in the same parishes there were eighty-two brothels also serving liquor to their clientele.[9] In 1791 a correspondent described the condition of the poor as "without relief, . . . without fuel, without food and the lawful means of procuring them." He appealed to the charitably minded to alleviate the miseries of the distressed part of their fellow creatures."[10]

Clearly, the eighteenth century was an age of drunkenness, violence, cruelty, coarseness, poverty, and disease in which there was little or no education for the common people. That said, it was not total darkness for, as J. W. Bready observed, "the multitude could still recognise nobility and respond to the touch of soul power."[11] It was into this environment that John Wesley came proclaiming the words of Jesus and doing the works of Jesus. He was indeed a challenging and thoughtful preacher and a man of deep social concern. In his discourse on the Sermon on the Mount, Wesley declared: "Christianity is essentially a social religion . . . to turn it into a solitary religion is indeed to destroy it. . . . [W]hen I say it is essentially a

---

8. Walpole, *Walpole's Letters*, Vol. 197.

9. Lecky, *History of England*, 487.

10. Wearmouth, *Methodism and the Common People*, 71–72.

11. Bready, *England before and after Wesley*, 137.

social religion I mean that it cannot subsist at all without living and conversing with other men."[12]

THE BEGINNINGS OF METHODISM

The originator of the Methodist revival was neither John nor Charles Wesley but George Whitefield (1714–70). For quite a time the British public regarded him as the movement's leader. Born at the Bell Inn in the city of Gloucester, he had risen to the position of "tapster" in that hostelry. From there he found his way as a servitor to Pembroke College, Oxford, at the age of eighteen. In this new environment he associated himself with the Methodists, led by John and Charles Wesley (on which, see later), and in 1735 underwent an experience that he afterwards described as the "new birth." He wrote, "I was delivered from the burden that had so heavily oppressed me. The Spirit of mourning was taken from me, and I knew what it was to rejoice in God my saviour." For some reason that isn't altogether clear, the Bishop of Gloucester took it upon himself to ordain Whitefield when he was below the canonical age of twenty-three, a step he soon had cause to regret. Whitefield proved a remarkable preacher, particularly in the open air. After his first sermon it was reported to the bishop that he had sent fifteen people mad. In truth, they had probably fallen under the Spirit and cried out for mercy. The bishop replied to the complainants that he hoped they would not recover before the next Sunday so that they might be spared a further dose.

From 1736–39 Whitefield was in America. He then returned to England and preached in the open air with remarkable effect, particularly to the colliers of Kingswood near Bristol. It was to Bristol that Whitefield summoned Wesley to come and engage in the work of field preaching.

John Wesley (1703–91) was one of nineteen children born to the Reverend Samuel and Susannah Wesley. Samuel Wesley was a Tory high churchman and incumbent of the Lincolnshire parish of Epworth. Young John nearly died in a fire, which appeared to have been started in the rectory by the active ill-will of certain local parishioners. He was, however, dramatically rescued from an upstairs window just seconds before the roof fell in and this was to the bystanders—and more especially to his mother, Susannah—"a sign of God's special interest in the boy." He was indeed, in the words of the prophet Zachariah, "A brand plucked from the burning." In consequence, Susannah resolved to be, as she put it, "more

12. Wesley, "Discourse on the Sermon on the Mount," *Works*, Vol. 3.

particularly careful of the soul of this child which God had so mercifully provided for."[13] It is no surprise that Wesley came to believe individuals might be "chosen" for certain tasks. Wesley regularly kept the anniversary of his rescue and had his name engraved under one of his portraits with the words "Is not this a brand plucked from the burning"?

After education at Charterhouse School John and his younger brother, Charles (1707–1788), went up to Oxford University. John was made deacon in September 1725 and ordained priest in September 1728. The following year he gathered together a group of very devout young people whose purpose was to encourage one another in the Christian faith. Later, in 1832, George Whitefield joined the group.[14] They regularly met together for prayer and study of the Greek New Testament and the works of William Law and Thomas à Kempis. They were devoted attendees at the sacrament of communion. It wasn't all piety however, and from the earliest days the group demonstrated their concern for the social well-being of others. Wesley and the members of the "Holy Club," as they were dubbed by their fellow students, visited the sick and the prisoners in Oxford gaol. Their methodical lifestyle earned them the nickname "Methodists." They agreed to observe a strict routine and method of study and practice in accordance with the statutes of the University.[15]

JOHN WESLEY

Missionary

Methodism owed much of its success and development to John Wesley's personality. Like his father, he was a Tory, a lover of the monarchy, and a high church Anglican. He was much influenced by the writings of Thomas à Kempis and William Law. Law's *Christian Perfection* and *A Serious Call* had a more profound effect on him than anything he had ever read before outside of the Bible.

In 1736 Wesley left England as a missionary to the new American colony of Georgia, having been tutor at Lincoln College from 1729–35. He had been invited by the governor, James Ogelthorpe, to be his chaplain. The American experience brought him to the realization that his own faith was lacking. On the outward journey, Wesley, along with other English

13. Semmel, *The Methodist Revolution*, 28.

14. Hattersley, *John Wesley*, 95.

15. Church, *Knight of the Burning Heart*, 48.

passengers on board the sailing vessel, *Simmonds,* was deeply impressed by the quiet behavior of a group of Moravian missionaries during a major storm (on which, see chapter 6). Once settled in the colony, Wesley caused friction by his rigid adherence to the Prayer Book formularies, refusing, among other things, to baptize infants except by immersion and excluding those he judged to be unrepentant from the Communion table. After two years he returned home disillusioned and sad. He wrote in his journal, "I went to convert the Indians; but, oh, who shall convert me?" Wesley still retained the memory of the Moravians who had been so calm during the storm and so, on his return to London, he decided to visit their chapel in Aldersgate Street; it was there that he experienced his evangelical conversion.

Evangelical Experience

Wesley's conversion took place on the 24th May, 1738. He later recorded it in the following words: "In the evening I went very unwillingly to a society in Aldersgate Street where one was reading Luther's preface to the Epistle to the Romans. About a quarter before nine, while he was describing the change which God works in the heart through faith in Christ, I felt my heart strangely warmed. I felt I did trust in Christ alone, for salvation; and an assurance was given me that He had taken away my sins, even mine, and save me from the law of sin and death."[16]

The key ingredient in this experience was assurance. For Wesley conversion was no longer a mere intellectual assent to an objective set of doctrines, it was also a subjective personal experience as the individual concerned encountered the living Christ who stood behind those doctrines. The experience of 1738 has been the subject of some discussion among church historians. There are those who are of the opinion that the year 1725 was his "first conversion" and that 1738 had to do with his assurance of that conversion. However, Wesley had, on his return from America, confessed himself unconverted, his words being, "Oh, who will convert me?" Nevertheless, Wesley had earlier written as follows at the time he was studying William Law in some depth, "But meeting now with Mr Law's *Christian Perfection* and *Serious Call* . . . the light flowed in so mightily into my soul, that everything appeared in a new view. I cried out

---

16. Davies, *Methodism,* 58.

to God for help, and . . . was persuaded that I should be accepted of Him and that I was even then in a state of salvation."[17]

Regardless of how we interpret Wesley's experiences, the fact is that 24th May, 1738, was a major turning point in his life. From this beginning the success of early Wesleyan Methodism can be traced.

THE APPEAL OF WESLEYAN METHODISM

After the Aldersgate experience of 1738 Wesley never seriously looked back. He preached wherever the opportunity arose, constantly stressing the need for personal salvation. Like his divine Master before him, the common people heard him gladly. Indeed, his message was to change the face of England. Wesley's success was due to a number of factors.

Wesley was a dynamic preacher and it is calculated that in the course of his lifetime he preached 40,000 sermons. He aimed always to preach "the plain truth to the plain man." A typical day in his life consisted of a journey of forty miles and four sermons. Thousands listened to him with rapt attention in the fields, on the streets, in churchyards, at pitheads, and outside factories. Wesley's proclamation brought people under conviction of their sinfulness and their need to seek Christ for forgiveness. Many were, to use Wesley's own words, "cut to the quick." Large numbers often sank to the ground and cried out for mercy. Others were reported to have lain motionless, as though dead. Bishop Joseph Butler of Bristol denounced Wesley's emphasis on spiritual gifts and his claim that demons could be exorcised as "a horrid thing, a very horrid thing."[18] Historians who have studied Wesley have put forward a variety of possible explanations for the falling phenomena. Some have suggested that some of the hearers suffered altered states of consciousness that had caused them to loose their hold on themselves. Others have suggested that the hearers were manipulated by Wesley's rhetoric or had been terrorized at the thought of hell or eternal damnation. The other possible explanation—that they were overcome by the Spirit of God—seems not to have been the explanation proffered by the majority of Wesley scholars. What cannot be overlooked, however, is that Wesley had a strong work ethic and that his other great gift was that of organization. In particular, he was able to arrange his followers into societies and train up people to be preachers and leaders. Each society was broken down into smaller groups, called classes, of a dozen or so members. Here,

17. Ibid., 48.
18. Hattersley, *John Wesley*, 151.

under the guidance of the class leader, who could be a man or woman, a weekly class meeting was held, at which each member was required to testify to their faith and teaching was given in an atmosphere of prayer and worship.

Wesley employed lay people at all levels in his societies and some he trained as full-time preachers. These he called "helpers." Such men and women were chosen on account of their personal knowledge of salvation. They were given a probationary period of one year with prescribed reading after which, if successful, they were appointed to a particular preaching place. In 1753 Wesley published *Twelve Rules for a Helper*, which set a demanding standard for those who were commissioned. Quite possibly as a result of his mother's influence Wesley took the radical step of choosing a number of female helpers, writing on one occasion, "God owns the ministry of women in the conversion of sinners and who am I that I should withstand God."[19] Some of Wesley's early helpers became quite well known, among them Thomas Olivers (1725–99), a Montgomeryshire shoe-maker whose hymn, The God of Abraham Praise, revealed a deep understanding of Scripture. Like Wesley himself, his helpers were plain spoken preachers; as the great Dr. Johnson of dictionary fame once observed, Methodist preachers were able to express themselves "in a plain and familiar manner, which is the only way to do good to the common people."[20]

FIELD PREACHING

One of the most prominent features of Wesley's mission was his open-air preaching. He began following Whitefield's invitation to come to Bristol and take up the work as he was about to leave once more for America. Although initially apprehensive, Wesley came to it as naturally as a duck takes to water. In 1782 Wesley declared that it was the main and constant business of a Christian minister "to preach Jesus Christ, and Him crucified."[21]

At this beginning time of Wesley's mission the great industrial revolution was already under way. Large crowds farm laborers were drifting from the countryside where they were no longer needed, on account of the more efficient methods of farming. These landless agricultural workers

19. Wearmouth, *Methodism and the Common People*, 227.

20. Semmel, *The Methodist Revolution*, 20.

21. Ibid., 56–57.

inevitably made their way to the new towns and cities. Here, in a new world of steam hammers and spinning jennies, they found work in the mills and factories of the new towns and cites that were springing up across the countryside. The established Anglican church was essentially rural and in these industrial heartlands there was, more often than not, no priest and no church. The need was therefore for unstructured preaching and teaching. Wesley's strategy was, in his own words, "to go to those who need you most." For this reason he concentrated his efforts on London, Bristol, the South West, and the North East. When no building was available to him he was always ready to preach in the open air.

Because of his focus on the towns and cities Wesley left large areas of rural Britain unvisited. He expressed a low view of farmers in general, declaring that "of all people they are most discontented."[22] Whether he was in town or countryside, Wesley was unconcerned about the parish boundaries. Needless to say, many local clergy were vehemently opposed to his excursions into what they regarded as their sacred territory. Wesley, for his part, responded declaring: "I look upon the world as my parish, thus far I mean, that, in whatever part of it I am, I judge it meet, right and my bounden duty, to declare unto all who are willing to hear glad tidings of salvation."[23] For legal good measure he added, "that as a Fellow of Lincoln College, he was ordained to preach at large."[24] In consequence of his extra parochial activities Wesley was asked on more than one occasion whether he thought it right to obey bishops. His reply was, Yes, in so far as conscience allows it.

ORGANIZATION

The Annual Methodist Conference of 1746 organized the existing Methodist societies into groups or circuits under the care of helpers who became known as travelling preachers. A circuit consisted of anything from twenty to thirty preaching places and the helpers moved round to each in turn, Sunday by Sunday. By 1753 there were twelve Methodist circuits and ninety travelling preachers. In 1756 there were twenty-six circuits and in 1776 the number had grown to fifty. The Annual Conferences exercised increasing authority over the affairs of the Methodist movement. The

---

22. Davey, *The Methodist Story*, 13.

23. Davies, *Methodism*, 78.

24. Hattersley, *John Wesley*, 152.

cohesion of the structure was further strengthened by grouping circuits together in districts. The financial support of the societies came largely from the members themselves. At the local level each society was broken down into smaller groups of twelve or thirteen known as class meetings. To be a Methodist member a person was required to take an active part in its weekly activities. As well as prayer and worship, each member was required to testify to their faith in Christ, relating evidence of it in the previous week. Each member contributed a weekly subscription of a penny, which was used to help the poor and to contribute towards travelling preachers' salaries, pension funds, and the building of new chapels. The class meeting created a powerful bond of friendship, care, and loyalty and enabled members to reinforce each others' Christian commitment.

In 1739 Wesley purchased a disused gun-foundry for £115 and converted it into a chapel and headquarters. About the same time two societies at Nicholas Street and Baldwin Street in Bristol set about building their own premises, which became know as the New Room. Wesley understood the power of property and from this moment on the Methodists were in the business of establishing buildings of their own on a wide scale, creating what was to all intents an ecclesiola or church within a church.

THE METHODIST EXPERIENCE

The uneducated poor were never going to be attracted or gripped by a religion that was largely intellectual and cerebral. They clearly needed a faith that was immediate, heart-warming, and experiential. It was here that Wesley's insistence on conversion of the heart and the witness of the Spirit were so vitally important. Conversions in early Wesleyan Methodism were almost always instantaneous. S. G. Dimond made a study of all the instances of conversion in John Wesley's journal. All but a handful of the 700 hundred or so conversion experiences described, he observed to be sudden. He summed up his findings in the following sentence, "In Methodism conversions are mainly instantaneous."[25] Wesley brought to evangelicalism the doctrine of the witness of the Spirit. Eighteenth-century Anglicanism sought to make its appeal to the intellect, the conscience, and the will,[26] whereas Methodism touched the feelings and the emotions with joy and compassion. As Wesley himself put it, "A Methodist is one who has the love of God shed abroad in his heart by the Holy Ghost given

25. Dimond, *The Psychology of the Methodist Revival*, 5.
26. Neill, *Anglicanism*, 423.

unto him." The distinguishing mark of Methodist conversion was its stress on the assurance of the Holy Spirit, whose presence strangely warmed the heart. Wesley stated it as follows, "the testimony of the Spirit is an inward impression on the soul whereby the Spirit of God witnesses with my spirit that I am a child of God; that Jesus has loved me and given himself for me; that all my sins are blotted out and I, even I, am reconciled to God."[27] On one occasion John Wesley wrote to his older brother, Samuel, "I believe that anyone who does not have the witness of God's Spirit with his spirit that he is a child of God should pray for it every day." Wesley's doctrine of conversion was also more consoling than the Calvinist alternative, which didn't offer such ready assurance. Indeed, in Calvinist thinking of the time the individual had to try and demonstrate to himself and others that he or she was one of the elect.

Perhaps the most debated aspect of Wesley's stress on experience was his doctrine of Christian perfection, the emphasis being that Christians can be perfected in the love of God. Wesley believed that this doctrine was taught in the *Book of Common Prayer*, most notably in the collect for purity at the beginning of the Communion service, which asks that the thoughts of our hearts may be so cleansed "that we may *perfectly* love Thee." Wesley didn't quite reach the point of teaching sinless perfection, but he clearly did believe that it was possible to reach a state in which temptation's power was diminished. The doctrine of Christian perfection was expressed in the following hymn.

> The thing my God doth hate
> That I no more may do.
> The creature, Lord, again create,
> And all my soul renew;
> My soul shall then, like thine,
> Abhor the thing unclean
> And sanctified by love divine
> For ever cease to sin.

FERVENT WORSHIP

Wesley's stress on Christian experience inevitably led to worship that was fervent and vibrant. At this point we must recognize the unique contribution of Charles Wesley, who must surely rank as one of the greatest

27. Rattenbury, *Wesley's Legacy to the World*, 97.

English poets. The words literally seemed to flow from his pen. In addition to his many preachments, Charles was the author of several thousand hymns, many of which have stood the test of time and are still sung to this day. Among them are "Hark the Herald Angels Sing"; "Lo, He Comes with Clouds Descending," and "O For A Thousand Tongues to Sing My Dear Redeemer's Praise." His hymns so aptly expressed the theology of the evangelical revival. This is seen, for example, in what is perhaps his greatest hymn:

> Love divine, all loves excelling
> Joy of heaven, to earth come down
> Fix in us Thy humble dwelling
> All Thy faithful mercies crown:
> Jesus Thou art all compassion
> Pure unbounded love Thou art;
> Visit us with Thy salvation
> Enter every trembling heart.

Many of Charles Wesley's hymns had repetitive choruses so that even those who did not read could imbibe the teachings of Methodism. For his reason Wesley described his hymn book as "a little body of practical divinity."

Another aspect of fervent early Wesleyan worship was the love feasts that Wesley had first encountered among the Moravian Christians he met in Savannah. Essentially they were the Agapēs, or love feasts. The central part of the Methodist love feast consisted in the sharing of a simple meal, which involved drinking from a loving cup and eating a small portion of bread or cake.[28] There was often vibrant singing and extempore prayers, which together with the eating and drinking served to create a strong bond of fellowship and unity among the worshippers. Love feasts were usually held quarterly and entry was normally by ticket. Wesley himself reported being present at a love feast on New Year's Eve, 1739, "where the power of God came mightily upon us, insomuch that many cried out for exceeding joy and many fell to the ground."[29]

---

28. See Baker, *Methodism and the Love Feast*, 15.
29. Hattersley, *John Wesley*, 145.

SOCIAL CONCERNS

From the very outset in the days of the Holy Club at Oxford Wesley had made the poor his particular concern. He frequently styled himself "God's steward of the poor." In 1757 Wesley said, "I love the poor; in many of them I find pure, genuine grace unmixed with paint [i.e., makeup], folly and affection."[30]

Wesley had a deep compassion for the needy. Just one year before his death we find him wading knee-deep through the snow on Bristol Streets collecting money and clothes for the destitute. In London he opened a dispensary for those who were too poor to afford medicine or medical help and he himself wrote a little book entitled *Primitive Physic*, which gives all kinds of remedies, practical help, and advice to counteract various ailments and sicknesses. Some of them seem strange, indeed almost superstitious remedies and have led to criticisms of Wesley's judgment.

Wesley was instrumental in starting a host of societies and benefit clubs for the needy and underprivileged. By 1850 a number of societies were giving basic medical care, making use of Wesley's remedies. Others lent small sums of money to their members or helped those who were unemployed find work. Such societies were later to become a marked feature of the evangelical world.

In addition to all of this Wesley was a constant writer. He used his pen to raise the issues of the conditions in the new towns, unemployment, the land question, taxation, the National debt, East India Company stock, the distribution of wealth, luxury, dress, money, intemperance, smuggling, the status of women, and above all slavery. He published an influential pamphlet on the subject entitled *Thoughts on Slavery*. He eventually passed the fight against the trade to William Wilberforce, who brought it to an end in 1807 after a lengthy parliamentary crusade. Wesley was perhaps the most powerful and active champion the working classes had during the eighteenth century.

LINKS WITH THE ESTABLISHMENT

This may be a debatable issue but it was probably the case that Wesley's success was due to the fact that he was a rebel within the established church. Once a person leaves an organization or an institution they lose

---

30. Anon., *British Methodism and the Poor 1739–1999* (MS in Methodist Archives, John Rylands Library).

the right to be heard and their concerns or criticisms are less likely to be listened to or taken note of. So rather than leave the establishment Wesley worked to reform it from within. He said on one occasion:

> I never had any design of separating from the Church. I have no such design now. I do not believe that the Methodists in general design it when I am no more seen. I do and will do all that is in my power to prevent such an event. Nevertheless in spite of all that I can do, many of them will separate from it. . . . In flat opposition to these I declare once more that I live and die a member of the Church of England, and that none who regard my judgement or advice will separate from it.[31]

He went even further and declared that "if ever the Methodist in general were to leave the Church of England, I would leave them."[32] Wesley was a curious mixture. He was a High Churchman and certainly no revolutionary. He kept a strict attachment to Church of England doctrine and valued the communion services, but he breached canon law and the parochial boundaries almost every day, preaching and forming societies—the "fresh expressions" of the day—in other people's parishes and on a widespread scale. Notwithstanding Wesley's commitment to the establishment, even before his death, Methodism had virtually become a denomination within it.[33] It had separate buildings and separate worship, including its own baptismal services. As early as 1755 Wesley discovered that some of his lay preachers were wanting to separate from the Church of England, and during his absence in Ireland in 1760 a number of them had begun to celebrate the Eucharist.

THE IMPACT OF WESLEYAN METHODISM

It has been calculated that Wesley left behind him more than 100,000 men and women organized into societies that were socially alive and concerned for the needs of the poor. In addition, it is recognized that four times that number of people were Methodists in heart and spirit and worshipped in Methodist congregations. The French historian, Elie Halévy (1870–1937), argued that it was for this reason that England was spared the bloody revolution that took place in France. Halévy asked the question, Why was it that

31. Baker, *John Wesley*, 322.

32. Armstrong, *The Church of England*, 62.

33. See for example, Chamberlayne, "From Sect to Church in British Methodism," 139–49.

of all the European nations England was most free of revolution? His answer was that the working classes and in particular their leaders had been captivated by Wesley's evangelical faith, which was opposed to revolution. In Halévy's own words, "the elite of the working class, the hard-working capable bourgeoisie, had been imbued by the evangelical movement with a spirit from which the establishment had nothing to fear."[34]

A number of others have echoed or supported Halévy's thesis. The sociologist, Ernst Troeltsch, in his *Social Teaching of the Christian Churches*, declared that Methodism was "one of the means by which the English World was rendered proof against the spirit of the French Revolution."[35] This view, that Methodism staved off a revolution, has also been supported by Marxists historians who regard religion as an opiate that inhibits the poor from rebelling against unjust social conditions. Edward Thompson, for example, in his *Making of the English Working Class*, wrote of Methodism's "box-like, blackening chapels" acting as "traps for the human psyche."[36] Again he wrote: "it is difficult not to see in Methodism in these years [1790–1840] a ritualised from of psychic masturbation. Energies and emotions which were dangerous to the social order . . . were released in the harmless form of sporadic love feasts, watch nights, band meetings or revivalist campaigns."[37]

Thompson was, of course, arguing that any proletarian revolutionary drive or energy that might have inspired the overthrow of an unjust social order was checked or channeled off by Methodist revivalism. In favor of this view that Methodism had a quieting influence are the following. Wesley was a High Churchman, an upholder of the status quo, and a lover of the monarchy. Both Wesley and Whitefield disapproved of revolution. Wesley indeed wrote tracts against the colonists of North America rebelling against English rule. Cornish Wesleyans, many of whom were tin miners, fishermen, and farm laborers nevertheless publicly expressed their pride that none of their number had taken part in any strikes during the early industrial period. It was observed that although Leicester was well known as a radical town with Luddite activists no Wesleyans had taken part in any radical disturbances. The governments of the day had noted that Wesleyans were loyal public supporters of the governing authorities. The Wesleyan Conference stood aloof from the militant and

34. Halévy, *History of the English People*, Vol. 1, 372.

35. Troeltsch, *Social Teaching of the Christian Churches*, Vol. 2, 721.

36. Thompson, *Making of the English Working Class*, 368.

37. Ibid., 369.

radical temperance movement, even though they were well aware of the dangers of alcoholic drink.

Some writers, however, have suggested that there were possibly other reasons why there was an absence of revolutionary fervor in the country. It has been argued that the governments of the day knew just how much downward pressure to exert on the working poor and when the moment was right to take the pressure off. The result of this was that there was no open rebellion. It has also been pointed out that there were large areas of the countryside where Wesley didn't go. The question then arises, Who or what quelled the revolutionary spirit in these areas? It has also been pointed out by W. R. Ward that far from exerting a conservative influence, there was a good deal of radical Wesleyan activity at grass roots level during the eighteenth century.[38]

Regardless of whether or not Wesley saved England from revolution, the fact is that Wesley changed the face of England. He made a major impact on the Church of England, opening its eyes to the plight of the poor, preaching a transforming gospel of hope, assurance, compassionate love, and practical action. His Methodist movement expanded hugely in the following nineteenth century and spawned a number of offshoots, including the more proletarian Bible Christians and Primitive Methodists in the first and second decades. Roy Hattersley summed up John Wesley as "one of the architects of modern England."[39]

FACTORS THAT MADE EARLY WESLEYAN METHODISM SUCCESSFUL

Dynamic Leadership

There can be no doubt that John Wesley was a dynamic and gifted leader. He combined scholarship with practical applied Christianity. He was an able communicator who, to use his own words, taught the plain truth to the plain man. Whether he was preaching in the streets or before the University, people flocked to hear him and they heard him gladly. The same is true of his writing, which was lucid and practical and covered the issues of life. Not only was Wesley a gifted communicator, he was also an able administrator and organizer. The Methodist structure that he established

---

38. Ward, *Methodism and Society 1790–1850*, 137–40.

39. Hattersley, *John Wesley*, 411.

held his converts together in fellowship and nurtured them in their new-found faith.

Experiential Religion

Wesley was an academic who lived in the age of enlightenment. He valued the rationalism of his day as was witnessed by his interests in the electrical experiment and medicine. At the same time, he was profoundly aware that cerebral religion of the Church of England was insufficient to meet people's deepest needs. Following his Aldersgate experience, Wesley was insistent on conversions that were definite and personal and that touched the feelings, "shedding the love of God abroad in their hearts." Wesley's Arminian gospel, in which the invitation to follow Christ was open to all, counteracted the fatalism of the age. No other form of Christianity was going to touch the poor, the majority of whom were unable to read or write, let alone understand a lengthy sermon or appreciate the liturgy. The witness of the Spirit of God implanted love and hope in the hearts of the ordinary people whom Wesley encountered in the streets, at pitheads, or outside the factory gates.

Social Action

Wesley was above all a social Christian who recognized that the words of Jesus alone are insufficient. For Wesley, right from his days in the Holy Club at Oxford, it was always the word and works of Jesus in concert. He made the cause of the poor his own. His was a dynamic, passionate, and caring Christianity that clothed the naked, fed the hungry, and defended the weak and marginalized. It is clear that the weekly class meetings provided group protection, mutual support, and encouragement, which sowed the seeds of later trade unionism. Wesley sought to apply the Christian faith to every level of society. We find him concerned over the increased population in the new towns, unemployment, taxation, the national debt, East India Stock, luxury, dress, intemperance, smuggling enclosures, and slavery, which he termed "the execrable sum of all villainies."

Lay Leadership

John Wesley's Methodism set a high value on every member ministry and lay leadership. At the class meeting the poor and uneducated learned the art of public speaking as they testified to their faith in Christ. With the passage of time, many began to read and write as they attended Sunday school. Wesley gave laymen and women the opportunity to lead and speak, both as local preachers and exhorters as well as full-time travelling helpers. All this resulted in a growing articulate working class who later raised up trade unions and organized co-operative stores and benefit societies. It was this fact that later caused Prime Minister, David Lloyd George, to remark, "The movement which improved the condition of the working classes, in wages, hours of labour, and otherwise, found its best officers and non-commissioned officers in men trained in the institutions of Methodism."[40]

40. Orr, *The Light of the Nations*, 91.

10 | The Primitive Methodists

IN THE TWO DECADES following the death of John Wesley Methodism became noticeably fashionable and prosperous and began to lose touch with its earlier roots among the poor. Indeed, John Wesley had referred to himself as "God's steward of the poor." An 1810 issue of the Tory journal, *The Quarterly Review*, highlighted this growing change, "Go into the collieries or the manufactures of Birmingham and Sheffield and inquire what are the practical consequences of Methodism wherever it has spread among the poor—industry and sobriety, quiet and orderly habits, and the comfort which results from it will be found."[1] Later in the nineteenth century people began to speak of Wesleyan Methodism having reached "the mahogany age," indicating that many of its members were sufficiently well off to buy expensive mahogany furniture. Around 1860 it was reported that crinoline dresses had conquered Wesleyan Methodist women and that in consequence numbers of them were finding difficulty getting through the door of their pews.[2] What all this meant was that by the beginning of the nineteenth century Wesleyan Methodism was becoming an establishment branch of the Christian faith and that the majority of its members were no longer willing to side with the poor and disadvantaged.

Wesleyan ecclesiology was adapting itself to this trend and becoming increasingly priestly and hierarchical, with many wanting a status for their preachers that would put them on the same level as the Church of England clergy. Many of the now upwardly mobile middle class congregational members had begun to fear anything that might hint of emotionalism or excess. Because of this changed attitude, those who were drawn to revivalism and wanted to see the fervency of early Christianity of the kind the Wesleys had preached began to be pushed out of the churches they had in some cases founded! Among those who suffered in this way were the Primitive Methodists. They were the largest offshoot from Wesleyan

1. *The Quarterly Review*, November 1810.
2. Obelkevich, *Religion in Rural Lindsey,* 208.

Methodism and were formed in 1811 by the joining together of the Camp Meeting Methodists and the followers of William Clowes.

The Camp Meeting Methodists owed their origins to Hugh Bourne (1772–1852). His father, Joseph, was a small farmer and timber dealer who lived life in the raw and was often drunk. He was also a stiff church-man and a derider of anything that might be described as vital religion. Inevitably, young Hugh Bourne grew up as a somewhat shy and retiring individual, but his mother, who was a God-fearing, gentle woman, spent quality time with him and taught him to read and write while she worked at her spinning wheel. Her nurturing created a real desire for learning in her young son and he eventually mastered the rudiments of Greek and Hebrew. In his early adult years Hugh Bourne worked as a carpenter, but his love of reading led to the event in 1799 that was to change his life. He recalled that one day, in his father's house, he surrendered his life to Christ. His words were:

> I sat reading in Mr Fletcher's *Letters on the Spiritual Manifesta-tion of the Son of God*, and realised the blessing named in John 14.21, where Christ says, "I will love him and will manifest my-self to him"; and He manifested Himself to me, and I was born again in an instant! Yea passed from death to life. The naughty was taken out of my heart and good put in . . . the Bible looked new; creation looked new; and I felt a love for all mankind.[3]

Following his conversion Hugh Bourne at once set about sharing his newfound faith in very intentional ways. He recorded in his journal that "my desire was that friends and enemies and all the world, if possible might be saved."[4] It was not long before Bourne succeeded in converting his cousin, Daniel Shubotham, who worked as a collier and together they engaged in some successful evangelism on the slopes of Mow Cop. As a result of their work a revival broke out in the small mining community of Harriseahead in 1801. It was a move of God that was to the dislike of the Wesleyan authorities. Harriseahead was, according to Kendall, "only slen-derly attached to the official Methodism of the area" and the general ethos was "much after the style of early Methodism."[5] One of its major features was "conversation preaching," rather than the formal pulpit proclamation favored by the Wesleyans. It was a kind of "in-your-face" speaking about Jesus. Cottage prayer meetings were held and many of them proved to be

3. Kendall, *History of Primitive Methodism*, Vol. 1, 12.

4. Ibid.

5. Ibid., Vol. 1, 31.

noisy affairs. Julia Werner noted that these gatherings were also popular because "they were held in rural areas where people were isolated and devoid of other forms of amusement."[6] Reflecting on these occasions, Hugh Bourne noted that "the people got to be, in a great measure Israelitish," by which he meant "noisyish." He quoted Ezra 3:12 and 13: "And the people shouted with a great shout . . . and the noise was heard afar off." Such was certainly the case of the meeting held in Jane Hall's cottage, where the door was left open and Elizabeth Baddeley, a miner's wife, clearly heard the prayer and worship coming from Harriseahead a mile away and was convinced of sin and her need of the Savior.

Bourne's ministry in this area was tolerated for a time by the Tunstall Wesleyan authorities and for a while his preaching places were listed on their circuit plans. Bourne was not a man who bent easily in the face of ecclesiastical pressure and events were soon to create a rift. Among them was his association with William Clowes (1780–1851), a man of similar spirit and vision. Clowes' mother, Ann, was a Wedgewood, related to the celebrated Josiah Wedgewood, and this family link enabled William to find employment at his uncle's pottery. Young William soon became an expert and found he could easily make twenty-one dozen plates in a day. His lifestyle, however, was raw and he spent much time dancing and visiting public houses, where he developed a reputation for gambling, fighting, drunkenness, and profanity. On one occasion, during a wake week, he even held a mock prayer meeting in a public house where the impiety was so extreme that many of the customers escaped into the streets with their mugs still in their hands. However, Kendal related that "where sin abounded, grace did much more abound" and in 1805 Clowes returned to his native area, clearly under the conviction of God. Clowes later recalled in his journal, "sometimes in sleep at night I have been agitated with terrible dreams, and starting up, I have been afraid of looking out of my bed, supposing the room to be full of damned spirits."[7] One of Clowes' friends, recognizing that he was in distress, took him to Bourne's new chapel at Harriseahead at a time when he had been reading the passage in 1 Corinthians chapter 11 in which the apostle warns of the dangers of taking the Lord's supper in an unworthy manner. When the bread and water of the love feast were being passed round Clowes mistook it for the Communion and feared that he was about to commit the unpardonable sin. The day

6. Werner, *The Primitive Methodist Connexion*, 180.

7. Clowes, *Journal*. In Kendall, *History*, Vol. 1, 54.

following he attended a cottage prayer meeting at which he committed his life to following Christ. Kendall recorded the event in the following lines.

> Conversion in his case was like some great upheaval of nature which changes the very contours of the landscape. His growth in Christian experience and knowledge was rapid. He discharged his debts, fasted and prayed, drew up rules for holy living, opened his house for prayer meetings, took part in efforts for repressing Sabbath breaking, became an active member of a Tract Mission, and as such walked many miles and did real evangelistic work in the houses of the people. He also became the leader of two classes, and in the course of time his initials appeared on the plan as an exhorter.[8]

At this point in time the revival around Harriseahead was much like a number of other local revivals on the margins of Wesleyan Methodism. However, Bourne had begun to take an interest in the reports in the *Methodist Magazine* concerning the frontier revivals in America, which related the great blessings that flowed from gatherings known as Camp Meetings. They were well advertised ahead of time and large numbers of people came with camping equipment and food for several days to these specially chosen sites. They were usually situated in quiet rural areas and the format was a mixture of fervent worship and prayer, revivalist preachers and exhorting sinners to the penitent form or pen at the front of the worship area. Bourne was particularly taken and impressed by Lorenzo Dow (1774–1834), who was one of the leading exponents of Camp meetings. It happened that Dow was on a visit to England and Bourne was able to invite him to Harriseahead. Dow, who had published a small pamphlet on the importance of Camp Meetings, urged on his hearers their great value both in stirring the sinner and in reviving those whose faith needed rekindling. After he had left the area it was decided to organize such a gathering and the venue chosen was Mow Cop. This celebrated and controversial meeting was held on 31st May, 1807.

The time at which it was held was one in which England was at war with France and there was still talk of revolution in the air. The authorities were understandably concerned about unlawful gatherings and were anxious to uphold *The Conventicle and Five Mile Acts*, which prohibited unlicensed preachers. Mow Cop was just the kind of event the Wesleyan Conference were trying avoid in order to portray themselves as upholders of government policy and the status quo. To make matters worse, some

---

8. Townsend et al., *New History of Methodism*, 563.

reports of the American Camp Meetings had made mention of instances of sexual license coupled with violent emotionalism, with people barking, jerking, and shaking. Although Bourne would probably have quashed any such behavior, the Methodist authorities were disturbed by the reports they heard and their Annual Conference at Liverpool in 1807 pronounced against Camp Meetings as "highly improper and likely to be of great mischief." Bourne, who was not one to be easily discouraged, soon organized a further Camp meeting at Norton-on-the-Moors, an event for which he was expelled from membership for breaking connexional rules.

Bourne now found himself responsible for preaching to and caring for thirteen places of worship. Undeterred by what had happened, he continued visiting and evangelizing the area and his group became known as the Camp Meeting Methodists. By 1809 things had progressed to the point where Bourne was able to engage James Crawfoot, as an itinerant evangelist. He paid him ten shillings a week and gave him instructions to labor alternately in East Cheshire and West Staffordshire. Crawfoot had been a local preacher on the Northwich Circuit, but had lost his position through having taken the pulpit for a group of independent Methodists at Warrington.

In June 1810 William Clowes, who had also been successfully evangelizing in the areas around Tunstall, was removed from the local preachers' plan, and in the following September his ticket of membership was not renewed for the reason that he too had attended Camp Meetings, contrary to the Methodist discipline. Many of those whom Clowes had brought to faith in Christ remained loyal and insisted on standing by him. They and others who subsequently associated with his activities were also removed from the Wesleyan class lists. Among them was James Steele, the Tunstall Sunday School Superintendent, and many of his members and scholars followed him. Clowes' followers became known as "Clowsites."

During the months following Clowes' expulsion he developed a close friendship with Bourne and some of his followers attended Bourne's Friday night revival services. Eventually, on the 30th May, 1811, the two groups held a joint meeting and agreed to come together and form the Primitive Methodist Church. The term expressed their desire to get back to the original Primitive Methodism of John Wesley.

HIGH VOLTAGE RELIGION

Primitive Methodists lived in a world in which Satan, heaven, hell, angels, demons, and witches were ever-present realities. Their religion was a high voltage experience. At its heart were powerful outpourings of the Holy Spirit accompanied by religious exercises such as jerking and shouting. Many of their meetings were focused on bringing the high power of God down on the assembled company through fervent singing, praise, and shouting. The experience of God's presence, which they tasted on these occasions, was more than enough to overcome the hidden fears and fetishes of rural superstition and haunted domains. Additionally, Bourne had discovered in 1809 that he had the gift of being able to impart the power of God's Spirit through the laying on of hands[9] and this, in turn, gave him the confidence to exorcise a demonic spirit from a woman in Harriseahead.[10] As a young man William Clowes had grappled with the Kidsgrove bogget (a female headless ghost) and later in life he had been disturbed by his encounters with a woman at Ramsor of whom Bourne wrote: "I believe she will prove to be a witch. These are the head labourers under Satan, like as the fathers are the head labourers under Jesus Christ. . . . For witches throughout the world all meet and have connection with the power of the devil."[11] Bourne related on another occasion how "he was struck down by the power of the Spirit" as he came home past "the praying place in Mr Heath's field." "I felt as if I was held by an irresistible power, and I sank down into nothing before it, and everything I did was contrary to God. I felt it die away. I gave myself up to God. Immediately came 'the spirit of burning,' and I was made 'a habitation through the Spirit.' I wondered at myself; I could scarcely believe what the Spirit witnessed."[12] These powerful experiences were fueled by a constant round of fervent revivalist meetings. William Clowes gave the following account of the way in which he encouraged religious exercises at the meetings that he organized.

> The class rapidly increased, until the house became so full, that there was hardly room to kneel. In leading my classes I used to get from six to ten to pray a minute or two each, and thus get the whole up into faith; then I found it a very easy matter to lead

9. Werner, *The Primitive Methodist Connexion*, 70.

10. Ibid., 70.

11. Ward, "The Religion of the People and the Problem of Control 1790–1830." Quoted in Cumming and Baker "Popular Belief and Practice," 242.

12. Ward, *Religion and Society*, 78.

> thirty or forty members in an hour and a quarter for I found that
> leading did not consist so much in talking to the members, as in
> getting into faith, and bringing down the cloud of God's glory,
> that the people might be truly blessed in their souls as well as
> instructed in divine things.[13]

Clowes went on to report that people who attended were converted in every room, including the larder. W. M. Patterson, writing in 1909, recalled a similar atmosphere in his account of some Primitive Methodist mission meetings in the North East of England: "the people fell in all directions and there was a strange mingling of shouts, groans and hallelujahs. During the revival at South Side, centres of gambling were broken up; confirmed gamblers burnt their dice, cards and books of enchantments; drunkards, hopeless sots were freed from the dread tyranny of fiery appetite. . . . The miracle was repeated again at Evenwood, West Auckland, and elsewhere, and at each place the converts became church workers and several of them local preachers."[14]

Some of this emphasis stemmed from Bourne's early association with James Crawfoot (1758–1839) and the "Magic Methodists" of the Delamere Forest, so called because they specialized in visions. Crawfoot was the youngest son of Thomas and Mary Crawfoot of the parish of Tarvin in Cheshire. He later wrote that "in the year 1783 in the twenty-fifth year of my age, I received the remission of my sins through faith in the blood of the everlasting covenant."[15] Soon after his conversion Crawfoot joined the Methodist Society and became a local preacher on the Chester Circuit. He was a great admirer of John Wesley and always went to hear him whenever he was in the city. The final words of Wesley's last sermon there were always in his mind: "Fellow labourers, wherever there is an open door, enter in and preach the gospel—if it be two or three, under a hedge or a tree: preach the gospel."[16]

Crawfoot focused his attention on the area around his home in the Delamere Forest and saw many sinners converted. He established a meeting in his own house on the last Saturday of each month for the promotion of holiness and those who attended became known as "Forest Methodists." At these occasions Bourne reported that "they increased their knowledge

---

13. Ibid., 77.

14. Patterson, "Northern Primitive Methodism." In McCord, *British History 1815–1906*, 123.

15. *The Primitive Methodist Magazine* 63 (1882) 355.

16. Ibid., 356.

of the deep things of God" and "learned how to bring down an influence that caused believers to thirst for more purity of heart." They also mastered the ability to remain in a state of "continual rest" in God and of "being clothed with majesty and power."[17]

After his exclusion from the Chester Wesleyans in 1807 James Crawfoot continued his endeavors in his local home area. It was at this time that both Bourne and Clowes got to know him and attended his meetings. During these occasions people often fell to the ground, some unable to rise until after the gathering had ended. This was called by those who attended "going into a trance or a vision."[18] Bourne accompanied Crawfoot on some of his local mission trips and found himself "greatly edified and blest with his conduct and conversations." Bourne wrote in the year 1810 of how "old James" opened many things to him and brought many souls to Christ.

It was also in that year that Bourne accompanied him on a journey to London to pray for Anne Chapman. She was a young woman who had been run over by a vehicle as she crossed the road in consequence of which she was unable to walk. Crawfoot had set his mind on this woman's healing and spent the whole night before his visit in prayer. Bourne recalled how on entering the room he pleaded and pleaded for her healing until his faith almost staggered. He appeared to see into her physical condition and "saw ulcers of the worst kind, with blood and purulent matter issuing from them." "Is it possible that God can cure this?," he kept asking. Then suddenly he called out, "O Lord God of Hosts, give the answer," and then he shouted, "I believe He can." Anne Chapman was powerfully touched and she was restored from that hour and the next day took a lengthy walk to attend a love feast where "she testified of the goodness of God and His power to heal disease, to pardon sin, and to sanctify the soul." Bourne called her healing "an astonishing miracle."[19]

Crawfoot served the Primitive Methodist Church as an itinerant for only four years but he continued preaching until his death in his eighty-first year. He died as he was out walking through a field with passers-by

17. *The Primitive Methodist Quarterly Review* 46 (1902), 587.

18. Ibid., 586.

19. Anon, "James Crawford: A Character Study," *Primitive Methodist Quarterly Review* 46 (1902), 583. It is interesting to note that the writer of this article suggested that Anne Chapman's healing was down to the fact that "Crawfoot possessed in a high degree this power of suggestion" (583) and again, "It is perfectly clear that Crawfoot had no knowledge of the results of the later psychical power which he possessed" (586).

hearing him shout out, "Glory! Glory! Glory!" moments before he fell to the ground. His very last words were, "Bless Jesus."[20]

It is not surprising that Primitive Methodism with its raw faith in demons and the world of unseen spirits lacked any sort of systematic theology. The "Prims" focused on a blunt dualism between heaven for the righteous and hell for the others. They had a strong awareness of the presence of evil and the demonic. Exorcisms and binding the forces of darkness were not infrequent. Writing of a later period, Robert Moore observed that the theology of the average Methodist adherent is "intellectually unsophisticated" and "totally unformulated."[21] Flora Thompson in *Lark Rise to Candleford* well captured the feeling of what Primitive Methodist meetings must have been like. She wrote that it was "a poor people's religion, simple and crude; but its adherents brought it more fervour than was shown by the church congregations and appeared to obtain more comfort and support from it than the church could give."[22]

STRATEGIES AND PROGRESS

Non-Mission Law

At first, the newly-formed organization made a deliberate decision not to try to expand too rapidly, but rather to confine themselves to the areas around Tunstall and Mow Cop. They felt God's call was that they should consolidate and build up their core following rather than engage in wide evangelistic activities that could have had the effect of weakening their home base area. This strategy of consolidating rather than immediate evangelism became known as the "Tunstall Non-Mission Law."[23] It was stated in the following lines, "Let us move cautiously; not weaken ourselves by covering too much ground, but confine ourselves within our present limits, and give our strength to building up our societies."[24] In 1814 Bourne put forward a series of rules that all the members were invited to

---

20. This information is drawn from the rest of the above article in *The Primitive Methodist Magazine* (1882) 356–58.

21. Moore, *Pitmen, Politicians and Preachers*, 118–19, 125.

22. Thompson, *Lark Rise to Candleford*, 125.

23. The term "Tunstall Non-Mission Law" was the name given to the strategy by those who were against it.

24. Kendall, *History*, Vol. 1, 189.

consider, change, or add too. They resulted in a church that was probably more democratic than any other in England at that time.

The "Tunstall Non-mission Law" was originally a term adopted by those who were opposed to it. However, with the passing of time, the policy was gradually ignored and Primitive Methodist preachers began to extend their endeavors along the river Trent.[25] In many ways this was an obvious strategy since roads were poor and rail travel had not yet been developed. By 1817 they had travelled as far as Nottingham and Newark and established bases in both places. From Newark missionaries pushed their way north, following the course of the Trent to Gainsborough, where they were able to start work in 1819. From these two points they were later able to fan out across the northern part of Lincolnshire and then move northwards into Yorkshire and up into the coalfields of Durham.

Other Primitive Methodist preachers continued southwards from Nottingham, possibly through Spalding and on to Kings Lynn, which became an established center in 1821. From there others went on to Norwich and Fakenham, which became independent centers by 1825. Other Primitive Methodist preachers and leaders headed southwards from Nottingham to Loughborough, which by 1822 became the center of a circuit that had forty-two preaching places on it, including Leicester and Coventry. By the middle of the nineteenth century Primitive Methodism was firmly established in four major areas: the South Midlands, the North West Midlands, East Anglia, including Lincolnshire, and the North East, embracing the coastal areas of Yorkshire and Durham. In 1811 the Primitive Methodists numbered only 200 members, but at their Conference in 1820 there were 7,842 members.[26]

Conversational Preaching

There can be no doubt that the importance Primitive Methodists attached to conversation preaching was an important factor in attracting new people into their congregations. The people who attended their gatherings were those whose education was minimal. They were not able to appreciate or stomach a carefully thought-out alliterated homily. Rather, they needed someone who could bring them face to face with the Jesus, who could release the power of his presence into their individual situations. Primitive Methodist local preachers were known, like John Wesley, as those who

25. Ibid., Vol. 1, 29.

26. Armstrong, *The Church of England and the Methodists*, 210.

preached "the plain truth to the plain man." Conversation preaching was a personalized way of relating the Christian faith to the issues of every day living at a time when Wesleyan Methodists were favoring more formalized pulpit preaching.

Charismatic Leaders

One of the key factors in the Primitive Methodist expansion was the number of dedicated and enthusiastic leaders they were able to produce. Although many were barely able to read, they were men and women of "charisma" (a term already noted, which the sociologist, Max Weber, used to describe individuals who had a captivating personality). They were men and women who were able to draw others after them and impart the vision. Such was John Benton (1775–1856). He was described by H. B. Kendal as "an unbending individual who would not be under anyone and who took his preachers' plan from no one."[27] On one occasion, when he was sent a copy of the circuit preachers' plan showing the places where he was appointed to preach, he returned it with the following lines scribbled on it.

> A plan from God I have to mind,
> A better plan I cannot find.
> If you can, pray let me know
> And round the circuit I will go.

Benton was virtually illiterate, to the point where a fellow local preacher once remarked to him, "You are bringing a scandal to the cause of Christ, you have no learning and you do not understand grammar."[28] A short while after this jibe Benton was delivering a Good Friday message based on the text, "It is finished." As he proceeded with his discourse, rough colliers started to fall under conviction on every side, eyewitnesses reporting that "some groaned, others shrieked and some fell from their seats." Benton, chancing to encounter the same local preacher who had scorned him, was unable to resist the temptation to say with decided emphasis, "This is grammar."

Robert Key (1805–76) was an early pioneer of similar caliber. Little is known of his early years save that he was born in the village of Upton-All-Saints on the Norfolk/Suffolk border and as an adult worked as a coal-heaver on the docksides at Great Yarmouth, where he kept company

---

27. Kendall, *History,* Vol. 1, 113.
28. Ibid., Vol. 1, 97.

with a gang of poachers, gamblers, and cock-fighters. He was converted to Christ in 1826 and became a travelling preacher two years later. In Victorian times he became known as "the apostle of mid-Norfolk" because he proved to be a major influence in the villages round East Dereham. He is recorded as trudging the roads and lanes of this isolated area often begging for hospitality. The years of 1825–42 were a remarkable period of expansion and advance in East Anglia. In 1825 the six Norfolk circuits had a membership of only 1,546 with thirteen ministers. By 1842 this had risen to a figure of 9,072 with fifty-nine ministers. Much of this expansion was down to Key's untiring labors.

Two others who illustrate the fervent early leaders of Primitive Methodism are William Braithwaite and John Stamp. Braithwaite, better known as "Hell-Fire Dick Braithwaite," was well known for his preaching and evangelistic endeavors in the regions surrounding Holderness. His message focused on the three "Rs," ruin, repentance, and restoration. Stories about him abounded. One convert reported that such was the power Braithwaite's diatribes that his (i.e., the convert's) hair stood on end to the point where his hat fell off! At the village of Appleby three men tried to push Braithwaite of the pedestal of the market cross, from which he was preaching. He responded to their violence by declaring that if any of the three died a natural death God had not sent him to preach that day. One fell from a church tower while drunk, another was gored to death by a bull, and the third was drowned.[29] John Stamp was a Primitive Methodist travelling preacher on the Louth Circuit from 1836 to 1839. He wrote of his years there, "I have walked more than 10,000 miles, have preached upwards of 1,500 sermons, and have visited near 6,000 families."[30]

Alongside the full-time preachers such as Key and Braithwaite, Primitive Methodism was, like the Wesleyan parent body, dependent on a host of lay preachers. In the case of the Primitive Methodists the majority of these men and women lived out their Christian faith in the fields, mines, and factories of rural and industrial England, where they worked long hours often in inhospitable and dangerous conditions. Yet they gave themselves unstintingly to preaching at the weekends, often walking many miles to their Sunday appointments. Flora Thompson described the way in which they formed the backbone of their church's mission: "They may have been unenlightened in some respects, but some of them had gifts no education would have given. There was something fine about their

29. Werner, *The Primitive Methodist Connexion*, 209 n. 44.
30. Obelkevich, *Religion and Rural Society*, 246.

discourses, as they raised their voices in rustic eloquence and testified to the cleansing power of the blood; forgetting themselves and their imperfections of speech in their ardour."[31]

Female Preaching

Following in the footsteps of John Wesley, Hugh Bourne, who authored a book in 1808 entitled *Remarks on the Ministry of Women,* was clear that women had an important role to play in both preaching and leading. Julia Werner pointed out that in 1818 one in five Primitive Methodist preachers was a woman.[32] Dorothy Graham in her study identified ninety female itinerants, and suggested that there may have been more.[33] Sarah Kirkland (1794–1880) was one of the first women preachers and although she was never formally appointed to a specific "station," she was held in high esteem, not least because she had been recruited by Bourne himself and played a significant role in establishing Primitive Methodism in a number of important places in the North Midlands.[34] R. W. Ambler observed that female preachers such as Ann Carr and Sarah Healand "linked early Primitive Methodism to the domestic lives of the rural workers of South Lincolnshire by helping to assert the role of women in providing a refuge against the stresses of social change through a religious experience in the home."[35] The high point of female Primitive Methodist preaching was probably the early 1840s since after 1842 no more women were appointed as itinerants, the last one being Elizabeth Bultitude who retired in 1862.

Camp Meetings

There is no doubt that the Primitive Methodist use of camp meetings was a very significant contributor to their successful evangelism. They were also a major cause of their separation from the Wesleyan parent body. While it was the case that William Clowes never took to camp meetings in the way that Hugh Bourne did,[36] they nevertheless were an important feature in

31. Thompson, *Lark Rise to Candleford,* 125.

32. Werner, *The Primitive Methodism,* 142.

33. Wilson, *Constrained by Zeal,* 206.

34. Milburn, *Primitive Methodism,* 15.

35. Ambler, *Ranters, Revivalists and Reformers,* 47.

36. Kendall, *Origin and History,* Vol. 1, 87.

the Hull diaspora over which Clowes presided. Julia Werner observed that in America camp meetings "reflected the vigour and rawness of frontier life" and that "rich and poor, black and white, farmer and townsman often came out of curiosity or to enjoy what was, after all, one of few major social events." She went on to observe that "both the pious and the scoffers were afflicted with the falling exercise and its variations, the 'barking exercise,' 'the laughing exercise,' and the jerks."[37] Werner also noted that, "although never recognised as an official institution of the American church, camp meetings were for more than a quarter of a century among the most powerful vehicles of frontier Methodism."[38] In rural England, where the Primitive Methodism took strong root, it was able to fulfill a similar social function bringing together those who otherwise would have lived isolated lives. Camp meetings were also the ideal vehicle to foster religious experience that brought excitement, catharsis, and wholeness to a segment of society who suffered long hours of work, harsh conditions, and had little in the way of joy or happiness.

IDENTIFICATION WITH RADICAL WORKING CLASS MOVEMENTS AND POLITICS

Trade Unionism

In the early days of Primitive Methodism the general view expressed by the Conference was that getting involved in politics had a damaging effect on people's spiritual life because unchristian attitudes would rub off on them. The Conference of 1835 asked the question, "What is the order of conference relative to speechifying or politics?," to which they made the reply, "That none of our travelling preachers be allowed to make speeches at political meetings, nor at Parliamentary elections. And it is strongly recommended to our local preachers to avoid such things." Conference then asked a supplementary question, "How shall the cause of piety be further guarded from injury?," and gave the response, "That none of our chapels or preaching rooms be lent on any account for either political or religious controversy."

However, as the decades passed it was soon abundantly clear that many chapels were giving this piece of legislation short shrift. Not only

37. Werner, *The Primitive Methodist Connexion*, 46.
38. Ibid., 46.

did large numbers of the local preachers enter the political arena to become trade union founders, leaders, and activists, so too did some of their full-time paid ministers. Primitive Methodists were at the forefront in the founding of mine workers unions in the Midlands, Northumberland, and Durham and the Agricultural Unions in Lincolnshire and East Anglia. Primitive Methodists were also active in the leadership of the Amalgamated Society of Railway Workers and in establishing some of the first Co-operative societies.

Total Abstinence and Teetotalism

Total abstinence was another cause with a political aspect[39] to it in which the Primitive Methodists took an active role. Somewhat surprisingly, the church did not finally establish its own temperance league until 1882 when members were encouraged to pledge, "I do hereby agree, by God's help, to abstain from all intoxicating drinks as beverages and will endeavour to promote the interests of this society." The reason for this late action was that from its very beginning the church had embraced temperance principles. Indeed, William Cutts had reminded Conference members in his Presidential Address of the same year that "from its very beginning the connexion has been on the side of total abstinence" and that "Mr Hugh Bourne was a total abstainer from all intoxicating drink before any total abstinence societies were formed in the country."[40]

The public start of total abstinence began on the 1st September, 1832, when "the seven men of Preston" made total abstinence pledges at the close of a temperance meeting.[41] Of the seven men, John King (1795–1885), Joseph Richardson, and Richard Turner (1790–1846) were Primitive Methodists. It was the last-named individual who was wont to say: "I am the happiest man alive for who can be happier than a teetotal Primitive Methodist!"[42] Significantly, several early missionaries who were sent out from Preston were also "Prims": James Teare (1804–68) was a Manx shoemaker who always spoke with an open Bible in his hands and Thomas Whittaker (1813–99) was often driven by images of hell that had remained

---

39. See Kent, *Holding the Fort*, 88, where the author points out that teetotalism had an appeal in that it enabled its followers to reject the social values and behavior of those they were supposed to regard as their superiors.

40. Scotland, *Methodism and the Revolt of the Field*, 163.

41. Kendall, *The Origin and History*, Vol. 2, 129.

42. Ibid., Vol. 2, 129.

with him since his Sunday school days. Another Primitive Methodist temperance worker was Richard Horne (1813–80), who hailed from Stoke-on-Trent. He took the pledge along with his father on 7th March, 1836. In 1845 he gave up his employment and worked full-time for the British Temperance League until 1876. Horne's diary records that in the year 1868 he delivered 234 temperance lectures, besides preaching most Sundays. He also noted that he had travelled 7,166 miles and that 62,140 attended his meetings, with 530 people signing the pledge.[43]

Other factors that contributed to the early success and growth of Primitive Methodism were the founding of the Book Room in 1821 at Bemersley in Staffordshire, with Hugh's brother, James, as its President, and the publication of the denominational magazine, with Hugh Bourne serving as editor until 1842. The Book Room printed a huge volume of spelling books, tracts, cheap literature, and Sunday school material.

PROGRESS AND IDENTITY WITH THE POOR AND WORKING CLASS MOVEMENTS

The Primitive Methodists expanded rapidly, reaching a membership of 33,507 by 1824, with 266,555 attending their places of worship on the last Sunday in March 1851, when the Religious Census was held.[44] The church continued to expand until the First World War. In 1932 it joined with the Wesleyans and the United Methodist Church in a major reunion scheme.

The one thing that can be said of the Primitive Methodists is that of all the churches in British history, they came the closest to winning the masses over to the Christian faith. The President of their 1875 Conference was absolutely right when he said, "No church in Great Britain is proportionately so largely connected with the working classes." If evidence were wanted for this fact it can be found by a cursory glance at almost any baptismal register of the mid-Victorian years. A survey of the Swaffam Baptismal Register for the years 1849–53 revealed the following occupations of the father of each family: laborers 67, shepherds 4, rat catchers 1, farming bailiffs 1, farmers (probably small holders) 2, mole catchers 2, woodmen 1, fellmongers 1, blacksmiths 6, sawyers 1, tanners 1, groom 1, railway laborers 1, shoemakers 7, carpenters 14, butchers 3, bakers 2, hucksters 2, brick layers 3, dealers 2, painters 1, plate layers 1, machine makers 1, publicans 1, pensioners 1, coopers 1, ministers 1, servants 1, and

43. *Primitive Methodist Magazine* 5 (New Series) 247–49.

44. Thompson, *Nonconformity in the Nineteenth Century*, 153.

footmen 1.[45] A. D. Gilbert also studied baptismal registers and found that Primitive Methodism had "almost twice the average representation among the unskilled."[46] It is certainly apparent from Kendall's account that in the 1820s Primitive Methodist missionaries were making effective inroads among the Luddites of the Midlands, the fishing communities of Filey and Flamborough and along the North Yorkshire coast, the miners of the midlands, Northumberland, and Durham, as well as the rick-burning farm laborers of Lincolnshire and East Anglia.

Methodism contributed in several ways to the growth of unionism, most notably by providing a basic training in public speaking and in business skills in a way that other denominations did not. In addition to the provision of Sunday schools, it gave men opportunities to stand in front of their fellows as exhorters, local preachers, and class leaders. Such offices as chapel and society steward provided a chance to learn simple business and administrative skills. In addition, Methodist conversion instilled in many ordinary men and women a sense of self-worth and dignity and gave them a desire to better their place in society. The result of all this was that many of the more articulate laborers were Methodists.

Methodist organization, with its three-tiered system of national Conference, circuit, and local chapel provided a model that many trade unions either adapted or used wholesale. Joseph Arch (1826–1919), a Primitive Methodist local preacher and champion hedge-cutter, founded the National Agricultural Labourers' Union, which had an annual conference, geographical districts somewhat akin to Methodist circuits, and local branches that often met in chapels. It is very likely that the union ticket derived from the Methodist class ticket. Trade union meetings in Victorian times often had the air of a Methodist chapel about them as members sang trade union hymns, uttered prayers, quoted Scripture, and concluded their business with the grace. A number of trade unions organized union camp meetings that were clearly inspired by the Primitive Methodism of their leaders. Many significant early trade union leaders came from the ranks of the Primitive Methodists. Among them were Thomas Hepburn (1795–1864), who formed the first mine-workers union at Durham, John Seaman (1865–1934), who founded the Wheelwrights' Operative Union,[47] and George Edwards (1850–1933), who founded the Allied and Agricultural Workers Union in 1906.

45. *Swaffam Primitive Methodist Baptismal Register.*
46. Gilbert, *Religion and Society in Industrial England*, 65.
47. See his obituary, *South Western Star*, 12th October, 1934.

FACTORS THAT LED TO THE SUCCESS OF PRIMITIVE METHODISM

Their Clear Mission Focus

Primitive Methodist Mission was sharply focused on one particular people group. From the very beginning their evangelistic efforts were focused on the working classes. Everything they did, in what James Obelkevich described as their "heroic age of missionary expansion" and "their age of revivalism and consolidation," was focused on the working poor.[48] They built chapels that were plain and much in the style and appearance of large versions of laborers' cottages, where the poor didn't feel uncomfortable or out of place. Their preaching was conversational in style and their content always straightforward and easily understandable. Their religion offered a fervent and immediate experience of the risen Christ and the intensity of their singing and praying offered a catharsis that was able to touch the lives of those who lived and worked in the raw environment of fields and the damp and heat mines and factories of the Industrial Revolution.

Local Leaders

From the very beginning, the Primitive Methodists trained and made use of local leaders who were largely drawn from the working poor whom they sought to reach with the Christian message. Some of their number could barely read or write. Such, for example, was Robert Waters, a trade union activist from Freethorpe in Norfolk. At the time when he preached his first sermon "he could only read very little, but so little that he had to confine himself to familiar hymns and portions of Scripture." One Methodist journal recorded some of his mistakes. "Behold I show you a great monster," he read out to the church one day, "that'll be the devil no doubt," was his comment. His wife who happened to be sitting near to the pulpit corrected him, "It's not monster but mystery." Robert apologized to the congregation, "I'm not learned, and I made a mistake, 'Behold I show you a great minister.' That's the Lord Jesus, there's no doubt!"[49] By taking on these local men and women the Primitive Methodist leaders were making use of those who could readily identify and relate to the people they were trying to reach. More importantly, they could explain the Christian

48. Obelkevich, *Religion and Rural Society*, 220.
49. *Primitive Methodist Leader*, 8th December, 1910.

message in a way that was in their idiom and their culture. In this respect they were, of course, following the model of Jesus, who himself chose his core helpers from the working men and women of his own locality. Too many Christian communities collapse because they become dependent on those who are brought in from outside their culture and community. They perhaps stay only for a limited period of time without ever really being able to embrace or understand the cultural setting in which they find themselves. Ideally, the local Christian community needs, like the New Testament churches, to be locally self-supporting and self-sustaining.

Their Involvement with Social and Political Issues

The working poor were drawn to Christ in large numbers by the Primitive Methodists on account of their involvement in political issues and most notably their founding and active support of trade unions. The laboring classes were aware that here were people who cared for their human rights and championed better working conditions on the basis of biblical justice. They felt a strong degree of solidarity with their local preachers, who were their leaders, stewards, and Sunday school teachers. This was their church that they felt they owned. Their preachers didn't engage in occasional acts of charity, like their Church of England counterparts, out of a sense of duty or because they were paid to. Rather, they fought for conditions that would make the charitable donations of broth and blankets unnecessary. Furthermore, many of their number did not give credence to a fixed social hierarchy, which believed that some were born to privilege and money while others had been decreed to labor for a mere pittance and be content, as Prayer Book Catechism put it, "with that state wherein God had been pleased to call them." The Primitive Methodist Sunday Schools and the experience of public speaking as local preachers or simply sharing a testimony at a love feast equipped men and women to be leaders in the worker-day world who could organize meetings and argue their case from the union or public platform.

11 | The Salvation Army

WILLIAM BOOTH (1829–1912), THE son of a pawnbroker, was converted in a Wesleyan chapel in Nottingham in 1844. He was a young man with high ideals and had been attracted by the powerful speaking of the Chartist leader, Feargus O'Connor (1794–1855), as he confronted the poverty of the industrial laborers who toiled in the mines and factories.[1] He was also powerfully influenced by the preaching of James Caughey (1810–91), an American revivalist who held meetings in Nottingham for six weeks in 1846. Young William was particularly struck by his variety of pulpit gestures and his ability to speak directly to certain individuals sitting in his congregations, which sometimes numbered as many as 3,000 people. Caughey preached for instant and absolute conversions and for sanctification, which could also take place in a single moment.

In 1852 William met Catherine Mumford (1829–90) and they were married on 17th June, 1855, in Stockwell Green Congregational Church. In 1854 he left the Wesleyan Reformers and joined the Methodist New Connexion, another Methodist offshoot that had been formed in 1797 by Alexander Kilham (1762–98). Booth was admitted into their Connexion as a full-time minister on Monday 28th May, 1858. However, even they were unable to hold him within their ecclesiastical system for very long and their 1861 Conference ordered him to desist from engaging in independent evangelistic work. It was not, however, in Booth's nature to respond to such a request and in August of that year he began a series of revival meetings in Cornwall. His time there demonstrated his remarkable powers as an evangelist with the *Wesleyan Times* giving the following report: "During the eighteen weeks Mr and Mrs Booth conducted their services in Redruth and Camborne at least 3,000 souls were brought to Jesus. . . . At Redruth we hear the Free Church has given £1,500 for ground and they are building immediately the largest chapel in the country. . . .

---

1. Begbie, *The Life of William Booth*, Vol. 1, 54–57.

Since Mr and Mrs Booth commenced their evangelistic work in Corrnwall 7,000 souls have been awakened and saved."[2]

Eventually, in June 1862, the Annual Conference of the Methodist New Connexion accepted Booth's resignation. By this time William had come to the view that the very poor were not going to be reached through the mainline churches or indeed the independent chapels. Catherine shared his opinion on the matter and wrote on one occasion, "The more I see of fashionable religion, the more I despise it; indeed, how can fashionable religion be other than despicable." In 1865, the Booths, who had settled in London, erected a tent in Whitechapel and so began what they billed as "The Christian Mission to the Heathen of Our Own Country." The East End was an area where the church was scarce and gin shops and poverty were close companions.[3] Booth wrote at that time, "I found my heart being strongly and strangely drawn out on behalf of a million people living within a mile of the tent, ninety out of a hundred of whom, they told me, never heard the sound of a preacher's voice."[4] In November 1868 William announced his plan to buy the People's Market in Whitechapel and turn it into the People's Mission Hall. By the close of the following year the Mission had thirteen preaching stations, which between them held 140 services per week. A variety of activities were organized, including reading, writing, and arithmetic. By 1870 the Christian Mission had twenty-nine separate missions, which were run by thirty full-time ministers.[5] At the end of 1878 there were twenty-nine Mission stations, 127 full-time ministers and evangelists, and an average Sunday attendance of 27,280.[6] In 1882 there were 440 Salvation Army Corps, staffed by 1,019 officers. In 1883, there were 634 corps and 1,541 officers. By 1884 the figure had reached 910 corps and 2,332 officers.[7] By 1882 the Salvation Army had outposts on all five of the world's continents. In the first appendix of his book, *In Darkest England*, William Booth spelled out "the position of our forces." In the United Kingdom there were "1,375 Corps or Societies with 4,506 officers and overseas there were 1,499 Corps with 4,910 officers."[8]

2. Hattersley, *William and Catherine Booth*, 135.

3. Collier, *The General Next to God*, 45.

4. Hattersley, *Blood and Fire*, 152.

5. Ibid., 213.

6. Ibid., 239.

7. Ibid., 284.

8. Booth, *In Darkest England*, Appendix 1, "The Salvation Army—A Sketch—The Position of Our Forces."

Booth commented that "the maintenance of all this system has, of course, been largely due to the unqualified acceptance of military government and discipline."[9]

Throughout these early days the Salvation Army encountered a good deal of opposition, not least from the Skeleton Armies that were founded in Exeter and Weston-super-Mare with the stated purpose of "disrupting meetings." The idea spread quickly and many others were established in different parts of the country, some of them backed by the brewers and encouraged by the lenience of the local magistrates. During the course of 1882 it was reported that mobs attacked the Army from Bath to Arbroath and from Guildford to Forfar, with William Booth complaining that 669 Salvationists, 251 of them being women, were injured and fifty-six Army buildings damaged.[10]

BOOTH'S VISION

William's heart was always for the poor. One day, following a late night walk through some of the East End slums, he observed that about every sixth building was a public house, many of them having steps at the bar so that little children could climb up and order gin. He related his experience to Catherine stating, "I seem to hear a voice sounding in my ears, 'Where can you go to find such heathen as these, and where is there so great a need for your labours?' Following which he exclaimed, 'Darling I have found my destiny!'"

Nevertheless, William and Catherine's vision was a soul-saving venture. It was forcefully expressed by Catherine in a letter to *War Cry* in July 1881: "Oh! How I see the emptiness and vanity of everything compared with the salvation of the soul. What does it matter if a man dies in the workhouse? If he dies on a doorstep covered with wounds, like Lazarus— what does it matter if his soul is saved?"[11] Two years later William wrote a letter to *the Pall Mall Gazette*, during the controversy over *The Bitter Cry of Outcast London*, in which he warned that it was not an issue that could be solved by bricks and mortar alone.

In order to bring London's East Enders to faith in Christ the Booths used assistants who were themselves genuine working men and women. Among their number were a blacksmith, a navvy, and a sailor. Two such

9. Booth, *In Darkest England*, Appendix 1, vii.

10. Hattersley, *Blood and Fire*, 276.

11. *War Cry*, 7th July, 1881.

men who became prominent in the Army's work were Elijah Cadman (1843–1927) and George Railton (1848–1913). Cadman was a chimney sweep and professional boxer. Like many working poor he was illiterate until his wife taught him how to write. When he first met William Booth he was said to have been so overwhelmingly impressed that he cried out, "I'm in love with him! He's a man!" As William saw it, these people could speak to the working men as those who belonged to the same class and had coped with the same experiences.

Like John Wesley, the founder of the Methodist Church from which he had come, William Booth was an able and passionate preacher. Like Wesley, he spoke "the plain truth to the plain man" and he spoke with passion and with power. As Roy Hattersley observed, "More often he insisted that scholarship stood between simple believers and uncomplicated belief."[12] Booth had a very strong sense of the presence of Christ in his life and his faith was simple and straightforward. He was in every way God's soldier truly and sharply focused on his vision to reach "the submerged tenth" with the Christian gospel. Despite every kind of opposition and discouragement, William Booth was driven onwards and upwards by his passion to save lost souls.

A MILITARY VENTURE

William Booth's Methodist background impacted much of what he did and planned for his new organization. John Kent has argued that the authoritarian, domineering behavior and decisions of the Methodist Conferences inclined and influenced Booth into becoming a dictator. In the early days of his Christian Mission Booth had styled himself as "the General Superintendent," but in September 1878 his journal described him as simply "the General" and went on to state that the Christian Mission had organized "a Salvation Army to carry the blood of Christ and the fire of the Holy Ghost into every corner of the earth."[13] The theme of the Mission's annual congress for that year was "Our War Congress."

Booth was not the only Victorian to think and organize his followers in a military way. It had been done by the Leicester Chartists—led by Thomas Cooper, who had formed Hallelujah Bands—and some of their members had even transferred their loyalties to Booth's organization. Additionally, some temperance pioneers had made use of warfare imagery

12. Hattersley, *Blood and Fire*, 4.
13. Begbie, *Life of William Booth*, Vol. 1, 437.

by styling themselves as "the Blue Ribbon Army" and requiring an army style pledge of total commitment and loyalty. This was, of course, the age of empire, in which British Imperialism was establishing colonies across the globe, many of them supported by garrisons of soldiers. The English church-going public was becoming both comfortable and familiar with things military. It was reflected in some of the popular hymns of the period. Among them were J. S. B. Monsell's Fight the Good Fight and Sabine Baring-Gould's Onward Christian Soldiers. Booth, like many young boys, had enjoyed playing soldiers and in his later life read and made frequent reference to the rules and regulations of the British military.

Not surprisingly Booth, like many sectarian leaders, became deeply committed to the value and necessity of dictatorship and in this he was enthusiastically supported by his closest assistants, George Railton and his son Bramwell. In his celebrated and best-known book, *In Darkest England*, Booth had written that "despotism is essential to most enterprises" and this was a principle that he came to practice on a wide scale. He could order an officer to move to an overseas posting of forbid marriage outside the army. He could tell officers how they were to organize meetings, right down to smallest details. In his later years, as Roy Hattersley has pointed out, this type of behavior was very difficult for some of his aids to cope with. Some critics were of the view that Booth's dictatorial leadership infringed the intrinsic rights of human liberty. His reply was that "liberty must be abridged if doing so would secure greater good."[14] The Mission's constitution gave Booth the right to continue as the General Superintendent of the Christian Mission for the rest of his life unless he decided to resign or was unable for some reason to discharge his duties.

Some objected to the military emphasis of the Salvation Army, feeling that it did not sit comfortably with Jesus' teachings of loving one's enemies and turning the other cheek. On the other hand, Booth's defenders were ready and quick to point out that the New Testament urged Jesus' followers to "put on the whole armor of God" and "to fight the good fight."

ARMY DOCTRINES AND STRATEGIES

Theology

As in any military organization, the Salvation Army's battle strategies had to be explicitly clear so that every soldier would know and understand

14. Booth, *In Darkest England*, 24.

what they were about. This meant that the Army's doctrines needed to be plain and straightforward. One of the army's early official catechisms stated that their beliefs could be summarized in the following lines, "Utter ruin through the fall; salvation alone from first to last through the atonement of Christ by the Holy Spirit; the great day of judgement with its reward of heaven for ever for the righteous and hell for the wicked."[15] Every soldier was also expected to maintain the highest moral standards. The *Articles of War*, which every soldier was required to sign, included a declaration to "abstain from the use of intoxicating liquor, from the use of tobacco in any form, and from the non-medical use of all addictive drugs." Another pledge was abstinence "from the use of all low or profane language and from all impurity, including unclean conversation, the reading of any obscene book or paper at any time, in any company, in any place." Each soldier also had to swear "that I will never treat any person whose life, comfort or happiness may be placed within my power, in an oppressive, cruel or cowardly manner; but that I will protect such from evil and danger so far as I can, and promote, to utmost of my ability, his present welfare and eternal salvation."[16]

In the early days of the Army there was a strong emphasis on the second coming of Christ, but with the passing of time Booth's focus was increasingly put on "present action" and working to improve the circumstances of the present. His social scheme, which he set up in 1890, was essentially a secular vision of a Utopian kind, which would be achieved by establishing a wide-ranging series of welfare institutions. Booth did, however, expect the return and reign of Christ "to be preceded by further and mightier outpourings of the Holy Ghost than any yet known," although he was also of the view that millennium "would consist of righteousness and the prevalence of love." In his later years his focus became increasingly non-millennial with the emphasis on the reign of Christ today.[17]

Brass Bands and Music

Alongside this clear teaching and strict moral code Booth developed worship that was at the same time both lively and appealing to the working poor. He realized the importance of fervent singing and, like his Methodist

15. Anon, *All About the Salvation Army*, 16.

16. *Articles of War*, declaration section.

17. Robertson, "The Salvation Army: the Persistence of Sectarianism." In Wilson, *Patterns of Sectarianism*, 73–74.

forbear, Charles Wesley, recognized that songs were the best way of instilling truth into the lives of those who were unable to read or write. On one occasion Booth exclaimed, "Why should the devil have all the best tunes?" He was not impressed by the more formal expressions of worship in some of the denominational churches and dropped the word hymn in favor of the word "song." In his later years he began to write words that would go with popular music hall tunes. In 1879 he opened his own music department in order to produce the particular brand of music that he felt would appeal to the masses. In keeping with the military ethos, Booth introduced military bands, the first of which was in Salisbury. Among other benefits, their capacity to drown out all music but their own proved to be an effective means of overcoming the opposition that often came from hecklers. The army's worship was often accused by his opponents of being mere music hall entertainment, to which Booth's response was that nothing else would make sufficient appeal. His own co-worker, Elijah Cadman, responded to the criticism that he made a lot of noise with the retort that there will be a great deal more in hell.

Advertising and Publicity

As well as their appealing music the Army began to make use of eye- and mind-catching advertising strategies, many of them being devised by William Cambridge. Among his best-known pamphlets were "The Hallelujah Railway Ticket" and "The Up-line to Heaven and the Down-line to Hell." He also wrote a little book that offered shares in the Salvation mine, which were "a hundred per cent guaranteed in this life" and with life everlasting in the world to come. John Irvine, in his biography of Booth, recounted the memorable tactics of the Wiltshire officer, James Dowdle, who would stand with his umbrella aloft to attract attention.[18] There were many Salvation Army advertisements on a military theme. One such was posted in Sheffield announcing various activities in the Attercliffe area. It was headed with the words "Reader—If you are not SAVED, you will go to HELL! 'Believe on the Lord Jesus Christ and thou shalt be saved." Underneath, the program of events began with the motto "BLOOD AND FIRE!" Followed by:

> LOOK OUT! LOOK OUT! CAPTAIN MORRELL and soldiers
> of the 37th Corps (Regulars) will challenge the DEVIL FOR War

18. Irvine, *God's Soldier*, Vol. 1, 357.

and make a SPECIAL ATTACK on his Territory. . . . Guns loaded at 7.00 a.m.: First Volley fired at 10.00 a.m., NEWHALL ROAD. Musical instruments in the Battle Field. Wounded picked up as we go along and handed over to THE GREAT PHYSICIAN. CAPTAIN MORRELL (Better known as the DEVIL DRIVER), from Leicester, letting the enemy have it right and left. Barracks at 11, with garrison kept by Captain Morrell. A HOST OF DARE DEVILS!! will repeat the firing on the Battle field. Again at PINFOLD LANE, at 2.00 p.m., right in front of the Enemy, And from thence march off to the VESTRY HALL, where they will arrive at 3.o'clock p.m.

Holiness Meetings

Those who accepted Booth's message and enlisted in his forces were encouraged to attend one of the army's holiness meetings. In a way this emphasis should not surprise us since his roots were still deeply embedded in Methodism and John Wesley had aimed to "spread Scriptural holiness throughout the land." Booth himself had been converted in a Methodist revival and retained a very strong sense of the presence of Christ in his life. That said, holiness and holiness meetings had become popular on both sides of the Atlantic, increasingly so after the end of the American Civil War, when many Christians had begun to feel guilt over the huge loss of life that had taken place in the struggle over the slavery issue. A number of revivalists came to England from America and held extensive meetings for sanctification. Among their number were Walter and Phoebe Palmer. John Kent has made the case that Mrs. Phoebe Palmer had a major impact on both William and Catherine, her first contact with them being in 1859, when William was serving as a minister with the Methodist New Connexion at Gateshead and she was leading revival services across the water in Newcastle Upon Tyne. Kent pointed out that Mrs Booth's letters "give a detailed account of her experience, and make it quite clear that she and her husband had completely accepted Phoebe Palmer's doctrine of holiness." Kent gives the following passage from Catherine.

> I struggled through the day until a little after six in the evening, when William joined me for prayer. We had a blessed season. While he was saying, "Lord, we open our hearts to receive Thee," that word was spoken into my soul: "Behold I stand at the door and knock. If any man hears my voice and opens to me, I will

come in and sup with him." I felt sure He had long been knocking, and Oh, how I yearned to receive Him as a perfect Saviour. But Oh, the inveterate habit of unbelief. How wonderful that God should have borne so long with me. When we got up from our knees I lay on the sofa, exhausted with the excitement and effort of the day. William said, "Don't you lay all on the altar." I replied in the language of the Holy Ghost, "The Altar is most holy, and whatsoever touches it is holy." Then he said, "Are you not Holy?" I replied in the language of the Holy Ghost, "The Altar is most holy, and whatsoever touches it is holy." Then he said, "Are you not Holy?" I replied with my heart full of emotion and some faith, "Oh, I think I am." Immediately, the word was given top me to confirm my faith, "Now are ye clean through the word which I have spoken unto you." And I took hold—true, with a trembling hand, and not unmolested by the tempter, but I held fast the beginning of my confidence, and it grew stronger; and from that moment I have dared to reckon myself dead indeed unto sin, and alive unto God through Jesus Christ my Lord. I did not feel much rapturous joy, but perfect peace, the sweet rest which Jesus promised to the heavy laden, I have understood the Apostle's meaning when he says, "We who believe do enter into rest." This is a just description of my state at present. Not that I am not tempted, but I am allowed to know the devil when he approaches me, and I look to my deliverer, Jesus, and He still gives me rest. Two or three very trying things occurred on Saturday, which at another time would have excited impatience, but I was kept by the power of God through faith unto full salvation.

And in another letter, written a little earlier, she said, "since that hour . . . although I have been tempted, I have not taken back the sacrifice from the altar, but have been enabled calmly to contemplate it as done."[19]

It will be seen from this quotation that this way of pursuing holiness is rooted in the altar of sacrifice in the Jerusalem temple. When a lamb or goat was bound to the temple altar it was considered to be holy because the altar was holy and anything that was laid on it was therefore held to be holy. The Booths' testimony is exactly in line with Phoebe Palmer's altar theology in which she urged her congregations to lay their all on the altar. Such surrender included every aspect of their lives, from the major issues of work, Christian service, marriage and family, to money, dress, and leisure activities. Then once having sacrificially surrendered their lives in

19. Both sources found in Booth-Tucker, *The Life of Catherine Booth,* 208–9. The first edition was published in 1892. In Kent, *Holding the Fort,* 326–27.

this way, usually at the conclusion of Palmer's revival meetings, kneeling at an altar rail or gathered round a communion table, those seeking holiness were invited to believe and receive the blessing by faith. These moments of total consecration could be highly charged with emotion as recipients sometimes wept, cried out, or fell to the ground.

The way in which both Phoebe Palmer's and the Booths' altar theology functioned is well illustrated by the following hymn taken from *Holiness Hymns*, a volume selected from various songbooks of the Salvation Army and specially adapted for use at Holiness Meetings and All Nights of Prayer.

My body, soul and spirit
Jesus, I give to Thee,
A consecrated offering,
Thine evermore to be,
Chorus: My all is on the altar,
I am waiting for the fire.

Oh, let the fire descending
Just now upon my soul
Consume my humble offering,
And cleanse and make me whole.

Chorus: My all is on the altar,
I am waiting for the fire.

I'm Thine, O blessed Jesus,
Washed by Thy precious Blood,
Now seal me in Thy Spirit,
A sacrifice to God

Chorus: My all is on the altar,
I am waiting for the fire.[20]

In some of the early Salvation Army meetings the atmosphere appears to have been a somewhat more raw experience than those directed by Phoebe Palmer. This was made plain in a note written by Bramwell Booth, possibly to George Railton:

I shall see you tomorrow some time and so need not write at length. The night (All Night of Prayer) was one of the most utterly wild I ever was at. Until this I have never seen either jumping or

20. *Holiness Hymns* (1880), 4.

> somersaulting to any extent. . . . This Rothwell is a decent fellow. Clever, quick, comic, can sing, talk, do anything—25—saved seven years—been a devil—Wesleyan of Rochdale, strong, wiry, squint eye, I should think daring and resolute![21]

Notwithstanding this somewhat extreme instance, this type of holiness teaching underlines the Salvation Army motto of "Blood and Fire," the "Blood" referring to the sacrificial death of Christ and the "Fire" to this experience of holiness.

The rules of Booth's Christian Mission, which were compiled in 1870, included number 28, which stated that meetings for holiness were to be held weekly and if possible on Fridays. At the last conference of the Mission in 1877, the year before the Army was founded, Booth made it plain that holiness was a vital concern:

> Holiness to the Lord is to us a fundamental truth; it stands to the forefront of our doctrines. We write it on our banners. It is in no shape or form an open debateable question as to whether God can sanctify wholly, whether Jesus does save his people from their sins. In the estimation of the Christian Mission that is settled forever, and any evangelist who does not hold and proclaim the ability of Jesus to save his people to the uttermost from sin and sinning I should consider out of place among us.[22]

A trap into which these meetings sometimes fell was to reduce the surrender to what were often, to all intents and purposes, domestic trivialities. This was well illustrated in another comment made by Bramwell Booth to his father:

> I preached last night at Sunderland. . . . After this we had an All Night of Prayer. . . . Of course we went straight on in the Holiness line. There were thirteen pipes, with several tobacco pouches, a scarf pin and a lump of twist, two or three cigars, two snuff boxes, ten feathers, a string of flowers and a brooch, voluntarily surrendered amidst a scene of sobbing and shouting rarely surpassed. . . . The fellows who have been bothering Blandy were at the penitent form or on the floor, ground to powder.[23]

Holiness, for the Salvation Army, included abstention from both alcohol and tobacco. This fact was well illustrated in 1870 when the *Christian*

---

21. Booth, *Bramwell Booth*, 109.

22. Sandall, *History of the Salvation Army*, Vol. 2, 53. In Kent, *Holding the Fort*, 321.

23. C. B. Booth, *Bramwell Booth*, 93.

Mission Magazine printed fifty-four reasons for avoiding tobacco. In the same year the Conference made total abstinence a requirement for all members. The *Orders and Regulations of Membership* stated that "No one shall be allowed to hold office in the Mission who is not a total abstainer from all intoxicating liquors, tobacco and snuff." However we regard these occurrences, holiness and the pursuit of holiness remained a central strategy and it was written into the Army's *Articles of War*: "We believe that it is the privilege of all believers to be 'wholly sanctified,' and that their 'whole spirit soul and body' may 'be preserved blameless unto the coming of our Lord Jesus Christ' (1 Thessalonians 5:23)."[24]

Preaching and Penitent Forms

Booth, like all revivalists of the period, studied ways and means of persuading individuals to get to that crucial moment where they would make a definite public commitment of their lives to Christ. He was strongly of the view that the more public such moments were the harder it would be to go back on the decision. He adopted the use of what was known as the penitent form. This was a series of wooden benches (or sometimes seats) that were left empty at the front of the meeting hall. Usually at some point near the close of the service those who were penitent about the state of their life were invited to come out publicly and take their place on the penitent form. Such moments were often times of great emotional release and catharsis. Richard Collier commented that "uninhibited converts, sensing a burden of guilt lifted from their shoulders would shout, 'I do believe—He does save me.' Some of the new converts who were ready to press Christ's claims on the willing and the unwilling alike doubtless stirred up or helped to provoke these emotional extremes."[25]

There can be no doubt that the penitent form was a powerful instrument that the Army used to great effect. It was estimated that between the years 1886 and 1906 at least four million people had knelt at Salvationist penitent forms.[26] Booth's advocacy and the Army's use of this procedure met with a good deal of criticism. Opponents claimed that those who came forward had done so because they had been captivated by emotion or put under strong group pressure to do so. From time to time Catherine was questioning of some of Williams pulpit rhetoric and urged him to "watch

24. *Articles of War*, section entitled Believing.
25. Collier, *The General Next to God*, 51.
26. Manson, *The Salvation Army and the Public*, 366–37.

against mere animal excitements in your revival sermons."[27] Many were of the view that these instantaneous conversions would not last. Others no doubt shared Bryan Wilson's view that this kind of euphoria amounted to a form of religious escapism for the working classes.[28] That said, there is evidence that the great majority of commitments lasted. Indeed, it was claimed in 1904 that "tens of thousands of worshippers enumerated under various Churches have first been got hold of by the Salvation Army."[29]

In summary, holiness was seen by Booth and his lieutenants as a deliverance from all known sin and the total and obedient submission of a person's life to the teachings of Jesus. There was no suggestion that Salvationists could reach a state of perfection. Booth's officers lived in the real world and were all too well aware of the consequences of the fall and the temptation to turn back into past ways and habits. Holiness at this level was frequently seen in terms of social habits and religious practice, such as Sabbath keeping, attendance at meetings, and issues of dress, clothing, smoking, drinking, and the theatre.

No Sacraments

One of the more controversial aspects of Booth's strategy was his rejection of the sacraments of baptism and the Lord's Supper. Initially the Lord's Supper was shared at all Booth's mission stations but then, for several reasons, he came to the view that the sacraments were not essential. In the first place, he was of the opinion that the sacraments led to an unbiblical concept of a special priestly class who would dispense them in a formalized ritual. William wrote on one occasion, "If I believed that my Lord Jesus Christ required of me that I should take so many pieces of bread and so much wine every day of my life, I should unhesitatingly carry out his commands. There is nothing that I am so conscious of that requires me to do that I left undone."[30] Catherine Booth was worried that their soldiers would come to rely on the ritual rather than on the reality of Christ's presence. Additionally, Booth feared that many of his converts, who had been habitual drunkards, would return to the past ways. Both William and Catherine felt strongly that the sacraments were a divisive influence

27. Hattersley, *Blood and Fire*, 91.

28. Wilson, *Patterns of Sectarianism*, 61.

29. Haw, "The Problems of Greater London." In Mudie-Smith, *The Religious Life of London*, 344.

30. Blinco, *Harvest of the Years*, 38.

in the church. Booth, it should be said, did not in the last analysis seek to prevent any of his soldiers from attending the sacraments elsewhere and publicly stated that any Salvationist who was seriously desirous of attending them would be given a letter of recommendation.[31] Significantly, in 1882 Edward Benson, the Bishop of Truro, who was impressed by Booth's organization and campaigns, persuaded the Convocation of Canterbury to consider making the army into a church organization. However, their overtures failed over this question of the sacraments.

Social Schemes

As the years passed Booth became increasingly concerned to meet the needs of the poor in practical ways. He was particularly concerned with their plight during the cold winter months and did his best ensure that the army's meeting rooms were kept warm. For the same reason he ensured that plenty of warm soup and other hot food and drink were readily available. On a single day in 1870 the soup kitchen and the Poor Man's Dining Hall in Whitechapel provided soup and other food for 2,000 men and women.[32] It was noted that in the years 1890–99 the Salvation Army provided 27 million cheap meals, gave lodgings to 11 million, and found work for 90,000 jobless people.[33] Booth was able to provide income support for this work from five "Food for the Millions" shops that he either owned or controlled in Limehouse, Brick Lane, Shoreditch, and Whitechapel.[34]

In 1890 William set out his most ambitious scheme for helping the poor in his famous book entitled *In Darkest England and the Way Out,* the title clearly having been borrowed from Henry Morton Stanley's (1841–1904) *In Darkest Africa.* Booth, it seems, had come to the realization that if a person was going to accept the Christian message, his or her immediate physical and social needs must first be dealt with. Indeed, he had written as early as 1869 that "no-one gets a blessing if they have cold feet and no-one ever got saved while they had tooth ache."[35] Booth's scheme, which he outlined in his book, consisted of a Household Salvage Brigade that would collect, once or twice a week, unwanted clothes and useable food and take

---

31. Booth, *Echoes and Memories*. In Blinco, *Another Harvest of the Years*, 37.
32. Hattersley, *Blood and Fire*, 184.
33. Barnes, *God's Army*, 72.
34. Hattersley, *Blood and Fire*, 189.
35. Booth, *All About the Salvation Army*, 70.

them to a local depot.[36] Attached to each depot Booth planned to set up a workshop where the unemployed would be able to earn sufficient to buy food. There were also cheap food depots and shops. Alongside these, Booth proposed a series of industrial and village colonies, a farm colony, and an overseas emigration scheme. There were also plans to help newly released prisoners, drunkards, and fallen women, and schemes to provide cheap or free legal advice, industrial schools, a Poor Man's Bank, and a Travelling Hospital. Booth's proposals have the feel of a utopian scheme, but the Army was able to put some of them into full effect. Many criticisms were directed against his scheme of social salvation. Thomas Huxley wrote a series of letters to *The Times* in 1891 in which he suggested that Booth had "failed to sort out the deserving from the undeserving."[37] Others suggested that Booth's philanthropic Christianity was an attempt to bribe people to accept his gospel by giving them food and shelter. Booth later became sensitive to this criticism and ruled that there should be no compulsion to attend the Army's services.

For the most part Booth's schemes, such as the homes for prisoners and the farm colonies, were well-received by the British public.[38] However, many were critical of the strict religious discipline that was imposed on those who joined them. That said, it was very probably the case that this kind of strict routine was exactly what many of them needed. It was also a fact that this type of framework provided stability and common purpose. Salvationists were also involved in other forms of caring and relief work. Both Catherine and Bramwell Booth supported Josephine Butler's campaign to repeal the 1864 Contagious Diseases Act, which allowed the police to arrest women who were suspected of prostitution in military towns and cities and take them to a hospital where they were examined for venereal diseases. If they were found to be infected they were compulsorily locked up until they were cured. There was no such requirement for the men.[39] *The War Cry* of 18 July, 1885, gave details of a petition to the House of Commons containing 393,000 names. It called for the age of consent for girls to be raised to eighteen and the procurement for immoral purposes to be a criminal offense. There is no doubt that the Salvation Army's campaign played a significant role in persuading MPs to pass the Bill which effectively outlawed brothels.

36. Ibid., *In Darkest England and the Way Out*, 117–18.

37. *The Times*, 2 January, 1891.

38. Ibid., 31 January, 1891.

39. It was reported that one out of every three soldiers on sick parades in 1864 was suffering from either gonorrhoea or syphilis.

An Equal Role for Women

One powerful aspect of the Army's strategy and organization was the equality they gave to women. From the very earliest days women were treated on equal terms with men and given the same opportunities as men to preach from the pulpit. The demand for female equality in the Army dated back to the time when William was a Methodist minister in Gateshead and Phoebe Palmer was holding revival services in Newcastle-on-Tyne. The Reverend Arthur Augustus Rees (1814–84), a former Anglican curate and later Independent minister, published a hostile pamphlet in which he denied, on biblical grounds, a woman's right to preach. Catherine wrote that "it was delivered in the form of an address to his congregation and would you believe that a congregation half composed of ladies would sit and hear such self-deprecatory nonsense? They really don't deserve to be taken up cudgels for."[40] Catherine herself responded with a published answer entitled, *Female Teaching; or the Rev A. A. Rees versus Mrs A. Palmer, being A Reply.* In it she argued that biblical passages cited to silence women were merely intended to restrict disorderly speech and to prevent the undermining of male authority.

> We think it a matter worthy of the consideration of the church, whether God really intended woman to bury her talents and her influence as she does now? And whether the circumscribed sphere of women's religious labours may not have something to do with the comparative non-success of the gospel in these latter days? We fear that it has, and the Lord of the Vineyard will require some more satisfactory excuses for our timidity and backwardness in his service than the one-sided interpretation of detached portions of Holy Writ and the *ipse dixit* of such men as Rev A. A. Rees.[41]

Women could hold any office in the Army, from Station Commander to General. Women also received equal pay. Catherine Booth herself said, "I believe one of the greatest boons to the race would be woman's exaltation to her proper position mentally and spiritually, who can tell its consequences to posterity."[42] Catherine launched her public preaching career in 1860 during a nine-week period when William was undergoing treatment

---

40. Booth-Tucker, *The Life of Catherine Booth*. In Kent, *Holding the Fort*, 325.

41. Booth, *Female Teaching: or the Rev A. A. Rees versus Mrs A. Palmer.* In Winston, *Red-Hot Righteous*, 21.

42. C. Booth, *Bramwell Booth*, 146.

for depression at a clinic in Matlock. She more or less acted as a New Connexion Methodist minister, taking over her husband's preaching and pastoral responsibilities. In the years that followed Catherine proved to be a sensational preacher, a fact that was well illustrated by her campaign at Ramsgate in the summer of 1868. There was no hall sufficiently large enough to hold all those who wanted to hear her and many people waited outside the entrance hoping for a word with her when she left the meeting. Roy Hattersley noted that by the end of the 1870s Catherine "was much more in demand than her husband in polite society and was preaching regularly in the West End."[43]

Section XII of the constitution of the Inaugural Conference of the Salvation Army stated, "Godly women in his Church; Godly women possessing the necessary gifts and qualifications shall be employed as preachers, itinerant and otherwise, and as class leaders and as such shall have appointments given them on the preacher's plan; they shall be eligible for any office and to speak and vote at all meetings."[44]

When the book of *Orders and Regulations for Staff Officers* was drawn up, chapter 4 was entitled "The Position of Women." It stated: "One of the leading principles upon which the Army is based is the right of women to an equal share with men in the great work of publishing salvation to the world. By an unalterable provision of our Foundation Deed, she can hold any position of authority or power in the Army, from local officer to that of General."[45] The Army's commitment to the equality of opportunity for women came at a time when women had difficulty obtaining any form of higher education and were barred from entry into many of the professions. Notwithstanding these hindrances, Booth directed that "all necessary forbearance and patience must be exercised towards woman in the drawbacks under which she labours in public life from physical weakness, marriage relationships, family cares, and other burdens which she is specifically called to bear."[46] In 1869 the Mission started a group of Christian Female Pioneers, whose primary responsibilities were to be with children. Ten years later they became known as the Army's "Hallelujah Lasses."

The Army's use of women was inevitably seen as extreme radicalism in an age in which women were regarded as inferior and, in middle class circles, regarded as being created only for the domestic sphere. John Kent

43. Hattersley, *Blood and Fire*, 242.
44. Ibid., 191.
45. Booth, *Orders and Regulations*, 8.
46. Ibid., 9.

wrote that it is clear that Mrs. Booth's ability and leadership drew a number of young middle class women to her in the 1878–85 period, "because she symbolised their own sense of revolt."[47]

DECLINING IMPACT

The Salvation Army is still alive and well, and its reputation for practical Christianity and compassion is still known across the globe. That said, it is a fact that even before the close of the Victorian era Booth's organization was beginning to lose its impact. In 1883 the *War Cry*, the Army's weekly paper, was selling nearly 350,000 copies a week in its English language edition. However, by 1890 the figure had dropped to 290,000.[48] John Kent argued that by this latter date the Army had largely lost its influence over the working class population of England and had little if any political influence at all.[49] In inner London, where the Army had its headquarters and where it concentrated its energies, attendance at its meetings declined from 53,591 in 1887 to 22,402 in 1903.[50] It was estimated in 1906 that the membership of the Army in the whole of the United Kingdom was of the order of 100,000,[51] with an estimated membership in London of 13,000.[52] Another estimate gave a membership figure of 115,000 for the British Isles in 1911, out of a world total of 256,950.[53] This decline is, of course, less dramatic when they are set against the pattern of a general decline in church membership in the last quarter of the nineteenth century. In 1851 church attendance in England and Wales had stood at just over 50 percent, but by 1900 it had dropped to 35 percent. The early years of the twentieth century saw a continued slowing down in the Army's growth with a brief upturn following the end of the First World War.[54] Roland Robertson noted in 1967 that the Salvation Army "is mainly lower-middle class" with its officers coming from the same background.[55]

47. Kent, *Holding the Fort*, 325 note 39.

48. *War Cry*, 17th May, 1890.

49. Kent, *Holding the Fort*, 335.

50. Inglis, *Churches and the Working Classes in Victorian England*, 196. Cited in Wilson, *Patterns of Sectarianism*, 101.

51. Robertson, *Patterns of Sectarians*, 102.

52. Ibid.

53. Ibid.

54. Ibid., 103.

55. Ibid.

The Salvation Army currently numbers over 1.6 million members worldwide in a 109 countries. In the United Kingdom there are over 800 Salvation Army Corps with 1,500 full-time officers and 54,000 members, which includes senior ranks, adherents, and junior soldiers. It has continued to carry forward much of William Booth's ideals and doctrine, still emphasizing the blood of Christ and the work of the Holy Spirit. Above all, the Army is still known beyond all else for its compassionate care given to believers and unbelievers alike. Salvationists have always taken pride in being "doers of the word and not hearers only." Food and shelter is offered to all alike and while the Army prays that it will help the recipients find faith in Christ there are no requirements to participate in their worship or other programs. The Salvation Army does not draw a line between the sacred and the secular. As they understand it, to give food to the hungry, drink to the thirsty, and a welcome to the stranger is an integral part of the work of the kingdom of God.[56]

FACTORS THAT MADE THE SALVATION ARMY SUCCESSFUL

William Booth's Compassionate and Dynamic Leadership

He was a man of the Spirit who had a lifelong and overwhelming sense of the presence of God in his life. Like all great leaders, he was a person with clear and straightforward vision that he pursued with relentless and passionate vigor. He was all about saving souls and he was not afraid to offend. Such was his charisma that he was not only able articulate his plans, but was able to persuade thousands on all continents of the globe to run with it. He was described as a "pyrotechnic preacher" who was able to communicate the Christian message with power and enthusiasm to the working poor in a way they could understand and embrace wholeheartedly. Along with most nineteenth- and early twentieth-century revivalists, William was always searching for new evangelistic methods by which to capture the hearts of those who came to hear him speak. One of the marks of Booth's giftedness as a leader was his willingness to take risks and try new strategies. Like John Wesley, whose influence he acknowledged on several occasions, Booth had the gift of organization and the energy to keep a watchful eye over the structures he set in place. While it was the case that Booth was an autocrat who, from time to time, came close to restricting the personal freedoms of some of his lieutenants, Booth was

56. Matt 25:35–36.

nonetheless a gifted strategist who kept in close touch with the commissioners he chose to supervise in the various nations of the world.

An Equal Role for Women

In his early days, William had come to recognize that women must be treated as being equal with men. In this opinion, of course, he had been greatly influenced by his wife Catherine. She had preached with much success on many occasions well before the Army had been founded. Indeed, she had run William's Methodist circuit for several months when he had been sidelined with depression. In consequence Booth had, from the very beginning of the Army, fully acknowledged the equality of women at all levels. Every position in the army was to be open to them from General downwards. Women were to have the same rights to preach as men and were to receive equal pay. Women played a significant role in the Army's work of speaking, singing, house-to-house visiting, and in practical and social care.

The Army Understood the Culture and Level of the Working Poor

Salvation Army worship was adapted to the culture of the working poor whom Booth's soldiers encountered on the streets of the world's major towns and cities. His vision of the church and its worship owed much to the life and practices of John Wesley, the founder of the Methodism in which Booth had himself been nurtured. Following the Wesleys, Booth recognized the power of corporate singing, especially if it was vibrant and joyous. It was the simplicity and fervent nature of the Army brass bands and their strong bouncing tunes that captivated the "submerged tenth" of London's East End in the closing decades of the nineteenth century. Booth's mission stations were minimalist in their structure and ceremonial. There were no priestly officers clad in clerical robes, who most artisans and unskilled workers regarded as hostile to their interests. There were no sacramental mysteries, which many in London and elsewhere regarded as either Romanish or superstitious and hard to understand. Salvation Army worship presented the plain truth to the plain man in joyous applied simplicity. The military style uniforms put everyone on the same footing and masked the difference between rich and poor.

All Members Were Active Participants in Mission

William Booth mobilized his converts. They not only got a uniform, they got a sense of identity and purpose as they were put to work testifying what the General had done for their lives. So they preached, testified, and sang in the streets.

A Holistic Theology

William Booth came to offer what was an increasingly holistic gospel that ministered to the needs of the whole person. When he first founded his mission his focus was on a soul-saving, but increasingly he came to the view that it was equally necessary to deal with the often immediate need for food and shelter. As he put it on one occasion, "No man got saved while he had tooth-ache." In the early days his method was characterized by three "s" words: soup, soap, and salvation. He also recognized that if his message was going to be heard, meeting rooms had to be warm and, where possible, floors needed to be of wood, which was a better insulator against the cold. The publication of his volume *In Darkest England* in 1890 marked Booth's commitment to social Christianity, or as one person expressed it, "social salvation." In the early days of the Christian Mission those who received food or help of various kinds were often expected to take part in the Army's prayers or worship, but in later times, following criticism, the requirement was ended. Booth recognized that Christian care should be extended without any strings attached.

12 | The Settlement Movement

THE FIRST SETTLEMENTS

What became known as Settlements first began to appear in some of the major towns and cities in England and the United States in the late nineteenth centuries. They arose partly out of a sense of duty and responsibility on the part of some Oxbridge clergy and prosperous Oxbridge University undergraduates and former students. They recognized that the churches had failed to make any significant impact on the working poor and felt strongly that something new needed to be attempted. The settlers were clear that a clergyman by himself was never going to have sufficient resources to impact the slums with the Christian message. What was needed was the same help that the squire gave to the rector or vicar in the countryside. No incumbent laboring on his own in the inner city or industrial town center was going to find the organizational and educational skills among his parishioners to run his parish. The strategy of the London Settlements in particular was therefore to invite a number of recent university graduates who were working in the city to live among the poor of the parish or local area and give two or three evenings a week helping to organize educational, social, and recreational activities.

SETTLEMENT VISIONS AND STRATEGIES

It was this taking up of residence or going to live among the poor that was the defining characteristic of the Settlement Movement. Whereas many evangelical groups such as the Salvation Army and City Missions just went into an area for an evening or weekend of evangelistic campaigning, the Settlers actually took up permanent residence in the area. It was presence before proclamation. One clergyman expressed it as follows:

The dwellers in the East End of our towns will not be converted by missionaries and tracts sent by dwellers in the West End. The dwellers in the West End must go themselves to the dwellers in the East themselves, share with the East those pleasures which give interest and delight to the dwellers in the West, and make up the fullness of their life. When the dwellers in the West go thus to the dwellers in the East they will themselves be converted, for they will have turned to Christ and accepted His yoke of personal service, and the dwellers on the East, recognising the true helpfulness of the Christian life, will be converted too.[1]

Presence before Preaching

The London Settlements, and indeed those elsewhere, had a variety of objectives and agendas, but the one basic and common agenda was this concept of a permanent residence or settling in the area of those engaged in the work. There were a number of settlements that can be classed as Mission Settlements for the reason that they were both a presence *and* in addition sought to advance a strongly Christian agenda. Some of the Tractarians, for example, felt that Toynbee Hall was too secular and they therefore founded Oxford House with its the distinct concern to foster and promote an Anglo-Catholic spirituality. Nevertheless, they followed Toynbee's warden, Samuel Barnett, in believing that a residential presence was vital. Their aim was that by Christian caring and compassion they would earn the right to speak the Christian message. Others of more liberal Christian views felt that they wanted to proclaim the Christian faith by presence rather than preaching. Barnett, for example, drew a sharp distinction between a "Settlement" and a "Mission." Speaking in 1897 he said: "A mission exists to proselytise, whereas a settlement is simply a base from which to build bridges to the working poor." Although he contended that Toynbee Hall would be "religious" in the best and broadest sense, there were many who felt unsure about his claims and wanted something more than the liberal Protestantism of Balliol College.

1. Moore, *The Attitude of the Church to Some of the Social Problems of Town Life,* 102–3.

Good Neighbors

The Settlers were mindful of Jesus' claim to bring good news to the poor and his command to love our neighbors as ourselves. They therefore put the emphasis on obeying this instruction by demonstrating practical care, improving people's quality of life, and so perhaps earning the right to speak of the Christian faith. Samuel Barnett, who has been called "the Father of the Settlement Movement," regarded the residential hostel as the base that fostered good neighborliness. The author of the *Handbook of Christian Settlements in Great Britain* aptly described Settlements as follows:

> Settlements vary in the aims and methods of work, but they have one thing in common, as their name implies: a number of men and women must have chosen to live in an industrial neighbourhood. They may live singly or in twos or threes, or they may live all together; they may live in private houses or in tenements, or they may live in a specially built hostel. The exact manner of residence is a detail, though an important one. The essential thing is that the residents should make themselves familiar with the district and should feel at home in it.[2]

The Settlers believed and hoped that by their presence they would be good neighbors to those in the locality by helping educate them, teach them public health and bring to them an appreciation of certain aspects of British culture.

Incarnational Theology

The great majority of settlers were men and women of Christian faith and worked from an incarnational theology. In simple terms, this meant that just as God did not stand aloof or at a distance from his creation but took human flesh and came and lived among his people, demonstrating care and compassion in works of helping and healing, so God's people are called to do the same. At a meeting that marked the beginning of the Oxford House Settlement in Bethnal Green, William Walsham How, the Bishop of Bedford, said: "As I long that on the one hand the foundation of your work should be faith in our blessed Lord, so I long too, that the outcome of the work should be the true acceptance of that fundamental doctrine of the incarnation, by which God and man are brought together."[3]

2. Anon, *Handbook of Settlements in Great Britain*, 5.

3. Inglis, *Churches and the Working Classes*, 157.

The members of the Settlements believed this to be a divinely inspired pattern and precedent and this is what led to their getting their hands dirty in all kinds of ways. Some members of settlements served on local boards of guardians or ran for office as borough council members. Others began to lobby the authorities about the poor state of drains, unhealthy sewers, and unacceptable working conditions. As Arnold Toynbee, who held very liberal Christian views, once put it, "the task of improving the masses is a profoundly religious task" and "any attempt to preach a purer religion must go along with attempts at social reform . . . and progress will never be organic until the religious spirit breathes through every act and institution."[4]

Civilizing

There was a belief on the part of many settlers that teaching and education with a practical and cultural emphasis was the way into the Christian faith for the majority of East Londoners. Put another way, if the poor could be civilized and raised to a better quality of life they would, in the process, embrace the Christian faith. Even the Mission Settlements that had an overt Christian agenda still placed much emphasis on social activities such as football, gymnastics, dancing, and a multitude of practical courses, ranging from English history and literature to simple hygiene and public health.

THE MOTIVATION BEHIND THE SETTLEMENTS

A number of different factors contributed to the emergence of Settlements. Prominent among them was the publication in October, 1883, of a penny pamphlet entitled *The Bitter Cry of Outcast London*. It was the work of the Reverend Andrew Mearns (1837–1925), the secretary of the London Congregational Union, and two other Congregational ministers. It was not an altogether original piece since at least some of the evidence was taken from a more racily written document produced by the journalist, George R. Sims (1847–1922), entitled, *How the Poor Live*. In the preface to a later edition, Sims pointed out that the author of *The Bitter Cry* acknowledged that he had derived the great assistance from *How the Poor Live* while compiling his famous pamphlet. Mearns stated bluntly that the

---

4. Toynbee, "Notes and Jottings," in his *Lectures on the Industrial Revolution*, 244.

churches were living in a fool's paradise if they really imagined that all the existing missions, temperance societies, and other reformatory organizations were doing more than a thousandth part of what needed to be done. To reinforce his point he quoted from some of the detailed researches that he had done in the area of Bow Common. He observed that out of a total of 2,290 persons living in consecutive houses, only eighty-eight adults and forty-seven children were connected with any place of worship.[5] In one district of St. George's-in-the-East only thirty-nine persons out of 4,235 attended a place of worship.[6] Mearns made the point that for the clergy to reach these people they will "have to penetrate courts reeking with poisonous and malodorous gases arising from accumulations of sewage and refuse scattered in all directions and often flowing beneath your feet."[7] Mearns' pamphlet was given instant and widespread publicity by W. T. Stead in his *Pall Mall Gazette* and by *The Daily News*, which highlighted "the great dark region of poverty, misery, squalor and immorality."[8]

The Wesleyans, Baptists, Presbyterian, and Congregational churches made a joint response to the *Bitter Cry* by calling a conference to discuss the needs and social conditions of the London poor. In 1884 Methodist ministers in London listened to a presentation by one of their number on the subject of "Outcast London."[9]

The Church of England response to the *Bitter Cry* was rather less united. It did, however, produce a number of thoughtful suggestions and considerably more action on the ground. Among those who were stirred was the Reverend Brooke Lambert (1834–1901), the Vicar of Greenwich, who had begun his ministry first as curate and then a Vicar of St. Mark's, Whitechapel, where he had set up a working men's club, a mutual improvement society, and established a penny bank. Lambert penned an article for *Contemporary Review* entitled "The Outcast Poor—Esau's Cry" in which he pointed out that London's poor, like Esau, had been deprived of their birthright and "have no blessing." He continued by making the point that the East London Esau may soon advance not with 400 but with 400,000 to meet us. They are men and women who live "shut out from faith, hope and love."[10] Lambert put forward a number of his own suggestions in much

5. Mearns, *The Bitter Cry of Outcast London*, 57.

6. Ibid., 57.

7. Ibid., 4.

8. Brock and Curthoys, *The History of the University of Oxford*, Vol. 7, part 2, 670.

9. Thompson, *Peter Thompson*, 33. In Inglis, *Churches and the Working Classes*, 68.

10. *Contemporary Review*, December 1883, 917.

the same way that Mearns had done considering the evils of bad housing, insufficient wages, and unscrupulous middle-men. He proposed various remedies, including better housing management and the development of co-operatives.

Lambert's friend, the Reverend John Richard Green (1837–83), had been engaged in similar work in the parish of St. Philip, Stepney. Among other things, Green had vehemently attacked the provision of indiscriminate charity and denounced William Booth, the founder of the Salvation Army, as "a ranting preacher" who combined "enormous breakfasts" with "revivalistic infusions."[11] About the year 1869 they had met together at the request of John Ruskin to consider the possibility of setting up a colony of university men to expand the type of work that they had both been attempting. They were both of the view that there was a need for educated men and women to take up residence in the poorer areas of London and other industrial towns and cities. Nothing of these hopes materialized and Green subsequently became ill and retired from the ministry. Lambert did, however, remember their earlier plan and in 1881 he addressed a group of students at Merton College, Oxford, and urged them to come down and help in his parish.

Another factor that impacted the emergence of Settlements was a growing sense of duty that it behooved the upper and middle classes to do something on behalf of the poor. This perception was a very strong aspect of Victorian life and had arisen partly from the evangelical conviction that each individual was answerable to God for the way in which they passed their days. Indeed a favorite text, which hung over many fireplaces in evangelical homes, was "Thou God seest me." It was this sense of duty that had prompted Brooke Lambert to minister in a working class parish in London. At Whitechapel, where he labored before going to Greenwich, he had been active in local government and been instrumental in forming secular clubs and societies.

One particular clergyman who was to be impacted by this sense of duty was Samuel Barnett (1844–1913), who was to become the most influential figure in the entire Settlement Movement. He had begun what became a regular practice of inviting undergraduates to spend part of their vacation in the neighborhood of St. Jude's, Whitechapel, and to involve themselves in the work of the parish. Among those who did so was the later to be social historian, Arnold Toynbee (1852–83), whose life was to

11. Mayor, *Churches and the Labour Movement*, 54.

become an inspiration to the Barnetts.[12] When Toynbee died at a comparatively young age Barnett planned and built the first settlement in his honor as a center where men who shared his spirit and concerns could live and work alongside the poor.

OXFORD AND CAMBRIDGE

A number of writers and commentators observed that in the later decades of the nineteenth century there was a changing atmosphere in the Universities of Oxford and Cambridge towards the needs of the poor. As early as 1850, senior academics were concerning themselves as to the role of the university to the nation as a whole. A little later in 1877, partly as a result of Benjamin Jowett's influence, a committee was established to promote extension lectures in large cities. On one occasion, when Samuel Barnett was addressing a meeting at Balliol College, Jowett unexpectedly turned up, commended the occasion, and advised every one who was present to make some friends among the poor.[13] K. S. Inglis wrote of Barnett that "at a time when English consciences were stirring uneasily over the condition of the urban masses, Barnett spoke in just the right tone of voice to some of the privileged members of his own university."[14]

This new mood became more visible when radicals such as Joseph Arch, the Agricultural Workers Union leader, were invited to give an address at Oxford Town Hall in 1883. Arch spoke on behalf of the union from a platform supported by several fellows and professors. Among other radicals who spoke in Oxford at this time were Ben Tillett, the Dock Workers' Union leader, the American, Henry George and the Socialist, William Morris. The *Oxford Magazine* for December 1883 commented that "above all it has been recognized . . . that Oxford has much to learn from the working classes as well as the working classes from Oxford." The same journal commented that, "the exceeding bitter cry of the outcast has been ringing in Oxford's ears for the past year."[15] Throughout 1884 there were reports on the work in East London.[16]

---

12. *Ninth Report of the Universities' Settlement in East London*, 1893.

13. Barnett, *Canon Barnett, His Life*, 305.

14. Inglis, *Churches and the Working Classes*, 154.

15. *The Oxford Magazine*, 7 March, 1884.

16. Ibid., 14 May, 226; 11 June, 297; 29 October, 355; 26 November, 431–32.

PUBLIC SCHOOLS

At the same time the universities were setting up their missions in East and South London, more than twenty public schools were active in forming very similar institutions. Nearly all the public school settlements were founded in the last quarter of the nineteenth century and had a specifically religious agenda. Indeed, some pubic schools formed their "missions" well before Toynbee Hall was established at Whitechapel. A range of different factors provoked the public schools to establish their missions. One of these was the "Muscular Christianity" movement, which seems to have come from the Christian Socialists, Charles Kingsley and Thomas Hughes, the latter advocating the lifestyle in his *Tom Brown's School Days* (1857) and *The Manliness of Christ* (1879). In the wake of this, games became a dominant focus in some schools and a number of them looked for headmasters who were accomplished on the sports fields. The image of the school was also important and governors wanted it to be seen that schools were making pupils aware of their responsibilities to the needy and providing opportunities for service.

Although Oxbridge Colleges established a significant presence in both the East End and in South London, the public schools were also set to make a considerable contribution to the origin and development of the Settlement Movement. Whereas there were less than twenty university settlements and settlement missions active in London by 1900, there were more than twenty-five such public school missions, well over half of which were located in the East End.

Many public school headmasters were themselves clergy who were acutely aware of the needs of the poor and the way in which the established church of the nation was failing in its mission in the inner city areas. Edward Thring, the distinguished headmaster of Uppingham, spent his first years after leaving King's College, Cambridge, working as a curate in the new parish of St. James, Gloucester. In this tough, unhealthy environment of poor housing on the eastern side of the city, where most worked as dockyard laborers or railway workers, Thring saw poverty first hand. Among other things, he assisted his incumbent, Thomas Hedley, teaching in the small three-roomed school alongside the church. There they did battle trying to teach the sons and daughters of the poor "the three Rs." The challenge was how the Cambridge honors graduate, for Thring was no mean scholar, was to get into the minds of these young disadvantaged children. But eventually he succeeded and there can be little doubt that St.

James' school was both the parent of Uppingham and the missions that were subsequently established in London. Years later Thring reflected in a sermon how much he also owed to Hedley. "I remember the great man," he said, "for he was a very great man, the quiet clergyman, under whom I had begun parish work." He said, "I never see a particularly disagreeable little boy come into my parish school without thinking here is someone I have to learn to love for Christ's sake."[17]

Many of the middle-class parents, who were sending their children to the newer public schools such as Uppingham, shared the same concern about social deprivation, crime, squalor, and immorality. They were more than happy to see that opportunities were being opened up to raise the quality of life of the disadvantaged sections of society and build bridges between classes. The establishment of missions would also help ensure that boys educated at public schools would not plead ignorance of the poor and would perhaps endeavor to do something to educate the nation's future rulers in their responsibilities to the working classes.

A number of schools were themselves acutely aware of these needs and invited priests who worked in slum areas to come and speak to the masters, boys, and old students. An 1887 issue of *The Berkhamstedian* captured the mood of the time. "There is," it reported, "a stronger spirit abroad and a greater desire to do something to benefit our fellow creatures."[18] Of the twenty-two schools that established Mission Settlements, fifteen did so in the 1880s and two others had been started before the decade began. As with the majority of university establishments, almost all the public school missions had some kind of specifically Christian agenda in which they sought to make the local people members of the Anglican church, or at the very least to Christianize the neighborhood in some way. They also aimed to provide educational and life-skill opportunities as well as providing recreational, health, and leisure opportunities. It is clear that the last two decades of the nineteenth century were the period of greatest enthusiasm for mission activity. By the Edwardian years conditions were beginning to improve and the beginnings of the welfare state were taking over some of the social and practical caring work that settlers had previously been undertaking.

In all of these developments one thing was not in any doubt and that was the impact of William Walsham How (1823–97), the Suffragan Bishop

17. Thring, *Addresses*, sermon 83, in M. Tozer, "The Readiest Hand the Most Open Heart."

18. *The Berkhamstedian*, March 1887.

of East London[19] and Anthony Thorold (1825–95), Bishop of Rochester from 1877–90, on the emerging university and public school mission settlements. Bishop How played the major role in establishing Oxford College and public school mission settlements in London's East End. Thorold, a pronounced Evangelical, despite being an Oxford man himself, was responsible for bringing Cambridge to South London as well as encouraging a small number of public schools into that area of his diocese.

TRACTARIAN SOCIAL CONCERN

The majority of Anglican, and indeed some Nonconformist settlement wardens, missioners, and residents, were motivated and inspired by the social theology of the second generation of Tractarians. Their earlier predecessors, despite living in an intellectual environment that was dominated by empiricism, sought to declare the biblical creedal faith of the undivided early Catholic church. Newman did constant battle with liberalism and used his intellectual capacity to undermine confidence in natural reason. The younger Oxford Tractarians, however, began to recognize the validity of at least some of the findings of the scientists and biblical critics, and they began to look for ways to reconcile them with their Catholic faith. Two factors helped them in this process. First, they began to renew their confidence in the New Testament documents, prompted by the work of Lightfoot and Westcott. Second, they found in the thinking and writing of T. H. Green a philosophy that countered the rationalism of the earlier nineteenth century.

Thomas Hill Green (1836–82)[20] had been taught by Benjamin Jowett but went on to part company with much of orthodox Christian belief. That said, he was a spiritual man who valued Jesus' teaching and example of sacrificial service. Green was essentially an "idealist," believing that ideas and ideals are products of the mind, as compared with the world around us, which is perceived through the senses. These ideals are, therefore, of a higher order of existence and linked with conscience, which Green regarded as the presence of God within man and therefore in the world. The true Christian, Green asserted, consults his conscience in order to discover the best way in which to know and honor God. Green believed that conscience, the spark of eternal consciousness, is present in everyone

19. This was a position created by John Jackson (1811–85), Bishop of London.

20. On Green, see the entry in *New Dictionary of National Biography*. His most important work, *Prolegomena to Ethics*, was published the year after his death.

and, arising from it, each person is concerned to aspire to do good. This led him to stress the importance of conduct and in particular the duties of citizenship. It was this that led him to become a role model serving as a member of Oxford Town Council and President of the Oxford Band of Hope Temperance Union. It was this aspect of Green's life that led K. S. Inglis to comment that "he deliberately set out to stir the civic consciousness of Oxford" and that "his teaching and example helped to make Oxford men think about living in a Settlement."[21]

The inner core of the second generation of Tractarians at Oxford included Charles Gore, a Fellow of Trinity, Edward Talbot, the Warden of Keble, and Henry Scott Holland, of Christ Church. Of these three, it was Scott Holland who was most influenced by Green. Indeed, he once remarked that Green "gave us back the language of self-sacrifice and taught us how we belonged to one another in one's life of high idealism." It was partly for this reason that Gore and J. R. Illingworth, another associate, came to focus on the incarnation. It was this doctrine more than any other that inspired the young men and women who took up the vision of Barnett and others to go and settle in the slum areas of the nation's capital in an attempt to incarnate the Christian gospel. J. W. Dickie noted: "incarnational theology recognised the need for efficient sanitation and healthy amusements not merely as means to an end but as themselves expressions of Christian fellowship."[22]

TOYNBEE HALL

Origins

In the context of one short chapter it isn't possible even to begin to consider settlements in any detail,[23] but some account of the founding of Toynbee Hall must be given since it became a pattern and model, at least in some degree, for almost all other settlements that followed it. Indeed, for this reason it has been called "The Mother of All Settlements."[24]

Toynbee Hall, which adjoined St. Jude's Vicarage, was opened in 1884, although its buildings were not completed until the following year.

21. Inglis, *Churches and the Working Classes*, 152.

22. Dickie, *College Missions and Settlements in South London 1870–1920*, i.

23. For a detailed account of Settlements in London see Scotland, *Squires in the Slums*.

24. Reason, *University and Social Settlements*, 52.

Residents had three duties: "to pursue some study, to consider other residents, and every week to do something, however small, which will help the ignorant, the sad, or the sinning, remembering always that the true man is he that serveth."[25] Those who took up residence bound themselves to stay for a term of not less than three months. The premises also contained a dining room, classrooms, and five little halls for educational and entertainment purposes. In addition, about a hundred non-residents at any one time were also involved in the work. The program for a typical week in 1890 comprised of ten lectures, four of which were in conjunction with the University Extension Society, nine reading parties, the meetings of two literary societies, thirty-five classes of various kinds, a concert, a party for a particular group, a meeting of a pupil teachers' association, and constant use of the library, which contained over 4,000 volumes.

Samuel Barnett Samuel had been curate in the fashionable London parish of St. Mary's Bryanston Square. There he opened a Club Room for working men, assisted in relief work, helped to found the first Charity Organisation Society, and engaged in education and club work. It was at St. Mary's that he also had the opportunity of working closely with Octavia Hill, who had opened a workroom for women. It was she, according to Barnett's wife, who gave him "new revelation of womanly potentialities, for which his dear mother and the women he had known at Bristol had given him no indication."[26]

Barnett's wife, Henrietta, proved to be the perfect match. James Mallon (1874–1961), one of Toynbee's later wardens, described them as "uniquely suited" and commented, "For forty years they thought and worked together, stimulating, balancing and supplementing one another . . . with the texture of their life so closely interwoven that their work and ideas belonged together."[27] His aim, which reflected the earlier Christian Socialist ideal, was "that everyone might know God as Father." Barnett had decided views as to why the poor absented themselves from traditional church. He soon began a service for children and went out visiting in "lay headgear" and "dressed as unlike a parson as he could well appear."[28]

As the Barnetts sought to grapple with these problems they recognized that help was needed from outside the parish bounds. This led Samuel to experiment with the idea of inviting undergraduates from his

25. Barnett, *Canon Barnett*, 405.

26. Ibid., 26–35.

27. Briggs and Macartney, *Toynbee Hall*, 27.

28. Barnett, *Canon Barnett*, 82.

university to come down to Whitechapel in their vacations and to give some of their time to helping with the parish organizations and clubs. Among the undergraduates who came to spend a summer vocation at Whitechapel in the 1870s was Arnold Toynbee. Though dissatisfied with many of the teachings of the Church of England, he believed it might somehow be capable of raising the poor to a better quality of life. His early death and his strenuous endeavors on behalf of the poor had a profound effect on his many friends and colleagues in the university and it was decided that the Barnetts' new venture should be called Toynbee Hall. Its central objective, which was set out in a "Memorandum of Association," was "to provide education and the means of recreation and enjoyment for the people of London and other great cities; to enquire into the condition of the poor and to consider and advance plans calculated to promote their welfare."[29]

As has been noted, in his approach to the problems of London's East End, Barnett wanted to avoid what he called "the machinery of religious missions." In the words of Briggs and Macartney: "His angle was very different from that of the Evangelicals anxious to convert the poor, or the Tractarians calling them to worship. He wanted not only settlement, but sharing of experience, not only contact but community."[30] The years that followed produced a constant flow of young men from Oxford who wanted to share in the vision. Among those who came were Arthur Sidgwick and Henry Scott Holland.[31] As the years passed and the work expanded, more and more men were needed and the Barnetts began to make regular term visits to Oxford, sometimes staying with the Master of Balliol College, Benjamin Jowett, who gave them active support.

Toynbee and Labor Concerns

Barnett was not one who could stand aside from the concerns of the working poor. Co-operation was the first working-class cause to appeal to Toynbee Hall and to be received with genuine concern and support. Benjamin Jones (1848–1947), the leading Co-operator, became a Toynbee Associate in 1886.[32]

29. *Memorandum of Association* printed in *First Annual Report of the Universities' Settlement in East London*, 1885.

30. Briggs and Macartney, *Toynbee Hall*, 5.

31. Barnett, *Canon Barnett*, 308.

32. *The Star*, October 1889.

Among other concerns, Barnett was a vigorous opponent of the system of casual labor that operated in the docks and elsewhere. He described it as "the hardest problem in east London."[33] It was, in his view, the main reason why so many East-Enders were poor and in constant need of relief. Toynbee settlers shared his concern over this issue and gave their support to a number of other East London labor struggles. In fact, from the earliest days Toynbee became the meeting place for a number of local trade unions. Prominent among them was the Dock Workers' Union. Toynbee provided a supper for Ben Tillett and Tom Mann and the dockworkers strike committee in September 1889. Several Toynbee residents became members of the Dock Workers' Union. Toynbee also investigated the conditions of the East London Slopworkers (Tailors and Tailoresses) and set up a committee to inquire into the terrible conditions at Bryant and May, which eventually led to a strike of 400 match girls.[34]

Barnett frequently intervened in trade disputes and in one year did so on fourteen separate occasions.[35] He personally chaired the first meeting of the Trafalgar branch of The Riverside Labourers' Union. The meeting was held in one of the lecture halls and about two hundred laborers were reported to be in attendance.[36] Tillett later claimed in his *Memoirs* that his inspirational leadership as a trade unionist owed much to a course of lectures he had heard at Toynbee.

The 1890 Annual Toynbee Report spoke highly of the value of trade unionism and noted that many of the new unions were holding their branch and business meetings on the premises. They included The Tailoresses Union, The Women Cigar Makers, The Stickmakers, The Tailors, Cutters, and Pressers,[37] The Railway Servants, The Furriers, The Shop Assistants, The Fellowship of Porters and Dock Labourers,' The Jewish Cabinet Makers, and Jewish Bakers.[38] In the summer of 1890 The Amalgamated Society of Shipwrights held its annual conference at Toynbee Hall. Barnett asserted, in what proved to be prophetically accurate words, that "co-operation and trade-unionism are the two forces that will make the twentieth century."[39] Toynbee was also active in supporting women's

33. Briggs and Macartney, *Toynbee Hall*, 47.

34. Mayor, *The Churches and the Labour Movement*, 59.

35. Ibid.

36. *The Toynbee Record*, 2.1 (October 1889) 8.

37. *The Times*, 31 March, 1891.

38. *Annual Report of Toynbee Hall*, 1890.

39. Barnett, *Canon Barnett*, 611.

trade-union activities and a number of female trade unions held delegate and branch meetings at the settlement. Among those who found the hall to be a supportive home base was The East London Tailoresses Society.[40] Thus, as L. Smith observed, "The Settlement was associated with the emergence of the New Unionism, which was attempting to organise the hitherto unorganised unskilled labourers and to extend unionism among the skilled and semi-skilled."[41]

Social Concerns

Barnett was strongly of the view that Toynbee men should be active in local government and social administration. He was vehemently opposed to harsh workhouses as a means of discouraging the lazy back to work. "It is not deterrence," he wrote, "it is education or training which will make people work; and education, be it remembered, includes discipline. The first thing necessary, is to replace the workhouses and casual wards with what may be called 'labour schools.'"[42] A number of Toynbee residents and associates were elected to various offices on local borough councils, particularly Stepney. Sanitary legislation was a key issue for Toynbee and a Sanitary Aid Committee was established that successfully campaigned for clean water after an outbreak of diphtheria and scarlet fever was found to have been caused by dirt from the East London Water Works. Barnett later claimed that Toynbee Hall had helped "to inspire local government with a higher spirit."[43]

Education at Toynbee

Barnett made education one of the central concerns of Toynbee's mission. He believed that only by educating the poor would they be in a position to lift themselves out of their down-trodden situation.

Toynbee was therefore concerned with education at all levels. It sponsored university extension lectures, but the fees were too expensive for most East Londoners. However, its applied courses enjoyed much greater patronage and success. Henrietta Barnett gave a list of 134 different classes that were taught during her time at Toynbee. They included such

---

40. See for example the report in *The Women's Gazette*, 14 June, 1890.
41. Smith, *Religion*, 65.
42. Barnett, *Canon Barnett*, 671.
43. Reason, *University and Social Settlements*, 22.

practical subjects as basket work, first aid, home hygiene, home nursing, human anatomy, life saving, sewing, shorthand, and reading, writing, and arithmetic.[44] One report in December 1891 asserted that "better proof of the hold that Toynbee's education schemes had taken on East London could not be had than the fact that a thousand students were in weekly attendance at the classes, not to speak of the large number of people who took advantage of the library, lectures and miscellaneous meetings."[45] The students were reported to be "both male and female, old and young, and, instead of being well-to-do, are nearly all poor."[46] The lectures, which were made as simple and practical as possible, were increasingly popular. Supporting local teachers was another of Toynbee's concerns and a number of Toynbee's members served on various school boards.

Barnett was a strong advocate for the equality of women and contended that the State should repeal all laws and abolish all customs that tempt men to lord it over women, or that interfere with the complete development of women's nature. In reply to a question as to whether the legal and clerical professions should be thrown open to women, Barnett said: "I do not think St Paul's prohibition of women speaking in the churches was intended to be a perpetual obligation. I am in favour of the removal of all legal restrictions on the occupations of women. They should have the same liberty as men to follow any calling and to vote at any election. Their present position of subordination develops the more brutal and selfish instincts of men, and at the same time provokes women to do acts and make claims which are unwomanly."[47]

Barnett was also concerned that the poor, who had little chance for relaxation during the week, should have the opportunity to enter galleries on Sundays. He made the point that "those who live in poor districts of great cities do not go short of material things only; they starve for lack of beautiful things." The result of this was that Toynbee entered into a controversy with the Lord's Day Observance Society over Sunday Art Exhibitions and Barnett wrote to the Bishop of London justifying Sunday opening.[48] While it is clear that Barnett was no sabbatarian, he was a strong defender of Sunday as a day for worship and rest from work. "Religion, it has rightly

44. Barnett, *Canon Barnett*, 330–31.

45. *The Scottish Leader*, 7 December, 1891.

46. *The Christian Union*, 18 September, 1890.

47. *The Bristol Mercury*, June 1894. In Barnett, *Canon Barnett*, 443.

48. Mayor, *Churches and the Labour Movement*, 64.

been said," he wrote, "depends on the Sabbath. Unless that is people break off from work they will not think about God."[49]

Barnett recognized the great importance of providing books for the poor, who had little opportunity to read and lacked sufficient resources to purchase any literature of their own. Toynbee's library therefore became a major priority and, despite the lack of grant aid, it continued to grow every year. In 1888 there were 3,878 volumes, in 1890, 5,216 volumes, and in 1900, 7,449 volumes. Eventually the pressure of Toynbee's campaigns came to fruition with the opening of the Whitechapel Public Library in 1892.[50]

Religion at Toynbee

In his Annual Report for 1890 Barnett stressed that Toynbee was nonsectarian in its ethos. He wrote that "among the residents of Toynbee have been found Churchmen, Nonconformists, Roman Catholics, Jews and unsectarians. . . . No man can say that Toynbee Hall has any narrow aim; it does not exist to increase any party, or bring honour to anybody."[51] That said, Barnett was clearly aware of his role as a clergyman of the established church and every morning there were prayers held in the settlement drawing room for all who wished to join in. Samuel Barnett "did not rush through a set of prayers as some clergy do," nor did he "gabble over a whole chapter of the Bible regardless of its length." His practice was to select a short passage and comment on it. This was followed by prayers and a hymn, which were carefully chosen.[52]

Notwithstanding his liberal views and broad theological sympathies, Barnett was distressed when a group of men from Keble College felt it necessary to establish a church settlement. However, with the passing of time Barnett overcame the wounds inflicted by rivalry and in the years that lay ahead he gave much time to encouraging the founding and promoting the growth of other settlements. Among those to whom he gave advice and support were Caius House in 1887, St. Hilda's for women in 1889, Mansfield House in 1890, Bermondsey Settlement in 1891, Canning Town in 1892, Browning Hall in 1895, Cambridge House in 1896, Passmore Edwards in 1896, and Plain House in Bristol.

49. Barnett, *Canon Barnett*, 491.

50. Kelly, *A History of Adult Education*, 241.

51. *Fifth Annual Report of the Universities' Settlement in East London*, 1889, 14.

52. Barnett, *Canon Barnett*, 490.

The Achievements of Toynbee

Henrietta Barnett was the perfect match for Samuel. The achievements of Toynbee were in almost every sense a joint affair. Some time in 1872, before they were married, he wrote to her that he could not conceive of there being another woman in the world "who will so meet my wants and stimulate my powers." At a later point, long after his death, when she had completed his biography, she could write, "I have loved living with my husband's spirit as I wrote his life and painted his character."[53] T. E. Harvey, Barnett's successor as warden, wrote of Henrietta that "her will-power harnessed men and women to tasks which would otherwise have been untouched that needed doing."[54] Barnett was constantly active in recruiting new residents. On 9 May he wrote to his brother Frank, "Oxford was good. On Sunday we had a meeting at Balliol. I once more fiddled on the Settlement string and found the men as ready as ever to dance. In fact the men altogether are as responsive as ever and put us in good heart." He went on to state that one really positive outcome of their stay was the relationship they formed with the Bishop of Ripon. Samuel noted that he understood "that high class men require intelligence rather than dogmas" and need to value rightness of life more than rightness of views.[55]

There was, consequently, a decided middle-classness about Toynbee Hall. It was noted that a characteristic of Toynbee tea was "one in which the maid brought in a trolley laden with buttered muffins and assorted cakes." Visitors to Toynbee felt it to represent too much of the ethos of a university college tucked away in East London. One guest noted the comfort of the drawing room with many easy chairs and hung with excellent portraits of great men such as Browning, Matthew Arnold, and Lord Shaftesbury. The dining room, he noted, "is rather sombre, with the arms of the Oxford and Cambridge Colleges decorating the walls."[56] A past resident wrote: "To old public-school and university men, Toynbee Hall, with its collegiate atmosphere, had a familiar feeling. There was the society of contemporaries, there was the kindly guidance and supervision of an elder man, there were the meals in common and community life."[57]

---

53. Ibid., 45.

54. Briggs and Macartney, *Toynbee Hall*, 25.

55. S. Barnett to Frank, 9 May, 1885, Barnett Correspondence, Ms F/BAR/25, London Metropolitan Archives.

56. *New York Herald*, 23 March, 1890.

57. Barnett, *Canon Barnett*, 434.

Toynbee Hall was indeed, in the words of Will Reason, "The mother of all Settlements." By this statement Reason referred to the fact that Toynbee became the model for almost all the differing settlements and mission settlements that followed in the years immediately after 1884. Toynbee undoubtedly gave major encouragement to university extension education and played a significant part in supporting trades unions in the East End of London. Perhaps above all, it demonstrated the ways in which the national church could and should be involved in championing the cause of the poor and disadvantaged. When Father James Adderley, who was the second warden of Oxford House, reflected on Barnett's death, he wrote: "I am convinced that in the death of Canon Barnett the Church has lost one of the very few prophets that we have had in our midst for a hundred years."[58]

OXFORD HOUSE

Oxford House in East London, which was established on the 8th September, 1884, was inspired by the Tractarians of Keble College, Oxford, under the leadership of Father James Adderley. Its aims were stated as follows: "Oxford House in Bethnal Green is established in order that Oxford men may take part in the social and religious work of the Church in East London; that they may learn something of the life of the poor; may try to better the condition of the working classes as regards health and recreation, mental culture and spiritual teaching; and may offer an example, so far as in them lies, of a simple religious life."[59] Oxford House had a distinctly Christian missional agenda that contrasted strongly with Toynbee Hall. Appealing on behalf of Oxford House, the Warden of Keble College, Edward Talbot, who had been chairman at the inaugural meeting, said; "One objective animates the whole movement—the preparation of character for . . . the reception of the religion of Christ, for the advancement of which Oxford House alone exists."[60] The leaders of Oxford House were of the view that if the Londoners of the East End were ever going to be won for Christianity then they, the Settlers, must be openly committed to the church in East London. They therefore became formally linked with the

58. *The Westminster Gazette*, 421.

59. *Oxford House Magazine*, 1894. In Ashworth, *The Oxford House in Bethnal Green*, 4.

60. *The Times*, 21 January, 1891, 13. In Inglis, *Churches and the Working Classes*, 157.

parish of St. Matthew's, Bethnal Green. When A. F. Winnington-Ingram became the fourth warden he was also appointed Rector of St. Matthew's "at the Bishop of London's special request." The bishop's view was that " the House will help the parish and the parish will help the House."[61]

Although the residents at Oxford House had a much more specifically religious agenda than Toynbee Hall, they nevertheless acknowledged that Barnett had given them the inspiration and relationships between the two communities were friendly.

Apart from differences in religion, many of the activities of Oxford House were very similar to those of Toynbee. There was a marked growth in the number of clubs and organization under the wardenship of Winnington-Ingram. There were university extension lectures and a program of social, athletic, and life-enhancing activities. Most of these activities came under the umbrellas of one of the three main clubs: The Oxford House Club for Clerks and Skilled Artisans, The University Club for Unskilled Working Men, and The Webbe Institute. The last of the three was named after the cricketer philanthropist, Herbert Webbe of New College. It provided activities for boys up to the age of eighteen. The work produced encouraging spiritual results such that by 1895 it was reported that, "we find 60 or 70 boys coming voluntarily to Bible Classes every week and a full Mission Service on Sunday night and always 200 or more men at the Club Service, and a small but growing body of club communicants meeting in the Oxford House chapel every Saturday night."[62]

The political views of Oxford House were perhaps more diverse than those of Toynbee Hall but all were agreed that no one was attempting to bias them in any particular direction. Residents actively involved themselves in a range of neighborhood, social, and governmental concerns and served on local Guardians and School Boards.[63] In June 1887, Harold Hodge of Oxford House took on the task of secretary of the Bethnal Green Sanitary Committee. Among other things, its findings revealed a very large number of houses that were defective in construction and objectionable from a sanitary point of view.[64] In 1888 Oxford House, like Toynbee, set up an Industrial Co-operative Society, which proved to be particularly

61. *Oxford House Chronicle* 9.8, August, 1895.

62. *Oxford House Annual Report*, 1895, 11.

63. Ibid., 12.

64. *Oxford House Annual Report*, 1887, 22.

popular venture. Each Saturday about a thousand customers personally purchased goods.[65]

OTHER OXFORD AND CAMBRIDGE SETTLEMENTS

Two other Oxford colleges faced up to the challenge of East London: Christ Church in 1881 and Trinity in 1888. Both were influenced by the ethos and personnel of Oxford House. The first Trinity Missioner was Luke Paget, who was described by James Adderley as "a most delightful combination of the cultured and the humorous and the busy."[66] The new Mission church of St. Frideswide, which seated 550, was dedicated by the Bishop of London on 15th July, 1890. The Trinity Mission House was founded in 1888 in a district carved out of the parish of St. John's East Stratford. The buildings consisted of a church that seated about 400, a large hall, a club, and rooms for the missioners.[67] The primary aim of both the Christ Church and the Trinity missions was to bring about religious commitment, albeit Tractarian in character. Darell Tupper Carey, who became warden of the Christ Church Mission in 1898, was a pronounced ritualist who was an active visitor and a captivating story-teller. He delighted in street processionals with fully-robed choir and enjoyed open-air preaching. "Tupper" was gifted with men and quadrupled the membership of his Working Men's Club.

SOUTH OF THE THAMES

While the Oxford Colleges, inspired by the influence of Toynbee Hall and Samuel Barnett's frequent visits to the University, focused their energies in the East End of London, Cambridge recognized that there was an untouched mission field south of the Thames. In this they were inspired, as were the public school missions, by Bishop Anthony Thorold, whose Rochester diocese extended right along the south bank of the Thames. He was always ready to assign an ecclesiastical district consisting of parts of several parishes to a new mission and he paid regular visits to all the college and public school missions that he had been established. St. John's

---

65. For a detailed account of the Oxford House Co-operative, see *Oxford House Annual Report*, 1889, 23.

66. Adderley, *In Slums and Society Reminiscences of Old Friends*, 69.

67. Legge, *Trinity College Mission in Stratford 1888–1889*, 11.

College Mission was located in Walworth, half a mile from the Elephant and Castle. Clare College Mission was established in the Dilston Grove district of the parish of All Saints Rotherhithe. Pembroke Mission was set up in an area in the parish of Stoke Newington, while the Corpus Mission was located in the parish of Christ Church, Old Kent Road.

All of these Cambridge Settlements in South London combined the Toynbee emphasis on residence and presence with an overt sharing of the Christian faith. The very fact that they were all ready to call themselves missions and styled their leaders missioners, rather than wardens, was indicative of their desire to be more up-front about their distinctive Christian agenda. The range of activities put on by the missioners was very similar in character to the East End settlements. The Gonville and Caius Mission reported an attendance at their meetings and classes of at least 1,000 every week.[68] The St. John's Mission ran a soup kitchen during the winter months, lent blankets to the poor, and opened a dispensary.[69] Activities at the Pembroke Mission included a Mother's meeting, a "Happy Evening" for boys of nine to thirteen years of age, a boys' club for fourteen to eighteen years, and a penny bank (Saturdays). Between 8th May and 30th September, 1886, 227 deposits were made at the bank totaling £17 17s. od.[70] The Missioners were always dependent on their respective colleges for funds and made regular reports of their work in college magazines and gave an annual sermon in the chapel to Fellows and undergraduates. Many missioners devoted long hours to their work and several were forced to retire as a result of burnout or breakdown in their health.

The twenty or so public school missions engaged in much the same activities as those established by the Oxbridge Colleges. Christ's Hospital ran the St. John's Working Men's Club, a men's Bible class, and Sunday school classes, social and musical evenings, a cricket club, debating society, and a library.[71] The Harrow Mission ran a mothers' meeting, a Church of England Men's Society, a boys' club with cricket and football sections, a girl's club "with about two hundred members of the rougher class," a musical society and gymnastic and drill classes.[72] Highgate School Mission could boast a Sunday School with 250 children, a lads' brigade, a penny

---

68. *The Caian* 3.2 (1893) 134.

69. *The Eagle*, Vol. 14, March 1886, 136.

70. *Pembroke College Mission First Annual Report*, 1886–7, 7.

71. *The Blue*, April 1893, 50–53.

72. Stogden, *Harrow in London*, 3–5.

bank, a gymnastic club, a reading and games room, a Brigade Band of Hope, and a weekly Bible Class.[73]

METHODIST AND CONGREGATIONAL SETTLEMENTS AND MISSIONS

Although the Anglicans led the way in establishing mission settlements, the movement also impacted Nonconformists. Wesleyan Methodists established a settlement at Bermondsey in South London in 1891 under the leadership of John Scott Lidgett (1854–1953). Lidgett, who came from the "High Wesleyan" tradition, went to Bermondsey following the Conference decision of that year to support the project. The main building, opened in January 1892, was to be the Warden's home for fifty-nine years. Lidgett set out a list of aims for the settlement, one of which was "to bring additional force and attractiveness to Christian work."[74] Although public attention was still strongly focused on the East End of London following the publication of *The Bitter Cry*, Lidgett chose South London for his settlement because, in his own words, Bermondsey was "at that time the most neglected neighbourhood of poorer London, as far as the purposes I had in contemplation were concerned."[75] It had not, Lidgett observed, been "written up" like the Mile End Road or the Ratcliffe Highway and "offered no field for slumming by society women."[76] Lidgett could doubtless have found people who would have supported him if he had been planning an evangelistic mission, but his vision for Bermondsey was altogether larger. "A settlement," he wrote, "is or should be a community of social workers who come to a poor neighbourhood to assist by the methods of friendship and co-operation in building all that is essential to the well-being of the neighbourhood."[77]

In 1895 the Congregationalists established both Browning Hall in Walworth and Mansfield House in Canning Town. The former institution came about during the long Walworth pastorate of P. J. Turquand (1826–1902). There the chapel, which had been for that day exceptionally dark and ugly, was transformed into the light attractive structure and

73. *The Cholmeleian*, July 1900, 209–10.

74. Davies, *John Scott Lidgett*, 53.

75. Ibid., 54.

76. Ibid.

77. Ibid., 55.

now worked as a Congregational Settlement under the name of Browning Hall.[78] Mansfield House was led by Percy Alden. Both institutions espoused Barnett's ideal of having residential helpers who would live in hostel accommodation and then devote their evenings and some of their spare time to clubs and other local community activities. In contrast to Toynbee, however, both Mansfield and Browning had rather more overt Christian agendas. Browning Hall was connected with a local Congregational chapel and offered non-sectarian evangelical teaching.[79]

An official account of Mansfield House stated that one of its key aims was "to bring the teaching of Christ to bear on all the problems of a poor man's life."[80] That said, it seems to have been the case that many of its residents were more concerned to engage in social action of various kinds rather than to try and convert the residents of Canning Town. The *British Weekly* kept a fairly tight watch over the two settlements in an effort to ensure that they didn't lapse into the "creedlessness of Toynbee Hall."[81] Notwithstanding, both came to be strongly associated with social and political reform. One of the leaders at Mansfield wrote, "To carry out Christ's teaching we felt that a vigorous attack must be made on the evil conditions of life in the district."[82]

In order to support this objective, committees were established on public health, education, poor law, and other matters. Browning declared their active support for the Labour Party and stated, "We stand for the endeavour to gain for Labour not just the good things of life, but most of the best things of life. Come and join us in the service of Him who is the Lord of Labour and the soul of all social reform."[83] Mansfield House can be credited with initiating the Poor Man's Lawyer Scheme and Browning Hall can claim to be the inspiration that led to the start of old age pensions.

The Roman Catholic Church didn't stand aloof from the challenge of London's poor. Newman House in Southwark opened in 1891 and was

78. *The Congregational Year Book,* 1903. In Mayor, *The Churches and the Labour Movement,* 65.

79. *British Weekly* 28 October, 1895, 89. In Mayor, *The Churches and the Labour Movement,* 65.

80. *Mansfield House Settlement in East London.* In Inglis, *Churches and the Working Classes,* 160.

81. *British Weekly* 28 October 1895. In Mayor *The Churches and the Labour Movement,* 159.

82. W. Reason, "A Week at Mansfield House" (1893), cited in Inglis, *Churches and the Working Classes in Victorian England,* 165–66.

83. *British Weekly,* 28 October, 1895.

in part a response to a call by James Britten to Catholic University under-graduates and public schoolboys to demonstrate a concern for the urban Catholic poor. The project received support and encouragement from Cardinal Herbert Vaughan. St. Philip's House, founded in 1894 in Mile End, was the first Catholic settlement in East London and testimony to Vaughan's concern for the Catholic poor.[84] Several other Roman Catholic settlements were established in the years that followed. They included St. Anthony's House in 1896 and St. Cecilia's in Albert Square, Commercial Road in 1900.

WOMEN'S SETTLEMENTS AND SETTLERS
OF MORE RADICAL VIEWS

A number of women's settlements were founded in the later Victorian years. Some were adjuncts to the men's settlements. Others were inde-pendent foundations. They included the Women's University Settlement at Southwark, Mayfield House in Bethnal Green, sponsored by Chelten-ham Ladies' College, and the Women's Settlements in Canning Town and Bermondsey.

The later Victorian years produced an increasing number of indi-viduals with radical and liberal views. Among those who were impacted by doubt and skepticism was Mary Augusta Ward, better known as Mrs. Humphry Ward. She was the granddaughter of Thomas Arnold and her father, also a Thomas, was remembered for having twice converted to the Roman Catholic Church. She was of the opinion that Christianity could be made palatable by ridding it of its miraculous content and focusing on the practical social aspects of the faith. These ideas she also set out in her highly successful novel *Robert Elsemere*, which was published in 1888. Elsemere, a country parson, felt his Anglican faith undermined by the new science of biblical criticism and so gave up his living to take on work among the London poor. In 1890 Mrs. Ward made her novel a real-ity when she was instrumental in establishing a non-sectarian settlement at University Hall in Gordon Square. It was based on a simplified ethical form of Christianity that emphasized social care. Mrs. Ward said on one occasion that one aspect of University Hall was to show that the faith of T. H. Green, Martineau, and Stopford Brooke was viable.[85]

84. Gleeson, "The Decade of an East End Settlement," *Month*, December 1904. In Inglis, *Churches and the Working Classes*, 160.

85. Inglis, *Churches and the Working Classes*, 161.

Philip Wicksteed (1844–1925), a Unitarian minister, was the warden for a brief period, but became disillusioned with the way in which the missionary and practical activities were segregated. After his resignation, the endeavor to nurture Unitarian religion was more or less given up. In 1898 Ward's organization subsequently developed into the Passmore Edwards Settlement and largely concerned itself with social and educational work. Ward's later years were somewhat less radical as she opposed the suffrage movement and supported her son as a Conservative candidate for Parliament.[86]

STATISTICS

In 1913 a student of the settlement movement counted twenty-seven Settlements in London, twelve in the rest of England and five in Scotland. Thirty-two of these were religious in their orientation. Eighteen of the settlements had university associations and others had university men and women living in them. In 1934 W. F. Lofthouse gave the statistics for residential settlements as twenty-nine in London and fifteen elsewhere in the country.[87] Settlements proved to be effective for a brief time span, but once the twentieth century began their influence and impact was gradually diminished. The main reasons for this were that many men began to be attracted to the new socialism that was emerging and the growth of the welfare state, which increasingly provided many of the social, medical, and recreational services that the Settlers had provided. From a religious point of view, Samuel Barnett observed that "Settlements had been inclined to become too much like the parish they were designed to supplement."[88] Probably the high point of the Settlement movement was just before the outbreak of the First World War.

86. Trevelyan, *Life of Mrs Humphry Ward*. In Mayor, *Churches and the Labour Movement*, 282.

87. Davies, *John Scott Lidgett*, 51.

88. Ellis, *Toynbee Hall and the University Settlements*, 167.

FACTORS THAT MADE THE SETTLEMENTS SUCCESSFUL

They Incarnated the Gospel

The Settlers may have been university men and women who at times appeared to be condescending in their attitudes and manner, but they were at least people who incarnated the gospel. They recognized the value of a Christian presence. They saw clearly that if Christians truly want to impact a locality the most important thing is that they should be resident within it. The Settlers lived out their Christian faith in ways that impacted the every day lives of the people who surrounded them. They involved themselves with the issues of sub-standard housing, public health, defective drains, insanitary sewers, and the need for fresh water. In short, they modeled Jesus' command to be good neighbors.

They Built Bridges into the Neighborhood

In the last quarter of the nineteenth century many churches were losing touch with the working poor and those at the margins of society. This was true of both ritualists (who the majority of working people suspected as being Roman Catholics in disguise) and also of many evangelicals (who were being impacted by the world-denying spirituality emanating from the Keswick Convention). The Settlers recognized that working people weren't going to come them; rather they, the Settlers, had to go to the poor and outcast. The Settlers recognized something that even William Booth, the revivalist founder of the Salvation Army, eventually concluded: that good news for the poor only comes through acts of loving kindness and practical care. In this they were, in reality, simply re-discovering the model that Jesus himself had exhibited, namely that his works demonstrated the truth and reality of his words.

They Established Communities

There is no doubt that the Settlements and Missions that were established in East and South London established genuine Christian communities in which those who joined the clubs and activities had a real sense of ownership and belonging. The hungry were fed, the disadvantaged defended, and the illiterate were taught to read and enjoy a rich variety of classes and lectures. There were penny banks, Christmas clubs, free concerts, lantern shows, billiards, bagatelle, country rambles, outings to places of interest, and even holidays. Indeed, literally hundreds of children were taken away by the Settlers every year for a week's holiday in the country or by the sea. All this made it much easier for the local residents to attend Bible studies and worship sessions with the Settlers because they knew, loved, and respected them and saw them several times every week.

They Recognized the Importance of Education and Recreational Activities

The Settlers were pioneers of adult education at a time when even secondary education was denied to most people. The education they provided was very wide-ranging and included both practical household and health matters as well as outlines of English literature, history, and painting. Without doubt, the education provided by the Settlers helped to produce a large number of more articulate trade union leaders, implanting in them Christian principles of self-respect and social justice. Settlements such Toynbee Hall and Browning Hall helped trade unions to organize themselves and to fight for better conditions of work and pay. One legacy of the Settlement movement, which has yet to be fully researched and recognized, was the way in which they identified the Christian faith with manly and sporting activities. It has been shown by Colin Kerrigan that it was the public school influence that caused many missions and settlements to take up football. Indeed, it is the case that the most popular Settlement boys' club activity was soccer and teams were often trained by missioners who had been gifted players at their pubic schools. Winnington Ingram was once asked what advice would he give to someone starting a boys' club and his reply was that the first thing to do was to start a football club. Perhaps one of the greatest legacies of the Settlement movement was that they introduced and gave the lads of East London a lasting desire to play and watch association football.

13 | The Pentecostals

THE BACKGROUND TO PENTECOSTALISM

THE WORD "PENTECOST" COMES from the Greek name given to the Jewish Feast of Weeks—*pentecoste hemera*, which means "the fiftieth day," because it fell on the fiftieth day after the Passover. Pentecost was the feast during which the first fruits of the corn harvest were presented. It was on this day that the Holy Spirit came on the early disciples in Jerusalem (Acts 2) and the first Christian church was born. The name "Pentecost" came to be adopted by the church for the celebration of this pneumatic event. It was a day when the Holy Spirit was given, accompanied by speaking in tongues.

Throughout the course of the history of the Christian church there have been times and periods when the Holy Spirit came to individuals and groups with special intensity, in some cases accompanied by spiritual gifts. Among those who spoke with tongues were the Egyptian monk, Pachomius (292–c. 348), the Jansenists, who followed the Dutch theologian, Cornelius Jansen (1585–1638), and the Irvingites, followers of Edward Irving (1792–1834).[1] However, it wasn't until the beginning of the twentieth century that the modern Pentecostal movement began, with a particular widespread emphasis on speaking in tongues and other spiritual gifts, most notably healing. The birth of this movement, as will be seen, occurred in a series of special meetings held in Los Angeles in 1906. Britain was first impacted in September the following year through Thomas Ball Barratt (1862–1940), a Methodist minister from Oslo. Having been influenced by Pentecostals in New York he was invited by Alexander Boddy (1854–1930), the incumbent of All Saints Parish Church in Sunderland,[2] to hold a series of revival gatherings. As a result, a number of small Pentecostal

---

1. Christie-Murray, *Voices from the Gods,* 37, 45, and 55–57.

2. For Boddy see Scotland, "Boddy, Alexander" in Larsen, *Biographical Dictionary of Evangelicals,* 59–60.

meetings began to spring up in various parts of the country, most of them led by lay people. On a world canvas, Walter Hollenweger analyzed five basic categories of Pentecostals: Black Oral, Evangelical, Catholic, Critical, and Ecumenical.[3] The first two are characterized by "orality," narrative theology, witness, a high level of participation, prayer for the sick, and dreams and visions in both personal and public forms.

The context in which Pentecostalism emerged was one of social and political turmoil following the end of the American Civil War. This was a conflict in which more American men were killed than was to be the case in the First World War, and it left many with feelings of guilt that this was a fight that had been fueled by different interpretations of the biblical teachings on slavery. Many felt a sense of failure and condemnation and this led to their determination to be more serious in seeking the face of God. While it was the case that there was no such suffering in England in the later decades of the nineteenth century, many of serious-minded, middle-class Christians began to feel they needed to beware of their increasing comforts and prosperity. Added to this was the fact that a number of holiness revivalists travelled from America and held extensive meetings in the "Old Country." Among their number were Walter and Phoebe Palmer (1807–74),[4] Amanda Berry Smith, and Robert (1827–99) and Hannah Pearsall Smith (1832–1911). The Smiths, who held meetings to enable people to receive holiness through faith, made a powerful impact at meetings they held at Broadlands, in Hampshire, and Oxford in the summer of 1874. Robert in particular stressed the need to feel the presence of the Holy Spirit in a physical way. The conference, which the Pearsall Smiths held at Brighton in late May and early June in 1875,[5] led to the founding of the Keswick Convention, which emphasized the importance of seeking a deeper experience of the Holy Spirit. During the closing years of the nineteenth century serious-minded Christians on both sides of the Atlantic had begun to speak and pray about the need for a new Pentecost for the church of the twentieth century. Teachers and Bible College students were asking, "What is the Bible evidence for Baptism of the Spirit?"

---

3. Hollenweger, "The Pentecostal Elites and the Pentecostal Poor: A Missed Dialogue"? In Poewe, *Charismatic Christianity as a Global Culture*, 201.

4. Scotland, *Apostles of the Spirit and Fire*, 118–38.

5. Ibid., 209–14.

LOS ANGELES AND THE AZUSA STREET REVIVAL

In a Bible College in Topeka, Kansas, run by Charles Parham (1873–1929), speaking in tongues was held to be the distinguishing mark of baptism in the Holy Spirit. In addition to his work in the Bible College, Parham—who is sometimes called "The Father of Pentecostalism"—began life as a Methodist preacher. In 1898 he moved to Topeka, Kansas, where he started a healing home and in 1890 founded Bethel Bible College. Parham held many large meetings at which numbers of those who came were converted, sanctified, baptized in the Spirit, and healed of sicknesses. Parham preached through the winter of 1903–4 in a warehouse seating several hundred in Galena, Kansas. In January, the Joplin, Missouri, *News Herald* reported that 1,000 had been healed and 800 had professed conversion.[6] Parham asserted that the purpose of Spirit baptism was "an enduement with power for service."[7] Parham continued to preach and hold meetings in various places in America until his death in Texas in 1929. One group of his followers later organized the Apostolic Faith churches, which began in Baxter Springs, Kansas.

One of Parham's pupils, a black preacher, William J. Seymour (1870–1922), was invited to Los Angeles by the woman pastor of a Black Holiness church. Seymour duly arrived and preached on Acts 2:4, "Anyone who does not speak in tongues is not baptized with the Holy Spirit." The majority of the congregation were unwilling to accept his teaching and Neelly Terry, the pastor who had invited Seymour, asked him not to return. However, some members invited him to hold meetings in their homes and on 9th April, 1906, the "fire came down" at a prayer meeting at 214 Bonnie Brae Street. Many people then experienced the baptism of the Spirit and Seymour hired an old African Methodist Episcopal church at 312 Azusa Street for $8 a month. By the close of 1906, the movement, which had several centers, claimed thousands of followers. On one particular day Seymour and some 500 people converged on one of the city's beaches and Seymour baptized 106 in the ocean.

This Asuza Street Mission is regarded by many Pentecostals as the place of origin of the worldwide Pentecostal movement. For three years, without interruption, prayer meetings took place there with speaking in tongues, singing in tongues, and prophecy. Originally, Parham was the main leader of the revival but, as Walter Hollenweger pointed out, from

---

6. Blumhofer, *The Assemblies of God*, Vol. 1, 86–88.

7. Ibid., *Restoring the Faith*, 50.

November 1907 his name no longer appeared on the letterhead. Blum-hofer observed that Parham had in fact attended no more than three Azu-sa Street services and "his long-harbored bitterness about the mission's success marked the beginning of his ultimate ostracism from main stream Pentecostalism."[8]

By the end of 1906 there were already nine Pentecostal assemblies in Los Angeles, some of which were not on good terms with each other. The Asuza Street Mission lasted until 1923. Hollenweger wrote of it:

> The "Pentecostal experience of Los Angeles" was neither lead-ing astray of the Church by demons (as the German Evangeli-cal movement claimed), nor the eschatological pouring out of the Holy Spirit (as the Pentecostal movement itself claims) but an outburst of enthusiastic religion of a kind well-known and frequent in the history of Negro churches in America which de-rived its specifically Pentecostal features from Parham's theory that speaking in tongues is a necessary concomitant of the bap-tism of the spirit.[9]

Significantly, Hollenweger, a world authority on Pentecostal his-tory, commented further that "I do not wish to assert here that the Holy Spirit was not at work in the Los Angeles revival. I agree with the pioneer British Pentecostal, Alexander Boddy, who wrote: 'It was something very extraordinary, that white pastors from the south were eagerly prepared to go to Los Angeles to the Negroes, to have fellowship with them and to receive through their prayers and intercessions the blessings of the Spirit. And it was still more wonderful that these white pastors went back to the South and reported to members of their congregations that they had been together with Negroes, that they had prayed in one Spirit and received the same blessings as they.'"[10]

Clearly, world Pentecostalism cannot be properly understood with-out reference to Azusa Street. The church attracted people from across the United States and reports drew and captivated people from around the world. The meetings were joyous and memorable. Following a summer camp meeting on the outskirts of Los Angeles, a reporter noted: "Many were the heavenly anthems the Spirit sang through His people. And he gave many beautiful messages in unknown tongues, speaking of His soon coming, invitations to come to the Lord, and exhortations from the word."

8. Blumhofer, *The Assemblies of God*, Vol. 1, 109.

9. Hollenweger, *The Pentecostals*, 23–24.

10. Ibid., 24.

Blumhofer noted that "Countless messages in tongues were interpreted to proclaim the imminence of Christ's return. 'Awake! Awake!,' they pleaded, 'There is but time to dress and be ready, for the cry will soon go forth. The Bridegroom cometh.'"[11]

PENTECOSTAL DENOMINATIONS IN AMERICA

Walter Hollenweger in his classic study of Pentecostalism[12] counted 200 Pentecostal denominations in the USA. Of these, two stand out as the largest and most influential: The Assemblies of God (white majority) and The Church of God Cleveland (black majority).

Assemblies of God

In the early years following Azusa Street there was very little in the way of formal links between the individual Pentecostal Assemblies. However, with the passing of time it became clear that some minimal organization was going to have to be put in place, if only to ascertain whether or not a particular speaker, pastor, or leader held to the orthodox Christian faith. Furthermore, the authorities required credentials for pastors if they wanted to make use of cheap rail tickets. Several of the early attempts to establish some minimal safeguards met with further complications. First, there was dispute over baptism when some of the leaders decided to follow the early apostolic pattern of baptizing only in the name of Jesus. A large number of the early leaders were therefore baptized a second time " in the name of Jesus." In 1915 those groups who had formed themselves into the Assemblies of God network rejected several practices. Among them were the use of wine at the Lord's Supper, the identification of regeneration with baptism in the Spirit, and the blurring of the distinctions between the Father, Son, and the Holy Spirit.

A number of pastors had come to the view that speaking in tongues was not the *sole* evidence of baptism in the Spirit. Nevertheless, this led to the 1918 meeting of pastors ruling that speaking in tongues had necessarily to accompany baptism of the Spirit. Indeed, they regarded tongues as the *initial* evidence of Spirit baptism.[13]

11. Blumhofer, *The Assemblies of God*, Vol. 1, 106.

12. Hollenweger, *The Pentecostals*, 29.

13. Ibid., 32.

In the early days most American Assemblies of God pastors set little store by formal education. They believed that Jesus' return was imminent and that evangelism was all that really what mattered. As a holiness church they made increasingly rigorous demands on the membership. Make-up, the theatre, the cinema, and even secondary high schools and universities were to be avoided. The Sunday school formed the real educational backbone of the Assemblies of God. Every age group from three years to the adults had its own Sunday school magazine. In 1961 the assemblies of God had 992,366 Sunday school pupils, against 514,317 members.[14]

The Assemblies of God seem to have communicated well with young people. In the later years of the twentieth century one of their most well known ministers was David Wilkerson (1931–2008). He went to New York in 1958 and began working with young drug addicts for whom he founded a recovery program known as *Teen Challenge,* an impressive project among deprived youth in Brooklyn, Chicago, and Los Angeles. In 1963 he co-authored *The Cross and the Switchblade* with John and Elizabeth Sherrill. It told the story of the conversion of gang member, Nicky Cruz, and sold over 50 million copies. In 1971 Wilkerson moved his ministry to Lindale in Texas, but returned to New York City in 1986 to found and pastor Times Square Church.

The Assemblies of God differed from most other American Pentecostal churches in that they regarded sanctification as a gradual process rather than an instantaneous work of grace. In 1916 their membership was 6,703, but by 1936 it had swelled to 148,043,[15] and in 1960 it reached 508,602.[16]

The Church of God

The Church of God began with a small revivalist group pastored by Ambrose Jessop Tomlinson (1865–1943), a colporteur of the American Bible Society. In 1907 the headquarters of the church were moved to Cleveland, Tennessee. In the early days there was a strict holiness theme and smoking was declared incompatible with membership of the church. There were reports of early converts rolling on the floor at some of his meetings and Tomlinson himself was known as "the beautiful screamer." In 1920 there was a major crisis when the Assembly accepted a proposal that all tithes

---

14. Ibid., 38.

15. Blumhofer, *The Assemblies of God,* 263.

16. Hudson, *Religion in America,* 346.

should be paid directly to A. J. Tomlinson, who would then pay each pastor. Tomlinson's self-adulation grew by leaps and bounds and before long he was simultaneously General Overseer, manager of the publishing department, editor-in-chief of the monthly journal, and head of the orphanage and the Bible School. By the same token he automatically controlled all salaries of the pastors and other staff. Eventually, Tomlinson's power complex proved to be too much for the people of the church he had founded and after court cases and a long struggle he was expelled from the little empire he had brought into being. However, notwithstanding this setback, he soon founded, with some of his loyal supporters, the Church of God of Prophecy, which grew quickly in both America and in the UK. The words "of prophecy" were added in 1952 to distinguish it from the Church of God from which it had originated. By the beginning of the twenty-first century the Church of God of Prophecy had congregations and missions in over 130 countries with over one million members world-wide. In the year 2006 its membership in the USA was 84,762 with 1,871 churches. The leadership of this church passed to his younger son, Milton Ambrose Tomlinson (1906–95).

Many churches in the USA named themselves, "The Church of God" so it became customary to add a distinguishing name in brackets. The original church that A. J. Tomlinson had founded became known as the Church of God Cleveland. After Tomlinson's departure it soon recovered and began to thrive under the oversight of F. J. Lee. Although records are sparse, particularly for the early period, growth was strong and by 1997 it had a membership of 4,648,497 with 26,416 churches.[17] The ethical rigorism continued with prohibitions on mixed-bathing, permanently waved hair, going to the cinema or theatre, and make-up.

PENTECOSTALISM IN BRITAIN

The Welsh Revival of 1904

The Welsh Revival played an important part in the origins of Pentecostalism. It began in Joseph Jenkin's church in New Quay on Cardigan Bay. Among those who were converted were Evan Roberts and his brother, Dan. Evan Roberts (1878–1951) was the son of a devout miner from Loughor in Glamorgan, near Swansea. He was converted by the preaching

---

17. Statistics of September 1997 from office of Business and Records, Church of God International.

of the Methodist minister, Seth Joshua, and later had an experience that he described as the baptism in the Spirit. He wrote of it in the following lines, "One Friday evening that spring [1904], as I was praying at my bedside before going to bed, I was taken up into a great expanse—without time or space. It was a communion with God. Up to that time I had only had a God who was far off. That evening I was afraid, but that fear has never come back. I trembled so violently that the bed shook, and my brother was awakened and took hold of me, thinking I was ill."[18]

He went on to relate that he woke each night about one o'clock and was taken up into communion with God for about four hours. "What it was I cannot tell you, except that it was God."[19] W. T. Stead questioned Evan Roberts at length about these experiences. Roberts was clear that he was not dreaming but was wide-awake and that he was speaking to God as Father Almighty but "as a man speaks face to face with a friend." Roberts acted on the basis of visions, one of which was of a check with the number 100,000 written on it as a sign of the number who would become Christians during the revival. As it happened, the tally of converts actually proved to be more in the region of 162,000. Needless to say, Roberts was greatly sought after as a preacher and received hundreds of imploring invitations to bring the revival to local towns and villages. From the middle of November 1904 he visited numerous chapels in the Welsh Valleys proclaiming the power of the cross and the joy of the Holy Spirit. He did not preach in the traditional manner but preferred to speak as he felt moved by the Holy Spirit. Roberts should not be regarded as the sole instrument of the revival; he was a firm believer in the priesthood of all believers and sent out mission teams to take the gospel message (his brother, Dan, was among those sent). Roberts valued and encouraged women and young peoples' gifts and among his early helpers were Sidney Evans, aged about twenty, Annie Davis, aged eighteen, Mary Roberts, aged sixteen, and Annie May Rees and Florie Evans, who were both fifteen. During the revival women happily led meetings while Roberts was present.

Ian Randall charted something of the significant impact of the Welsh revival outside the principality.[20] He noted that in 1905 a large meeting of ministers was convened in London at Christ Church, Westminster Bridge (where F. B. Meyer was minister), to consider the impact of the revival.

18. Hollenweger, *The Pentecostals*, 179.

19. For a full account of Roberts' early years see Jones, *An Instrument of Revival; The Complete Life of Evan Roberts, 1878–1951.*

20. Randall, "The Breath of Revival," 196–205.

Among those who participated were Campbell Morgan of Westminster Chapel, Thomas Spurgeon of the Metropolitan Tabernacle, and Dinsdale Young of the Methodist Westminster Central Hall. J. W. Ewing from the large Rye Lane Baptist Chapel, Peckham, London, said in January 1905, following his personal experience in Wales, "I seemed to be searched through and through by the white light of the Spirit of Holiness."[21] Randall noted that "large numbers of local churches across Britain, as well as in many other countries, were affected."[22] Among other places where the revival had a major impact was Charlotte Baptist Chapel, Edinburgh, where there were two years of revival and growth and a substantial number of people converted.

Significantly, in 1905 F. B. Meyer spoke for eight days to large audiences in Los Angeles about revival and, as Randall and others have pointed out, this made a significant contribution to the beginnings of Pentecostalism.[23] His accounts were endorsed by Joseph Smale, the pastor of First Baptist Church, Los Angeles. He had been a member of the Metropolitan Tabernacle in London and then trained for the ministry at Spurgeon's Pastors' College. He had visited the revival and brought back glowing reports to his congregation. Smale later founded the First New Testament Church where speaking in tongues occurred on Easter Sunday, 1906.[24] It is clear that these events played a significant part in the emergence of Pentecostalism in both England and America.

All Saints Sunderland

The father of the British Pentecostal movement, Alexander Boddy (1854–1930),[25] took part in the Welsh revival and worked with Evan Roberts. He was adamant that the Pentecostal movement was a direct continuation of the Welsh revival. On hearing that there had been an outpouring of the Spirit in Norway, Boddy went out to witness it for himself. As a result he persuaded Thomas Ball Barratt (1862–1940), a Methodist minister working in Oslo, to come to Sunderland. Ball arrived on the 31st of August and

21. Ibid., 196.

22. Ibid.

23. Bartleman, *How Pentecost Came to Los Angeles*, 11.

24. Randall, "The Breath of Revival," 204–5. Bartleman, *From Plough to Pulpit*, 22.

25. Scotland, "Alexander Boddy," *Biographical Dictionary of Evangelicals*, 59–60. Blumhofer, "Alexander Boddy and the Rise of Pentecostalism"; Lavin, *Alexander Boddy: Pastor and Prophet*.

stayed till the 2nd December. Meetings were held in the parish hall of All Saints, Sunderland, where he was the incumbent. During the period from September 1907 to April 1908 about 500 seekers who came experienced the baptism of the Spirit with speaking in tongues, including the Bradford plumber, Smith Wigglesworth (1859–1947).

The Assemblies of God in the British Isles

On 9th January, 1909, only three years after the events of Azusa Street, a small company gathered at All Saints Vicarage in Sunderland to form The Pentecostal Missionary Union. Alexander Boddy chaired the meeting, which elected Cecil Polhill (1860–1938)[26] as President. Polhill-Turner, the squire of Howbury Hall, had been at Eton and was one of the "Cambridge Seven," a missionary group that included Charles Studd (1860–1931), the England Cricket Captain. He had earlier gone out as a missionary to Tibet. He had visited the revival in Los Angeles and was baptized in the Spirit at a prayer meeting in a private house there. For a number of years he organized conferences in Kingsway Hall in London that brought together independent Pentecostal churches from across the country. Eventually, the Pentecostal Missionary Union of churches under Polhill's presidency was dissolved to become the *Assemblies of God* in 1925.

A leading figure in the British Assemblies of God was Donald Gee (1891–1966). Originally a Congregationalist, he was converted under the ministry of Seth Joshua. His first experience of Pentecostalism took place when he came into contact with a Baptist group in 1912. He described his baptism in the Spirit as follows, "Increasingly glory now flooded into my soul in the meetings as well, until I began to speak in new tongues publicly. Also, I would sing very much in the Spirit in new tongues, when the little Assembly would be moved in this way by the Holy Spirit during our times of prayer and worship."[27]

For a long period Gee was the pastor of the Assembly of God congregation in Edinburgh. From 1934–44 he served as vice-chairman of the British Assemblies of God, and from 1948 onwards he was chairman. He undertook long journeys throughout the world as a Bible teacher, though not as an evangelist. From 1947 onwards he became the sole ex-officio member of the Committee of World Pentecostal Conferences. Up to 1964

26. For Cecil Polhill-Turner, see Pollock, *The Cambridge Movement*, 73, 78, and 83–86.

27. Hollenweger, *The Pentecostals*, 208.

he was also in charge of the Assemblies of God Bible School in London. Among other roles, Gee was also a writer of some distinction and his book *Concerning Spiritual Gifts* was translated into many languages and has remained a classic. Even critics of the Pentecostal movement have taken his works with seriousness. Gee advocated co-operation with the World Council of Churches, but remained firm in his commitment to classic Pentecostal beliefs. He wrote in 1925, "The doctrine that speaking with other tongues is the initial evidence of the baptism in the Holy Spirit rests upon the accumulated evidence of the recorded cases in the book of Acts where the experience is received."[28] Speaking at the Fifth World Pentecostal Conference in 1958 he put forward the same view.

> To teach a presumed Pentecostal experience without emotional manifestation is to emaciate the doctrine beyond all recognition as being according to the Scriptures. . . . There must be some outlet for deep feeling. Why not accept the form of outlet that God in his wisdom has ordained? . . . that speaking in tongues is the scriptural evidence of baptism with the Holy Spirit. . . . The soul becomes intoxicated with such a divine ecstasy that it is beyond ordinary forms of speech. . . . [W]ith all due respect we refuse to be satisfied that so-called Pentecostal experiences without physical manifestation are valid according to the scriptural patter of common logic.[29]

By 1979 there were 550 Assemblies of God churches in England alone.[30] By 2012 the figure had risen to over 600 with more than a thousand full-time leaders. In September 1999 the Hillsong churches, which were founded in 1983 in Sydney, Australia, had planted a congregation in London. Other congregations have been established.

The Elim Pentecostal Churches

Another important arm of British Pentecostalism was brought into being through the labors of George (1889–1962) and Stephen Jeffreys (1876–1943). The two brothers came from a very simple home in Wales. Their father was a miner and at the age of twelve Stephen had to go down to the coalface with his father to earn a living. His brother, George, was originally a salesman with the Maesteg Co-operative Society. Both brothers

---

28. *Redemptorist Tidings*, 1 December, 1925
29. Hollenweger, *The Pentecostals*, 209.
30. Bebbington, *Evangelicals*, 262.

committed their lives to Christ in the Welsh revival of 1904 in Shiloh Chapel. On 3rd June, 1910, George testified to "the Spirit falling upon me, then speaking through me in other languages, according to Bible evidence. Bless His name." In 1914 he went to Bible School and became a Congregational minister. By the time he was twenty-seven he was so famous that he commanded audiences of thousands and filled some of the largest halls in the country. In 1915, while in Ireland, he founded *The Elim Evangelistic Band,* an evangelistic team to assist him in his large-scale missions. The first Elim church was established shortly afterwards in Belfast. In 1926 Stephen became a full-time evangelist with the Assemblies of God. He travelled the world visiting, among other places, New Zealand, Australia, South Africa, and the United States. His final years were spent preaching in his beloved Wales. With the rapid growth of the Elim churches, a former Redemptorist Convent was purchased in 1925 and became the movement's headquarters and Bible College. Up until 1934 George Jeffreys remained the undisputed leader of the Elim Movement, acting without any official structure or organization. It was then decided to have an executive committee and from that point on they began to exercise increasing control over the movement. However George Jeffreys' view of church polity was essentially a congregational one and he felt strongly opposed to any form of centralized control. The result of this was that in 1934 he eventually parted company with the denomination that he himself had founded. About ten other ministers joined him and together they founded the Bible Pattern Church. Eventually, in 1944, Jeffreys signed over some fifty-six properties of which he was still a trustee to the Elim Trust Corporation. By 1979 the number of Elim churches had reached 350.[31] By 2010 there were more than 600 congregations in the UK, the largest of which is Kensington Temple in London.

After Jeffreys' departure the Elim Church continued the process of institutionalization under their secretary, Pastor E. J. Phillipps. In this process local churches no longer had title or trust deeds, but handed them over to the central administration. The sociologist Bryan Wilson described the change in Elim as being from a "tribal community" drawn together by a single leader to a denomination with a complete organizational structure.

The Elim Church has emerged as one of the most moderate Pentecostal churches. It teaches the inspiration of the Bible, but not in any way that asserts that the apostles were mere pens in the hand of the Holy Spirit. The doctrine that speaking in tongues is the initial sign of the baptism in

---

31. Bebbington, *Evangelicals*, 262.

the Holy Spirit is rejected as "not valid." The gifts of the Spirit are practiced, but are restricted in accordance with carefully defined criteria. In
the matter of the healing of the sick, Elim maintains the rational principles
set out by Jeffreys that "There is no authority in Scripture for the view that
every saint who is suffering from sickness and disease is out of line with
the will of God."[32]

Although he was not officially connected with either the Assemblies
of God or the Elim Church, Smith Wigglesworth (1859–1947) has become a legend among Pentecostals and Charismatic Christians, largely on
account of his healing ministry. Wigglesworth's education was neglected
owing to his parents' poverty and he had to go to work at the age of six,
pulling and cleaning turnips. He was converted in a Wesleyan Methodist
chapel at the age of eight. He married Mary Jane, known as Polly, in 1882
and together they engaged in Christian work, including healing meetings
at the Bowland Street Mission, which they founded in Bradford (where
Smith also worked as a plumber). A number of dramatic healings took
place even in the early days, including that of the local Baptist Minister's
wife who got up almost immediately from what her friends had described
as her deathbed.

When Smith heard about speaking with tongues at the meetings at
All Saints, Sunderland, he travelled there to investigate. In September 1907
he received what he now called "the real baptism in the Holy Spirit" with
the sign of speaking in tongues. The following Sunday Smith preached
at his own Mission Hall and his address was so powerful and clear that
it caused his wife to remark, "That's not my Smith, Lord, that's not my
Smith." From that time onward Smith's reputation and career became international as he travelled the world conducting healing campaigns. The
basis of Wigglesworth's healing ministry was faith. He once said, "If you
prayed for something six times you prayed five times in unfaith." Smith
believed all sickness to be of the devil and described cancer as "the devil
incarnate." For this reason he often kicked, punched, or slapped those who
were sick as a means, along with prayer, of driving the devil out of their
bodies. He later claimed that he had seen three people raised from the
dead as well as the restoring of sight to the blind.

32. Hollenweger, *The Pentecostals*, 200.

Later Twentieth-Century Pentecostalism in Britain

Fresh impetus was given to the Pentecostal movement with the arrival of immigrants from the West Indies, who brought with them their own churches, most notably the New Testament Church of God and the Church of God of Prophecy. These two groups both expanded rapidly, putting down strong roots in London, Birmingham, and the Midlands in particular. Later arrivals from West Africa brought a strong influx of other of independent Pentecostal groups to London and elsewhere. The most significant is the Kingsway International Centre, which was established in 1992 with 200 adults and 100 children. The church, which was located in Hackney in the East End of London and pastored by Matthew Ashimolowo (b. 1952), has in the region of 12,000 people in attendance at the main Sunday services.

CHARACTERISTICS OF PENTECOSTALISM

A God to be Experienced

Pentecostals have been, and are known for their insistence on the necessity of *experiencing* God through the Holy Spirit. The early Pentecostal pioneer, Donald Gee, stated that the central attraction of the movement "consisted purely of a powerful individual experience." The stress was not on any system of doctrine and Arminians and Calvinists both found themselves on the same platforms. Teachers with diverse views on holiness and eschatology were conscious of a new, deep, fundamental unity in spirit. Because the emphasis was on the Spirit rather than systems of government Pentecostalism promoted a temporary ecumenism.

Worship

Since its very beginnings Pentecostal worship has had a strongly cathartic aspect. During the fervent singing and vibrant worship, participants are lifted out of themselves and away from their trials and the painful and stressful experiences of life. As Waldo Cesar discovered in his study of Brazilian Pentecostalism, "all parts of the service emphasize the miraculous and feed the souls along their path in the world." As he saw it, the experience of baptism, which converts experience powerfully, communicates the presence of the Holy Spirit and a sense of the supernatural.[33] Researches have shown that Pentecostal worship offers a sustaining force that enables its participants to cope with the adversity of their daily lives. As the Chilean theologian, Juan Sepulveda, put it, "Daily life has penetrated more and more into worship, at the same time that worship has become the sustaining force in a stubborn action in face of adversity."[34]

From the beginning, Pentecostals have recognized and appreciated the power of music in attracting converts. Parham's associate, Howard Goss, stated that "without it the Pentecostal movement would never have made the quick inroads into hearts that it did."[35]

A Literal Interpretation of Scripture

Pentecostals are people of the book. Early Pentecostals were marked by their exactness in following a literal interpretation of Scripture. On a worldwide canvas the majority operate out of a fundamentalist kind of literal biblicism. When they have seen something in the New Testament church they have taken it as applicable for today, whether it be healing, power encounters, speaking in tongues, or other spiritual gifts. They sought to be people led by "The Book" and by the Holy Spirit. One of the early Azusa Street preachers, Frank Bartleman, recalled: "In the beginning of the Pentecostal outpouring I remember preaching for three hours one evening and the people still wanted more. Those were days of great hunger for the word of God." A Church of God minister, C. M. Padgett, wrote in the December 14th, 1918, issue of the Church of God *Evangel* about the results of the Holy Spirit baptism. One of them will be, "The Word of God will be prized above all reading, to your soul it will be the book of books; other reading matter will be secondary. The Newspaper will not be allowed to crowd out the word of God." Pentecostal biblical literalism was, and indeed is, well illustrated by the snake-handling Pentecostals of Kentucky and Tennessee. The practice began by George Went Hensley in 1909, particularly at the Dolley Pond Church of God with Signs Following. Based on a literal interpretation of Mark chapter 16, dangerous rattle snakes are handed round at a point when the meeting reaches a high emotional pitch.

33. Shaul and Cesar, *Pentecostalism and the Future of the Christian Churches*, 36–37.

34. Sepulveda, *Estandarte Evangelico* 3 (1991) 91. In Shaul and Cesar, *Pentecostalism*, 143–44.

35. Blumhofer, *The Assemblies of God*, 145.

Death from snakebite occurs from time to time, including Hensley himself in 1955. Although various attempts have been made to prohibit snake handling, the practice continues in a number of American states.

The Baptism of the Spirit was Power for Service

Pentecostals believed that the new experience of the Holy Spirit was an enduement with power for witness and service. William Seymour put it as follows in one of his earlier writings: "There is a great difference between a sanctified person and one that is baptized with the Holy Ghost and fire. A sanctified person is cleansed and filled with divine love, but one that is baptized with the Holy Ghost has the power of God on his soul and has power with God and men. Power over all the kingdoms of Satan and his emissaries . . ."[36]

Aaron A. Wilson, a pioneer Pentecostal preacher, "felt the call to preach from a child, but when filled with the Holy Spirit such a burden for lost souls came upon me!"[37] Gary McGee rightly claims that, "The history of Pentecostalism cannot be properly understood apart from its missionary vision."[38] Agnes Ozman, who had a remarkable baptism in the Holy Spirit at Azusa Street, related how this missional drive arose: "The next night after I received the Holy Ghost . . . I with others went down to a mission at Topeka and my heart was full of glory and blessings. I began to pray in English and then in tongues. At the close of the service a man who is a Bohemian said he understood what I said in his own language."[39] This phenomenon, recorded by Ozman, of speaking in a *known* language that the person had not learned by mechanical methods' is known as Xenolalia. Some researchers refer to this phenomenon as Xenoglossolalia. People who were part of the Azusa Street revival left Los Angeles for every corner of the world, believing the Spirit had equipped them to communicate in foreign languages. Some of this early evangelistic zeal was characterized by sending personnel out without pre-arranged financial help.

Charles Parham, leader of the revival at Topeka, Kansas, and later a participant for a brief period in the Azusa Street Revival, firmly believed in the special missionary role of tongues. *The Apostolic Faith* for 1906 reported: "The gift of languages is given with the commission, 'Go ye into all

36. *Corum* 2.13 (1981) 3.
37. Dempster et al., *Globalisation of Pentecostalism*, 37.
38. Ibid., 32.
39. Blumhofer, *The Assemblies of God*, 83.

the world and preach the gospel to every creature.' The Lord has given languages to the unlearned, Greek, Latin, Hebrew, French, German, Italian . . . in fact the Holy Ghost speaks all the languages of the world through His children." Before long, however, many Pentecostals questioned the missionary use of tongues and emphasized that the Pentecostal baptism was an avenue of praise and intercession to God provided by the Holy Spirit. Periodicals then began to urge the need for language study as a prerequisite to study for the Mission Field. Thus, in the words of David du Plessis, "Sparks or shall we say 'tongues of fire,' from Azusa Street were blown in every direction from the Pacific to the Atlantic Coast and from the Gulf of Mexico to the Great Lakes."

An Imminent Second Coming of Christ

The early Pentecostal preachers believed that they were proclaiming an "End Time" message. In 1916 Aimee Semple McPherson (1890–1944) toured the southern United States in her "Gospel Car" emblazoned with the slogan, "Jesus is coming soon. Get Ready!" Pentecostals are, and always were, people who lived in expectation of the Lord's return, and this has been a strong motivational factor in their evangelism and missionary enterprise. They felt, as many have done since, that the Pentecost that they were experiencing was God pouring out his Spirit in the last days. They believed that theirs was the last and final revival before the Lord returned. Thomas Ball Barratt, one of the first leaders, wrote in the Preface to his *When the Fire Fell*, "I am convinced that this Movement is the last call to all ere Christ comes."[40] Some saw the Pentecostal outpourings at Azusa Street and in Wales as the beginnings of the Latter Rain of a promised end-time revival. Early Pentecostals had a fervent belief in the premillennial return of Christ and the secret rapture that would see them snatched away to safety before the Man of Lawlessness (referred to in 2 Thessalonians 2) came rampaging through the earth.

THEOLOGY

In the matter of theology, Pentecostals have tended to act now and theologize later. Pentecostal theology has often been "theology on the move." That said, Pentecostal theology has some basic underlying assumptions.

40. Barratt, *When the Fire Fell*, 3.

One of its stresses is immediacy. For Pentecostals it's not just "a God who is there"; the stress is on "a God is there *now!*" God is not an idea, but a presence and a power. Pentecostals are also people of the Spirit. The Holy Spirit and his gifts and ministries are at the center of Pentecostal theology. Pentecostals emphasize the baptism of the Holy Spirit as an indispensable source of power for service. They also exalt Jesus as the baptizer in the Holy Spirit. From the very beginning Seymour had a strong Christology that centered on the giver of the Spirit rather that the gift.[41] Early Pentecostal missionaries were driven by an intense last-days theology, which in many cases was linked with the belief that the early twentieth century would see the promise of the "latter rains" fulfilled in their endeavors.

The "Jesus Only" Dispute

A number of early Pentecostals discovered that baptism in the book of Acts was always in the name of Jesus and came to the view that this was the correct way to carry out the command of Matthew chapter 28. A large number of early Pentecostal leaders were therefore re-baptized "in the name of Jesus." Those who followed this teaching were, in effect, teaching a modalistic view of the Trinity. They taught that Jesus was the name for God the Father, God the Son, and God the Holy Spirit.

Concern for the Poor

When Pentecostal experience, worship, and theology are put together it comes as no surprise that the poor have readily been drawn into its congregations. Marginalized men and women have found there the power they needed for physical, mental, and spiritual renewal. In countries such Brazil, Chile, Kenya, and Nigeria this has enabled them to overcome the destructive and downgrading forces that surround them. Pentecostalism has empowered the poor and in many places it has enabled them to stand for their human and political rights. The message of liberation theology took strong root among Pentecostals, particularly in Chile, where many supported the socialist President Salvador Allende (1908–73). In recent times nowhere has this concern for the poor been more powerfully in evidence than in the ministry of Heidi and Roland Baker. In 1995 they went to Mozambique where they have seen miraculous healings, thousands of

41. Frodsham, *With Signs Following*, 38.

conversions, hundreds of new churches planted, medical stations established, orphanages built, Bible colleges founded, and local pastors trained for the ministry.

Sunday schools were a high priority from the beginnings of Pentecostalism. Not only were they a major aspect of evangelism, they performed an educative role by offering the poor and those with minimal education the chance to read and write. This enabled them to grow in confidence and self-respect and to better their lot economically. Blumhofer's observation that at least 2,080 Sunday schools were started by the Assemblies of God in America between 1937 and 1939 illustrates this point well.[42]

WORLD PENTECOSTALISM

Estimates of its size in 1906 ranged from 13,000 to 15,000. Fifty years later Pentecostalism had reached 10 million people worldwide and had become known as the third force in Christendom. By 1982 it had reached 51 million.[43] By 1999 Pentecostalism was growing by 19 million a year and 54,000 new adherents every day.[44] Margaret Poloma, a sociologist who spent more than twenty-five years studying Pentecostal Christianity, wrote in 2001, "the approach known as Pentecostal Christianity today has an estimated 500 million followers, comprising 30% of the world's Christian population."[45] She was, of course, including in this estimate the many millions within the historic denominations who share a Pentecostal experience.

FACTORS THAT MADE PENTECOSTALISM SUCCESSFUL

Life Transforming Power

Perhaps the most appealing aspect of Pentecostalism is that it is able to demonstrate that the Christian faith has power to transform people's lives. Many individuals who have joined Pentecostal churches have found their lives possessed of a new energy and vitality. This has been evident from

42. Blumhofer, *The Assemblies of God*, 268.

43. Barrett, *World Christian Encyclopedia*.

44. Dempster et al., *The Globalisation of Pentecostalism*, 47.

45. Poloma, "A Reconfiguration of Pentecostalism." In Hilborn, *Toronto in Perspective*, 101.

the earliest days of the Azusa Street revival in Los Angeles. Pentecostalism empowers and enlivens its participants in encounters with a supernatural God. These power encounters don't merely end in the experience of individuals; in many cases they have strengthened believers to fight for social justice in countries like Chile, Brazil, and Mexico. It was, in part, the Pentecostal spirit that fueled the struggle of the black communities against racism and apartheid in the USA and South Africa.

Vital Worship

Pentecostal worship is notable for its vitality and spontaneity, indeed it has been said that a Pentecostal meeting where you know what is going to happen is "backslidden!" Pentecostal worship is fervent, exhilarating, and often forceful. It exhibits a capacity to lift its participants out of themselves and away from their burdens, pains, and daily concerns. It also has a strongly cathartic or healing dimension that touches the whole person, whereas traditional evangelical worship frequently touches only the mind and fails to engage the heart or the body. Pentecostal worshippers feel an "impartation" of the power and presence of God. This comes through the preaching and more directly as the pastors pray for God's Spirit to come down on the congregation or invite God's presence on individuals with specific needs. People often leave Pentecostal worship feeling stronger in their faith and sensing they are closer to God.

The Reality of Jesus

In much of the world's Christianity Jesus is a figure of history whose teachings people seek to apply and put into practice in their daily lives. There is often little or no sense or consciousness that Jesus is the living God whose power is vital and transforming. For the Pentecostal, knowing Jesus only with the mind or intellect is insufficient. Pentecostalism, in the words of Donald Gee, "made Jesus intensely real."[46] The Pentecostal Jesus is "the same yesterday, today, and for ever." His power to bring good news to the poor, heal the sick, and cast out demons is unchanging. When Heidi Baker was asked the reason for the remarkable transformation that has taken place in Mozambique she responded: "Our own pastors tell us that it is

---

46. *Christian Missionary Alliance*, 22 September, 1906, 177. In Blumhofer, *The Assemblies of God*, 143.

the miracles that bring the people. They go where Jesus heals them, loves them, and does things for them. They don't want to go where they can't feel or appreciate the presence of Jesus; . . . they don't want to exchange their powerful witch doctors for a powerless church. They want a living God involved with their lives."[47]

Intentional Evangelism

Since its inception in Los Angeles, Pentecostalism has been noted for its strong emphasis on evangelism. Indeed, as has been observed, several of the early pioneers were of the view that the gift of tongues had been given to aid them in proclaiming the Christian message in other nations and cultures. William Seymour's pastoral admonition was, "Try to get people saved." What was perhaps of greater significance was the sentence that preceded it. Seymour said, "Now, do not go from this meeting and talk about tongues, but try to get people saved."[48] David Hesselgrave has underlined "the deep-seated missionary motivation" of the Pentecostal movement "that has propelled it into its present role as perhaps the most missionary-minded segment of world Christianity." He wrote that "if anything is generally characteristic of Pentecostal churches worldwide, it is an ethos of growth. In a time of defeatism, stagnation, and retreat in many churches, a growth climate may prove to be one of the great bequests of Pentecostalism to the larger church of Christ."[49] Many Western Christians have become so over-weight with intellectual and biblical knowledge that they find it a struggle to go out and exercise their faith. Pentecostals, on the other hand, have a personal story to tell and they tell it not waiting and imagining they will get answers to all their ultimate and theological questions. At the center of the Pentecostal missiology is the experience of the Holy Spirit. As J. Roswell Flower, an early editor of *The Pentecost*, observed: "The baptism of the Holy Ghost does not consist in simply speaking in tongues. It has a much deeper meaning than that. It fills our souls with the love of God for lost humanity, and makes us much more willing to leave home, friends, and all to work in His vineyard, even if it be far away among the heathen."[50] Pentecostal mission was also generated

47. Poloma, *Main Street Mystics*, 231.

48. Dempster et al., *Globalisation of Pentecostalism*, 35.

49. Hesslgrave, *Today's Choices for Tomorrow's Mission*, 118. In Dempster et al., *The Globalisation of Pentecostalism*, 32.

50. Dempster et al., *Globalisation of Pentecostalism*, 36.

by their close attention to Scripture. They regard their experience as the fulfillment of Acts of the Apostles chapters 1–2. This has led to what Donald McGavran termed, the "people movement" approach to missions, as opposed to the "mission station" approach.[51]

---

51. McGavran et al., *Church Growth Bulletin*, Vol. 3., 97. In Dempster et al., *The Globalisation of Pentecostalism*, 43.

EARLY HISTORY

THE FIRST VINEYARD CHURCH came into being when Kenn Gulliksen brought together two Bible study groups that were meeting in the homes of the singer-songwriters Larry Norman and Chuck Girard.[1] By the beginning of 1975 there were thirteen such groups holding meetings at the Beverley Hills Women's club, a number of which were attended by celebrities of the entertainment world. In 1974 Gulliksen, who was an associate pastor at a Calvary link church, together with his wife, Joanie, started a link congregation in Los Angeles which they called "Vineyard," from Isaiah 27:3, "Sing about a fruitful vineyard; I, the Lord watch over it; I water it every moment lest anyone damage it. I guard it night and day."[2] Their vision was to practice the gifts of the Holy Spirit, emphasizing speaking in tongues, prophecy, and healing. Carol Wimber described Ken Gulliksen as "a natural church-planter" who "had the most charming personality of anyone I have ever known."[3] His gift seemed to be to go to an area, plant churches, and then moving on.

In 1977 John Wimber (1937–97), a former Quaker minister, affiliated his Friends congregation at Yorba Linda with Calvary Chapel. However, after only a short duration his teaching on healing and the gifts of the Spirit led him into disagreements with the Calvary leadership. Chuck Smith, the Senior Pastor of Calvary Chapel, put his hand on John's shoulder, blessed him, and told him to call his congregation "Vineyard." This, as it happened, was the same name Gulliksen had taken for his small group of churches, and John and Carol checked with Ken to be sure that he was

1. Jackson, *The Quest*, 78.
2. C. Wimber, *John Wimber*, 151.
3. Ibid.

happy that they too should be called "Vineyard, because if one day he discovered he didn't like us, we would never change our name again."[4] At this point Gulliksen's network consisted of about six congregations. However, by this time John's congregation numbered about five thousand and had moved to a large warehouse complex in Anaheim.[5] So, in view of the dynamic drive and growth of Wimber's ministry, Gulliksen gave the leadership of his movement over to Wimber.[6] In later times he expressed some regret at having done so, stating that his decision had been brought about by his own insecurity.

JOHN WIMBER

Robert Schuller, the founder pastor of the Crystal Cathedral and world-wide televangelist, called John Wimber "one of the twelve most influential Christian leaders of the twentieth century."[7] John Wimber was born in Peroria, Illinois, in the American Midwest on 25th February, 1934. It was a dysfunctional family, with his father leaving the home when young John was only a year old. In the early boyhood days that followed, his maternal grandmother was a significant and positive influence. His mother later re-married.

In the middle of his lonely teenage years John found solace in the world of music. He was blessed with an excellent tenor voice and soon found he had an ability to play and enjoy several instruments, including piano, string, and wind, his first love being the saxophone. Still in his teenage years, John enjoyed playing at various gigs and local jazz clubs in California's Orange County. By this route he found his way into making a living by providing musical back-up for Hollywood films.

In 1955 John met and married Carol, the eldest daughter of a medical doctor, who was a non-practicing Catholic. Life was pressurized and their marriage ran into difficulties; divorce appeared to be on the cards for a while in 1961. The stress levels no doubt increased the following year when John formed a music group which took the name "The Righteous Brothers." They became a widely acclaimed and highly popular band and

---

4. Ibid., 157.

5. Scotland, *Charismatics and the New Millennium*, 201. See also C. Wimber, *John Wimber*, 151.

6. For a detailed account see Jackson, *The Quest*, chapter 4, "How John Wimber's Calvary Chapel Became a Vineyard."

7. Pytches, *John Wimber*, 9.

reached the top of the charts on two occasions. However, John and Carol held together and in 1963 they were brought to faith in Christ through Dick and Lynn Heying, a couple who had only recently themselves become Christians. Dick recognized the importance of giving new Christians further instructions and he entrusted the Wimbers to the care of Lawrence Gunner Pain, a part-time evangelist. They both began attending his Bible Studies and in a short while John professed "to have found the pearl of great price" and prayed, "OK Lord, you can have my career." In 1964 John Wimber was filled with the Holy Spirit. At the time Gunner and his wife were moving from the area, John was talking out loud to the Lord about his concerns when he suddenly realized he couldn't understand what he was saying. As Carol put it, "The words were coming out all wrong. He was speaking in tongues."[8] He kept the experience under wraps for a while, but he then shocked the Righteous Brothers by announcing that he was leaving them and later the same year he enrolled in a biblical studies course at Azuza Pacific University. John greatly enjoyed his studies and took particular delight in church history, which, according to Carol, "saved us a lot of grief!" In her words, "there aren't any new truths, just old error!"[9]

Pastoral Ministry

John and Carol began to evangelize their friends and did so in a very effective manner such that by 1970 he was leading eleven Bible study groups each week. In August of that year he was taken on to the staff of the Yorba Linda Friends Church where his brother-in-law, who was married to Carol's younger sister, was a youth pastor.[10] John was called an Associate to the Pastor, then Associate Pastor, and finally Co-Pastor, although Carol noted that "he didn't care what they called him."[11]

In 1974 John enrolled in Peter Wagner's Doctor of Ministry program at Fuller Seminary.[12] It didn't take Wagner very long to recognize that John had a distinct gift as an evangelist as well as a thorough grasp of the principles of church growth. In view of this, he persuaded Wimber to take on the role of director of the new Charles E. Fuller Institute of Evangelism

8. C. Wimber, *John Wimber*, 74.

9. Ibid., 89.

10. Ibid., 91.

11. Ibid.

12. Ibid., 96.

and Church Growth. Besides lecturing, a substantial part of this role included consultancy and advisory work. He became fascinated by those churches that were growing for no apparent reason. It wasn't that they had dynamic teaching or wonderful ministries, "it was just plain God."[13] During his three and a half years in the post Wimber calculated that he had engaged at some level with some 40,000 pastors coming from twenty-seven different denominations and nine para-church organizations. During this period of time John and Carol remained members of the Friends Church, although relationships were becoming strained because of their emphasis on the Holy Spirit.

Although the work was challenging and rewarding, the travel proved to be very tiring. A crisis point finally came during his Fuller role one winter's night in 1977 when he made a late arrival at Detroit airport and discovered that there was no one there to meet him. Feeling totally exhausted he decided in consequence to book into the Metropolitan Hotel. Before turning in he knelt at his bedside, prayed, and read Psalm 61. During the night he sensed God speaking to him and saying to him, "John, I've seen your ministry. Now I want to show you mine."[14]

It was not long after this incident that Wimber came into conflict with the elders at Yorba Linda Friends church. They were deeply concerned that there had been speaking in tongues in the congregation and they wanted to know what part he had had in it. Despite Wimber's insistence that "it was not about tongues but about the Holy Spirit," they were not satisfied. The upshot was that Wimber and about sixty left to start a new work.[15] The new church had its first meeting on Mother's Day, 1977, with Carol recalling a talk on Mary the mother of Jesus, a delightfully happy hour of worship with joyful songs, children dancing, a puppet show, and coffee and doughnuts. From this very first occasion the worship was characterized by the casual dress code and intimate singing that was to become synonymous with the Vineyard.

CORPORATE RENEWAL

The newly ejected Quaker congregation grew rapidly and affiliated with Chuck Smith's Calvary Chapel. People were experienced salvation, baptism in the Holy Spirit, and healing. One occurrence that had a major and

13. Ibid., 106.

14. Pytches, *John Wimber*, 25.

15. C. Wimber, *John Wimber*, 120–21.

lasting impact on John Wimber took place during this time in which he was pastoring the Calvary Chapel affiliate congregation. For a while John had heard about the ministrations of Lonnie Frisbee (1950–93), who was sometimes referred to as "the Modern day Samson." A former nudist-vegetarian-hippie, Frisbee claimed that Jesus appeared to him in 1967 while he was "high on acid." He joined the House of Acts who discipled him, following which he was taken on to the staff of Calvary Chapel working in their House of Miracles. His presence and ministry had an extraordinary impact, with the congregation skyrocketing from 150 into the thousands "within two years."[16] Indeed, Chuck Smith stated that Calvary Chapel had been instrumental in 20,000 conversions and eight thousand baptisms.[17] Despite being uncertain about Frisbee's soundness as "one of God's irregulars" Wimber nevertheless invited him to speak at the evening worship service on Mother's Day, 1980. Just as the service was coming to an end Frisbee invited all those under the age of twenty-five to come to the front of the building, then he quite simply called the Holy Spirit to come down on them in the name of Jesus. What followed was later described as "holy chaos" as about four hundred people fell to the floor and others, who did not believe in speaking in tongues, spoke loudly in unknown languages. Others groaned and cried out. Frisbee wandered among the congregation praying for people, many of whom fell to the ground.

John Wimber sensed that what he had witnessed was good, but he had reservations and was particularly concerned to protect the young people in his congregation from being led astray. He spent the night following avidly reading accounts of the world's past great revivals to see if he could find similar phenomena. Finally, exhausted, he gave up and called out, "Lord if it is you, please tell me." A short time afterwards he received an unexpected phone call. He recognized a voice at the other end as a friend from Denver, Colorado, several thousand miles away. He begged forgiveness for ringing at such an inappropriate time and went on to say, "I have something very strange to pass on to you. I don't know what it means, but God wants me to tell you simply, 'It's me, John!'" It was all Wimber needed to know and from that time forward he was never afraid to invoke the Holy Spirit's presence on a meeting or apprehensive about outward manifestations.[18]

16. Jackson, *The Quest*, 387.
17. Ibid.
18. Pytches, *John Wimber*, 31.

It was clear that the Wimbers were on a collision course with the leaders of Calvary Chapel and the inevitable happened in 1982 when Chuck told Wimber to disaffiliate and change the name of the congregation to the Vineyard. "It was Mother's Day 1982," Carol Wimber recalled, "that we officially took the name Vineyard."[19] The church continued to grow rapidly such that new and larger premises were needed. In consequence, they held their Sunday worship in Canyon High School in the Anaheim Hills. However, it was not long before this also proved to be too small and a warehouse complex at La Palma, Anaheim Hills was purchased. The Anaheim Vineyard Christian Fellowship could seat more than three thousand worshippers and contained several halls, lecture rooms, office space, and storage areas. Anaheim also became the home for Vineyard Ministries International Music and the base for Mercy Ministries, where huge quantities of food were stored. In time they came to give away thousand dollars worth of food every year.

MC510 SIGNS, WONDERS, AND CHURCH GROWTH, AND POWER EVANGELISM

During this very busy and transitional time Wimber taught his controversial and highly acclaimed MC510 Signs, Wonders, and Church Growth course at Fuller. He was able to use his Anaheim experience to practically demonstrate and reinforce the content of his teaching. Wimber typically spent three hours lecturing, "followed by an optional hour of clinic, with no predetermined format."[20] The content of this course formed the basis of Wimber's book, *Power Evangelism*, which was published in 1986. The authors are given as John Wimber and Kevin Springer, but it was Springer who wrote the book from Wimber's notes.[21] Bill Jackson observed that Springer played a key role by making Wimber's teaching available to people across the globe. Springer also edited *Equipping the Saints*, which became an important Vineyard publication.

The significance of Wimber's teaching was his focus on the Gospels. Whereas historic Evangelicalism was largely rooted in the New Testament epistles, Wimber took the evangelical church back to the Gospels where Jesus taught his disciples to pray, "Your kingdom come." How is this to be achieved? His answer was: by doing what Jesus did. Wimber's contention

19. C. Wimber, *John Wimber*, 158.

20. Jackson, *The Quest*, 110.

21. Ibid., 111.

was that whilst Jesus never surrendered his divine nature during his earthly ministry, he nevertheless elected to live as a man anointed by the Holy Spirit. In so doing he became our role model and example for today.

Two key factors provided the basis of Wimber's *Power Evangelism*: his experience of an overwhelming demonstration of God's power through the ministry of Lonnie Frisbee and his study of George Eldon Ladd's *A Theology of the New Testament*. Ladd's thesis was that Jesus came to set the kingdom of this present world free from the dominion or rule of Satan and to break the hold of sin, sickness, suffering, disease, and the demonic. He maintained that by casting out demons and healing the sick Jesus demonstrated that this process had begun and God's kingdom was coming near. One of the key texts that Ladd cited and which makes this point is Luke 11:20, "If I by the finger of God cast out demons then is God's kingdom come among you." Ladd went on from this to assert that Jesus' followers have been commissioned to take part in this same work of driving Satan back by performing these same works that Jesus did and proclaiming the presence of God's kingdom.

Basing his study on Ladd in particular, Wimber began to teach, preach, and practice what he termed "power evangelism." He was adamant that if gospel preaching is going to be effective it must go hand in hand with demonstrations of God's power, which will cause the hearers to believe. It was his belief that the *works* of Jesus caused people to respond to the *words* of Jesus.

A very short while after Wimber began this teaching there were reports of many hundreds of people being converted and others receiving remarkable healings. During one period of three and a half months Wimber estimated that 1,700 people were converted to Christ. Wimber published this theology in his book entitled *Power Evangelism: Signs and Wonders Today*. In chapter 3 Wimber contrasted "power evangelism" with "program evangelism." Without the assistance of charismatic gifts, programmatic evangelism aims to convince the minds and hearts of the people. Programmatic evangelism is usually characterized "by message-centred communicators who present the gospel primarily through rational arguments. . . . There is an emphasis on organisation and technique."[22] Wimber continued that "by its very nature and assumptions, programmatic evangelism tends to have as its goal decisions for Christ, not disciples. Many

---

22. Wimber, *Power Evangelism*, 56.

people who make these decisions do not encounter God's power, and thus frequently do not move to mature faith."[23]

Wimber went on to point out that there is an element of listening and spontaneity involved in power evangelism so that whereas in programmatic evangelism, the Christian says, "In obedience I go. Holy Spirit bless me." In power evangelism, the Christian says, "As the Holy Spirit tells me to go, I go."[24]

Wimber was not saying that programmatic evangelism is wrong; rather, he was contending that it could be enhanced and made more effective if, at the same time, people were able to see a demonstration of power. In developing this theory Wimber also drew material from Dr. Peter Wagner's book, *Frontiers in Mission Strategy*. In it Wagner outlined three common styles of evangelism. First, there is Presence Evangelism, where people are helped to faith by good and charitable things done for them. Second, there is Proclamation Evangelism, which adds good *words* to the good deeds. Finally, there is Persuasion Evangelism, which incorporates an element of discipleship. Wimber's concern was to take people one further step and the key, as he saw it "is the demonstration of God's power."

To drive his point home, Wimber cited the passage in Luke chapter 7 where Jesus answers a question brought to him by John the Baptist's disciples soon after he had raised a man from the dead in the city of Nain. Their query was, "Are you the one who was to come, or should we look for someone else?"[25] Jesus didn't try and convince them with some good reasons, he merely demonstrated that he was the Messiah by the works that he did. He told John's disciples, "Go back and report to John what you have seen and heard: the blind receive their sight, the lame walk, those who have leprosy are cured, the deaf hear, the dead are raised, and the good news is preached to the poor."[26]

In the same section of the book, Wimber went on to underline the fact that the New Testament reveals that Jesus spent more time healing and casting out demons than preaching. Thus, out of a total of 3,779 verses in the four Gospels, 727 (or 19 percent of the total) specifically relate to the healing of physical and mental illness and the resurrection of the dead.

The practical outworking of this theology soon became visible at Wimber's Vineyard churches and conferences. Wimber believed God

23. Ibid., 56–57.

24. Ibid., 57.

25. Luke 7:19.

26. Wimber, *Power Evangelism*, 59.

could empower any believer in any situation to engage in power evangelism. His conviction was that, technically, the "baptism in the Spirit" takes place at conversion and any subsequent experiences are "fillings" and therefore any Christian can "do the stuff," by which he meant the works of Jesus.[27] On other occasions Wimber said that in God's kingdom work "everyone gets to play."[28] In other words, the ministry is not for the chosen few, but everyone is called to take part. "Doing the stuff " simply means inviting the Spirit to come on people who want the Lord's help for healing, guidance, deliverance from evil or any other situation of need. Doing the stuff can be done at the end of a worship service or conference talk or equally out on the street or in any other suitable place. After someone has prayed "Come Holy Spirit" people are urged to wait for a minute or two, at least to allow the Lord time to minister before they start praying. Wimber's approach to "doing the stuff" was to be relaxed and laid back and allow the Lord to do it. Those praying should pray simple prayers blessing what God is doing and asking for God's kingdom to come and for more of God's presence. How do those ministering know if God is moving in power? The most obvious way is simply by asking the one who is receiving prayer if he or she feels any different. Often there are other indications when people feel bathed in love, cleansed from their past, freed from fear, resting in peace, or perhaps sense they have had a healing touch. Sometimes people shake, feel a sensation of heat, or even fall to the ground.

Peter Wagner coined the term "Third Wave" to distinguish this "move of the Spirit" that he, Wimber, and others were promoting, from what he took to be two earlier and yet distinct moves of the Spirit. The first of these was the Pentecostal movement, which was followed by the earlier Charismatic movement. All three waves he regarded as being part of one major move of the Spirit within the twentieth century.[29] It was this equipping of all the saints to engage in ministry that was one of the distinctives of the "third wave." Bishop David Pytches summed it up, following a visit from John Wimber and a Vineyard team to his church in Chorleywood. He wrote: "We have had many visiting preachers who have blessed us and when they have gone they have taken their ministry with them but John Wimber came and left his ministry with us."[30]

27. Jackson, *The Quest*, 115.
28. See Wimber, *Everyone Gets to Play*, 11.
29. Springer, *Riding the Third Wave*, 122.
30. Pytches, *Living at the Edge*, 261.

Power evangelism as promoted by Wimber has become a very prominent and valued form of ministry, not just in Vineyard churches, but right across the denominational spectrum. It has had a significant impact on church life in the United States, Britain, and other parts of the world. In the British Isles Wimber-style ministry has become common place in charismatic churches, including a wide section of the Church of England and the so-called "new churches," which came into being in the 1970s and 1980s.

Power evangelism has not been without its critics. Prominent among them has been Martin Percy who himself grew up in a Charismatic church and is currently Principal of Ripon College, Cuddesdon. He came to the view that Wimber primarily engaged "in his own particular holy war with weak, powerless or dead churches."[31] Wimber's opponents claimed that he made too much use of the concepts and motifs of power. All the talk, so they claimed, was of "power healing," "power evangelism," "power ministry," "the dynamics of spiritual life," and so on. There is, his critics have argued, insufficient attempt to entertain the other side of the Christian message, such themes as suffering, cross bearing, trials and testing, and the day of small things. Martin Percy argued strongly in his *Signs and Wonders and Church Growth* that John Wimber's use of "power stories" and powerful personalities, together with other power metaphors may be "alienating the sick, the poor, the helpless and the handicapped from the church."[32] He pointed out that when the Apostle Paul was with the weak he became weak.[33] Not so by implication John Wimber. His church, Percy maintained, is portrayed as a "powerful body." It is "a mighty army and the agent of God's power." Its role is strongly fortified by success-orientated spiritual warfare songs that proclaim that the church is the army of the Lord.[34] Others have added their concerns that power healings were limited in scope and number and this can be very disconcerting to those who come to meetings and conferences with high expectations and are not healed. Wimber, some claimed, had no theology of suffering, at least in the early days of his ministry. Wallace Benn and Mark Burkhill made the point that the Great Commission in Matthew 28:18–20 "does not mention healing, so ministers in particular need to think carefully about where

---

31. Percy, "Signs, Wonders, and Church Growth," 7. Scotland, *Charismatics*, 207–8.

32. Percy, "Signs, Wonders and Church Growth," 42.

33. Ibid., 60.

34. Ibid., 167–69

Wimber's theology is leading them."[35] In fairness to Wimber, it might be countered that Matthew 28 verse 20 does say "teaching them everything I have commanded you," which presumably included healing. Benn and Burkhill also argued that too much was made of the bodily manifestations[36] when people are "doing the stuff." They maintained that it needs to be recognized that fluttering eyelids, involuntary muscle movements, and warm sensations may be psychological or even demonic.[37] They were also of the idea that too much emphasis was put on Satan. Thus, when the Church of England evangelist and friend of Wimber, David Watson, died, it was reported that "Satan got him." More controversial was Wimber's contention that Christians can be "demonized."[38] This latter concern was raised by Donald Kammer, an Assemblies of God pastor, in a much more irenical *Churchman* article, published in 1992. He wrote that "the possibility of Christians being demonised was one factor which caused negative reaction to Wimber"[39] who had stated in *Power Healing*, "I believe believers and non-believers alike can be demonized."[40]

Benn and Burkhill wrote in 1987 and Percy completed his thesis in 1993 and it needs to be said that Wimber, who was essentially a man on a journey that led him through some treacherous theological territory, both responded to and answered many of these criticisms. Wimber certainly did exhibit a deep concern for the weak and the alienated and established Vineyard churches in places like Soweto where there has been a real witness against racism. Care for the poor has been, since the earliest days, one of the Vineyard's core values. From the very beginning, Mercy Ministries has been at the heart of every Vineyard fellowship, feeding literally thousands every week in all parts of the globe.

Wimber graciously responded to the harsh and brutal criticisms of Philip Jensen and other Sydney Christian leaders who "wished he would go to hell" and acknowledged that he had failed to give full place to the cross.[41] Wimber, in fact, called the Vineyard's main songwriters together and exhorted them to put out more songs demonstrating the centrality

---

35. Benn and Burkhill, "A Theological and Pastoral Critique of the Teaching of John Wimber," 105.

36. Ibid., 107.

37. Ibid., 107–8.

38. Jackson, *The Quest*, 138.

39. Kammer, "The Perplexing Power of John Wimber's Power Encounters," 50.

40. Wimber, *Power Healing*, 121–23.

41. Jackson, *The Quest*, 157.

of the atonement. A number of songs flowed directly as a result of this gathering, among them, "It's Your Blood that Cleanses Me," "You Gave Your Body," "At the Cross," "The Blood of Jesus," and many more.[42] Wimber tempered his views on the demonic and in 1985 found himself in strong disagreement with Peter Wagner over the extent and influence of principalities and powers. Wimber had come to the view that the "strong man" had already been bound in the ministry of Jesus and that there was therefore no need for praying against regional powers. At a major conference at Anaheim in 1993 all the Vineyard leaders were instructed to follow Clinton Arnold's counsel, who stated: "I can find no Scriptural evidence suggesting that we have the right or authority to 'serve notice,' 'evict' or 'bind' spirits over cities, regions or nations."[43]

On the matter of healing, while it is the case that many who came with great expectations were not healed, there were times when significant numbers of people received what they understood to be a real touch from God. In a book entitled *Healing: Fiction, Fantasy, or Fact?*, Dr. David Lewis, a social anthropologist, critically examined the claims of healing that were alleged to have taken place at the Harrogate Conference in 1986. There were 2,470 registrants, of whom 1,890 returned the questionnaire used to quantify experiences. Lewis and other professional scrutinized the data for more than a year. They found that although there were only sixty-eight reported cases of physical healing, a further 748 had received prayer for spiritual or emotional healing, of whom almost 80 percent testified to experiencing some measure of healing. While it is the case that Wimber raised some major questions over the issues surrounding divine healing, he also represented a major challenge to the Christian church as to how much of the supernatural it should expect to see. It was not correct to assert, as some have done, that Wimber had no theology of suffering. He explained that the reason why some were not healed was simply that the kingdom of God had not yet fully come on earth and indeed would not do so until the second coming of Christ.

MISSION AND GROWTH

From its inception mission and church growth have been at the very heart of Vineyard DNA. Indeed, church planting has been listed as one of the Vineyard's core values. One statement put out by the leadership reads as

42. Scotland, *Charismatics and the New Millennium*, 208.
43. Arnold, *Spiritual Warfare*, 183.

follows, "We believe God has called us to raise up 10,000 Vineyard or Vineyard churches. Most of these will come through the work of church planting in metropolitan areas. This is the New Testament pattern."[44] In 1984 John Wimber and Bob Fulton arranged a seminar at Anaheim for all intending church planters, at which they set out a very simple strategy. In short, when people came to faith in Christ they were put into small or kinship groups. When two or three of these were established they were encouraged to worship together on a Sunday night. If such gatherings reached between fifty and a hundred, the time had arrived to meet on Sunday mornings and a church was considered to have come into being.

With such a strategy in place it was inevitable that the Vineyard movement would grow quickly, and such proved to be the case. In January 1985 the Vineyard movement was located in Southern California and consisted of approximately seventy churches. By December of the same year there were church plants along the East coast and some in the Midwest and Northwest with an overall number of 139 churches. In 1986 the organization was strengthened with the inauguration of *The Association of Vineyard Churches* (AVC). The organization was designed among other things to facilitate church planting, to raise and release funds for church planting, and to oversee existing fellowships. By the end of that year the Vineyard had grown to about 200 churches.[45] Between 1988 and 1998 the Vineyard saw an increase of nearly 400 percent, from 236 churches in three countries to 819 churches in fifty-two countries.[46]

Wimber's links with the British Isles began in 1981 when Eddie Gibbs, who was on the faculty at Fuller Seminary, urged Canon David Watson, who was a guest lecturer, to visit a church near Anaheim and it was there he made contact with the Vineyard. That same year Wimber took a team of over thirty people to England. They went first to St. Andrew's Church in Chorleywood where there were remarkable scenes and some significant healings. This began a longstanding bond between the Vineyard and many of the English churches. Despite David Watson assuring his fellow Anglicans that the Vineyard did not intend to plant churches on English soil, John Mumford, who had been curate at St. Michael's Chester Square in London, and his wife Eleanor, were convinced that England needed Vineyard churches and they set up what became known as the South West London Vineyard in Putney. Other Anglican clergy joined

44. Jackson, *The Quest*, 107.

45. Ibid., 139.

46. Kay, *Apostolic Networks*, 164.

them, including Rick Williams, who established a congregation at Twickenham, and Martyn Smith, who planted in Manchester and Chris Lane at St. Albans. Their example quickly caught on and Vineyard was soon enjoying a rapid growth in England. In 2012 there were more than a hundred Vineyard church in England. In March 1996 John Mumford was publicly installed by Wimber as the director of Vineyard Churches UK. Gradually, an organizational structure has been emerging, although it is still at a fairly minimalist level of local pastor, regional overseer, and national director. William Kay has seen in this an emerging episcopal structure in which the local leadership can draw on the services of the national leadership because they recognize and share its values (not because they are *obliged* to do so).[47]

In 1986 Wimber and the Vineyard began a drive to extend their overseas missionary outreach and conferences were organized in Brighton, Wembley, and Harrogate in England and also at Frankfurt, West Germany, where more than a thousand attended.[48] A team of 130 was sent out to New Zealand where they ministered to over 6,000. In total, Vineyard teams did thirteen major conferences and attracted attendances of 76,000.[49] Local congregations are autonomous and are responsible for their own finances, although each is asked to give 5 percent of their income to a national central fund.[50]

THE VINEYARD AND THE PROPHETIC

As the Vineyard movement grew and expanded it inevitably began to embrace and adopt a number of individual independent congregations who either shared its values or were looking for some kind of relational oversight. Among those with whom the Vineyard came into contact was the Kansas City Fellowship, whose congregation included a small group of prophets. For a period of two years they became deeply entwined with Wimber and the Vineyard movement. Indeed Bill Jackson found it very painful having to recount this chapter in his history of the Vineyard.[51]

47. Kay, *Apostolic Networks*, 172.

48. Jackson, *The Quest*, 142.

49. "Equipping the Saints," *Renewal News*, Spring 1988, 22. In Jackson, *The Quest*, 142.

50. Kay, *Apostolic Networks*, 172.

51. Jackson, *The Quest*, 175.

The links between Wimber and the Kansas City Fellowship (KCF) began in 1988. Early in that year Bob Jones, who was recognized as one of the prophets, told the lead pastor, Mike Bickle, that John Wimber would be calling him and that this would result in a shared future ministry. Five days later Wimber did call him and later that year the two of them ministered together. Controversy was not slow in coming because Paul Cain had been assistant to William Branham who had preached the "Latter Rain" doctrine, which asserted that the "former rain" of James 5:7 was the Day of Pentecost (Acts 2) while the "Latter Rain" was the last great outpouring of the Holy Spirit that would immediately precede the return of Christ. Associated with the Latter Rain movement was the doctrine of the "Manifested Sons of God" who would oversee the church in the run up to the millennium. Some of their number would even receive a resurrection body and be able to move at will from country to country. That said, it should be noted that there was no evidence that Bickle or his assistant, Paul Cain, had themselves shared Branham's views. Cain, as Jackson pointed out, did maintain that the prophecy in the Old Testament book of Joel about a powerful army that the Lord would raise up in the last days referred to a group that the Lord would raise up in this final period of history. Many Vineyard pastors, including Jack Deere, shared his new interpretation.[52]

Some of the pronouncements made by the Kansas City prophets had a ring of truth and reality about them. Others seemed off the wall or erroneous. Paul Cain told the registrants at the Anaheim spiritual warfare conference "that God had given him a torch with which to initiate the 'last days' ministry" and "that God had instructed him to offer the torch to the Vineyard." He then gave a whole series of very accurate words of knowledge to individuals, during which there were said to be power surges.[53] His most controversial Anaheim prophecy, which was heard by the 9,000 registrants from all over the world, was that "the first shot [of revival] is going to be fired when John [Wimber] comes to England the next time."[54] Many other prophecies were given, which Bill Jackson has listed out in detail in his history of the Vineyard.[55]

Cain's most controversial prophecy took place "when he called out John and Eleanor Mumford (whom he did not know), the pastors of

52. Jackson, *The Quest*, 199.

53. Ibid., 204.

54. Wimber, "Revival Fire."

55. Jackson, *The Quest*, 206–8.

the S.W. London Vineyard, and, in the context of prophesying for them, closed by saying, "and I believe that revival will probably find its starting point somewhere there [in England], when the Lord will just start to move throughout London and throughout England."[56] Mumford, according to Jackson, assumed that the revival would begin in London in October 1989. Although there was no sign of anything that looked like a revival during October John Mumford refrained from making any judgment because of Cain's good track record of accuracy. In January David Parker, who was one of Bickle's leadership team, was in London and listened to the tape of Paul's prophecy and then pointed out that he had not specifically mentioned the year. However, for many Vineyard pastors this was simply an exercise in "back-peddling." In March 1990 Mumford then told a gathering at St. Andrew's Church in Chorleywood that he had added a false interpretation that the revival had been due to start in the October of 1989. However, by this time Bickle had let it be known that five people had separately received a word that the Lord would strategically visit London and that the revival would then move on to Germany and other parts of Europe.[57] He then revised his prophecy to be "revival, tokens of revival."[58]

Wimber embraced the Bickle prophecy wholeheartedly in a period that Jackson described as "the prophetic honeymoon."[59] In a surprising move in May 1990 Wimber announced that Kansas City Fellowship was going to become part of the Association of Vineyard Churches. In this same year David Pytches raised the profile of the Kansas City Prophets in England with the publication of his book, *Some Said it Thundered* in which he was particularly impressed by some of their nature prophecies. At the same time, Wimber set about organizing a series of conferences in London and other parts of the British Isles, including Wales and Scotland. In high expectancy he took his whole family to England convinced that a breakthrough of major proportions was about to take place. Before the opening meeting at the Docklands Conference in London Wimber told his team members, "This week is the most crucial moment in the Vineyard. It is the most important task in Vineyard history. If we have success here, it will give us momentum for the next two decades." Happy Leman, senior pastor of the Vineyard in Champaign, Illinois, stated that Wimber

56. Ibid., 208.

57. Ibid., 209.

58. Ibid., 224.

59. Ibid., 210.

believed that this could be a turning point in history.[60] While there were some powerful moments at the Docklands gathering it was clear when the conference had come to an end and in the months that followed that there had been no revival. As Bill Jackson put it, "The whole affair set up many for disillusionment."[61] It was not just those in America who felt misled. Indeed, there had not even been any "tokens of revival." Roland Howard reflected on the disillusionment that followed this failed prophecy, but pointed out that what was worse is the tendency to forget the mistake "and to continue until the next big name, offering Charismatic experience or portents of revival comes to town."[62]

It was not just the American leadership who were disappointed and led astray by Cain's prophecy, as many English church leaders had also trusted in the veracity of what had been promised. The Canadian psychiatrist, Dr. John White, who had taken a period of leave to study the Vineyard, had rated the Kansas City prophets very highly. "No charge of sexual misconduct or acquisitiveness or arrogance," he wrote, "can be laid at their doors."[63] A number of prominent English charismatic leaders who had witnessed the ministry of Paul Cain, Bob Jones, and John Paul Jackson issued a statement in their support, which was published in *Renewal* magazine in October 1990: "We believe they are true servants of God, men of sound character, humility and evident integrity. . . . We observed their radical commitment to the word of God. . . . We have no doubt about the validity of their ministry . . . and encourage as many as possible to attend the conferences to be held in Edinburgh, Harrogate and London in the autumn of this year, at which they will be ministering."[64] Signatories included Gerald Coates (Pioneer), Graham Cray (St. Michael-le-Belfry), Roger Forster (Icthus), Lynn Green (YWAM), David McInnes (St. Aldates, Oxford), John Mumford (South West London Vineyard), Bishop David Pytches, Bishop Brian Skinner, Teddy Saunders, Barry Kissell (St. Andrews Chorleywood), Terry Virgo (Clarendon Church and New Frontiers International), Anne Watson (Belfrey Trust), Rick Williams (Riverside Vineyard, Teddington).[65]

---

60. Jackson, *The Quest*, 225.

61. Ibid., 226.

62. Howard, *Charismania*, 40.

63. *Renewal*, vol. 172, 1990.

64. *Renewal*, vol. 173, 1990, 7.

65. Ibid.

Yet less than a year later Mike Bickle stood alongside John Wimber at a leaders' conference in London while John read out a statement of apology.[66] In the fall of 1991 the tragic news of Bob Jones' sexual sin became public knowledge and he was removed from his ministry. The allegations included "using the gifts to manipulate people for his personal desires, sexual misconduct, rebelling against pastoral authority, slandering leaders and the promotion of bitterness within the body of Christ."[67] This, plus the accusations of Ernie Gruen, the pastor of another church in Kansas, seemed in Jackson's words, "to put the final nail in the prophetic coffin for many."[68] Bob Jones was then put under the pastoral authority of Larry Alberts and was eventually released by him to minister at large again in 1994. The Vineyard still continued to refuse Jones to engage in any from of ministry in its churches.[69] Paul Cain also left the Vineyard for reasons connected with unity.[70]

For a while it seemed as if the Vineyard might have done with prophecy altogether. Yet despite making mistakes and getting their hands burnt through their links with the Kansas City prophets, Wimber and the Vineyard continued to teach and encourage the churches to develop a prophetic future vision. They also made widespread use of "the word of knowledge," the gift of the Spirit mentioned in 1 Corinthians 12:8, understanding it to be god-given knowledge of someone else's need or condition implanted in the mind of a Christian believer. Often at the end of meetings and conferences those praying for another person would be urged to listen in the quietness of their own heart for a "word of knowledge," which would then lead them to pray into the real needs of the individual concerned.

The prophetic gifts had been largely dormant in the Christian church since the end of the second century, surfacing only occasionally and usually in the hands of extremists. The Vineyard fellowships, and Wimber in particular, called the churches back to the importance of trying to listen to the voice of God, both for individuals and more importantly for both local and the national churches. In more recent times the Vineyard practice has been to recognize that prophecy is not an exact science and that we only prophesy in part and that therefore no one gets it all correct. Generally,

66. *Renewal*, vol. 183, August 1991, 21.

67. *Renewal*, March 1992, vol. 190, 1992. See also Moriarty, *The New Charismatics*, 102, and Jackson, *The Quest*, 233.

68. Jackson, *The Quest*, 233.

69. Ibid.

70. C. Wimber, *John Wimber*, 237, note 3.

speaking, the attempt is made to convey prophecy in words that indicate that what is being said comes in the form of an impression, which is believed by the speaker to come from God. This then opens up the possibility for people to scrutinize and assess the usefulness of what has been said.

CONTINUING MISSION

Bill Jackson reflected that "the immature way we had responded to prophetic ministry had all but halted our forward progress."[71] Yet one of the truly impressive things about the Vineyard (and John Wimber's leading of it) has been and is their ability to pick themselves up after a dysfunctional episode and move on with the central agenda, which is to engage in mission and to plant Vineyards. Indeed, John Wimber believed that planting new churches was part of the Vineyard's genetic code. At the Denver Leaders' Conference in 1991 there was a new emphasis in missions and Bob Foulton was appointed to be Coordinator for the International arm of AVC. Importantly, the Denver Conference re-articulated the Vineyard's core values "reaffirming who we are and where we are going."[72]

> The Bible taught as the Word of God
> Ministry to the poor, orphans, widows, etc.
> Evangelism tied to social concerns if possible
> Healing the sick and casting out the demons
> Commitment to small groups
> Equipping the saints in things such as serving, giving, doctrine,
>   family, finances, etc
> Interaction with pastors and churches
> Worship that reflects the values God had given us such as
>   intimacy, being natural, etc
> The exercise of spiritual gifts
> Commitment to missions[73]

INTIMATE WORSHIP

One of the Vineyard's most impacting core values has been their stress on intimate and personal worship. Almost all evangelical churches have

71. Jackson, *The Quest*, 247.

72. Ibid., 246.

73. Ibid.

adopted Vineyard songs, many of which are in the soft rock tradition. Wimber's conviction was that worship songs need to be personal in nature and addressed *to* God rather than *about* God. Central to Wimber and Vineyard thinking is the importance of singing a block of songs without pausing between them. In this way the congregation is helped to focus on the Lord and personally encounter his presence. Many Vineyard songs, particularly those written in earlier years, were simple in construction and the words reflected a concern to express devotion and love for Jesus. John Gunstone suggested that these songs were designed to open up the individual both psychologically and spiritually to the forgiving and trans-figuring power of God.[74]

Jackson wrote that after 1991 the AVC task forces began to redefine their identity in terms of mission. The Vineyard strategy was to return to the local church as the base for missionary action. This was in keeping with the New Testament pattern where Paul and Barnabas were sent out by the local church. Beginning in the nineteenth century there was a gradual move away from the local church to para-church organizations and societies, even though the financial support still came from local and parish churches. The result was that enthusiasm for missions began to diminish. Bob Foulton's strategy was to get small clusters of American Vineyard churches to take on responsibility for reaching particular overseas areas.

The new strategy resulted in fresh moves to evangelize and plant new congregations outside America 1993. Wimber ministered in Australia. Carl Madearis of the Colorado Springs Vineyard responded to God's call and went out with his family to Beirut as a missionary. Fred Colloms, a real estate tycoon from Peoria, Illinois, began to make trips to Mexico and was installed as director of Vineyards in Mexico. John and Carol Christian, who were originally from India, returned to their homeland with a team from San Jose and established a Vineyard church plant in Madras.[75] The Vineyard grew from 377 churches in eight countries in 1992 to 819 churches in fifty-two countries in 1998.[76]

In the 1990s the Vineyard structure necessarily had to develop in order to cope with the expansion of the movement, both in America and overseas. In addition to National Directors and Coordinators, Regional Overseers, and Coordinators, two task-orientated categories of leadership were added. These were titled Generalists, who were people-orientated

---

74. Quoted in Pytches, *John Wimber*, 231.

75. Jackson, *The Quest*, chapter 15, "Birthing Missions."

76. Ibid., 340.

leaders whose primary role was to build up relationships and community. A second category, who were to be known as Specialists, were people with the ability mobilize people to reach a particular goal or objective. John Wimber remained the international director of the movement until his death in 1997. After this it was agreed that the members would decide his successor. In the event Wimber was succeeded by Todd Hunter.

TORONTO AND THE AFTERMATH FOR THE VINEYARD

In October 1994 John Arnott invited Randy Clark, the leader of the Vineyard at St. Louis, Missouri, to hold a series of meetings at his Toronto Airport Vineyard Church. Clark held his first gathering on 16th January, 1994, expecting his stay to be a short one. As it happened he remained there until the 26th March, a total of forty-two days. Clark, along with many others, had been deeply impacted by the ministry of Rodney Howard-Browne (b. 1961). For a number of years Howard-Browne had been active in Kenneth Hagin's *Rhema Ministries* in South Africa. He was also associate pastor with Ray MacCauley at the Rhema Mega Church in Johannesburg until 1987 when he felt called to take up residence in the United States. This was a big step of faith as he and his wife, Adonica, arrived with only four suitcases and $300. Howard-Browne felt strongly that God had told them to prepare the churches for the coming revival. Along with many other big name charismatics, he claimed it was the "last days outpouring of the Holy Spirit" and that God appeared to him personally. He wrote of his encounter as follows: "It felt like liquid fire—like someone poured gasoline over me and set me on fire—the best way I can describe it is that it was as shocking as if I had unscrewed a light bulb and put my finger in the socket. I knew it was God."[77]

By any standards, Howard-Browne's ministry must be termed remarkable. He travelled extensively in the United States during the course of 1993 and attracted large audiences, which he "would bring under the power."[78] Believing himself to be just "the Holy Ghost's bartender" he ministered in a manner similar to Benny Hinn. During ministry times whole sections of his congregations fell to the ground as a result of his blowing on them. He did and still does this as he walks up and down among his audiences. According to Clifford Hill, one of his outspoken critics,

77. Howard-Browne, *Manifesting the Holy Ghost*, 16.

78. "Rumour of Revival," *Alpha*, July 1994. Airport Vineyard had changed its name to the Toronto Airport Christian Fellowship.

Howard-Browne's particular speciality "is to have those who fall down begin to laugh uncontrollably, supposedly with the joy of the Lord."[79] Howard-Browne was apparently himself bemused on one occasion when people laughed as he spoke on the subject of hell. Some of those who were smitten down were apparently unable to get up and described their condition as "feeling like a block of cement." A crucial factor in so far as Toronto was concerned was the fact that his ministry was and is about "impartation" of the power and presence of God." It was this impartation and the phenomena of Howard-Browne's meetings that were to feature so strongly and to become the focus of so much controversy, particularly within the Vineyard movement.

Clark had been "touched" at one of Howard-Browne's meetings in Tulsa, Oklahoma. It was this outpouring that led John Arnott to ask him to come as a conference speaker from Thursday 20th to Sunday 23rd January, 1994. In the event it became a worldwide movement and by 1996 one million people had visited the Toronto Airport Vineyard Church to drink from the refreshing waters of their "wells."[80] By 1997 8,000 prodigals had recommitted their lives to the Lord and 6,000 had made first time commitments at Toronto Airport Church alone.[81]

Notwithstanding this remarkable outcome, many were critical of the meetings because of the phenomena that were taking place. Many of them were similar to those which had taken place at Howard-Browne's meetings and indeed had been seen in other revival times including that under Jonathan Edwards at Northampton, Massachusetts in the middle years of the seventeenth century. In particular, people's doubts were raised by the so called "holy laughter," which looked like a form of drunkenness, falling to the ground, the jerks, animal noises, including roaring like a lion, jumping, pogoing, and running on the spot.[82] Others were not happy with the idea of people being encouraged to lie down and soak in the Spirit or having hands laid on them to receive the impartation of this experience. Many of the critics felt there was too much rhetoric and auto-suggestion as people were asked to stand in lines to receive the Spirit with specially trained catchers behind them.

79. Hill writing in *Prophecy Today*, vol. 10.5, 5. See also Roberts, *The Toronto Blessing*, 85.

80. Chevreau, *Catch the Fire*, 20.

81. Ibid.,7.

82. For a detailed explanation of these phenomena and possible ways of understanding them see Scotland, *Charismatics*, chapter 10.

By the late Spring of 1994 Wimber felt that he needed to speak about what was happening in Toronto and he set out his thoughts in his *Reflections* magazine. He urged smaller churches not to wear out their people by holding too many meetings, and he made it clear that he had serious reservations about training catchers and putting tape on the floor so that people could fall down in what looked like individual parking spots. He was concerned that too much emphasis was being put upon the manifestations, with those who experienced them being regarded as first-class Christians who were truly open to God's Spirit. He strongly advised Vineyard leaders and others to pastor the renewal and if necessary to put a stop to "holy" laughter if it was disrupting the preaching. In his Winter edition of *Reflections* he spelt out six things that must be going on in a local church, whether it was in renewal or not. These were teaching the Word, administering the ordinances of baptism and communion, pastoring people's needs, equipping the saints for ministry, leading worship, and doing the work of evangelism. In his opinion any minister who neglected these key aspects of ministry to pursue renewal was making a serious mistake.

In September 1994 Wimber called a board meeting at Anaheim to discuss the situation. Randy Clark, who wasn't able to stay for the whole time, expressed his concern that too much of the discussion was on animal noises, which had not been a feature at his meetings. John Wimber became increasingly disturbed at the animal noises and early in December 1995 the board made the decision to withdraw its endorsement of the Toronto Airport Vineyard. In a somewhat confused state of affairs the Toronto leadership anticipated that Wimber's decision to come and visit them in December 1995 was to work things out. In the event Wimber began by announcing that the Toronto Airport Vineyard (TAV) was being asked to separate from the Association of Vineyard Churches. For his part Wimber made it clear that the AVC believed the renewal to be a genuine move of the Holy Spirit but that it had been poorly pastored.[83] Arnott and the TAV leadership were shocked and felt that the AVC board hadn't been straight with them about their feelings in the preceding months. News of the decision was posted on the internet and quickly spread around the world. Randy Clark expressed how hurt he was by the decision that had been taken, and forty other churches left the Vineyard.[84] Ted Haggard, the Pastor of a 5,000 member church in Colorado, accused the AVC of injustice saying: "You just can't spank your children until they thoroughly

---

83. Jackson, *The Quest,* 329.
84. Ibid., 331.

know what they are doing wrong and what the punishment will be if they continue."[85]

THE VINEYARD IN RECENT TIMES

Following John Wimber's death, Todd Hunter became the National Director of the Vineyard in January 1998 and served in that capacity until he resigned in 2000 to become a priest and then a bishop with Anglican Church in America (AMIA).[86] In 2007 the National Board of Directors appointed Bert Waggoner of Sugar Land, Texas, as the new National Director. He was followed in October 2011 by Phil Strout, who is the Senior Pastor of the Pathway Vineyard. At the present time the Association of Vineyard Churches includes over 1,500 churches around the world still with a strong focus on church planting and advancing the kingdom

FACTORS THAT MADE THE VINEYARD SUCCESSFUL

Kingdom Focus

Numbers of peoples have tried to analyze the Vineyard movement and to pinpoint what it is and what has made it successful. One thing can be said is that from the very beginning it has been a *kingdom-focused* movement. In their theology the Vineyard has remained committed to George Elton Ladd's kingdom theology of "the now and the not yet" of the kingdom. This has been the motivating factor for the signs and wonders teaching that miraculous works (exorcisms and healings) are a sign that, in a limited way, God's kingdom is being established now. It is these works that are necessary to validate and generate a response to the spoken message. It is also "the now and the not yet" of the kingdom which helps to explain why some situations are transformed and others are not and why some people are healed and others are not.

Servant Evangelism

Wimber and the Vineyard recognized that Jesus' way of reaching people was through acts of service and that he had taught that his followers were

85. Ibid., 332.

86. See *Christianity Today* 53.9, September 2009.

to copy his example and to be servants both in the Christian community and outside of it. The setting up of *Mercy Ministries* and of feeding and caring for the poor and marginalized lies at the heart of the Vineyard DNA.

Church Planting

From its inception the Vineyard has been committed to planting new congregations. This is seen as the New Testament pattern of doing mission and stimulating church growth. The Vineyard has always been flexible, recognizing that some congregations may simply be in the Lord's purposes for a season or a short period of time and that it may also be right to give churches away to other denominations or groups or networks. From the beginning Wimber led the Vineyard to love and bless the whole church in all its differing denominations and expressions. It was for this reason that he blessed the Anglican Church in the UK by setting up a fund that gave birth to New Wine and the Kingdom Power Trust.

A Minimalist Church

During his time as church growth consultant at Fuller Seminary Wimber doubtlessly encountered many out-of-touch leaders and church growth bureaucrats, which led him to do his best to ensure that the Vineyard began, and remains, a minimalist church. To a large extent he succeeded, although Bill Jackson later reflected that many Vineyard pastors and leaders "wrongly followed John's 'benevolent dictator' model of leadership."[87] Places of worship, whether they were warehouses, pubs, bars, or high school halls, were always plain and unadorned. If there was a Communion table there would be no cross or candles. Indeed, in some places you might even find plates of doughnuts alongside the bread and wine. The Vineyard principle was always that everything should be such that people walking into a meeting would find nothing strange or cringe-worthy that would cause them embarrassment or difficulty. There would be no books with pages to find and flick backwards or forwards according to the month or season of the Church's year. Everyone would dress down and come in casual attire. Those leading the worship or meetings wouldn't wear special clothes that might set them at a distance from the rest of the people. The talks that were given were and are Bible-based, straightforward, and

---

87. Jackson, *The Quest*, 369.

practically applied. Wimber wanted a church that was centered on the five-fold ministry of Ephesians 4:11 with apostles, prophets, evangelists, pastors, and teachers.

The Emphasis on the Holy Spirit

The Vineyard still looks back to Mother's Day, 1980, when Lonnie Frisbee invoked the Holy Spirit on the congregation at Calvary Chapel in Yorba Linda. It was this moment that taught Wimber, and consequently the Vineyard movement, the importance of giving the Lord time to move in a situation or a person's life. To wade in with one's best prayers the moment a sick person asks for our help was, in most cases, simply not allowing God to minister. Wimber and the Vineyard helped the whole church to see part of what being a "priesthood of all believers" is about. Ministry is not merely for the specially ordained few, but for all the people of God. Any believer can invite God's Spirit to come and bring healing or help. As Wimber put it, "everyone gets to play." To use the title of Rich Nathan and Ken Wilson's book Wimber "Empowered Evangelicals."

A Deep Commitment to the Bible

Wimber emerged from the American fundamentalist tradition, but he moved to a less-rigid view of Scripture. He had a deep commitment to the Bible as "the inspired word of God" and the priority of preaching the gospel. And although Wimber was profoundly attached and rooted in Scripture, he always sought to remind people that "the Bible is the Menu and not the meal." He urged Christians everywhere to hunger for the Spirit and "not to be satisfied with just studying the menu." For Wimber it was always the Word and Spirit together and he never tired of underlining the fact that we live in time when the Spirit empowers the ministry of Jesus in the world.

15 | Drawing on Christianity Outside the Box

QUINTILIAN, THE ROMAN MASTER of oratory, once said: "It is a good thing to know, and always keep in mind, the things which were illustriously done of old." Epicurus, the Greek philosopher, advised his disciples continuously to remember those of old time who lived with virtue. The purpose of this final chapter is simply to draw together the key factors that contributed to the success of the movements studied in the preceding chapters, some of which are still in existence and actively promoting the kingdom of God. The fact that others are now no longer active, at least in the same recognizable form, is no necessary reason to consider them to be failures. Indeed, some of them may have been intended in God's purposes only for a season or limited periods of time. Others, such as the Montanists, Donatists, Waldensians, and the Lollards, have merged back into the mainstream denominational churches and impacted them with fresh injections of spiritual life.

Each of the movements studied in the previous chapters of this volume focused on some of the distinctive characteristics of the movements examined, many of which the contemporary Christian churches would do well to incorporate into their life and worship. The Montanists, for example, emphasized the gifts and power of the Spirit and stressed the value and importance of the prophetic. The Donatists highlighted the necessity of having Christian leaders who are men and women of integrity and who hold fast to the faith in times of trial and suffering. The Waldensians and the Moravians were both missionary-minded people who upheld the biblical creedal faith and established caring and compassionate communities. The Lollards recognized the supreme authority of the Scriptures as the sole basis of faith and practice. The Puritans and the Society of Friends stressed the vital importance of the home and a Christian business ethic. The Puritans underlined the necessity of hard and conscientious work, and the Friends stressed the Christian duty of care for all employees. John Wesley's Methodists set before the world the importance of evangelism and social Christianity. The Primitive Methodists fueled working-class movements such as Chartism and the trade unions by giving them articulate leaders and imbuing them with a Christian spirit. The Salvation Army came to stand for hand-in-hand evangelism and compassionate care. The Settlement movement has reminded the contemporary churches of the importance of being a presence in a locality and the Christian requirement to be good neighbors before attempting to preach to them. The Pentecostal movements recalled the churches to the importance of baptism in the Spirit and healing and wholeness, while the Vineyard churches have demonstrated the centrality of intimate worship and a kingdom vision.

Leaving these more significant individual traits to one side, it is also clear that, taken together, all of these movements had some marked core characteristics that made a significant contribution to their success. It is these that all sections of the Christian church, but particularly the historic denominations, would benefit from regularly re-visiting. Let us consider some of them.

LEADERSHIP

The most obvious factor in the success of all of these movements was their leadership. Each of these groups were led by men and women of "charisma," a term first enunciated by the sociologist, Max Weber. By this word he meant that they were people who were, by nature, visionaries with a gift of personality who drew others after them, who came to share their goals and embrace aspirations. Such individuals were not respected first and foremost for their status, office, or position; rather, they were followed for who they were and the ways in which they lived out their vision. Those with "charisma" also had the ability to communicate their vision in an effective and understandable way.

Much of what is currently spoken of as leadership in the contemporary Christian world is, in reality, simply management. In essence, mangers are those who devote their time and energy to preserving and maintaining what is already in place. Leaders, on the other hand, pursue that which is beyond the existing institution and structures. The men and women who played significant roles in the Christian groups considered in these chapters were leaders in the sense that they set out and invited others to sign up to a new but straight-forward, biblically informed, vision with clear doctrinal, spiritual, and social objectives that they pursued with boldness and determination, often in the face of opposition and hostility.

Montanus, Donatus, John Wycliffe, Peter Waldo, Nicholas Zinzendorf, George Fox, John and Charles Wesley, Joseph Sturge, William Booth, Samuel Barnett, Arthur Winnington-Ingram, Smith Wigglesworth, David Du Plessis, and John Wimber and others whose lives have been considered here, were all individuals with a resolute determination and outward vision. Like the leaders in the book of Acts, they were all also radically focused and seriously devoted followers of Jesus who kept a personal walk with him. Donatus, for example, was determined that those who had denied Jesus in the persecutions should be required to begin the Christian life again with full public repentance and a fresh re-entry into the Christian community. He was resolute in his opinion that Christian ministers and leaders in Christ's church should not be compromisers that had denied the faith. His concern was therefore to ensure that if such men and women wanted to return to church leadership, or even simply re-enter the Christian churches, they should have a period of serious repentance and basic Christian teaching and then undergo another baptism, the rite of entry into the Christian church. For more than four hundred years the greater part of North African Christians followed the lead that he had given.

John Wycliffe and his followers were resolved that *whatever the cost* they were going to see an English Bible in the hands of every man and woman. George Fox was totally set on freeing men and women from what he regarded as the nominal, compromising religion of the Church of England's steeple houses so that they could find new life in God's Spirit. Count Nicholas Zinzendorf, the Moravian leader, declared that he "had only one passion, and that is He," by which he meant Jesus Christ. John Wesley dedicated his entire life to preaching the "new birth in Christ" and spreading scriptural holiness through the land. William Booth summed up his life in an interview with King Edward VII when he declared his "one passion was the souls of men."

Whereas dioceses, district chairman, and area ministers often rule over their congregations, the majority of the leaders considered in these pages were by nature servant leaders. They were men and women of compassion who served both their leadership teams as well as those they encountered beyond their communities of faith. John Wesley called himself "God's Steward of the poor." At the 1841 annual meeting of the Methodist Society he reminded members that "many of our brethren and sisters have not needful food . . . [and were] destitute of convenient clothing . . . sick and ready to perish." By way of a solution, Wesley proposed "first that each bring what clothes they could spare" and "second that each give a weekly penny or what they could afford for the relief of the poor."[1] Just a few months before his eighty-second birthday he waded ankle-deep in snow collecting food and blankets for the people of Bristol. He recorded in his journal, "At this season we usually distribute coats and bread among the poor of the society. But I now considered that they wanted food as well as clothes. So on this, and the four following days, I walked through the town, and begged two hundred pounds in order to clothe them that needed it most."[2]

William Booth may have been a dictatorial leader who was even on occasion accused of infringing personal liberties, but his heart was always for those he termed "the submerged tenth," that section of society who were so marginalized that no one else cared for. His book *In Darkest England* launched what was, and still is, the most consistent, serving, and compassionate expression of practical Christian care for the world's poor and the needy. The Society of Friends leader, Joseph Sturge, gave the greater part of his lifetime to fighting slavery in both England and in the American colonies. His fellow Quaker, the chocolate manufacturer, George Cadbury, refused to buy Cocoa beans that had been produced by slave labor and, at home in England, he built a model village for his work force at Bourneville consisting of 370 solid houses. He also provided employees with a gymnasium and swimming pool for recreation, and a well-cooked meal was served to each employee every working day.

All the leaders mentioned in these chapters were also men and women of moral integrity. They recognized the truth of Oswald Chambers' maxim that a person's value to God in public is what they are in private. Not one of these founding leaders suffered a moral lapse with either money, sex or power. They were highly regarded as exemplary role models by those who followed them. It is true that John Wesley and William Booth were rather dictatorial, but it needs to be remembered that they were loved and respected by those who followed them. Both men, it should also be noted, lived in times that were hardly democratic and certainly not imbued with values of social equality.

From these brief comments it will be apparent that effective Christian leadership is servant leadership that is also compassionate and practically caring. No leadership in the contemporary church is going to touch people's lives with the presence of Christ unless his command to serve is actioned.

1. Wesley, *Journal*, 7 May, 1741.
2. Ibid., 4 January, 1785.

Contemporary Christian leaders wear a host of different hats and are often busy in a variety of different roles, such that consequently the central objective and focus of their ministry is frequently lost in a melee of circuit meetings, deanery synods, sub-committees, and related activities. These issues, though they are often laudable in themselves, result in a loss of energy and what the sociologist Max Weber termed "the evaporation of charisma." The leaders of the movements considered here were men and women of singular purpose who recognized the need to concentrate sharply on what they perceived to be their primary divine calling. They would all have endorsed John Wesley who, when once reflecting on his achievements, declared, "I think I am an example of what God can do with a person who concentrates on one thing at a time."

One thing seems abundantly clear: all of these movements flourished and were effective because they had strong, vibrant leaders who were visionaries. They were able to set out an agenda that was biblical in its principles, doctrine, practical care, and compassion. They were men and women who inspired their following to buy into it and run with it. They had enthusiasm, which in many cases captivated and fired up their people to persevere even in times of intense suffering and opposition.

TRAINING

Many contemporary parochial clergy and church ministers are able and talented individuals who have been well trained in universities and seminaries. Consequently, they often run their church or community very well with the help of a small number of staff or co-leaders. That said, a key issue is what happens when they move on, run out of energy, or even die? To guard against such eventualities they need to heed the New Testament exhortation to go and train men and women who could teach others also.[3] The fact of the matter is that if the leader's vision is a kingdom vision, then a small team will never be sufficient. Indeed, it will always be necessary to follow St. Paul's injunction to keep teaching and training up as many others as possible to assist in carrying forward the vision.

One characteristic that all the leaders of these groups shared in common was that they all gave time and attention to teaching and training those who would assist in carrying forward the vision both in the present and subsequently when they had either died or run out of steam. Wycliffe trained and mobilized assistants who became known as Lollards. For more

---

3. 2 Tim 2:2.

than a hundred years following his death they copied portions of his Bible and moved around the English countryside reading them privately in people's homes or in discreetly chosen out of the way locations. Along with other leaders of these movements, Peter Waldo resourced his Waldensian helpers. He had begun life as a wealthy merchant and sunk a large portion of his personal funds into producing copies of the Scriptures and other materials for his missionaries. By nature he was a caring, compassionate individual who also gave much time and attention to addressing the needs of the poor and by working alongside his chosen co-workers.

From their early beginnings, the Moravians have been an education movement, with Bishop John Amos Comenius recognized as "the Father of the Elementary School." On the continent of Europe, Moravian schools flourished in Germany, Switzerland, Holland, and the Baltic provinces. Zinzendorf likewise was totally committed to training his followers and he himself often travelled and worked with his foreign mission teams. Moravian settlements were widely known for their mutually supportive and caring communities. Wesley, in a large measure, had the gift of administration and trained full-time leaders who he designated "helpers." In 1753 he issued *Twelve Rules for a Helper*. It included the following advice:

> never be unemployed a moment; never be triflingly employed. Converse sparingly and cautiously with women; particularly with young women in private. . . . A preacher of the Gospel is the servant of all. Be ashamed of nothing but sin: not of fetching wood (if time permit), or drawing water. . . . Therefore spend and be spent in the work. Observe. It is not your business to preach so many times . . . but to save as many souls as you can. Therefore, you will need all the sense you have, and to have your wits about you.[4]

One of the great strengths of Wesleyan Methodism was the training it provided for leadership. Not only did the ordinary poor learn to read and write in Methodist Sunday Schools, they were assisted in public speaking by being given experience first as exhorters and then as local preachers. Within the environment of the Methodist Circuit they also learned the skills of management and handling finances. Wesley himself issued other guidelines to his full-time assistants regarding such matters as marriage, preaching, and reading.

William and Catherine Booth in their military style Salvation Army recruited and trained officers and indeed rank and file members, men

4. Davies, *Methodism*, 81.

and women who were enthused both by them and with their message. A unique aspect of Booth's strategy was that he even used men and women as leaders who were drawn from the ranks of the very poor.

One of the great strengths of the Vineyard churches is the way in which they have trained their leaders and indeed huge numbers of other laymen and women who share their values. Part of Wimber's legacy, which has also rubbed off on New Wine and other Apostolic networks, is the way in which they have organized high-quality conferences on key issues of ministry such as healing, holiness, the prophetic, and kingdom theology. But Wimber in particular always engaged the Vineyard in the practical aspect of the teaching that he gave. Their leaders didn't merely instruct their congregations in the ways that Jesus taught his followers to preach the gospel, heal the sick, and cast out the demons, they also went out and did it with them. Wimber recognized that Jesus trained his disciples, not by leaving them at a local synagogue for a year or two to assist the Rabbi, but by taking them with himself out onto the streets of towns like Jericho and Decapolis. There they engaged the needy in conversation, prayed for them, and gave them practical help whenever possible. As Wimber put it so clearly, "the meet is on the street" or again, "the meeting place is the market place."

The Settlement and Pentecostal movements were very different in their ecclesiologies, but education and training were a major priority and indeed a significant factor in their success. Both the Settlers and the Pentecostals were deeply involved and engaged in compassionate ministry to the poor and marginalized by teaching and training them. In summary, we learn from the movements considered in these chapters that the effective and obvious missional context in which to train disciples is not the religious work of the local parish, circuit, or Christian fellowship but out on the streets and in the community centers, cafés, gyms, clubs, pubs, and shopping malls; in short, the world outside the church context, or to use Jesus' own words, out in the "highways and byways."

Contemporary Christian leaders need to take note of this principle of training others because in doing so they will not only come to understand the vision, they will buy into it and own it. To train others in this way is to respect and empower them as individuals and at the same time draw them into commitment to the cause. Additionally, all visions need honing and refining, and by sharing them in this way with questions and debate that opportunity becomes a possibility.

FEMALE LEADERS

It is important to underscore the fact that women played an active role within the life and effectiveness of these movements. Indeed, one of the reasons why Montanism was so strongly attacked was because of the significant leadership roles held by Priscilla, Maximilla, and other women. We know from prosecutions that took place in the early sixteenth century that women were also active in the leadership of the Lollard movement. Down through the Christian ages women have also been active in leadership in the Society of Friends. It began with Margaret Fell, who preached in public in the seventeenth century when no women were accorded the right to speak in church. Other strong female leaders included the prominent missionaries Rachel Metcalfe and Esther Butler. Elizabeth Fry was a distinguished prison reformer and Catherine Gurney was another able Friends leader who founded the Christian Police Association. Women were prominent in the leadership of Wesleyan Methodism and Primitive Methodism in particular where they served both as full-time preachers, local preachers, and circuit officials. At one point in the early history of Primitive Methodism a third of all local preachers were women. Women were given remarkable place in the Salvation Army, where from the very beginning they were able to hold every position from General downwards and were paid the same as male officers. William's wife, Catherine, was almost his co-leader in the early days and preached with powerful effect. Their daughter, Evangeline Booth (1865–1950), was the fourth Salvation Army General from 1934–39. A number of women played prominent leadership roles in the London Settlements and Settlement missions, including Henrietta Barnett, Edith Langridge, Catherine Newman, and Mary Augusta Ward.[5] Women were also to the fore in leadership roles in the early phase of Pentecostalism and have continued to be so. Of particular note are Aimee Semple McPherson and Kathryn Kuhlman. Women's ministry has been welcomed and publicly stated in the Vineyard movement. Many Vineyards tend to be led by husband-and-wife teams, a pattern that has been adopted in a number of churches within the New Wine Network. The contemporary churches need to recognize the biblical principle that in the beginning woman was created to stand alongside the

5. Scotland, *Squires in the Slums*, chapter 7.

man, not under him,[6] and that many women were active in leadership in the churches of the New Testament era.[7]

AN OUTWARD KINGDOM FOCUS

Sociologists have observed that churches, indeed all institutions, have a capacity to become "idolatrous." By this the following is meant: when they first came into being they did so to serve a particular need or purpose. They were a means to an end. However, with the passage of time all institutions have the potential to lose sight of that original purpose and to become an end in themselves. In this way a church, group, or community of people that originally came into being to extend God's kingdom can begin to overlook the initial vision and its goal instead becomes its own self-existence or survival. Thus, rather than putting its energies into extending the message of the kingdom of God, the focus moves to nurturing, building up, and improving the community of people as well as developing its structures, hierarchy, and rituals. The theological focus of attention has now become a *maintenance* rather than a *missional* ecclesiology. The energy is now channeled into enhancing and maintaining the institution rather than using it as a vehicle to achieve a missional goal or vision. Vance Havner has charted the fourfold passage of an institutional decline. It begins with a man who initiates a movement that eventually turns into a machine and then steadily declines until it has become a monument.

It seems clear enough that the groups studied in this book were essentially movements rather than institutions, simply for the reason that they began and continued with mission and then developed structures to support that mission. In contrast, established denominational churches are essentially institutions by definition since they invariably start with a structure of diocese and parish, district or circuit, presbytery or area, and then allow that to govern and shape their mission. All the groups examined in these pages were missional movements, at least in their early years, and most of them remained so for considerable periods of time. While they kept moving their focus and energies forward in the direction of their vision they proved to be effective. Decline set in for some of them, however, almost from the moment when they first began to let go of their goal to move forward and out beyond themselves. Such, as we have

6. Gen 1:27 and 2:18.

7. See for example, Rom 16; Acts 16:40; 21:9; Phil 4:2.

seen, was the case with a later section of the Society of Friends. Clearly, therefore, we learn from this that it is of vital importance for Christian churches to retain a minimalist ecclesiastical structure, which will enable a pioneering kingdom vision to develop with suitable flexible structures. Once the energy and appetite for this has been lost all that remains is their own community and they have already begun the all too familiar journey from mission to maintenance.

The fourteen movements studied in this book all put continuous energy, thinking, and planning into mission and outreach. They were not concerned with ecclesiastical office or territorial circumscribed districts or parishes restricted to a geographical area. Nor were they were primarily focused on devising ways to bring people into their institution or community. They were all primarily engaged with people and macro issues in the outside world beyond themselves and their religious communities. They were not apprehensive or fearful of the prevailing cultural, societal, and political issues that surrounded them. On the contrary, they endeavored to redeem them by active engagement. The Celtic Christians demonstrate this well. They didn't reject all the Druid customs that surrounded their villages and settlements. Some they embraced, such as respect for the creation, and others they transformed into Christian festivals and practices. Wesley, like the Celts, embraced the surrounding culture of his age. Indeed, it has been said, and even argued by some, that not only did Wesley change the face of England, he saved the nation from a bloody revolution such as had taken place in the American colonies and France. He did so because the movement he birthed brought significant changes in the culture of English society. The Society of Friends changed the culture of many factories and businesses in the eighteenth and nineteenth centuries in both England and America.

These groups also took seriously the biblical injunction to heal the land, and they therefore aimed, wherever possible according to their means and resources, to bring divine wholeness to human relations and activities. In some instances, their focus was on the world of work and business. Such was the case with the Moravians and the Society of Friends. Moravian and Quaker employers believed that the way they did business and treated their employees was at the very heart of their duty to God. The Primitive Methodists gave major attention to educating the poor and combating the evils of drunkenness and gambling. Samuel and Henrietta Barnett and the Settlements and missions that they inspired aimed to raise the whole quality of the life of the poor of London's East End and other urban centers. They sought to achieve it by education, by engaging with local authorities, campaigning for pure water, better sewers, just wages, and reasonable hours of work. It is for this reason that John Wesley's Methodists and the contemporary Salvation Army and the Vineyard churches spent and spend time on the streets giving out food and offering clothes and shelter to the homeless. In these ways they not only conveyed the Christian faith as they understood it by compassionate care, they also earned the right to explain it more fully in words.

The reason that these movements were outwardly focused was in large measure down to their leadership. They were all men and women who followed Jesus' injunction to "go into all the world" and who believed they had been given a message for those beyond and outside of their faith communities. Most of them were also convinced that they have been called to a particular people group or ministry. The contemporary church needs leadership with a specific outward focus and vision and a budget and resources to support it. Indeed, it needs to take serious note of Mike Ruhl's article entitled "Smelling the Coffee: Seven Sins of a Dying Church," in which he researched a large number of churches and found that 95 percent of their budgets were spent on ministries for church people! The challenge down through the ages has been, and will continue to be, to get out of the church environment and to put money and resources into an outward kingdom vision.

MINIMALIST CHURCH

A common factor among all these movements was their minimalist ecclesiology. Their focus was not on the institutional and doctrinal development of the church, but on the church as an outgoing community of believers. They sat lightly when it came to buildings, rituals, robes, and ecclesiastical ceremonies. They believed that energy and focus devoted to these things can both obscure the heart of the Christian message and sap energies and focus away from promoting the kingdom of God in the outside world. They were also clear that they wanted people to have a living encounter with Christ and not an induction into an institution or an initiation into a system of rituals and disciplines. They recognized in the past, as the churches must in the present, that if and when new people ventured into a place of worship they needed something that was straightforward and readily understandable. They required, in the words of John Wesley, "the plain truth for the plain man."

It's not easy to convince people that a local or neighborhood church is a Christian family in which all are equal in the sight of Christ when leaders sit at the front of the building in big seats on a raised platform and walk around in long robes. Jesus himself, in fact, warned against both and urged that no-one call a leader "father." Not all the groups in these chapters were completely free of ecclesiastical hierarchies, but they nevertheless sat light to them. Even in the Vineyard, which has been particularly noted for its minimalist structures, there have been exhortations to beware of hierarchies and titles such as Senior Pastor and Head of Youth Ministries.

It is also vital that a church's vision or goal is kept in a simple and clear format. John Wimber once related an encounter with a man who had just listened to him speak at a meeting. When are you going to start giving us the deep stuff? he asked. Wimber replied: "Who was the best Bible teacher ever?" The man's immediate response was Jesus. Wimber then asked: "What is Jesus' best sermon that the Holy Spirit saw fit to cause the New Testament writers to include in the Gospels?" After a moment or two of hesitation the reply was, the Sermon on the Mount. Finally, Wimber retorted, "So what is deep about it"? He then went on to state that, "it's simply a gorgeous picture of kingdom living" and urged all the conference registrants to keep the Sunday stuff simple. "If people want to do the Tabernacle or Leviticus," he said, "let them do it on their own!"

Most of the movements that make up these chapters, with the possible exception of the some of the London Settlements, retained a vision and objectives that was readily understandable. It seems so obvious and yet it is so easily missed that if churches want people to become part of their vision, it has to be plain, straightforward, easy to understand, and set in a culture with which they are comfortable. All of the groups considered here recognized that the churches and denominations from which they emerged had, to some extent, lost their focus on Jesus and his kingdom and become, in various degrees, idolatrous; that is, they were turning in on themselves. They had lost sight of that for which they originally came into being. The new version of church with which they then started was minimalist. It was in the culture of the age and its structures and rituals were just enough to fulfill and engage with the vision they established. Thus for most, ritual and ceremonies were at a minimum. Sacraments such as baptism and the Eucharist tended to be plain and unadorned. In the case of the Society of Friends and the Salvation Army, baptism and the Lord's Supper were dispensed with altogether. Clerical hierarchies, vestments, and titles were not seen as important. In most of these organizations the leaders didn't become "a race apart," rather they operated very much in the manner of ordinary laymen and laywomen, which facilitated a more effective and easier communication.

MEN AND WOMEN OF THE SPIRIT

It is abundantly clear that the fastest growing sections of worldwide Christianity are the Pentecostal and Charismatic churches, which emphasize the presence and empowerment of the Holy Spirit in the life of the believer. It seems obvious enough that throughout Christian history, beginning with the apostolic age, that the most vibrant churches have always been those who have sought the outpouring of the Spirit of God. Each of the founding leaders of these movements were individuals whose affections were awakened and impacted by the Spirit of God and were consequently impelled into action by feelings of love, compassion, and concern for the marginalized, the suffering, and the needy.

Montanus had a dramatic conversion experience in which he was overcome by the Spirit of God, which led him to practice and promote the gifts of the Spirit. Among many others, his movement attracted Tertullian, himself a man of the Spirit and one of the most significant theologians of the early church. From the beginning of their movement the Donatists laid a strong emphasis on the Holy Spirit and the power of the third person of the Trinity. This was undoubtedly a key factor in their becoming the religion of the whole of the North Africa within a generation. The Puritans were men and women who cried out to the Lord for the presence of God's Spirit in their lives. They constantly looked for the witness of God's Spirit in their daily living. The great Puritan theologian, John Owen, wrote *The Work of the Holy Spirit in Prayer* (1682) and *Two Discourses on the Work of the Spirit* (1693). His writings gave the Puritans extended teaching on the importance of spiritual gifts. The Moravians were reborn under the leadership of Nicholas Zinzendorf when the Holy Spirit came on their whole community as they gathered for the Eucharist on 13th August, 1727. They were people whose spirituality included regular watch-night services in which they waited for the Spirit of God to come on the assembled company. It was at one of their meetings in 1738 that John Wesley's heart was "strangely warmed" when the Spirit of God came upon him as he listened to a talk on the Letter to the Romans. George Fox and the early Friends were people who often trembled under the presence and power of the Holy Spirit at their early gatherings. Both Hugh Bourne and William Clowes, the co-founders of the Primitive Methodism, had dramatic conversion experiences in which they were deeply conscious of the Holy Spirit's presence. Their ministry and church, which touched the English working classes in a way that no other did, was focused on bringing down the power of God on their congregations. William Booth was from first to last a man of the Holy Spirit. Indeed, the motto of the Salvation Army is "Blood and Fire," the fire being the fire of the Spirit of God, which came on the first Christian tongues of fire on the day of Pentecost. It goes without saying that both the Pentecostals and the Charismatics, as their name suggests, were people of the Holy Spirit.

People at the present time are living in a complex world that is characterized by instant service, fast foods, short-term contracts, divorce on demand, and immediate access to the internet. It is reckoned that a quarter of the population in the Western world have some kind of addiction, the root cause of which is emotional pain. People are therefore in search of an overwhelming experience that will deal with their hurts and bring them wholeness and well-being. One of the major reasons why the majority of the movements in this book so readily attracted followers from the marginalized sections of society was because they brought men and women into an experience of God's Spirit that touched and transformed their lives in a deep and lasting way. So if the contemporary churches are ever going to touch a large section of their generation for Christ it will have to be in and through the power of the Holy Spirit.

DEEP AND PRAYERFUL SPIRITUALITY

Integrally related to the life in the Spirit that these movements fostered was their deep and serious spirituality. Their mission, planning, and strategies were surrounded with prayer. The Montanists for example, were serious and rigorous in their devotion to Christ, often fasting and eating sparsely in order to keep spiritually alive. The Celts were people whose lives were punctuated by many simple and short prayers. Theirs was a domestic spirituality in which nothing was either too small or too great to commit to prayer. George Fox and the early Quakers prayed long and hard as they waited on the Spirit of God for guidance. The Moravians held watch-nights in which they prayed though the hours of darkness seeking divine presence and direction. The Methodists, who were greatly influenced by them, adopted the Moravian practice. Cottage prayer meetings were also a major feature in both the Wesleyan and the Primitive Methodist circuits.

The Salvation Army, the early Pentecostals, and indeed all the movements discussed in these pages knew prayer was basic to their progress and effectiveness. Clearly, intercession of every kind has to be a first priority for the contemporary churches as it was for these outside-the-box movements.

ROOTED AND GROUNDED IN SCRIPTURE

It is clear that all these fourteen movements were rooted and grounded in Scripture. Despite some of the hostile and biased press the Montanists and the Donatists received, and continue to receive, both were solidly orthodox in their beliefs and endorsed the rule of faith and the early Catholic creedal statements. In the face of bitter persecution from the medieval Catholic Church, the Waldensians fought to preserve the New Testament faith, particularly the doctrines of baptism and the Eucharist. Wycliffe and the Lollards were totally given to translating, copying, and promoting the study of the Bible, which they regarded as the supreme authority. The Puritans were known as people who went by the book. Their preachers constantly urged the study of its pages and their people were told to read it as families in their homes. The Bible was central in the teaching and preaching of George Fox and the evangelical sections of his followers. Wesley and the Methodists similarly regarded the Scriptures as the inspired word of God and therefore the one sure foundation for their life, worship, and practice. Wesley and his early helpers preached the Scriptures in a way that few others have done. The Salvation Army Articles of War declare that "the Scriptures of the. Old and New Testaments . . . constitute the divine rule of Christian faith and practice." Contrary to the views of some, we have noted that from the very beginning, preaching the Bible has played a central part in the life of Pentecostal and Charismatic communities.

RADICAL HOSPITALITY

It is important to note that the majority of these movements made considerable use of the home. The Montanists and Donatists must have done so since they operated at a point in time when Christianity was a persecuted minority and official church buildings were few in number. For the Waldensians, Moravians, and the Lollards, home-based meetings were also essential for the same reason. It is clear the Lollards established what was, in effect, a network of underground house churches in parts of late fifteenth-century England. Both the Wesleyan and the Primitive Methodist churches grew by means of Cottage-based prayer meetings, watch-nights, and love feasts. This suggests that perhaps the contemporary churches need a re-think concerning the place and value of the home as the base for missional activities. The church is, after all, described in the New Testament as "the household of God" and "the family of God," which implies that the home needs to be recognized as a base and vital instrument for advancing the kingdom of God. Indeed, contemporary Christianity needs to re-visit the church of the early sixteenth-century Puritans who taught that the home is a church in miniature. The phrase "Christianity begins at home," which derived from the Puritans, suggests this should be the starting point from which the kingdom of God is advanced.

DENOUEMENT

Throughout the centuries the worldwide church has been constantly in debt to movements of "Christianity outside-the-box," such as those considered in this book. In fact, each of these groups exemplify a principle enunciated by the missiologist, Wilbert Schenk: "that the Christian faith has been saved repeatedly in nearly two thousand years of history by moving from an established heartland to a new environment." These groups, from the Montanists to the present-day Charismatic network churches, remind us that new "outside the box" movements have played, and indeed are still playing, a vital role in extending Christ's kingdom because they call the wider denominational and national churches back to their original vision and biblical roots. They also cause them to seek a renewal of their spiritual life, and in many cases stir and provoke them to a kingdom vision that stretches beyond their own communities.

Select Bibliography

Adamnan. *Life of Columba*. London: Penguin, 1995.

Adderley, James. *In Slums and Society: Reminiscences of Old Friends*. London: Fisher Unwin, 1916.

Ambler, Rod. W. *Ranters, Revivalists, and Reformers*. Hull, UK: Hull University Press, 1989.

Ames, William, *The Marrow of Theology*. Translated by John D. Eusden. 1629. Reprint. Boston: Pilgrim, 1968.

Anon. *All About the Salvation Army*. London: n.p., 1883.

———. *British Methodism and the Poor 1739–1999*. Methodist Archives, John Rylands Library, University of Manchester.

———. *Handbook of Settlements in Great Britain*. London: The Federation of Residential Settlements and Educational Settlements, 1922.

———. *Lives of the British Reformers*. Rev. ed. London: The Religious Tract Society, n.d.

———. *Mansfield House Settlement in East London*. London: Canning Town, 1892.

Armstrong, Anthony. *The Church of England and the Methodists*, 1700–1850. London: Rowman and Littlefield, 1973.

Articles of War. London: Salvation Army, n.d.

Ashworth, Mandy. *The Oxford House in Bethnal Green*. London: Oxford House, 1980.

Augustine. *Contra Cresconium*. In *Post-Nicene Fathers of the Christian Church*, Volume 4, edited by Philip Schaff, 55–56. Grand Rapids: Eerdmans, 1956.

———. *Letters*. In *Post-Nicene Fathers of the Christian Church*, Volume 1. Grand Rapids: Eerdmans, 1956.

———. *Sermons in Connection with the Donatist Controversy*. Edinburgh: T. & T. Clark, 1872.

Aune, David. *Prophecy in the Early Church*. Grand Rapids: Eerdmans, 1983.

Baker, Frank. *Methodism and the Love Feast*. London: Epworth, 1956.

Barnes, Cyril. *God's Army*. Oxford: Lion Husdon, 1978.

Barnett, Henrietta O. *Canon Barnett, His Life, Work and Friends*. London: Murray, 1921.

Barratt, Thomas. B. *When the Fire Fell*. Olso: Hansen and Sonner, 1927.

Barrett, David B. *The World Christian Encyclopedia*. Oxford: Oxford University Press, 1982.

Bartleman, Frank. *From Plough to Pulpit*. Los Angeles: Bartleman, 1924.

———. *How Pentecost Came to Los Angeles*. Los Angles: n.p., 1925.

Baxter, R. *Treatise on Conversion*. London: Simmons, 1658.

Bebbington, David W. *Evangelicals in Modern Britain*. London: Unwin Hyman, 1989.

Bede. *Ecclesiastical History of the English People*. London: Penguin, 1990.

————. *Life of Cuthbert*. In *The Age of Bede*, edited by D. H. Farmer, translated by J. F. Webb. London: Penguin, 1983.

Begbie, E. Harold. *The Life of William Booth*. London: Macmillan, 1920.

Benn, Wallace, and Mark Burkhill. "A Theological and Pastoral Critique of the Teaching of John Wimber." *Churchman* 101.2 (1987) 101–13.

Blinco, Sidney A. "Another Harvest of the Years." In *Echoes and Memories*, edited by Bramwell Booth. London: Hodder and Stoughton, 1925.

Blumhofer, Edith. *Restoring the Faith: The Assemblies of God, Pentecostalism, and the American Culture*. Chicago: University of Illinois, 1993.

Booth, Bramwell, editor. *Echoes and Memories*. London: Hodder and Stoughton, 1925.

Booth, Catherine. B. *Bramwell Booth*. London: Rich and Cowan, 1933.

————. *Catherine Booth: The Story of Her Loves*. London: Hodder and Stoughton, 1970.

Booth, William. *In Darkest England and the Way Out*. London: Salvation Army, 1890.

————. *Orders and Regulations*. London: Salvation Army, 1878.

Booth-Tucker, F. de L. *The Life of Catherine Booth, the Mother of the Salvation Army*. London: Salvationist Publishing and Supplies, 1924.

Bownde, Nicholas. *The Doctrine of the Sabbath*. London, n.p., 1595.

Bradley, Ian. *Celtic Christianity*. Edinburgh: Edinburgh University Press, 1999.

————. *Enlightened Entrepreneurs*. London: Weidenfeld and Nicolson, 1987.

————. *The Celtic Way*. London: Darton, Longman & Todd, 1993.

Bready, J. W. *England before and after Wesley*. London: Hodder and Stoughton, 1938.

Brigden, Susan. *London and the Reformation*. Oxford: Clarendon, 1988.

Briggs, Asa., and A. Macartney. *Toynbee Hall*. London: Routledge and Kegan Paul, 1984.

Brock, Michael G., and Mark C. Curthoys. *The History of the University of Oxford*, Volume VII, Nineteenth Century, Oxford, Part 2. Oxford: Clarendon, 2000.

Byefield, Nicholas. *The Marrow of the Oracles of God*. London: n.p., 1630.

Calder, William, M. "Philadelphia and Montanism." *Bulletin of John Rylands Library* VII (1923) 59–91.

Cannon, William R. *History of Christianity in the Middle Ages*. New York: Abingdon, 1960.

Carlson, Leland. H. *Writings of Henry Barrow, 1590–91*. London: Allen and Unwin, 1966.

Chadwick, Owen. *The Early Church*. London: Penguin, 1993.

————. *The Reformation*. London: Penguin, 1964.

Chamberlain, J. H. "From Sect to Church in British Methodism." *Journal of Sociology* 2 (1964) 139–49.

Chevreau, Guy. *Catch the Fire: The Toronto Blessing: An Experience of Renewal and Revival*. London: Marshall Pickering, 1995.

————. *Share the Fire: The Toronto Blessing and Grace-Based Evangelism*. London: Marshall Pickering, 1997.

Christian, John T. *A History of the Baptists*. Texarkana, TX: Bogard, 1922.

Christie-Murray, David. *Voices from the Gods: Speaking with Tongues*. London: Routledge and Kegan Paul, 1978.

Church, Leslie F. *Knight of the Burning Heart*. London: Epworth, 1945.

Clowes, William. *Journals of William Clowes*. London: Hallam and Holliday, 1844.

Collier, Ronald. *The General Next to God*. Glasgow: Fontana/Collins, 1977.

Cragg, Gerald. R. *Puritanism in the Period of the Great Revolution 1660–1688*. Cambridge: Cambridge University Press, 1957.

Cumming, G. J., and Derek Baker, editors. *Popular Belief and Practice.* Studies in Church History 8. Oxford: Blackwell, 1972.

Cyprian. *Letters.* In *Ante-Nicene Fathers of the Christian Church*, Volume 5. Grand Rapids: Eerdmans, 1956.

D' Aubigné, J. H. Merle. *The Reformation in England.* London: Banner of Truth, 1962.

Dandelion, Pink. *An Introduction to Quakerism.* Cambridge: Cambridge University Press, 2008.

Davies, C. S. L. *Peace, Print, Protestantism 1450–1558.* Paladin History of England. 1976. Reprint. London: Fontana, 1995.

Davies, Rupert, editor. *John Scott Lidgett.* London: Epworth, 1957.

———. *Methodism.* London: Penguin, 1964.

Davis, John F. *Heresy and Reformation in the South East of England 1520–1559.* London: Hart Davis, MacGibbon, 1976.

De Paor, Liam. *St Patrick's World.* Dublin: Four Courts, 1993.

Dempster, Murray W., et al., editors. *The Globalisation of Pentecostalism.* Oxford: Regnum, 1999.

Dickens, Arthur G. *The English Reformation.* London: Fontana/Collins, 1978.

Dickie, J. W. "College Missions and Settlements in South London 1870–1920." B.Litt. diss, Oxford University, 1976.

Didymus. "Concerning the Trinity." In *God's Self-Confident Daughters: Christianity and the Liberation of Women*, edited by Anne Jensen. Louisville: Westminster John Knox, 1996.

Dimond, Sidney G. *The Psychology of the Methodist Revival.* London: Milford, 1926.

Drummond, Andrew L. *German Protestantism since Luther.* London: Epworth, 1951.

Ellis, L. E. *Toynbee Hall and the University Settlements.* London: n.p., 1948.

Elton, Geoffrey R. *Policy and Police: The Enforcement of the Reformation in the Age of Cromwell.* Cambridge: Cambridge University Press, 1972.

Epiphanius. "Panarion." In *God's Self-Confident Daughters: Christianity and the Liberation of Women*, edited by Anne Jensen. Louisville: Westminster John Knox, 1996.

Ervine, St. John G. *God's Soldier: General William Booth.* London: Heinemann, 1934.

Eskenazi, Tamara C. Harrington et al. *The Sabbath in Jewish and Christian Traditions.* New York: Crossroad, 1891.

Esler, Philip F., editor. *The Early Christian World.* 2 vols. London: Routledge, 2000.

Eusebius. *The History of the Church.* London: Penguin, 1989.

Everts, William W. *The Church in the Wilderness, or Baptists before the Reformation.* Nappanee, IN: Baptist Bookshelf, 1986.

Fifth Annual Report of the Universities' Settlement in East London. London: 1889.

Foakes Jackson, Frederick J. *The History of the Early Church.* London: Allen & Unwin, 1965.

Foxe, John. *The Acts and Monuments of John Foxe.* 4th ed. London: The Religious Tract Society, n.d.

Frend, William H. C. *The Donatist Church.* Oxford: Oxford University Press, 1952.

———. *Saints and Sinners in the Early Church.* Wilmington, DE: Glazier, 1985.

Fries, Adelaide L. *Customs and Practices of the Moravian Church.* Winston-Salem, NC: Board of Christian Education and Evangelism, 1973.

Frodsham, Stanley H. *With Signs Following: The Story of the Pentecostal Revival in the Twentieth Century.* London: AOG, 1949.

Gilbert, Alan D. *Religion and Society in Industrial England, 1740–1914.* London: Longman, 1976.

Graham, Dorothy. "Chosen by God: The Female Itinerants of Early Primitive Methodism." PhD diss., Birmingham University, 1987.

Green, John R. *Short History of the English People.* London: Macmillan, 1912.

Goodwin, Thomas, *The Works of Thomas Goodwin, DD.* London: Nichol, 1866.

Greenslade, S. L. *Schism in the Early Church.* London: SCM, 1964.

Haigh, Christopher. *English Reformations.* Oxford: Clarendon, 1995.

Halévy, Elie. *History of the English People.* London: Benn, 1913.

Hardinge, Leslie. *The Celtic Church in Britain.* Slough, UK: Street, 1972.

Hassé, E. R., *The Moravians.* London: National Council of Evangelical Free Churches, 1911.

Hattersley, Roy. *John Wesley: A Brand Plucked from the Burning.* London: Abacus, 2002.

———. *William and Catherine Booth and their Salvation Army.* London: Abacus, 2009.

Hesslgrave, David J. *Today's Choices for Tomorrow's Mission: An Evangelical Perspective on Trends and Issues in Missions.* Grand Rapids: Zondervan, 1988.

Hilborn, David, editor. *Toronto in Perspective.* London: Acute, 2001.

Hill, Christopher. *Society and Puritanism in Pre-Revolutionary England:* New York: Shocken, 1964.

———. *The World Turned Upside Down.* London: Penguin, 1991.

Hollenweger, Walter J. *The Pentecostals.* London: SCM, 1969.

Hood, A. B. E. *St. Patrick: His Writings and Muirchu's Life.* Exeter, UK: Phillimore, 1978.

Howard, Roland. *Charismania.* London: SPCK, 1997.

Howard-Browne, Rodney. *Manifesting the Holy Ghost.* Louisville: RHBEA, 1992.

Hudson, A. *Lollards and Their Books.* London: Hambledon, 1985.

———. *The Premature Reformation.* Oxford: Clarendon, 1988.

Hudson, W. S. *Religion in America.* New York: Scribner's Sons, 1965.

Hughes, Philip. *The Reformation in England.* 3 vols. London: Macmillan, 1951.

Hunter, G. G. *The Celtic Way of Evangelism: How Christians Can Reach the West Again.* Nashville, TN: Abingdon, 2006.

Hurstfield, Joel. *The Reformation Crisis.* London: Arnold, 1965.

Inglis, K. S. *Churches and the Working Classes in Victorian England.* London: Routledge and Kegan Paul, 1963.

Jackson, Bill. *The Quest for the Radical Middle.* Kenilworth, SA: Vineyard, 1999.

Jenson, Anne. *God's Self-Confident Daughters: Christianity and the Liberation of Women.* Louisville: Westminster John Knox, 1996.

Jerome. *Letter 41.* In *Nicene and Post Nicene Fathers of the Christian Church,* edited by Philip Schaff, 55–56. Grand Rapids: Eerdmans, 1979.

Jones, Brynmor P. *An Instrument of Revival: The Complete Life of Evan Roberts 1878–1951.* Gwent, UK: Bridge, 1995.

Kammer, Donald. "The Perplexing Power of John Wimber's Power Encounters." *Churchman* 106 (1992) 45–64.

Kay, William K. *Apostolic Networks in Britain.* Milton Keynes, UK: Paternoster, 2007.

Kelly, T. *A History of Adult Education in Great Britain.* Liverpool: Liverpool University Press, 1992.

Kendall, Holliday B. *History of Primitive Methodism.* London: Dalton, 1906.

Kent, John. *Holding the Fort: Studies in Victorian Revivalism:* London: Epworth, 1978.

Knappen, Marshall M. *Tudor Puritanism.* Gloucester, MA: Smith, 1963.

Knox, D. *The Lord's Supper from Wycliffe to Cranmer*. Exeter, UK: Paternoster, 1983.

Knox, Ronald. *Enthusiasm: A Chapter in the History of Religion with Special Reference to the XVII AND XVIII Centuries*. Oxford: Clarendon, 1957.

Lambert, M. *Medieval Heresy*. Oxford: Blackwell, 1992.

Lander, John K. *Itinerant Temples Tent Methodism 1814-1832*. Milton Keynes, UK: Paternoster, 2003.

Larsen, Timothy, editor. *Biographical Dictionary of Evangelicals*. Leicester, UK: InterVarsity, 2003.

Leatham, Diana. *Celtic Sunrise*. London: Hodder and Stoughton, 1951.

Lecky, William E. H. *History of England in the Eighteenth Century*. London: Longmans, Green, 1890.

Legge, H. *Trinity College Mission in Stratford 1888-1889*. Trinity College Archives, Cambridge, undated.

Lewis, Arthur J. *Zinzendorf the Ecumenical Pioneer*. London: SCM, 1962.

Lewis, Peter. *The Genius of Puritanism*. Haywards Heath, UK: Carey, 1975.

Loades, David. *Revolution in Religion The English Reformation 1530-1570*. Cardiff: University of Wales Press, 1992.

Moriarty, Michael. *The New Charismatics*. Grand Rapids: Zondervan, 1992.

Maitland, Samuel R. *History of the Albigenses and Waldenses*. London: Rivington, 1832.

Manson, John. *The Salvation Army and the Public*. London: Routledge, 1906.

Mayor, Stephen. *The Churches and the Labour Movement*. London: Independent, 1967.

McCord, Norman. *British History 1815-1906*. Oxford: Oxford University Press, 1993.

McGavran, Donald, et al. *Church Growth Bulletin*, 3. Santa Clara, CA: Global Church Growth, 1982.

McGrath, Patrick. *Papists and Puritans under Elizabeth 1*. London: Blandford, 1967.

Mearns, Andrew. *The Bitter Cry of Outcast London*. London: Clarke, 1883.

Meek, Donald. *The Quest for Celtic Christianity*. Edinburgh: Handsel, 2000.

Memorandum of Association. In *First Annual Report of the Universities' Settlement in East London*. London: Penny and Hill, 1891.

Midgley, C. *Women against Slavery: The British Campaigns, 1780-1870*. London: Routledge, 1992.

Milburn, Geoffrey. *Primitive Methodism*. London, Epworth, 2002.

Moore, Robert. *Pitmen, Politicians and Preachers*. Cambridge: Cambridge University Press, 1974.

Moore, E. de W. *The Attitude of the Church to Some of the Social Problems of Town Life*. Cambridge: Cambridge University Press, 1896.

Morgan, Irvonwy. *The Godly Preachers of the Elizabethan Church*. London: Epworth, 1965.

Moreland, Samuel. *The History of the Evangelical Churches of the Valleys of Piedmont*. Paris, AR: The Baptist Standard Bearer, 2001.

Mudie-Smith, Richard. *The Religious Life of London*. London: Hodder and Stoughton, 1904.

Murray, Iain. *The Reformation of the Church*. London: Banner of Truth, 1965.

Murray, Stuart. *Radical Christian Groups*. Cheltenham, UK: Open Theological College, 1998.

Muston, Alexis. *The Israel of the Alps: A History of the Persecutions of the Waldenses*. London: Strand, 1852.

Neill, Stephen. *A History of Christian Missions*. London: Penguin, 1964.

Nickalls, John. *The Journal of George Fox.* Cambridge: Cambridge University Press, 1952.

Ninth Report of the Universities' Settlement in East London, 1893. London: Penny and Hull, 1895.

The Noble Lesson. In *The History of the Evangelical Churches of the Valleys of Piemont*, edited by Samuel Morland, chapter 18. London: Hills, 1658.

Northbrooke, John. *A Treatise on Dicing, Dancing, Plays and Interludes with Other Idle Past Times.* London: n.p., 1577.

O'Loughlin, Thomas. *Celtic Theology: Humanity, World and God in Early Irish Writings.* New York: Continuum, 2000.

Obelkevich, James. *Religion and Rural Society in South Lindsey 1825-1875.* Oxford: Clarendon, 1976.

Orchard, G. H. *A Concise History of the Baptists.* Watertown, WI: Baptist Heritage, 1988.

Orr, J. Edwin. *The Light of the Nations.* London: Paternoster, 1965.

Packer, James I. *Among God's Giants.* Eastbourne, UK: Kingsway, 1997.

Parker, T. L. H. *The English Reformation.* Oxford: Oxford University Press, 1952.

Patrick. *Confessions of St Patrick and Letter to Coroticus.* New York: Doubleday, 1998.

Paz, D. G. *Nineteenth-Century English Religious Traditions: Retrospect and Prospect.* Westport, CT: Greenwood, 1995.

Percy, Martin. "Signs, Wonders and Church Growth: The Theme of Power in Contemporary Christian Fundamentalism with Special Reference to the Works of John Wimber." PhD diss., London University, 1993.

Poewe, Karla. *Charismatic Christianity as a Global Culture.* Columbia, SC: University of South Carolina Press, 1994.

Pollock, John C. *The Cambridge Movement.* London: Murray, 1953.

Punshon, John. *Portrait in Grey: A Short History of the Quakers.* London: Quaker Home Service, 1984.

Pytches, David, editor. *John Wimber: His Influence and Legacy.* Guildford, UK: Eagle, 1998.

———. *Living at the Edge.* Bath, UK: Acadia, 2002.

———. *Some Said It Thundered.* London: Hodder and Stoughton, 1990.

Rattenbury, John E. *Wesley's Legacy to the World.* London: Epworth, 1928.

Ray, David B. *The Baptist Succession.* Gallatin, TN: Church History Research Archives, 1984.

Reason, William. *University and Social Settlements.* London: Methuen, 1896.

Richard, H. *Memoir of Joseph Sturge.* London: Partridge, 1864.

Roberts, David. *The Toronto Blessing.* Eastbourne, UK: Kingsway, 1994.

Robertson, Roland. "The Salvation Army: The Persistence of Sectarianism." In *Patterns of Sectarianism*, edited by B. Wilson, 49–105. London: Heinemann, 1967.

Sandall, Robert. *History of the Salvation Army, 1865-1878.* London, Nelson, 1950.

Saxby, Trevor. *Pilgrims of a Common Life.* Kitchener, ON: Herald, 1987.

Scotland, Nigel A. D. *Apostles of the Spirit and Fire.* Milton Keynes, UK: Paternoster, 2009.

———. "The Charismatic Devil." In *Angels and Demons*, edited by P. G. Riddell and B. S. Riddell, 84–105. Leicester, UK: Apollos, 2007.

———. *Charismatics and the New Millennium.* Guildford, UK: Eagle, 2000.

―――. *Methodism and the Revolt of the Field in East Anglia, 1872–1896*. Gloucester, UK: Sutton, 1981.

―――. *Squires in the Slums: Settlements and Missions in Late-Victorian London*. London: Tauris, 2007.

Seaver, Paul S. *The Puritan Lectureships: The Politics of Dissent 1560–1662*. Stanford, CA: Stanford University Press, 1934.

Semmel, Bernard. *The Methodist Revolution*. London: Heinemann, 1934.

Shaul, R., and Cesar, W. *Pentecostalism and the Future of the Christian Churches*. Grand Rapids: Eerdmans, 2000.

Shepherd of Hermas. In *The Ante Nicene Fathers of the Christian Church*, vol. 2, edited by Philip Schaff, 30–33. Grand Rapids: Eerdmans, 1979.

Simpson, Alan. *Puritanism in Old and New England*. Chicago: University of Chicago Press, 1956.

Springer, Kevin. *Riding the Third Wave*. London: Marshall, Morgan and Scott, 1987.

Stevenson, J. *Creeds, Councils and Controversies: Documents Illustrating the History of the Church, AD 337–461*. London: SPCK, 1987.

Stoeffler, F. Ernest. *The Rise of Evangelical Pietism*. Leiden: Brill, 1971.

Stogden, E. *Harrow in London*. Harrow, UK: Harrow Mission, 1909.

Sundkler, Bengt, and Christopher Steed. *History of the Church in Africa*. Cambridge: Cambridge University Press, 2000.

Sykes, John. *The Quakers: A New Look at Their Place in Society*. London: Wingate, 1958.

Sykes, Norman. *Church and State in England in the Eighteenth Century*. Cambridge: Cambridge University Press, 1934.

―――. *The English Religious Tradition*. London: SCM, 1961.

Tawney, R. L. *Religion and the Rise of Capitalism*. Bellmawr, NJ: Harcourt Brace, 1998.

Tertullian. *Against Praxeas*. In *Ante-Nicene Fathers*, Volume 3. Grand Rapids: Eerdmans, 1957.

―――. *De Fuga*. In *Ante-Nicene Fathers*, Volume 4. Grand Rapids: Eerdmans, 1956.

―――. *On Exhortation to Chastity*. In *Ante-Nicene Fathers*, Volume 4. Grand Rapids: Eerdmans, 1956.

―――. *On Fasting*. In *Ante-Nicene Fathers*, Volume 4. Grand Rapids: Eerdmans, 1956.

―――. *On Monogamy*. In *Ante-Nicene Fathers*, Volume 4. Grand Rapids: Eerdmans, 1956.

―――. *On the Resurrection of the Flesh*. In *Ante-Nicene Fathers*, Volume 3. Grand Rapids: Eerdmans, 1957.

Trevett, Christine. *Montanism, Gender, Authority and the New Prophecy*. Cambridge: Cambridge University Press, 1996.

Thompson, A. C. *Moravian Missions*. London: Hodder and Stoughton, 1883.

Thompson, Edward P. *Making of the English Working Class*. London: Gollancz, 1963.

Thompson, Flora. *Lark Rise to Candleford*. London: Penguin, 2008.

Thompson, David M. *Nonconformity in the Nineteenth Century*. London: Routledge & Kegan Paul, 1972.

Thring, Edward. *Addresses*. London: n.p., 1887.

Tierney, Brian. *The Middle Ages: Sources of Medieval History*. New York: Knopf, 1974.

Townsend, William J., et al., editors. *A New History of Methodism*. 2 vols. London: Hodder and Stoughton, 1909.

Toynbee, Arnold. *Lectures on the Industrial Revolution*. London: Rivingtons, 1884.

Tozer, M. "The Readiest Hand, the Most Open Heart: Uppingham's Mission to the Poor." *History of Education* 18.4 (1989) 323–32.

Trevelyan, G. M. *English Social History*. London: Longmans, Green, 1944.

Trevelyan, Janet P. *Life of Mrs Humphry Ward*. London: Constable, 1923.

Troeltsch, Ernst. *Social Teaching of the Christian Churches*. Madison, WI: University of Wisconsin Press, 1984.

Verey, David. *Diary of a Cotswold Parson*. Gloucester, UK: Sutton, 1978.

Vickers, John. *A Dictionary of Methodism in Britain and Ireland*. London: Epwroth, 2000.

Walpole, Horace. *Letters*. London: Everyman, 1926.

Ward, W. Reginald. *Religion and Society 1790–1850*. London: Batsford, 1972.

Warneck, Gustav, and George Robson. *Outline of a History of Protestant Missions from the Reformation to the Present Time*. Edinburgh: Oliphant, Andersen and Ferrier, 1906.

Wearmouth, Robert F. *Methodism and the Common People of the Eighteenth Century*. London: Epworth, 1945.

Werner, Julia. *The Primitive Methodist Connexion, Its Background and Early History*. Madison, WI: University of Wisconsin Press, 1984.

Wesley, John. *Journals*. London: Conference Office, 1811.

Wilson, Brian, *Patterns of Sectarianism*. Oxford: University Press, 1990.

———. *Religious Sects*. London: Weidenfeld and Nicolson, 1970.

Wimber, Carol. *John Wimber: The Way it Was*. London: Hodder and Stoughton, 1999.

Wimber, John. *Power Evangelism: Signs and Wonders Today*. Sevenoaks, UK: Hodder and Stoughton, 1985.

———. *Everyone Gets to Play: John Wimber's Teachings and Writings on Life Together in Christ*. Boise, ID: Ampelon, 2009.

———. *Power Healing*. London: Hodder and Stoughton, 1986.

———. "Revival Fire." *Renewal* 184 (September 1991) 26–29.

Winston, Diane. *Red-Hot Righteous: The Urban Religion of the Salvation Army*. Cambridge: Harvard University Press, 1999.

Woolman, John. *The Journal of John Woolman*. London: Melrose, 1848.

Wylie, James A. *The History of Protestantism*. London: Cassell, Petter and Galpin, 1870.

Zarek, Otto. *The Quakers*. London: Religious Book Club, 1945.

Index

Index

Lightning Source UK Ltd.
Milton Keynes UK
UKOW050617270113

205411UK00001B/9/P